VINTAGE MORRIS

Tall Tales but True from a Lifetime in Motorcycling

By Lester Morris

Yesterday with Lester

You've met Lester Morris. Perhaps not in person, but in a movie, a musical or perhaps a TV show or advertisement. Remember those terrific electricity ads with the tall linesman and the short customer? Lester was the short bloke; you will have noticed that he gave the role a bit of an extra dimension – he does that with everything he touches.

I have read and used Lester's material in four motorcycle magazines now. There were always people who came up to me and said, "The only reason I buy your magazine is because of Lester." There were also always people who said, "He's bloody got it wrong, you know..." but there were always more of the former than the latter. And I don't think anybody ever claimed he wasn't funny.

Lester's sense of humour is very gentle, but you're still not likely to miss the joke. He makes sure of that...

Not only does he bring the past alive, but whether he's being washed away in a flash flood at the Bathurst races or nearly being squashed by his (then) wife's sidecar exploits (see the cover), Lester finds humour in everything. Would that we could all do the same; we might enjoy our lives as much as Lester enjoys his.

So you might have seen Lester Morris on TV, in a movie or a show. You might have heard his voice, commentating on races at Amaroo Park or Mount Panorama. You might have bought a widget from him at the immortal Omodei's motorcycle parts and accessories emporium.

And now you can carry him around in your pocket.

I'm glad you've bought this book, and I'm sure that you will be too.

Peter "The Bear" Thoeming
Editor Emeritus,
Australian MOTORCYCLIST Magazine

Foreword

Some unfortunate souls don't live seventy years, and many of those who do live their allotted 'three score years and ten' and sometimes more, may not have experienced the joys, the sorrows, the hurts and the sheer pleasure of spending much of that time flashing about the countryside while mounted upon a large variety of motorcycles. How sad that is, for they know not what they have missed!

As it happens, from my tentative beginnings as far back as 1947 to the time of writing these words, I have spent almost seventy long years doing just that: riding an enormous number of motorcycles over a great variety of surfaces. These surfaces varied from paved roads and smooth road-race circuits to choppy, pot-holed and rock-strewn dirt tracks, deep snow and ice – yes, snow and ice in Australia – and over some quite good road surfaces which had recently been strewn with a thin coating of nigh-invisible sand and/or gravel, or accidentally sprayed with a liberal coating of near-liquid animal waste material from ambulatory, if quite ill, bullocks.

I worked in the motorcycle trade in a variety of establishments (one of which was my own) for nearly thirty of those years, from large motorcycle distributors in Sydney and Melbourne, to smaller suburban agencies, and during that time I might ride anything from three or four to several more motorcycles almost every day of the week. They would come in a variety of types and sizes, some of them – in view of my short stature at just on 5'-3"(1.6M) – quite a bit too large for me.

Small mopeds and scooters with miniscule engines and doughnut-sized wheels I have been forced to ride are cheap-and-cheerful and super-economical to own, and thus earn their place – as Honda, among others, have clearly displayed over a great many years. But these little commuters can be more dangerous to ride than powerful machines if only because they can unintentionally become like mobile chicanes.

On the other hand, the much larger motorcycles I have ridden over very many years are safer on the roads than people who haven't ridden a motorcycle give them credit for. They are more manoeuvrable than motor cars, they provide a much smaller target, and can brake hard or accelerate far more quickly than any other form of motorised vehicle. The motorcycle rider also enjoys an all-round, unrestricted vision denied to all other road-going vehicles, even if there is an element of danger in riding them. As a bonus our controls are better laid out than saloon cars as well.

Some of the large motorcycles which provided a challenge for me included the WLA Harley-Davidson; the early CB750 Honda and later 750cc three-cylinder GT750 two-stroke Suzuki 'Water-Bottle'; 750cc Moto-Guzzi 'California' Cruiser from 1974 ; the two six-cylinder CBX Honda and frightful shaft-drive Z1300 Kawasaki models; and the monstrous, 1300cc, 125BHP, OHC Super-Sports Munch Mammoth. I wrote a long in-depth road test report on that huge German machine for a local magazine in 1975, and sent a copy of the report to a Dutch enthusiast who is compiling a history of Munch machine. I don't know how he found me!

Heavy and cumbersome some of them were, and thus very hard for me to wheel about easily once I was forced to clamber off them, but once underway they could be thrown about through corners with some abandon because, in effect, they became almost weightless at speed.

But large or small, brand new or very old, good, bad, dangerous, too fast or two slow, evil-handling, or running on rails, if it was powered and on two wheels, or sometimes on three, it was my job to ride them. It could be a machine which a rider might offer as a trade-in on a newer model; a new machine to be ridden for registration to the local Motor Registry; a bike offered for a diagnosis of a possible fault, or a road test of that same motorcycle after it had been repaired, or serviced, in the store's workshop; perhaps a smash repair which had just been straightened out and re-assembled. It could often be a motorcycle I borrowed from the showroom floor just to ride home upon.

From the early sixties, and for almost 20 years I was on-course commentator at Bathurst's Mount Panorama circuit during the Easter motorcycle racing carnival, but this was interrupted on occasion because of Theatre commitments which might see me on tour with a stage production for some months. Happily, I was always welcomed back with open arms.

It could be very busy at times at Bathurst and even more often at Sydney's Amaroo Park on a weekend, where I would be commentating on

> *"If you want to blame this book on anyone, then you can blame quite a number of people, but there are two in particular who should bear the brunt. The first is a fellow motorcycle scribe called Bob Guntrip, and the other is the legendary Peter (The Bear) Thoeming..."*

the events on-course, while furiously scribbling notes between races for a race report I had to write for most of that Sunday night. The report would have to be in the hands of the lay-out artist on the Monday morning, to be type-set and printed in a publication which was to be on the stands by the middle of the week! This applied, in particular, with my own motorcycle newspaper, 'Australian Motorcycling' which the great photographer, Bill Meyer and I published for some ten issues from the late seventies. Bill was the driving force behind the publication, I was its Editor/writer.

It was often my great privilege to share these on-course race reports at Bathurst and Amaroo with the legendary commentator, Will Hagon, a man of wit and wisdom, and a fine motor race commentator of many years' standing.

Will and I shared the commentary box at Amaroo Park many times, while at Bathurst I was in the commentary box on Skyline Corner at the top of the descent of the Ess-bends, with Hagon in the Control Tower at the bottom of the circuit, near the pit area.

One of my happiest achievements was to make use of the detailed, highly-successful British RAC/ACU Motorcycle Training Guide (the entire programme of which was swiftly air-mailed to me from England upon my request) when I opened the Motorcycle Learner Training Scheme in 1972 which bore my name. There had been other schemes for training Army and Police motorcyclists prior to this, but mine, as far as I could ascertain, was the first of its type to be employed in the training of civilians. Instructors from my store trained almost 200 people with input from me, with another 800 or so said to have gone through the scheme after I left the scene. The Training Scheme was finally picked up by a major motorcycle Club in Sydney, which I believe trained many, many hundreds of riders thereafter.

I have been involved in a parallel career in Theatre, Film and Television as actor/singer from the early sixties, almost at the same time as I was pursuing a career as a specialist motorcycle writer, with much of my later road test reports written in Melbourne in the seventies during the day, while performing on stage or Theatre Restaurant at night, with the occasional gig on TV commercials or drama, which usually necessitated daytime filming. This carried on later in Sydney from the late seventies, and continues to this day. At that time, I began another career as a Stage Director, and later again directed Operas for the semi-pro Rockdale and Sydney Independent Opera companies.

Many people have asked over the years how many motorcycles I have owned outright and it has always surprised my enquirers to learn that I have only owned just five (5) machines in all that time! I may of course make an exception of the eight or ten motorcycles which were on display in my own, short-lived motorcycle store in Sydney in the early seventies.

One of the bikes I owned later was a C70 Honda step-thru, which was the butt of many a joke. I was forced to mention to the scoffers that the little bike was a very handy unit to use when attending casting sessions for film and TV in the city in areas where parking was nigh-impossible. I could also leave the bike at many out-of-the-way motorcycle warehouses for a week or more when picking up a machine for a road test report. Better that than arguing with my current nearest and dearest about leaving the family car behind.

My first road test report was of the brand-new Z1 900cc DOHC Kawasaki, which arrived in Sydney in 1972, the report published in the Sydney-based, long-defunct 'Motorcycle Sports' newspaper. It was many months before the exciting machine's appearance anywhere else outside of Japan. This was entirely due to Australia's geographic advantage, of course, for its close proximity to Japan guaranteed this, as it did when Honda first arrived in Australia in April, 1958, almost a full year before it arrived in Europe, England or America. And, as you will read in my piece on Honda's Arrival under the Chapter in 'Ryde Motorcycles', I was there at the time! It was the C71, 250cc OHC twin which was the first bike to land in Oz, the little step-thru arriving – hot off the production line – in late August of that same year; again, well ahead of everyone else on earth.

My all-time, favourite motorcycle, the 1974 Moto-Guzzi 850T. I road tested the bike for Two Wheels magazine, finding it to be a perfect 'fit', to deliver bags of mid-range grunt, displaying great handling, with powerful brakes and, as a nice bonus, to be comfortable in the extreme, 'naked' though it was.

The 750SS (Super Sport) 'Desmo' Ducati coming onto the apex of the fastest corner on the Kew Boulevard in Melbourne. The sweeping, well-built access roads were laid down long before the up-market Housing Estate they serviced was even begun. It was thus a fine 'race' circuit if, sadly, an unofficial one, and for much too-short a time.

If you want to blame this book on anyone, then you can blame quite a number of people, but there are two in particular who should bear the brunt. The first is a fellow motorcycle scribe called Bob Guntrip, and the other is the legendary Peter (The Bear) Thoeming, another specialist writer whose interest in motorcycles and motorcycling in general extends, as mine certainly does, back, back, into the dim dark ages. As a serious journalist, Thoeming's numerous short stories and cartoons about his many, many years touring through little-known lands, while camping-out in fair weather and foul, in some most unsuitable places, the while brewing strange meals from whatever victuals he could manage to scrounge up, have been published many times over, and are the stuff of either legend or nightmares.

Thoeming showed more than a little interest in this project, suggesting that he may have the expertise and the contacts to make such a project actually happen. He edited several Nationally-successful magazines for which I wrote a number of road test and race reports, along with many 'Tall tales and True', while at a race meeting one weekend, Guntrip demanded to know when I was going to write my memoirs of what he so aptly described as " A Lifetime in Motorcycling"

Guntrip edited the occasional magazine to which I contributed Classic motorcycle test reports and/or humorous columns, and has written for several publications other than his own while remaining to this day an active writer on the subject.

I have written many road test reports over many years, including the first road test of the all-new R90S BMW, which I reported upon for three different publications, as well as over television for the ABC/TV 'Torque' programme when I was the TV show's motorcycle compere in the seventies. There have been more than thirty of my reports published in several magazines on a range of genuine Classic motorcycles as well. These include Black Shadow Vincent, Gold Star BSA, Ariel Square Four, 1935 Matchless OHC Vee-Four Silver Hawk, Scott Squirrel, Rudge Special and many other once-famous motorcycles. Many of them are now eagerly sought-after classics, one or two of which I might have once sold when they were brand new!

There were a series of road safety and simple maintenance articles I wrote for 'REVS' motorcycle newspaper in the mid-sixties, then a column called 'Small Bore' for 'Motorcycle Rider and Mechanic', followed by several issues of the Sydney based 'Motorcycle Sports' as Assistant Editor/Advertising Manager, while writing my fortnightly 'Chain Chatter' motorcycle column in the early seventies for Sydney's major daily newspaper, the Daily Mirror.

Several years later, while in Melbourne, I wrote several road test reports for 'Two Wheels' magazine; including an in-depth report on my all-time favourite motorcycle, the shaft-drive Moto-Guzzi 850T. I also wrote pieces for 'The Bike Book' in 1974-75, including a long piece called "European Thoroughbreds", the 4000-word epic an all-day affair conducted on the Calder circuit which included the R90S BMW, Laverda Jota, Ducati 750SS, M7 Moto-Guzzi Sports, and the rare MV 'California', attended by some of the machines' owners. That issue also featured my article on the history of BMW, a test report on the Moto-Morini 3-1/2, while I was involved in two other feature stories.

Foreword

Three of those Bike Book publications featured some of my pieces, including a full road test report on a 1959 BMW R60 with Steib saloon sidecar, and the first Ducati 750 Sports to arrive in Australia, which was followed shortly thereafter by the exciting 'Imola replica' Ducati 750SS and later again by the enlarged 900SS version. An all-new Japanese machine I road tested for REVS fortnightly newspaper – and which was another 'world-first' – was the OHC 'flat-four' GL1000 Honda, which arrived in Oz in 1974. It was too big for me, and its odd handling was a feature brought about by having a low-slung engine with gearbox and fuel tank mounted so low that riding the bike briskly was not easy.

Just like those clowns with their long, lead-lined boots which one can't push over, I initially found it hard to crank the bike over through corners because it always wanted to pop right back up again, and had to be held down quite firmly. Once used to this quirk the bike became an easy, relaxed machine to ride. It proved to be an effortless open road cruiser, and ended up being a great success in America.

Hopefully there are a few pieces of great interest within these covers, as well as some little-known information. It has been suggested to me that anybody who ever threw a leg over a motorcycle anywhere on this earth, and lived to tell the tale, should readily identify with the stories I have written on this subject. This may help to explain why these various columns, which glorified in the titles: 'Small Bore'; 'Short Torque'; 'Chain Chatter'; 'Lester We Forget' and 'The Wild Half' have proved to survive the test of time and been read by many, many riders both here in Australia and beyond.

Why the 'Wild Half'? The Bear suggested, when discussing my new column for his very successful "Australian Road Rider" magazine, that he knew I always wanted to be a 'Wild One', but he said that I was far too short (Eh?): so a Wild Half I thus became! My new column in The Bear's latest magazine, 'Australian Motorcyclist', is now called 'Classic Morris,' for better or for worse.

We finished this book at Omodeis, Sydney's Nationally-famous spare parts and accessory house, in 1968, – which still leaves much unsaid – although I have mentioned many odd incidents which happened in later years in some of the earlier stories. I left the trade at that time to pursue a successful 'full-time' career in Theatre and TV, in which I am still closely involved, so there was a break of some three years before it all fired up again, which it did in Melbourne and which continues to the day. We ran out of room as well, but there will certainly be much more of my published material to be collated, and that will happen sooner rather than later.

So come along for the ride and you don't need to own a bike at the moment to do so. In fact, even if you haven't ridden for many years, have never ridden a motorcycle at all, or are in the process of thinking that one day you might, then come along as well. There are said to be more than a few giggles within these pages; but there might also be a loud belly laugh or two.

Lester Morris,
Sydney, Australia.
November, 2016

BMW's space-ship-like R100RS. It was an effortless, swift machine which went exactly where it was pointed, was comfortable in the extreme and was fitted with one of the finest fairings of its era. It 'trapped' some engine noise and vibrated a little, due I assume, to the action of the large, horizontally-opposed alloy pistons.

What's this thing, then? Well, I did say, 'the biggest and the smallest', didn't I? This rare, 1979 50cc CBA Gilera moped was very handy for a half-hour squirt in bumper-to-bumper traffic, but could be a mobile chicane anywhere else, were I to attempt to ride it elsewhere. It was nippy for its tiny size, and handled on rails; as you would except from Gilera (yes, Gilera!)

Contents

Introduction – *by Peter "The Bear" Thoeming*	1
Foreword – *by Lester Morris*	2
Early Days	7
Hazell & Moore	20
A.P. North	67
Indian Outfit	77
Ryde Motorcycles	89
Omodeis	169

Acknowledgements

After so many years in motorcycling there must be many people I have met along the way to whom I owe my thanks, and indeed there are. I could begin by thanking the proprietors of the stores in which I have been employed during my pimpled youth, and for many years thereafter, but they are long gone, and their businesses with them. I thank them, anyway. The exception is **Ron Angel**, who came to the rescue by offering me a job when the Musical in which I appeared in Melbourne was canned earlier than everyone expected.

To the many motorcycle magazines to which I have contributed over nearly half a century, my thanks, although most of those publications have long gone as well. However, '*Two Wheels*' presses on with great vigour, as it has for nearly half a century, while '*AMCN*' goes from strength to strength, and is very much older. Though some earlier publications are gone, some of their highly-steamed editors remain: to **Peter (The Bear) Thoeming**, an iconic figure in the industry for a great many years edited several magazines which published my work in years past, and who now presses on with his latest publication, '*Australian Motorcyclist*', I offer my sincere thanks.

Bob Guntrip, editor of '*Classic Bike*'- among several other notable publications – is still busily involved with numerous published articles of his appearing in a variety of specialist publications, and seems to be as keen and unassuming as ever. **Mac Douglas**, a former long-term editor of *Two Wheels*, is yet another who published many of my pieces, and my regards to both of them as well.

What of the photographers whose work greatly enhances everyone's stories, and without whose artistry the published works would not be nearly as interesting? Ah yes, those 'never-satisfied' photographers!

The late, great **Bill Myer** is high on that short list, along with the late **Ray Ryan**, Melbourne's **Rob Lewis**, the staunch **Graham Munro** from Sydney and the legendary **Bill Forsythe**, also from Sydney; and just about everywhere else on earth. Each of them have my undying gratitude. Others whom I only met once or twice, but whose names were mentioned only briefly at the time, ought to be congratulated as well.

The book's cover cartoon from '*Classic Bike*' is by **Brendan J. Akhurst**, whose illustrations have greatly enlivened many of my stories in *Two Wheels*, while featuring heavily in many other stories in the magazine, and, of course, elsewhere. Well done, Brendan: great artistic flair and a fine sense of the absurd.

Closer to home, my wife Lyn helped save my Music Hall production and kept us on the go for over 30 years: there is no way known I could have done all that alone. And **Christine Kelleway**, who played in the Music Hall for most of that time and toured with me in '*Snow White*' through WA, NSW and New Zealand? These girls had little to do with motorcycling, but their support in several other artistic endeavours which were well removed from motorcycling knew no bounds. It's all encouragement, folks, and every little bit of it helps in this life.

This book's designer, graphic artist **Paula Garrod**, has designed many magazines and numerous books for years. I thank her sincerely for her great work in designing this one, and for cutting and shutting where necessary.

For anyone else out there whom I have met over the years, or owe a kindness to, but have not mentioned here; you are not forgotten, just out of mind at the moment but, I truly hope, soon to return. My thanks to you as well, and my apologies.

Lester Morris has asserted his moral right to be identified as the author of this work.

ISBN 978-0-6482885-0-3 (MOBI)
ISBN 978-0-6482885-1-0 (EPUB)
ISBN 978-0-646-96233-7 (Soft Cover)
Printed in Singapore by Markono Print Media Pte Ltd

1947

Early days

Squelch

There was a small grocery shop several blocks from my old school, Darlinghurst Junior Tech, which I found to be very interesting indeed. In the first place, it was the only shop just about anywhere in Sydney where I could (very) occasionally hand two pence over the counter to buy a small white bag which hid just two of the entirely delicious Arnotts Chocolate Monte biscuits. Those great treats, along with many similar delicacies, which are to be found by the boat-load on every one of the Nation's grocery store's shelves these days, were to be found nowhere else during the War years; at least nowhere else of which I was aware. I never asked where he managed to get them from, it was quite enough to be able to nibble them slowly, just as a mouse might nibble a piece of ripe cheese, thus ensuring that each one of the tasty morsels would last a very long time.

Looking back, I think I was favoured by the shopkeeper because of my **second** interest in his store, which was his gleaming motorcycle, which leaned on its footrest outside the store every day. It was a 1934 500cc Square Four Ariel – I was later to learn from my brother Don – but I certainly didn't know much about it then, although at the time the bike's owner did tell me a little about the engine, while the brand name was clearly emblazoned on the sides of the fuel tank panels. It fairly gleamed in the sunshine, from its bright scarlet and chrome petrol tank to its highly polished alloy primary drive case and timing case covers and the beautiful alloy casting which concealed the overhead camshaft drive chain. Even the contrasting black frame and mudguards shone. And they were well augmented by the pair of long, chrome plated exhaust pipes which terminated in a pair of similarly gleaming fish-tailed mufflers.

> *"I wouldn't sit on that if I was you, son" he said, not unkindly. "If it fell on you it might kill you."*

I had stumbled upon the bike entirely by accident, for the small grocery shop was off the schoolboys' beaten path a bit, and I wasn't long before I was perched on the bike's saddle, swaying about from side to side and looking off into the distance as though I was out there somewhere on the open road, the bike roaring away underneath me, the wind whistling through the hair I still had in abundance back then. He came out of the shop almost at once, and with a grin on his face. "I wouldn't sit on that if I was you, son" he said, not unkindly. "If it fell on you it might kill you. If it fell on me, the worst it would do would be to break my leg. But it would kill you."

All of about 14 years of age, I nonetheless thought his pronouncement was overly dramatic, but I climbed off the bike and stood looking at it with more than a little envy. "What's that red 500 doing on that shiny thing?" I asked, pointing to the highlighted number which was cast into the overhead cam-chain case cover.

"That's the size of the engine, lad," he announced. "It's got four cylinders and it's a very fast bike, and this one's usually got a 600 written there. But you can ask for one to be on special order which is a 500." I had no blind idea what he was talking about, but it struck me even then that surely a '600' whatever-they-were would be at least 100 better than a '500' would ever be? The same rule of thumb probably exists even today – or does it?

My brother Don had recently left school and had started work in a specialised workshop called Palmer and Goodsell, in Sydney's Foveaux Street, where he had hoped to be apprenticed as a motorcycle mechanic. They were not especially interested in training mechanics at that time, so he left there some time later and went to work with Bennett and Wood, where he stayed for many years. But before he left he introduced me to a bloke called Alec Quelch, who worked in the garage, and who *was* a motorcycle mechanic. Oddly, his all-abiding passion was, of all things, the Square Four Ariel, or 'Squariel' as they were known in those days. Apparently Alec was well known in the industry (and so was his love for the Squariel) and he glorified in the nickname "Square Four Quelch" which was quickly corrupted to "Squelch."

Early days

I told Squelch about the Ariel I had seen in Barcome Avenue, near the school, and he apparently knew all about it, because I recall him telling me that the owner always had the bike service by him. He told me the 500 -whatever that was – should have been a 600 (whatever *that* was) because the bigger engine was the standard machine, the 500 only made to 'special order.' He didn't seem to understand why the owner went to the added expense of ordering the smaller capacity bike, when the 600 was much more readily available, and when I told him the owner said it was a fast bike, he replied that yes it was, but the 600 was even faster. He shook his head sadly as he said that, and I didn't understand why… that is, not until many years later.

> *" I could wear the gear if I must, but I was never to ride that bike anywhere. "*

At that time I had had very little to do with motorcycles, even though I enjoyed more than a passing interest in them, and in fact was to buy my very first machine, a 1929 ES2 Norton, a year or so later while still at school, purchasing the bike with part of the proceeds from selling newspapers on (and off!) the trams in Kings Cross. I spent some more of the money I had stashed aside on some seemingly-useless War surplus items like a paratroopers (steel) helmet, a pair of hugely oversized pilots' shoulder-length leather gauntlets and an even larger pair of enormous, heavy duty boots intended for use by adult, motorcycle-mounted Dispatch riders. Oh, and there was also a box which contained a pair of brand-new US air-force Polaroid goggles, complete with a spare elastic strap and several spare lenses of various colours, from dark and light green to yellow, amber and a couple of clear ones as well. This lot completed my ensemble.

Perhaps I couldn't ride the bike anywhere, because my parents – or at least my mum – declared themselves dismayed at these asinine purchases and threatened me with a near-death experience if I was ever to be **seen** riding the old Norton about. I could wear the gear if I must, but I was never to ride that bike anywhere. Well, I did ride the thing on occasion, but was never seen by *them*, so a perverse logic dictated (at least to me) that those entirely illicit, brief rides, while my folks were across town by tram and thus gone for quite some time, didn't really count, so I was thus spared the grim experience with which I was threatened. At least for the time being!!

My slowly developing passion for powered two-wheelers (as against the ME-propelled pushbike I already owned) was piqued when Don foolishly mentioned he was going to the Sydney Royale on a Saturday night for one of the very first Speedway meetings to be held after the war, where he was to meet Squelch on the first level of what he called the 'main, or open, stand.' Of course I insisted on going as well, but as usual he didn't want to know about that, for I was at that time – and may still be, for all I know – a pain in the arse younger brother who was always trying to tag along with him.

Well, by some stroke of good fortune, to which I remain forever indebted, I managed to go with brother Don, the while having absolutely no blind idea of what I was going to see when I got there.

There was a huge crowd at the Sydney Showground that night, which was 'estimated' to be at 50,000 – later said to be closer to 30,000 – but this was still an enormous number of people and was claimed to be the largest crowd to attend ***any*** sporting fixture in Sydney back in the late forties. I was later to learn that Speedway racing had already been held on the nearby Sports Ground (now the Sydney Football Stadium) in 1946, but this was to be the first meeting on the huge, 1/3rd mile oval in the Showground since before the war, the venue hosting its first speedway event there almost twenty years previously.

The air was electric, the sights and sounds of this enormous, highly excited crowd added to by the harsh sounds of several engines being warmed up in the pit area, situated directly under the large concrete stand which stood right opposite the ' main stand' in which we were only to find room to *stand* and watch. Suddenly, to an enormous cheer, the pit gates opened and six black-clad riders rode out and made their way to a set of white ribbons which had been lowered across the track at what was clearly the start line halfway along the finishing straight. The air was suddenly alive with sound as the bikes then moved slowly to the tapes, their engines on full song with clouds of white smoke in the air behind them when suddenly the tapes flew up and they were away!

Vintage Morris

1947

I had never, ever, seen (or heard!) anything like that before as the riders, who were close enough to each other to be covered by a King-Size bedspread, howled sideways into that corner at ever-increasing speed, to then spear down the 'back' straight opposite the finish line, obviously gaining speed with every meter covered. They flew through the corner underneath the main stand at break-neck speed and howled onto the finishing straight at a speed which looked to be almost half as fast as before, to again fling themselves headlong into that fast, wide sweeping bend, apparently at an impossible pace. I stood there open-mouthed in utter amazement as the six riders hurtled shoulder-to-shoulder down that straight and again negotiated the fast sweeper underneath the concrete stand over the pits and flew sideways onto the finishing straight.

It was all over in three short laps, but the crowd was still bubbling with excitement when yet another six riders emerged from the pits, their black leathers and coloured helmets offset by bikes agleam with lashing of chrome and copper plate, the engines again snarling like six wild beasts just under control, impatiently waiting to be unleashed as those which had gone on before them had been.

For some unaccountable reason, the spectators who stood on ground level stood well away from the high fence which surrounded the arena and I frankly couldn't understand why. As the riders flew out of that first corner after the start of the second race, I rushed down to the fence to get a better look at the action, and in fact climbed up onto the so-called 'Bull Pens' on the apex of that first corner to be closer to the action.

Well, I couldn't get any closer to the action than that, even if I was on the track itself and right in the midst of it all, for as the riders flew into that corner on the next lap, broadside on, they pelted several cubic meters of Dolomite clay from each of the six spinning rear wheels. And they flung it all *straight at me*! And at an extremely high speed, to boot.

I have never before, nor since, felt anything like it as I was mercilessly pelted with tons of the stuff, which felt as though I had been the victim of several very large labourers who were lined up, in close company but one at a time, to viciously pelt me with several shovel loads of blue metal and other pain-inducing road base materials. The stuff those bikes showered me with ended up in my eyes and ears, up my nose, in my mouth and down my neck, inside the front of my shirt, matted into my hair, and up the leg of my schoolboy's short trousers.

The next thing I can remember was lying on the ground while being dragged away from the fence by several concerned patrons who helped me to my feet and began brushing me down, as I howled in shock like a new born babe.

Hey, how was I expected to know how dangerous climbing onto that fence would be? After all, it was only the second Speedway race I had ever witnessed, and I was still a young schoolkid, so I couldn't be expected to know that those rooster-tails of flying Dolomite pelted over the fence from the machines' rear wheels could slam into someone with such violence. And above the din of the racing machines screaming back to the bend to administer another dose I could hear the huge crowd still shrieking with laughter at this idiot of a kid who had jumped on top of the fence to get a better look at the action, only to be rewarded for this absurd behaviour by being thrashed savagely with a high-speed layer of the loam with which that track had been so recently been re-surfaced.

One surprising thing which took my immediate attention as I was raised blubbering to my feet, was that the little semi-circular dickey-door with which the front of young schoolboys' short pants were thoughtfully adorned, was standing agape! I never found out why, because for a kid who was very shy and even more careful to close that handy little trapdoor after it had served its stated purpose, it was simply never, ever open like that unless it simply had to be; and usually for only a short period of time at that.

Like much of the large crowd in that huge stand, Squelch found the whole episode very amusing, but brother Don was visibly upset. I thought he was concerned for me, of course, but as he went to some pains to point out, he was much more concerned about what would happen to *him* if this incident ever reached the ears of my father. He was, after all, my older brother and should have been looking after me, pain in the arse though I was.

That Speedway meeting was just one of many hundreds of similar meetings I was happy to attend for many seasons on Friday nights at the Sports Ground and on Saturday nights at the Speedway Royale on Sydney Showground. But I never ventured anywhere near that safety fence again, even though I sat close enough to the fence to occasionally feel the light wisp of some powdered loam dust, and of course to gleefully inhale the heady aroma of burning castor oil.

Vintage Morris

Early days

My brother Clyde

The eldest of my three brothers was an odd character. For some inexplicable reason the description has been leveled at me on several occasions over the years, and there may be a reason for this somewhere, if I could only find out what it is. But Clyde was something else again; a rebel, a gifted artist; a man who seemed imbued (or cursed) with the 'wanderlust', which decreed that he was always searching for that elusive something, somewhere, which might make his life more complete, and he spent much of his early life vainly seeking it. He seemed to be a reasonable sort of person, if a bit elusive, one of his odd quirks being to suddenly disappear whenever a Circus or other travelling sideshow came to town.

We would hear nothing from him for months, or sometimes years, at a time, which must have concerned my mum greatly, although I cannot say I ever heard her mention it – at least not to me.

He was a very fine painter, and made a quite good living later in his life as a commercial and display artist, but as he grew older he became even stranger. Among many other things he achieved at the time, he was chiefly responsible for an almost complete re-vamp of the place while painting the Luna Park area back in the mid-forties when he was in his twenties.

When the Hollywood block-buster movie 'The Ten Commandments' was about to be released in this country during the fifties, he was commissioned by MGM to mount a large display in one of the city's major Cinemas, and his life-sized, cut-out figures of the various leading actors, allied to his own background painting, was hailed far and wide, resulting in him fielding several offers to go to Hollywood to repeat his ground-breaking displays. None of us seemed to know how he got the gig in the first place, but for some unaccountable reason he simply didn't want to know about any of the offers which seemed to arrive daily by post or phone.

Today these types of highly-colourful promotional displays are seen in every Cinema chain everywhere, often to augment the more simple, full-colour posters which adorn the walls of these establishments, and they are prominently positioned to promote movies which may be several weeks away from being screened. It is entirely possible that brother Clyde was a pioneer in this field in the early fifties, because this type of promotion was apparently unknown prior to that time.

His other works – like designing and building a miniature display during the early War years of a three-storey College complete with gymnasium, heliport (for the new-fangled helicopters), and viable Theatre, while simultaneously writing and rehearsing a Theatre revue he called "Shake it, Don't Break it", seemed to him to be nothing out of the ordinary. The stage production almost made it to the Tivoli in Sydney, but was finally quashed by the Theatre during rehearsals because of lack of funds. This was all remarkable stuff to us little kids, but he remained almost a stranger to us all, in particular to my dear old mum.

None of us knew where he got these skills from; he just seemed to pluck them out of the air around him.

He was gone for some months in the later forties, but a long-lost, black sheep cousin of ours from New Zealand turned up unheralded and unannounced at our door one day (how he knew where we lived has always been a Family Mystery) to breathlessly convey the news that Clyde was working at the Royal Easter Show in Sydney, and he was appearing with the frightening Globe of Death, promoted by a family called the "Daredevil Durkins."

The Globe of Death was a two and a half ton steel-mesh sphere some six meters in diameter which had been built out of latticed steel – I believe as far back as in 1931. A small panel underneath the sphere allowed for entry and exit, while the whole device was built in easily dismantled panels, welded, bolted and/or hinged together. The sphere was supported by a series of strong steel poles which were secured to the structure at various points and it seemed secure enough but it also vibrated and wobbled alarmingly as the (several)motorcycles within it were ridden up the walls, sideway in a kind of 'figure-of-eight' movement and over the top as well.

It had taken the Durkin brothers, Herb (a former noted speedway rider who won several Speedway Championships) Frank and Stan almost four years to practice inside the thing and to reach a reasonable level of skill and safety. They had previously devised the Wall of Death, by comparison a 'simple' timber circular chamber like a vertical wall, around which they flashed on their motorcycles, and this had proved to be a very successful fairground attraction.

The Globe of Death was an entirely different matter, for it then allowed the various motorcycles which were ridden therein to not only run along the side walls but also to loop the loop over the top as well, and this was done not only in solo but with at least two – and sometimes three! – motorcycles running about inside the cage at the one time.

It has been suggested that sometimes there have been as many as **seven** machines in there together, but there seems to be no evidence of this and I seriously doubt if it would be in any way possible for this to occur. But as a Grand Finale there was also a (very) midget car zipping about in there with two or sometimes three motorcycles, and I have actually seen this at an earlier Easter Show, the tiny four-wheeler driven by Noreen, the wife of Herb Durkin. She was included in the act from around 1934, not long after she unaccountably married Herb. Incidentally, that car was so tiny the steering wheel had to be removed before Noreen could get into the thing, then her knees were under her chin somewhere, her elbows flapping about like eagles' wings, and she was so firmly wedged therein that there is no way she could get out again until some-one removed the steering wheel again and prised her out with what looked like a large tyre lever!

How she would have coped in the inevitable event of an accident is anyone's guess, but I assume they would have to open the cage up, bundle the lot into an ambulance together and then have to carry out a surgical operation to remove her from the vehicle, or the vehicle from her!

As far as I am aware there is no record anywhere of how Herb – or anyone else – actually persuaded Noreen to risk life and limb by wedging herself into that tiny little thing in the first place, but she was at that time a very well-known Tivoli showgirl, and a versatile solo artiste (she was, in fact, the sister of the famous Theatrical entrepreneur Garnett H Carroll) so if you were brave and clever enough, and enjoyed sufficient talent to make a successful career out of that tough on-stage job back in the thirties before TV arrived, then I suppose you could do anything, no matter how dangerous it may seem to be.

So members of the our family, my two brothers, Don and Andy, my mum and myself, trudged off to the Sydney Showground and made our way to the Globe of Death, its presence heralded by the bellowing sounds of the open megaphone exhausts of an all-black motorcycle sitting atop a set of meter-wide rollers it was driving.

The rear wheel was contained within a pair of rollers, which safely located the bike, while a long chain drove another pair of rollers upon which the front wheel sat. A small, thin man wearing a pair of leather breeches with stout lace-up boots and black body-belt, the *ensemble* topped by a flaming red shirt with billowing, puffed sleeves, stood poised upon the motorcycle's single saddle, his arms outstretched sideways at shoulder-height.

The bike, which seemed to be only just under control, was sliding from side to side to the very edge of the rollers, apparently teetering on the brink of falling out of them and crashing to the ground several meters below him. It was all very dramatic stuff, the crowd "Oohing" and Ahhing" at the bloke who was so obviously endangering life and limb upon his dangerous perch. I noted that the machine was a near-new 350cc Triumph 3T, the poor relation to the first of the 500cc Triumph twins which had just begun to arrive in Australia. It was soon after the war and I was still at school, so it must have been around 1947.

> *"No Health and Safety Rules in those days, folks, and you can bet there was not much life insurance either."*

I had seen the Globe often enough at earlier venues some years previously (for many years it was a fixture in numerous country and major city Agricultural Shows and had even played **on stage** in the Melbourne Tivoli Theatre several times!) but in those days the machines were all pre-war Coventry Eagle 250cc two-strokes – again with open exhausts which rent the air around with a frightful din. I had also watched spellbound as the riders would often ride side-saddle(?) when they rode around the walls of the Globe, and often when looping the loop were riding 'hands off', with arms either outstretched to their sides or firmly crossed over their chests. No Health and Safety Rules in those days, folks, and you can bet there was not much life insurance either.

But apart from the interesting 3T Triumph motorcycle, it was the *rider* who suddenly took all of my attention because, as I finally focused upon him I was shocked, thrilled, amazed and then horrified – or it could have the other way

Early days

> "*Clyde,*" *she trumpeted for the entire Showground to hear. "Get down off that thing at once, you fool. Do you want to break your neck? Get down from there at once, I say, you bugger of a kid!!*"

around, for I was momentarily stunned – to see it was my brother Clyde up there smirking at his enthralled audience, his life clearly in peril!

But if I had taken a beat or two to notice it was him, then mother was very much quicker than me, as mothers are of course inclined to be. My mum was half a head shorter than me (yes, that is possible!) and she had been a very feisty readhead in her much younger days. Her hair was no longer red, but the feistiness remained with her to the end of her days. She swiftly elbowed her way through the throng until she was directly below the bellowing motorcycle and I can still hear her voice to this day as it rang out above the din of that raucous exhaust.

"Clyde," she trumpeted for the entire Showground to hear. "Get down off that thing at once, you fool. Do you want to break your neck? Get down from there at once, I say, you bugger of a kid!!" The crowd may have thought mother was a stooge of some sort because for the most part they thought it highly amusing, laughing uproariously. At first, that is, but she soon put a stop to that nonsense.

"This is no laughing matter" she announced to nobody and everybody at the same time. "How would you like it if your son was up there making a fool of himself?" She turned upstage again and shouted to my brother anew, but with even more bluster. "Get down from there, I said."

Somewhere through the fog her voice emerged into his consciousness, and he looked down to see what all the fuss was about, losing his concentration as the bike wobbling about even more alarmingly than before, in fact apparently threatening to topple off its unstable perch.

A man dressed in similar attire to Clyde's strode over to mother as if to harangue her, but she said something to him that stopped him in his tracks and which caused him to make the throat-slashing gesture to cut the bike's engine, which Clyde did and it sobbed with relief as it sputtered to a stop. Clyde bowed to the applauding crowd and climbed down from his lofty perch to face his irate mum, while we stood about wondering whether or not we should try to disappear somewhere; at least for the time being.

But all was forgiven because they tearfully embraced as they disappeared into the nearby tent which seemed to be the office of the Durkins, to emerge a little later arm-in-arm and all smiles. There was one more performance to be given, Clyde assured us, and then he could gladly come home with us, his long tenure with the Durkins over and with no recriminations from any of the people involved.

But mother was far from placated because his final performance, which we saw for free, involved the tiny car and three motorcycles in the Globe at once, the car being sent on its way by an assistant who held the little vehicle in position from the centre of the base of the Globe to control it as is slowly rotated until it picked up sufficient speed to be able to negotiate the sphere under its own steam. Naturally, that assistant could not leave the inside of the sphere while the various machines were looping the loop, performing figure-of-eight maneuvers or running about the sides of the sphere, *and then alternating their places and movements*, but he had to continuously change his position in the base of the Sphere as the machines flew about inside it, missing him by mere inches. That person could have been thoroughly splattered at any time, and with no warning at all.

That sprightly assistant was of course, my brother Clyde, who gladly came home with us after that final performance.

As a post-script to this story it was some 20 years later, when I was working in Omodies, that a man came in to purchase five pairs of heavy lace-up boots, five body-belts and five pairs of black leather breeches. He was of course a descendant of the Daredevil Durkins, continuing that tradition which had been founded way back in the very early thirties. He asked for, and was given, a discount on his purchases, and was in fact greeted like a long-lost relative by the store's Manager.

Clearly he had visited the place several times

Vintage Morris

in the past, for the pair seemed to know one another well. Perhaps I should have mentioned my brother Clyde to the man, but there was no opportunity to do so, for he suddenly shook hands with manager, bundled up his large pile of goods and quickly departed.

Statues in the park

We played soccer for my school in Sydney's Centennial Park on Tuesday every week in winter in the days when I was a simple, puling schoolboy during the early forties. We played the game in a fairly haphazard way (who wanted to know about soccer all those years ago?) upon a small field which was located at the base of a small slope which lead down from a pair of massive, heavy gates of the park to the vast area beneath.

Just inside that set of gates there used to be a pair of pseudo-Classic white 'marble' statues which framed the entrance road, the duo posing imperiously upon their separate plinths. Sadly, they were removed some years later because the local idiots were vandalising the poor, defenceless buggers to death. One of them was the large near-nude statue of a Greek wrestler – from **Ancient** Greece thankfully – who seemed to be forever sniffing his own armpit as he stood with one iron-clad forearm resting on top of his head, the other covering his kidneys. There was a statue of an equally near-nude discus thrower standing directly opposite him.

The discus thrower was apparently just about to hurl his discus into the adjacent bushes, as he was bent down to the task, his legs spread apart his huge, gross fig leaf (which was all both athletes wore) fondled into a nigh shapeless blob by decades of giggling, itinerant schoolgirls. The girls, I might add, used the Park in their hundreds on sports days as well. On one notable occasion, I saw that the hapless discus thrower had been expertly made up (I assume by one or more of the girls, or perhaps a soft boy) with scarlet lipstick, beautifully rouged cheeks and heavy eye shadow, eyebrows neatly arched, his eyeliner very cleverly applied. The statue was clearly embarrassed by this unwarranted attention, the frowning wrestler opposite looking upon him with disdain, if not downright suspicion. A week later the man's face was once again a virginal white, which I'm sure was a relief to him.

There were other statues scattered about the park, one of which was a statue of a seated Diana the Huntress with her shield, part of whose longbow had been snapped off by an earlier generation, but whose apparent lack of expertise with the weapon when it *was* complete was evidenced by the pencil-thin greyhound which attended her. Of course it may well have been the more slender *Italian* greyhound, or even a whippet, but that larger than life hound was nonetheless a bit on the slim side.

Those three statues in particular were the butt of many an earthy jibe as they grimaced upon the passing parade from their positions just inside the main gates, the two athletes opposite one another on the Bondi Junction entrance, Diana upon her more lonely plinth just down from the larger, main gates at the Moore Park end. Unhappily, these three statues, along with most of the others which were such a feature of Centennial Park from the late 1880s, were removed in 1971.

It was to the poor Diana that I once unintentionally turned my attention on the occasion when I had one of my very first solo rides upon a motorcycle. I am still at odds to understand why the bike's owner Billy Galloway actually allowed me to ride his year old 1946 Speed Twin Triumph at all. Perhaps he'd learned I recently bought my very first motorcycle, a 1929 Norton ES2, which I had managed to secure by spending much of the money I had earned after school hours by selling newspapers while leaping on and off the speeding trams in Kings Cross

It was during a sports day in the Park, and we had just finished playing a losing soccer match, which was quite normal for us, as Darlinghurst Junior Technical School was a bit of an easy beat. Billy's younger brother Bob was one of the team members, his lack of expertise with the round ball by no means unusual. For some obscure reason, I could kick a ball fairly well, and with either foot, while our inside right half was fairly good at the game, but in a team of eleven it was never enough. Both the inside right – whose name escapes me now as it did even then – and myself were selected to play for the State in a Junior soccer carnival while at school, if that means anything to anyone, but the rest of the team were, to put it mildly, not up to scratch.

Billy had rolled up just prior to the game ending, and he expressed his dismay at our loss, which at 3-nil was a little less than usual. He called me to come up the steep grass hill from the football field to where his gleaming Amaranth Red Triumph sat proudly on its rear

Early days

stand, gave me some very simple instructions and fired the engine up. "Four speed gearbox, mate" he said proudly, "One down, three up. Not like all the others, which are one up and three down."

In passing, Billy looked more like The Fonze, of "Happy Days" fame, than the Fonze ever did, with his hair in almost exactly the same style, the same type of open leather jacket, and he wore the much-maligned "working men's dungarees", which were later to achieve widespread and everlasting fame as the Blue Jeans people wear with such fervour today. But Billy's hair was quite a different colour than Fonzie's, for it was a flaming red, just like his younger brother's. Billy actually preceded the endearing character from the popular TV sit-com by the best part of 25 years

He seemed much more confident than I was about allowing me to ride the bike, and I realised some time afterwards that he must have thought I was actually riding the Norton about, even though I was some two and a bit years shy of being able to legally ride anything on two wheels other than a bike powered entirely by the efforts of whoever happened to be pedalling the thing. He was half-right, because I wasn't allowed to ride the old Norton at all, at least not while my folks were anywhere in sight, but I had been known to fire the thing up and take it for an illicit squirt on more than one occasion when I discovered I was alone.

So Billy kicked the Triumph engine into life and helped me into the saddle, which I thought a bit un-necessary because I was about the same height then as I am now and the single saddles on those early British motorcycles were always easy enough for me to reach and to sit upon. Naturally I stalled the bike a couple of times before I was instructed to 'open her up a bit', which I finally did as I dropped the clutch and sped off, snapping my neck like a carrot in the process.

"Just keep turning to the right," I heard him shout as I sped away, "and you'll end up back here."

And so I did just that, riding to the bottom of the tar-sealed road, and then turned right onto the main boulevard, riding in a clockwise direction. Another right hander, by now in third gear, and that right hander took me up the hill on the way towards the main gates on the Moore Park end. Next, I peeled off to the right again to negotiate the tight corner where the imperious Diana held Court and which was to lead along a side road back towards the road upon which I had begun my perilous and entirely illegal ride. For some reason I managed to remember to change back to second gear before I entered the corner, but of course I had no blind idea of the speed at which that corner could be safely negotiated, or what the correct line through it should be.

I peeled off early and came out late, instead of the other way round, with the inevitable result that I was rewarded for this lack of expertise by mounting a small grassy mound, sliding sideways across the verdant sward and clouting Diana side-on right on her plinth – a very painful spot indeed. If not for Diana herself, then certainly for me!

It was a bit of a blur back then, and not much better right now, but I dimly recall I was pelted out of the saddle, bounced onto it and out again in one hit, came down again with my knees on the petrol tank (boy, didn't that hurt!) and we then speared across the grass back onto the roadway, my feet by now off the footrests and trailing along behind. The bike then decided to take me back onto the grass on the opposite side to where Diana sat shaking her head sadly at the scene which was dramatically unfolding in front of her. And then, the throttle still wide open and flat out in second gear, we leapt across the series of high, buttressed roots of a monstrous Moreton Bay fig tree which had been thoughtlessly planted in my way almost a century earlier.

Again I was pitched out of the saddle, the only part of me still attached to the Triumph a pair of white-knuckled hands which steadfastly refused to un-curl themselves no matter what might happen. I landed again a few seconds later, this time between the sprung saddle and the rear mudguard, my arms at absolutely full stretch, then was pelted back into the saddle for the last time. Clearly quite sick of this accidental display of advanced gymnastics, the Triumph finally decided it had had enough, turned on its heel and climbed the small hillock we had been rapidly descending, then headed back onto the comparative safety of the sealed road.

Be well assured, the bike did this on its own for it was entirely unaided. I'm sure I had no input at all, because I frankly didn't know what was going to happen next, but I was quite in awe of the machine's ability to execute such a neat manoeuvre. In fact I had little idea of what had just happened, although I knew too well how close I came to disaster. I was very lucky to be still sitting on the bike, as it had been entirely out of my control and could easily have pelted

Vintage Morris

1947

> *"If I were you" he said with a wink just before he roared away, "I'd give up riding motorbikes. You're a bit on the small side for 'em. They're not for everyone, you know."*

me off at any time during the last 10 seconds or more.

We proceeded along that road for a few seconds, the engine screaming for mercy before I suddenly realised this and changed into third gear. For the first time in my life I actually heard a motorcycle engine sigh with relief, as the bike and its half-terrified rider at last settled down for the ride back to where its proud owner was patiently waiting. The bike settled itself down almost immediately but I certainly didn't because I was well aware of how lucky I had been. Both knees were aching badly and my backside was as sore as if someone had bent me over and kicked me up the behind several times with the toe of a size 10 steel-capped workmen's boot.

Suitably chastened, I rode up the slight incline to the top of the Park, turned right and right again, and then rode down to where Galloway was standing, by now surrounded by several of the team players.

"How did you go?" he asked, as the boys crowded around, "I heard you really turning the wick up once you were out of sight. Goes well doesn't she?"

"Yeah, it was great fun." I lied. I wasn't brave enough to tell him the bike was still only in second gear as it was revving its poor guts out when he heard it, and that it was totally out of control on a slippery grass surface while I was clinging onto the thing for dear life, with absolutely no idea what was going to happen next. I think he cottoned onto this however, because he then pointed out a few grass stains on the bikes wheel rims and then turned his attention to my shoes.

"What's wrong with your Saint Louis Blues, mate?" he asked, grinning at me and pointing to the badly scuffed uppers on the near-new full-box brogue shoes I had thoughtfully put on after I had changed from my football boots.

"Ran off the road onto the grass," I replied, "but it was all right, I didn't come off."

"Yeah, thought so. Thank Christ for that. More by good luck than good management, I reckon," he laughed.

The he gave me a piece of friendly advice I have thankfully chosen to ignore.

"If I were you" he said with a wink just before he roared away, "I'd give up riding motorbikes. You're a bit on the small side for 'em. They're not for everyone, you know."

We moved well away from our war-time home in the wharf-side suburb of Woolloomooloo a few years after I left school and I never saw either of the Galloway brothers again. I doubt if Billy ever knew how I took absolutely no notice of his admonition, even though I must admit that there has been many a high-performance motorcycle which has clearly been much too big for me to push about. I didn't say 'too big for me to ride', because I have only ever come across three machines which have almost beaten me; the CBX1000, six-cylinder Honda, that Monstrous, ill-handling, six-cylinder Z1300 Kawasaki and the awe-inspiring Munch Mammoth.

Perhaps I could have added the water-cooled, 750cc three-cylinder Suzuki 'Water Bottle' two-stroke to that list, but I rode it as almost daily transport for several months while working with Ron Angel in Melbourne and I could finally pelt it about like a roller skate – that is until I had to climb off the bike and wheel it about: it then became quite a handful to control, let me tell you!

First Bike

My first motorcycle was not a 1935 GTP Velocette, that sweet little 250cc two stroke single with twin exhausts, huge external flywheel, foot gear-change and throttle-controlled oil-pump. Throttle-controlled oil-PUMP on a pre-war British two-stroke, did I say? Most people might assume the Japanese were first with that 'advanced' method of two-stroke engine lubrication back in the late '60s, but in fact they were not

Yes, it was going to be the Velocette but, sadly, that was not to be.

The bike was for sale in Lakemba and I lived in Woolloomooloo, which meant I had to ride my pushbike out there and come home on the Velo – possibly with the pushbike slung over my shoulder. Yes, you can do that, if you're stupid enough; I did it once when I bought a new pushbike and rode home with the old one hung over my shoulder.

Vintage Morris

Early days

What an idiot I was! I must have looked like a variation on a Hermit Crab, wearing an alternative mode of transport instead of a lichen-and weed-encrusted sea shell. A motorist zooming past in one of the first-ever Holdens leaned over and shouted: "I've heard of a spare wheel, but this is ridiculous!" How right he was!

Perhaps fortunately, I couldn't find the address and, in fact, was looking for a place called Kanimbla, which may not even exist in this country for all I know. Thinking back, it was just as well. I had never ridden a motor-cycle before and was too young to hold a licence, anyway. I had the money, because I'd sold newspapers as a schoolkid by leaping on an off the speeding trams in Sydney's Kings Cross trams for many months, but I cringe at the thought of the disaster that return journey could have been. Assuming the owner of the little Velocette had been fool enough to sell me the thing, that is.

I made do, instead, with a totally different machine for my first bike – a 1929 Model 18 Norton 500cc single, the pre-cursor to the later ES2. The nomenclature 'ES' referred to the enclosed (valve)springs. According to my father, who was faintly amused at my new toy, the machine was known universally as the Mankiller Norton in view, I was later to learn, of its evil handling when pushed hard.

There was, rumour had it, an invisible hinge in the middle of the frame just under the single saddle, around which the tail-end would pivot and wag about like an eager puppy dog. I searched in vain for this hinge but never found it, although you could feel it working well the moment the bike was ridden with any degree of enthusiasm.

Cornering at speed was a bit odd in view of the bike's slow handling, courtesy of its extremely long wheelbase, plus the machinations of the invisible hinge and an almost total lack of suspension. On the positive side, the footrests were mounted very high and could never be made to touch the ground. It wasn't much, but it was something.

The centre-stand was another matter entirely, for it eagerly ground itself away to a razor's edge, and the gear-lever would sometimes dig in – yes, the gear-lever! – on right-handers, which was very off-putting in every sense of the expression.

The bike was fitted with a three-speed Sturmey-Archer gearbox, the gear-lever initially hand-operated. It was a long, flat steel lever with a round wooden ball on its end, but its mounting

> *"The various gears were easy to find, be it understood, for they announced their selection with such alarming graunches and grinding noises that they rendered the horn unnecessary as a warning device."*

position could be altered so that it was much closer to a rider's foot, which made for much quicker – if not too certain – gear-changes. First gear was gained by lifting the lever by foot to first gear almost level with the petrol tank, with second gear at footrest level and top gear with the lever almost dragging on the ground. Oh, and you had to find the gears for yourself; it was very much 'hit-and-miss' for there was, of course, no positive-stop mechanism to select the gear for you.

The various gears were easy to find, be it understood, for they announced their selection with such alarming graunches and grinding noises that they rendered the horn unnecessary as a warning device.

Another odd thing about the Norton was its incandescent exhaust pipe, which could light your way home after dark as it glowed white at the exhaust port and tapered off to cherry red as it curved towards the gearbox. How was I to know at the time that the engine was over-heating because the ignition timing was slightly retarded and that the owner of the machine was similarly inclined?

Valve gear was not enclosed and you could run into the back of a bus as you watched, mesmerised, the valves opening and closing before your very eyes. The pushrods were similarly naked and you could watch them jiggling up and down as the engine ran – if you weren't interested in the traffic around you! Thankfully there wasn't much of that to be found, and I didn't ride the bike very often anyway, certainly not while my folks were anywhere to be seen!

You could – well, I could – pluck the inlet pushrod from its mount while the engine was running, if you felt like it. I never touched the exhaust pushrod, I'm happy to say, and I've wondered occasionally just what would have happened had I done so. That's interesting to think about, isn't it?

That Norton handled very badly, and I shouldn't have been riding the thing anyway, but I learned to tame it, more or less. This made the first bike I could actually ride legally a true joy to own, even though it wasn't much to shout about in the performance stakes.

This first 'legal' bike was a near-new 1951 James Cadet, a trim little 125cc Villiers-engined, plunger-sprung lightweight which I owned for some five years and which I rode just about everywhere. If its performance wasn't in the same league as the Norton's, it was at least very much more comfortable and dead reliable – except for one or two little quirks.

It had been raced at Bathurst in the first, long-forgotten Ultra-Lightweight event at the OCTOBER Bathurst meeting in 1951 and, though outwardly standard, was still in full race trim internally, with an alloy-filled cylinder head giving a much higher compression ratio, a slightly larger carburettor – from the 200cc model – and some judicious work on the ports. It would easily blow off a hard-ridden James 'Captain', the 200cc variant, and had a clear edge on the frightful 250cc BSA singles some fools were persuaded to buy.

However, it had the disconcerting habit of snapping the two top mudguard stays with no warning and dropping the front guard onto the tyre. The guard would then pivot around the rear stay – which would always remain intact – and sometimes whip the guard under the font wheel. If this happened, it would lock up everything and allow you to skate noisily along with a steel front tyre underneath your wheel until you fell off.

The noise was frightful, so much so that it would empty local pubs while strong men blanched visibly and little old ladies suddenly could hear clearly again – if only for a short time.

This happened to me no fewer than *three* times and it may be of interest to note that the Spare Parts Department at Hazell and Moore, for whom I worked at the time, had two full racks of front guards in stock, to service the small number of machines that were sold. And yes, I recall that I fell off on two of those occasions and shunted a taxi up the backside on the other.

Amazingly, the problem didn't occur with the larger, 200cc variant.

When I fitted the third mudguard, I mounted the quarter-inch Cycle thread bolts to the forks with thick rubber washers in a bid to muffle any errant vibrations which might have been causing the problem. They were actually the Triumph motorcycle's tank-mounting rubbers, but they made not a whole lot of difference: the guards did last a lot longer, but still gave way after a while.

Another odd quirk of that little bike was a tendency for the engine to seize with little warning when ridden flat out – it was in race trim, after all – but this was easily overcome by a couple of squirts of Red-Ex in the tank when filling up with petrol/oil (petroil) mixture – if I remembered to do it, which was not always the case.

I never did find out what the magic ingredient in that long-forgotten fuel additive was; enough to say it worked perfectly, so that I could pound that poor little 125 as hard as it could be ridden with Red-Ex added to the oil in the fuel tank, and it never gave an ounce of trouble.

Not so easy to overcome was a problem with rear axles, which could snap like carrots now and again on the machines which employed plunger-sprung rear ends – particularly when emerging from small bomb craters in tramlines. This did not seem to occur on James machines with no rear suspension. No-one I spoke to ever knew why this was the case.

Oddly, this would have no apparent effect on the handling, which was never the James's strong point, anyway, and was only apparent when the rear wheel would cock itself over in the frame and begin to rub lightly on the rear guard stays. Happily, unlike the front guards, the latter never fell onto the tyre. Hazell and Moore's spare parts manager, Vic Peace, had a brother who was a noted engineer who enjoyed a nice little earner is supplying the company with 125cc sprung-frame James rear axles on a regular basis.

Ah, yes, one's first motorcycle. It should be remembered with some affection. I can easily remember that awful Norton which I should not have ridden at a too-early age (and only when my parents were away for a day or so, of course) and the little James, which I rode quite legally from the tail-end of 1951. It was not amongst the fastest, nor the best handling, nor the prettiest, nor the most comfortable, nor......... but, hey, it did the job it was supposed to do, and it did this from some five years thereafter. I don't remember it with much affection, I'm afraid. But then again....

Early days

GPO

Several months before my first job in the motorcycle trade at Hazell and Moore in late 1948, I was employed as a telegram messenger boy working out of Sydney's GPO in Martin Place. During the day shifts I would stroll about the city dropping of telegrams at a large variety of businesses, with the occasional foray to more outlying areas on my PMG pushbike; my ever-faithful, if overly-heavy, Number 465.

At night I rode that pushbike all over Sydney, from Garden Island Naval Base in Wooloomooloo to Kings Cross, North Sydney and many inner-city suburbs like Redfern and Darlinghurst, with longer rides at night as far afield as Leichhardt and Summer Hill on several occasions. Those latter suburbs were between about eight to twelve kilometers from Sydney's CBD. I recall I once had to walk all the way back to the GPO at night from Leichhardt with the rear chain looped over the top frame rail, because the connecting-link had mysteriously fallen out. That was a real bummer, for it seemed to take forever.

And no, I couldn't ride the bike because the only brake it had was on the rear wheel and it was the so-called 'back-pedal' type, which would not work if there was no chain to back-pedal against. I couldn't ride the bike and jam the heel of my shoe against the rear tyre as a brake, either – as I so often did with my own push-bike – because the PMG bike was thoughtfully equipped with large, heavy mudguards on front and rear wheels.

I must say I knocked poor old 465 about a bit (or was it the other way around?), because I was seen on several occasions to be lying face-down on the roadway with the bike mangled nearby due to the sudden, unexpected opening of a near-side car door, or some half-blind pedestrian suddenly appearing under the bike's flashing front wheel. I had a 1929 Model 18 Norton motorcycle at home which I rode occasionally when my folks weren't around, but that pushbike in heavy city traffic was something else again.

But the worst incident of them all was when I was riding the bike back to the GPO from Circular Quay one day along the busy George Street, Sydney's main arterial road, as I was rapidly (?) approaching a large, un-laden International semi- trailer. The semi was equipped with one of those old-fashioned mechanical signalling device which consisted of a large metal hand, painted bright yellow, which was located at the far end of an articulated arm. When it was necessary to do so, the driver could raise the out-stretched hand on its metal rod to indicate whether the vehicle was to stop or make a right-hand turn.

On this occasion, as he approached the tight, left-hand corner into Hunter Street the driver raised that hand to give the 'right turn' signal to indicate he was moving into the centre of the road from the gutter, which he did, and this clearly allowed me to dive underneath him to triumphantly emerge on the other side, pedalling furiously ahead of the large truck.

Of course, it didn't end up that way, because I couldn't see the sudden change in the signal from that confounded yellow hand, which now stood upright to indicate to those with enough brains to see it that he was actually turning left into Hunter Street and had swung wide to ease the turn. I was in the wrong place at the wrong time as the semi swung into the corner, the rear wheel closing in on the gutter and on a collision course with me and poor old 465.

Naturally, the driver couldn't see me through his tiny, round rear vision mirrors with their restrictive vision, nor did he see me suddenly grab the nose of the bike's saddle to propel the bike forward and myself in the opposite direction to watch, horrified and from my worm's eye view, as poor old 465 was mangled underneath the semi's rear wheels. You can't get much closer than that and live to tell the tale!

I had to carry that sausage-shaped bike back three city blocks to Humphrey, the bike mechanic at the GPO, and try to explain what had happened, for that semi continued on its way with never a backward glance from the driver, even though I saw a pedestrian running after it waving his arms about frantically: perhaps he thought I was still sliding along under the vehicles wheels?

Perhaps I could have said that good old 465 was the original machine I rode for several months in the job but, as it had had several new wheels, a couple of sets of handlebars (one day half a handlebar snapped off at the mounting bracket and spat me off as a result, but that was hardly my fault) and one brand-new frame, that statement could hardly have been correct.

Many, many years later – some thirty years or so, in fact – I was instantly reminded of that (apparently) long-forgotten event with 465 and that old International on the corner of George and Hunter Streets. I was again mounted upon two wheels, but on a very different machine; this time, it was a high-performance motorcycle.

1947

A new Law had recently been passed, which allowed a large semi-trailer to use two lanes when entering or leaving a major road, as well as two lanes – if they were available, which they usually are – on the exit, which clearly gave these very large vehicles plenty of room to manoeuvre. But as ever, it was up to the driver of the vehicle in question to make it *very* clear what his intent may be, and to make the appropriate signals safely via his large, intimidating array of amber blinking lights which we were in place to notify other road users of exactly where he was headed. He would have been assisted in this pursuit by the huge, now-obligatory rectangular rear vision mirrors which currently adorn these large vehicles.

> *"I was alongside him at the time, so I had to brake very smartly and duck back into the left lane again."*

I was closing very briskly on the large semi in front as it was approaching the turn out of the two-lane Greystanes Road on to the three-lane Prospect Highway when the driver, who was in the inside lane at the time, indicated a left turn. I knew there was plenty of road to use when he turned onto the much wider, three-lane Highway and so, assuming stupidly that he had plenty of room for this manoeuvre, I whipped very smartly into the right lane. So did he almost immediately, and without any indication that he was about to do so for his *left* blinker was still flashing about. I was alongside him at the time, so I had to brake very smartly and duck back into the left lane again.

As the left-hander approached, with me by now in the inside lane and with a small car displaying a large red P-Plate just ahead of me, I was suddenly reminded of the George Street incident as the driver of the car in the now-vacated inner lane saw an opportunity to cut ahead of the truck. I could see exactly what was about to happen, because it had happened to me all those years ago, for the car driver suddenly accelerated towards the corner hoping to take advantage of the now-vacated inside lane.

By the way, the semi still had its large blinker lights clearly indicating a *left* turn coming up, while making use of the *right-hand* lane to ease his turn onto the wide Prospect HIghway.

It was entirely legal for him to do so, of course, although his first effort at blinking for a left corner then spearing across into the right lane in front of me without signalling his intent was not – in fact it was not only illegal but a bloody stupid thing to do.

OK, it sounds complicated and it was, for the truck was in the outside (right-hand) lane with his left blinker showing his intent to turn left, and about to use both lanes in doing so, while that small car was closing rapidly upon it in the inside lane, with – I thought – no idea that the semi was almost certain to cross his bows very soon. The car driver was perhaps too intent on beating the truck to the corner – or was unaware of the new Law having recently being passed to (legally) make the large truck's cornering much easier – for he kept on, his speed unabated, as they both neared the corner.

Meanwhile, I had of course moved well back into the right lane again to watch as the drama quickly unfolded, for I wanted to be well clear of whatever was about to happen, as the vivid memory of George Street and bike number 465 continued to flood my mind.

As the small car neared the corner, with the traffic light still bright green, the large semi, which was still moving at a fair clip, began to move into the inside lane where in fact there was nowhere for him to go, because the inexperienced car driver had stuffed his vehicle right into the large truck's entry line. The semi's driver had not spotted the small car yet – which he could be forgiven for not expecting to be there at all – but the young driver of the car suddenly spotted the Juggernaut bearing in on him, and prudently slammed the brakes on as hard as both feet could manage.

The rig sliced into the apex of the corner and on the inside lane much too quickly, the tail-end of the long vehicle almost clipping the inside curb, where it missed the car by little more than a tissue paper, while the car's warning device bleated feebly at the monster. I could not see how close the rig came to the vehicle, but as I swept round the left hander behind the truck I could see how close it must have been to a disaster. In looking back in both mirrors, and then a quick look over the shoulder (which is so often worth twenty mirrors) I didn't see the car emerge from the road and it didn't appear until we were well along the Highway several seconds later.

I know how that driver must have felt after that very close shave, but I knew he couldn't have leapt out of his car as I was able to nimbly jump off poor old PMG 465 all those long years earlier.

Hazell & Moore

First job...

The first job I endured was serving for a few months as a Telegram delivery boy stationed at the GPO in Sydney in 1948. The first job I enjoyed in the motorcycle industry was later in that year when, as a kid almost straight from school, I answered an ad for a Junior Spare Parts Assistant with the Triumph motorcycle importers and distributors, Hazell and Moore, in Sydney. I knew the place well enough, for I had often pressed my nose against the show-room's display window at night to admire the gleaming Norton, Triumphs, Panther, James, NSU and flashy Indian machines that littered the floor with some profusion.

Of course, I didn't know what a spare part was, but I was the proud possessor of my ancient Model 18 Norton, so I knew what a motorbike was, and that was apparently enough for the company. I will never know why they decided to employ me, but I was leaping out of my skin to get into the industry and I suppose there was more than a little of my rampant enthusiasm on display. It must have counted for something.

In those days, spare parts were a little hard to come by and the industry was still struggling back to its feet after the war, with companies like this one often making do as best they could.

Tyres, for example, were in very short supply and I know of one instance in which a colleague of mine bought an old Ariel he didn't want for 30 shillings (that's a princely three Oz dollars, folks) so he could transfer the near-bald tyres to his equally old Norton. I shudder to recall that he threw the Ariel onto a rubbish tip when he had removed the tyres and a few other odds and ends!

My first task was to cut rolls of drive chain to specified lengths, a task accomplished by grinding through the top plates and driving the pins out with a small punch. The chain was German A&S (Arnold and Stolzenberg) and was actually an industrial chain designed to drive various machines. It was *not* intended to transmit power, but was, I assume, easier to come by than the correct motorcycle chain, certainly cheaper and apparently in some abundance.

In passing, the British roller chain manufacturers, Renolds, acquired A&S in 1963. The so-called roller ('bush') chain was invented by Hans Renolds in 1880, and every drive chain manufactured in the world today, including heavy-duty industrial chains, uses his original design – if with some later improvements.

There were stacks and stacks of these rolls, all in 25-foot lengths, from which one could extract around five rear chains. Naturally, I had to be shown how to do this, but once I knew the drill it was easy enough. A chain breaker wouldn't look at the stuff; it would just skate off, assisted by the 'whale oil' that liberally coated the chain and smelled like an Afghan camel-driver's knickers.

It smelled even worse when heated and fried by the bench-grinder, but a peg on the nose and breathing through my ears and tightly clenched teeth helped a little. Not much, let me say, for the out-stretched chain I had so carefully measured would slowly uncoil itself under the vibrations of the bench grinder and, snake-like, playfully wrap itself around my waist.

There was nothing I could do about this, because I was more interested in grinding the chain away than grinding myself away. To make matters worse, as I got towards the end of the large roll of chain, I would often be attacked by both ends at once.

This was my job for the first couple of weeks and it was pretty tough stuff, because I smelled like a semi-tropical, inland fish market and was not socially acceptable to anyone in the spares department or the workshop; or at home, either.

During the second week I scored a dustcoat, which kept the chain off my clobber but did nothing for the pong, which became a full-blown stench when I hung the coat in the hot sun one day in the hope of removing at least some of the foul odour.

I didn't think the industrial chain was much good (but what did I know?) because it seemed to last most owners only a few months or so. It was not unusual to see mechanics peeling the chain off the sprockets like unwinding a coil of heavy fencing wire and then holding the things out at arm's length like a broom handle. What this did for a machine's performance is anyone's guess.

1948-1954

> *"Don't ask how I come to remember this, but the very first customer I actually spoke to nearly sent me out of the industry forever."*

The best thing that could be said about A&S chain all those long years ago was that Hazell's sold a whole lot of it!

When the British Renold's chain began to arrive and we could dispense with the industrial stuff, it was very much easier to cut to length, so I graduated to opening hundreds of heavy crates of Indian motorcycles spares the company had bought from the Army at auction.

It was all packed in what they called 'Tropical Pack', a tarred paper wrapped around the items which was then then dipped in wax. The spare parts inside were again liberally coated with whale oil, but this time the stuff – while it was protecting the items themselves well enough – had apparently gone off.

If I thought the stuff on the frightful chain was on the bugle a bit, the gunk that covered the Indian parts was half as bad again! Impossible? You should have been there, dear reader.

Imagine the scene: New kid on the block, eager to learn, flung into the deep end doing the chores which, it was plain to me even then, no one else wanted to do ... and then to find I was so ripe – well, rotten, really – that no one wanted to get too close to me. That new job was a giant relief from that festering German chain, of that you may be well assured, but was still more than a little on the nose!

I was asked to make lists of the contents of the crates and it was there I began to learn what the parts actually were, where they went and what they did. It was great stuff, really, and exciting enough because nobody knew what was inside any of the crates and it was little me who discovered it all.

One crate had two large saddles, three pairs of large leather saddle bags and a huge – and very heavy – box filled with old screws, nuts, bolts, jets, spindles and literally thousands of smaller items. On my list I made the note "One Box Miscellaneous" and took the list to the guy in charge of my unpacking the crates. He looked down the list and asked "One box, miscellaneous, what does that mean?"

"Miscellaneous means made up of a variety of parts or ingredients," I informed him patronisingly.

"I know what the bloody *word* means, goat!" he shouted, "What I want to know is what's in the thing!"

"I dunno," I shouted back, "It's a box full of a variety of parts or ingredients."

"Then list them all in detail, mate," he said, patting my elbow and smirking as he strolled off to enjoy his morning tea.

It transpired that the huge box was filled with spares for the Schebler carburettors the Indian motorcycles employed, and it took days to list them all. It also happened that the company had very few of these parts and management was thrilled and delighted to discover the unknown treasure trove. Almost as if I had opened King Tut's tomb, I was thus raised from the status of ineptitude to faintly promising, and then to a position of lurking, terrified, behind the high spares parts counter.

Don't ask how I come to remember this, but the very first customer I actually spoke to nearly sent me out of the industry forever. It was morning tea time and the counter was more or less unattended as a grinning, blond-haired character sidled up to me and leaned forward conspiratorially.

"FU2F82521CR4ATR5A?" he asked, grinning like a school-boy. I felt it was more of a question than the utter gibberish it sounded like, because he finished the recitation with an upward inflection.

Of course, I favoured him with 'Stunned Mullet Expression Number One', which I have used many times since to good effect on stage, but at that time it was no act. I didn't have a clue what the hell he was on about. I felt it was a secret code or some form of English, because I recognised the numbers and letters, but it was still gibberish.

"Eh?" I said, which is all I could manage.

"Very good," he said in English "You'll go far."

Then he said it again, this time with more emphasis.

" F.U.2.F.8.2.5.2.1.C.R.4.A.T.R.5.A? T.R.5. O.K? A?"

"Don't give the kid a hard time, Snowy." said the voice of the spares manager over his teacup, "He's only been here a few weeks."

My first customer was that great character Snowy Newell, and he was playing silly buggers again, which, I was later to learn, he did very well indeed.

"Tell him what you want," my boss continued.

"OK," he said, grinning at me. "I'll translate".

Hazell & Moore

"Have you two off 8.25:1 compression ratio pistons for a TR5 Triumph. Eh?"

Now that certainly made more sense as I had opened enough crates of Indian spares to know what a piston was, and I also knew the TR5 was an all-alloy 500cc off-road Triumph twin with fat knobby tyres and upswept exhausts. Of course, what I didn't know at the time was that the Triumph was one of the very first off-roaders of its type and pre-dated the almost-iconic Yamaha DT1 by some 20 years. I was in good company, for no one else knew that in 1948, including the Japanese!

Snowy gleefully departed the scene with the pistons under his arm and I was happy to see him go, because I was very much the Laugh of the Week. I was to get my own back on him several months later when I saw his grinning face at the counter again. By then I was, of course, much more relaxed and at ease with customers. In the interim, I had eagerly pored over a fistful of spare parts manuals, and knew a whole lot more of what the long list of spare parts actually were, where they went, what they did and what their longevity was expected to be.

I saw Snowy sidling up to my end of the spares counter again with that grin on his face, and I knew I was likely to be the butt of another gag of his, but this time I was well and truly ready for him! I slipped a small speedo globe into my hand as he beckoned me over and ordered a set of cam followers for a Speed Twin Triumph. I feigned a huge sneeze and shoved the base of the globe up one nostril, leaving just the glass bulb hanging out.

"Bless you!" he said, as I straightened up to face him, sniffing, the glass bulb by now looking like a bubble-boogie hanging out of my nose.

"Oh, phew!" he said, puckering his face up and shuddering slightly. "You filthy bugger."

"Sorry about that, sir," I said, removing the bulb and holding it up for him to see. "Could you use some of these?"

"Smartarse kid," he said, shouting with laughter "That's one on me!"

The counter manager, that all-round good guy and father figure Harry Steadman, took me to one side.

"Promise me," he said, desperately trying not to laugh in my face, but with little success. "Please promise me you will never do that again."

I promised him I wouldn't, but I have done it several times since then, as I worked in various motorcycle stores. It's a bit naughty, but it's not a bad gag. And it has always worked well.

Old days

If we head way, way back to what today we might refer to 'the good old days of motorcycling' in this country, which, in this case, would be the first five years or so after the Second World War, it might surprise many modern-day enthusiasts to discover that Australia was the biggest importers of British motorcycles in the world.

There were no Japanese motorcycles to seen anywhere outside of Japan (and precious few in that country, either) while there were very, very few machines at all from Europe, except for the occasional single-cylinder 250cc ohc NSU from Germany, the rare 250cc single-cylinder BMW, an even smaller handful of Zundapp flat-twins, and….. well, that was about your lot!

The slumbering giant America would not be fully awakened until 1950, when the first of the newly designed vertical-twin, 650cc Triumph Thunderbird motorcycles appeared, with their very austere battleship-grey colour scheme and almost total lack of chrome plate. The new Triumph stood cheek-to-jowl with the new 650cc A10 BSA twin, a machine which saw its Genesis in the 1933 650cc, 6/1 Triumph twin.

It was called 'Austerity Time' in Britain, the country struggling to climb back to its feet after the war, the motorcycle industry assisted in no small measure by the demand from Down Under for almost every machine the Nation could build. Hard to believe though it may be, that's simply the way it was just after the war.

It was the 'Austerity Progamme' which resulted in the new 650cc Triumph looking so dull, but its introduction came about because of the burgeoning demand from America for larger capacity motorcycles from Britain other than 500cc Triumph 5T and the sportier Tiger 100 which they had begun to discover. Both Triumph machines were dwarfed by the large, bumbling American twins, Harley-Davidson and Indian. America was becoming more and more aware that there had been a huge range of entirely acceptable motorcycles made in other countries around the world, long before any of us were aware that Japan and Europe were soon to appear on the scene.

British motorcycles were King in those days, glorifying in such once-famous names as BSA, Matchless, Royal Enfield, Sunbeam, AJS, Triumph, Velocette, Douglas, Francis-Barnett, Excelsior, Norton, Ariel, James ... and Panther.

There were, of course, many others whose

1948-1954

main claim to fame was as small commuter machines, the likes of which are not often seen these days, or are hidden like retarded kids almost out of sight – usually in the dimmer recesses of local showrooms.

Enfield is still made in India, along with a few Villiers-engined lightweights we hear very little about, while Triumph soldiers on as never before, some say thinly-disguised as a Japanese import (if you can't beat 'em?) and Norton battled on for some time with its unpopular rotary-engine road-burner for some inexplicable reason, but now is on the boil again. Thankfully! The rest have, very sadly, disappeared, though fortunately not without trace.

I recently spotted and old-time favourite of mine, a 1949 Panther 100, the 600cc single with its long-stroke sloping cylinder forming the frame's front down-tube, with its slim Dowty Oleomatic front forks and its prodigious pulling power.

As a single-cylinder 'thumper' the Grunter, as it was so often called, was very much an ideal sidecar machine, as it would pull a heavily-laden sidecar like a freight train – thanks, in part to its soft cam timing, smallish carburettor and 33-pound flywheels. Yes, thirty-three pounds, or 15Kg, a lot of inertia to get underway, but a hell of a lot more to stop once spinning freely.

The engine would idle like a wrist watch, and – with no tacho to help – if you counted the sucks through the carburettor and the exhaust 'flooomphs' which followed shortly thereafter, while timing it carefully on your watch's second-hand, you could calculate that the engine idled at just 350rpm! Yes, that's 350rpm, not 3500rpm!!

At the time these machines were brand-new I worked at Hazell and Moore, the Panther importers in Sydney, who also imported Triumph, Norton, Indian, James, NSU (the German machine, as we have noted, as rare at that time as Zundapp, Guzzi, and, indeed, BMW!) and the French Mobylette.

One of the Panther's features was a wet sump – well, not really a wet sump but a compartment under the crankcases which contained the oil – and it fell to my lot one day to check the oil level on a new 600 single which was being serviced for the first time.

The dipstick was attached to the filler plug on the front of the crankcases, so I simply unscrewed the thing and peered inside. I was rewarded for this folly by an extremely flatulent outburst, followed by a large quantity of warm oil, which spread itself with some glee over my face and down the front of my new shirt!

Look, I was only a kid not long out of school, what did I know back then? I certainly didn't know you should turn the engine off before you check the oil level in a wet-sump engine!

The Dowty Oleomatic front forks were a bit odd, because you pumped them up with a pushbike pump to whatever level you wanted, and then you took your chances. There were no springs, the suspension only as good as the air seals allowed it to be. The forks were also used on early Velocettes, Scott and the 350cc two-stroke EMC, which I nearly forgot. To digress, the latter were large two-strokes, the Scott a 500 or 600cc twin, the EMC a 350cc split-single, with two pistons, the same number of cylinders, one big-end, a two-piece con-rod and one combustion chamber. (Eh? I'll explain it again another time.)

Dowty Oleomatics were used in the twenties on the under-carriage of light aircraft, and are still used to this day on much larger, commercial jet airliners, but this suspension system was less than successful when applied to motorcycle front forks.

There was a case in point with a Panther 350 we had on the showroom floor. I attempted to demonstrate to a customer how simple it was to pump up the Dowty forks, so I let all the air out of the Schrader valve on top of the forks and waited for the front end to subside gracefully.

It didn't subside at all, so I nudged the handlebars sharply, whereupon the bike demonstrated the brilliance of its 'Easy roll-on rear stand' by easily rolling off it again as the now air-less forks collapsed with a crash and the bike sprang gleefully forward. I don't know why, but the man bought the bike anyway, even though we had to pull him out from underneath the thing. Look, what did I know, I was just a kid?

After spending some time in the Spare Parts department I was placed in charge of a new accessories counter which was built in the motorcycle showroom, and I had some fun times down there, let me tell you.

A Panther 600 solo pulled up outside one day and two odd characters climbed off to shuffle up to the counter and demand to look at the leather flying helmets I had on display. (Crash – for crash read 'safety' – helmets were rare in those days and mostly confined to racing circuits, believe it or not!) Those close-fitting helmets came in a variety of colours; Virginal White, Orifice Brown and Inside-the-Closet Black, and endowed their wearer with a bullet-shaped head, a self-conscious air and about another five mph top speed.

Vintage Morris

Hazell & Moore

The rider chose the white job, his pillion passenger the more Macho black; they looked at one another, blushing and giggling like schoolgirls – which they were impersonating very well, I might add – and they remarked, almost as one "Don't tell me I look like that!!" as they buckled their chinstraps tightly.

With their new-found image, they puffed their respective chests out like pouter pigeons and strolled (I could say 'minced' but I won't) to the bike, perched on its rear stand, the tail-end pointing skywards like an eager chicken.

The rider sprang to the kick-starter, his passenger settling on the Lycetts sprung pillion seat – there were few dual-seats around in those days – with his legs dangling towards the ground. As the engine fired, the rider selected first gear, revved the long-stroke single to within an inch of its life, rolled the bike off easy-roll on rear stand and dropped the clutch at the same time.

I have yet to see a Panther 600 leap away as quickly as this one did (except for a Speedway racing sidecar of fond memory) and I'm sure the passenger would say the same thing, for the bike speared off, the pillion seat's raised lip whipping him over into a near-perfect backflip.

With the bike by now several meters up the road, the pillion rider executed a brilliant five-point landing on hands, knees and nose; not bad when you consider he probably had little, or no, rehearsal. It was very neatly done, however unintentional it might have been.

It was a Saturday morning, so there was the traditional 50 or more riders on the footpath outside, their bikes angle-parked tail-end to the kerb. The air was suddenly rent by a series of huge, ironic cheers, with a spontaneous burst of applause and several whistles as the riders rushed to lend aid or to offer their congratulations.

Still on his hands and knees in the middle of the road, the guy in the black helmet lifted his head and looked straight through the window at me with the most amazed expression I have ever seen on anyone's face. There was a red spot on the tip of his nose and even from where I was, I could see a small flap of skin hanging from it like a huge boogie.

I must say I expected him to stand up and bow to the laughter and applause of the madly cheering crowd – I would assuredly have done so to acknowledge the spontaneous plaudits, ironic through they were, had it been me! – but he was red-faced and clearly throbbing with embarrassment as well as pain. I couldn't help yelping with laughter at the poor guy's plight, even though I tried manfully (boy-fully?) not to do so, as he was still staring at me through the shop's front window. He seemed Ok, and his mate, who by now had trickled the Panther quietly back to the footpath, was obviously very contrite indeed.

They were both wearing their sisters' shorts, leather Roman sandals and Chesty Bonds singlets which we may have thought Butch in those more innocent days but were probably not.

With both incumbents by now settled, the Panther made a much more leisurely exit to little more than a smattering of polite applause, but I did notice, as the bike slipped out of my sight, the pillion passenger fetched the rider a thump in the kidneys for his pains. It was, I felt at the time, no more than he deserved.

I never owned a Panther, but I had access to one which we had trouble shifting from the suburban shop in which I spent several very happy years. It was a 1950 model, still with the Dowty forks, and it was fitted with a Murphy double-adult sidecar which was wide enough to take my wife and small son.

We went on several camping trips, with mum and the kid in the sidecar and Loudly Complaining sister-in-law on the pillion. Loaded down with the essential tent, sleeping bags, cooking gear and provisions that bike hauled us with some vigour up hill and down dale with great ease, including a particularly noteworthy trip into the depths of the Megalong Valley and briskly out again.

Imagine my amazement when it came time to replace the primary drive chain when I discovered that the bike was still on solo gearing! The engine sprocket should have been replaced with one at least two – preferably three – teeth lower, but the bike pulled so well, and so effortlessly, that I simply replaced the chain and left the gearing as it was!!

Perhaps we could argue that it is just as well nobody makes motorcycles these days the way they built motorcycles back in the forties, because many of those bikes were in essence designed some twenty years previously, but it should be noted that there were quite a few outstanding machines 'Made in England' which were entirely acceptable in those days, both in Oz and in America.

Even with the astounding designs of new motorcycles from many, many countries, which leave those old bangers in the shade on a direct comparisons, we might still acknowledge some of the fine British bikes which were on the world's roads long before many of these latter-day motorcycles were thought of.

Bikes like the 1000cc Square Four Ariel – the only series-production four-cylinder motorcycle readily available in those days – the even finer Vincent Vee-twins and the earlier Gold Star BSA, were not amongst the most popular bikes in those days but, because they are even rarer today, have become the stuff of Legend.

It was not amongst the most popular motorcycles of its era, but there has never been a slow-revving, stump-pulling Big Thumper quite like the Panther, even more so with the later machines, the Panther 120, which were 650cc singles from about 1963 onwards. Sadly, the last Big Panther left the Yorkshire factory in 1966.

Cucciolo

Other people who live in many Nations remote from the Great Southland might be very surprised to discover that the 'Island/ Nation/ Continent', or 'Down Under' – as Australia is so often called – is not only by far the biggest island in the world, but that its area is almost exactly the same as the land mass of North America, if one excludes Alaska. It's true, because it is almost the same distance from Darwin, in the Northern Territory, to Adelaide in South Australia as it is from America's Great Lakes to New Orleans. It is also nearly the same distance from Perth in Western Australia to the Nation's most populous city, Sydney, in New South Wales, as it is from New York to Los Angeles.

But there the comparison ends, because America has a population of some 350-odd million, while Oz has a population of just over 23 million people, most of whom are living almost in the water on the Nation's east coast, with a few settlements a little further inland. On the other side of the huge Island, Perth, the capital city of Western Australia sits almost alone as it remains the most isolated major capital city on earth.

In pointing out these facts, I am reminded of the executive from the small, newly-established Ducati motorcycle factory in Italy who arrived in Australia in the early fifties with the all-new 65cc Cucciolo 'Turismo' ultra-lightweight motorcycle with a plan to ride from Sydney to Melbourne on the miniscule device as some sort of publicity stunt to help promote the machine. It was clear from his statements to the Press at

> *" Ducati had arrived in Australia in early 1948 with the announcement that its new, bolt-on engine called the Cucciolo... "*

the time that the Ducati factory executive had no blind idea of just how huge our land mass was, or how far he had to ride the little bike on his long journey from Sydney to Melbourne. He could also have had no idea how long it would take at the little biker's stated 44mph (50Km/h!) top speed – downhill?- when he announced his intention to introduce his new, ultra-lightweight machine to the Australian public.

This was of course in the very, very early history of Ducati in this country, for it had crept into Australia, as it did into other countries, without publicity or fanfare. The company had been formed as far back as 1924, but had originally been involved in the manufacture of radio parts, the new lightweight Cucciolo machine its first serious foray into the manufacture of motorcycles.

Ducati had arrived in Australia in early 1948 with the announcement that its new, bolt-on engine called the Cucciolo ('Little Pup', or 'Puppy', depending on who you were talking to at the time, and named after its 'yapping' exhaust note) was imported into NSW by Nock and Kirby, which was then the biggest hardware store in the country. Nock and Kirby was looking to diversifying its interests and was spreading its wings into new territory with the adoption of this new engine kit for pushbikes as well as a number of inboard marine and outboard engines imported from England.

The little Ducati engine was a 48cc four-stroke with exposed overhead valves operated by **pull-rods,** not pushrods, a one-piece cylinder head and barrel, a large, external flywheel behind which its magneto lurked, a two-speed gearbox, and its spark plug pointing directly ahead, waiting to be doused by road spray in wet weather. The neat little power-plant was intended to be clamped to your ordinary pushbike where the pedal cranks were, to provide a miniscule power source. There was a set of pedals fitted to the engine which could be used to start the device and then they were held in different positions to change from the low first gear to the (not much) higher second gear. I rode one of these things back then, which was quite an experience, but I cannot remember exactly where the pedals were supposed to be. I think they were at quarter-to-three when you took off, and at quarter-past-nine for the higher gear, or it might have been at six o'clock for one gear and half-past-twelve for the other, but I must say I can't remember if this is right or not. But what I do remember was the stern admonition to never turn the pedal-cranks backwards, but I am not sure why: I suspect it might have confused the gear-change 'mechanism'.

If I don't know the exact position of the bicycle pedals in selecting one gear or another, what I *do* know is that any English Vicar's obese and elderly maiden aunt could probably blow one of these 'powered' pushbikes into the weeds while normally seated on a Raleigh pushbike with 'sit-up-and-beg' handlebars, and do so without raising a sweat.

It has been suggested that the little engine – which was designed in 1945 by Aldo Farinelli and built by Ducati from 1947 onwards, after its original manufacturer S.I.A.T.A couldn't keep up with demand – was said to be a surprise package in its performance, and perhaps the 'Little Pup' might beat pedalling your steed everywhere you went. But not by much, I suggest, because I remember you still had to stand on the pedals to provide much needed assistance to the engine on most 'reasonable' gradients. You would probably have to leap off and trot alongside your pushbike in low gear on anything steeper.

In the normal process of evolution there was – God help us! – a 60cc road-race version of the Cucciolo engine fitted into its own frame, but without pedals, and it in fact won quite a number of races – including a nine-day (9 DAY!!) event held in Italy. I don't know what these pocket rockets were actually racing *against*, but it's a fair bet the things were not overly endowed with anything from great speed to even greater handling or brakes, though fuel consumption (which was said to be an astounding 225 mpg!) was probably not much of a problem.

A larger, 55cc version of the little 48cc Ducati engine shortly appeared as a complete machine with a slightly heavier frame, drum brakes, pedals and lightweight front forks. It is said that somewhat more than 200,000 Cucciolo were sold by 1950, I assume as bolt-on kits just prior to the introduction of complete machines. This would have greatly helped the Ducati coffers, and almost certainly established the factory as a serious manufacturer of a series of lightweight

> "*This is the machine our earnest Italian was going to ride from Sydney to Melbourne, poor bugger.*"

motorcycles. The success of the little engine may have provided the reason for the Italian's executive's promotional visit to Sydney.

Further into the Cucciolo's evolution, the 65cc upgrade in 1950, which the Italian visitor rode, had the bigger engine mounted into a 'proper' lightweight frame, and it was fitted with a modern looking swing-arm rear suspension and slightly heavier telescopic front forks. Though not far removed from a heavy pushbike, it was nonetheless built as an ultra-light **motorcycle**, with a power output from the 'larger' engine of some 2 (that's TWO) horsepower. Valve gear was now enclosed, the cylinder head detachable, with the bicycle pedals removed and a three-speed gearbox incorporated.

This is the machine our earnest Italian was going to ride from Sydney to Melbourne, poor bugger. If he had no idea how far this distance was, then he was soon to find out as he was pointed in the right direction one morning and waved away from Sydney's GPO, replete with floppy, black felt hat and large overcoat, a photo of the event carried in one of Sydney's morning newspapers. Quite some time later – probably three or four days later! – he arrived in Goulburn, and asked one of the friendly natives if this was indeed Melbourne! According to legend, he was told that he had just covered less than *one fifth* of the journey, but there is no record of how he felt about that, or what he did.

I cannot recall hearing any more about this brave soul, but can only assume he may have managed to get a lift back to Sydney, with his bike either flung savagely into the roadside bushes or tucked underneath his arm. For all I know he may still be on the road somewhere between both cities, a bit like a precursor to Forrest Gump, who, if you remember the film, started running away one day and didn't know how to stop again for some considerable time.

If this was the case, by now the hapless Italian may well have been heavily bearded and unkempt, his large felt hat bleached by the sun to an ugly grey and stiff as an ironing board, his large, flapping coat tattered and filthy with age. He would by then have every right to be twitching and muttering to himself, the while still searching the horizon with bloodshot, red-rimmed eyes, aching for his first glimpse of this Great Southern Metropolis.

He may also have the shards of many an overtaking semi-trailer's mirrors adorning his garments, or even the powdered rubber of numerous shredded tyres glued to his face.

What an absurd scenario I hear you groan, as the highly-steamed Editor of this odd piece has assuredly done – and not for the first time.

On the other hand, of course, our hero probably told us all to get stuffed and simply flew back home again. In the first available DC3 aircraft!

If he had waited two years until 1953 he could have given the new Ducati Cruiser motor scooter a squirt and enjoyed a somewhat quicker, and certainly more comfortable, ride. The smart looking new scooter employed a 175cc, 12BHP, four-stroke engine, with electric starter and automatic transmission. It was amongst the best of its time, and would have been amongst the fastest as well, but was too expensive to compete with the biggest selling machines, the Vespa and the infinitely better Lambretta, both of which also hailed from Italy.

Ducati managed to manufacture just 2000 of their fine scooters, the other two Italian scooters accounting for many millions between them. Vespa, of course, survives to this day, while Lambretta, made under licence in Germany for years as the NSU Prima, and in nearly a score of other countries, including India, is currently in limbo, with vague promises of someday re-appearing in all its glory.

As a postscript to this story, Lambretta once announced a world-wide competition for the longest single ride on one of its scooters, and offered several million lira (which was probably worth about Twenty Five Pounds ($50 then, but about $1000 in today's money) to the stalwart who could manage to achieve this feat. A local lad, who must have been at once desperate and should have known better, decided the simplest way to achieve his fortune was to ride his little scooter half-way around Australia, which he then proceeded to do.

It wasn't too bad, he said, (I suggest it wasn't too good, either) when riding along sealed roads but the device must have been more than a handful on the unsealed road across the Nullarbor Plains back in the early fifties, where potholes hidden in loose bulldust and long stretches of corrugations were a challenge to the skateboard-sized 8" wheels and short-travel, rudimentary damped suspension system.

Again, he would have had nothing to grip with his knees, other than his wedding tackle – which he probably gripped by hand every now and again for a swift, relieving massage, particularly after negotiating several potholes and numerous other irregularities into which the little scooter's wheels would surely have plunged. Perhaps he carried a ten-gallon fuel tank on the machine's footboard to ensure he managed to cross the forbidding stretch of track without running out of fuel. He could certainly grip *that* with his knees, but at what cost to the little bike's handling?

I (very) dimly recall reading something about the bloke's ordeal, in which he related, as he was just near the end of the Nullarbor Plain at the first sighting of some foothills near Kalgoorlie, that he spotted a small cloud of dust which seemed to be descending a small hillock in the middle distance. As the cloud approached it proved to be a pack of wild dogs: not dingoes, he said, but previously domestic canines which were probably wild because someone had dumped them on the side of the road and then driven off. They were barking like crazy and looking not only mean but *lean* as well.

With the throttle wide open and the little bike gyrating underneath him like a Mallee bull with a flank strap attached, he ploughed – why put a pun in at this stage of the drama, you might ask? – through the dirt ahead, hoping against hope that one of the three most likely things that could happen wouldn't happen. He could (a) fall off the bloody thing, and be consumed on the spot; (b) the engine could overheat and seize or have the spark plug conk out; (c) the spark plug could grow a whisker across its terminals and conk out anyway; (d) he could run out of petrol; or (e) be overtaken by the swiftest of the meat-eaters and be plucked from his scooter. That's five I know, but (f) he said he was about half-a-mile an hour quicker than the fastest of the pursuers, and was just able to keep them at bay, though I am sure he would not have looked over his shoulder to see how far behind they were!

He rode that thing as far and as fast as he could before pulling up for a rest to void his loins or to throw up his lunch at the side of the road, and there can be no doubt he was mightily relieved (Please, not another pun!) to find no sight, or sound, of his erstwhile pursuers.

To traverse this large Island Continent from one side to the other, or one *end* to the other on two wheels has always been a daunting task, but to have attempted the feat on a small, softly-sprung, mini-wheeled, under-powered scooter over a mostly unmade, pot-holed, corrugated and dust covered 'road' more than sixty years ago? That would have to have been an act of either supreme courage, or the act of a hare-brained crackpot, for it was said at the time that there was no support vehicle of any type to accompany the youth.

Quite apart from the distinct possibility of being gleefully consumed by a pack of ravenous wild dogs at some point of that long and perilous journey, it remains a wonder that he managed to survive that journey to tell the tale.

Happily, the Island Continent of Australia is not peopled by predatory animals like lions, tigers, leopards, bears or other dangerous man-eating critters, while the inquisitive Dingo or large (herbivorous) kangaroo can be shooed away fairly easily, but there are sometimes small packs of 'wild' dogs to be seen which can be quite menacing. It was probably quite a surprise to our enterprising youth to have come across such a small pack of ravenous creatures which were camped just outside that first glimpse of civilisation at Kalgoorlie, but it might have been a different matter had they crept up to his flickering camp fire in the dead of night to descend savagely upon him!

Rowe Street

If, for some inexplicable reason, anyone should decide to pursue a career in the entertainment industry, especially if one inclination is to pursue that career in Theatre, it behoves upon that person to either seek professional help from a learned psychologist or, if this doesn't work, to take the necessary steps to find out how to go about learning one's craft. This doesn't mean for a second that there is any guarantee of any form of lasting success, or indeed any success at all, but if one must strut one's stuff upon the stage, it makes good sense to find a good Training Institute to join and then to sit still and learn as much as possible about your craft.

That is precisely what I did, because when the bug bit me, which it did almost as I began work in the motorcycle trade, there were no training institutions anywhere which catered to the person who wished to become a performer in Musical Theatre, to hopefully follow this with the (very) occasional gig in film and the appearance, perhaps a little more often, on Television as well.

Rowe Street Musicals was one of the very early amateur companies I joined in the early fifties which enabled me to seriously study the multi-faceted art of the live Theatre actor-singer. Since 1985 it has become known as Ashfield Musical Society: in passing, it was in Campsie-Ashfield Musical Society in which, as a pimpled youth, I first became involved in live Theatre. But it was just one of seven of these companies in which I was to appear in an ever-growing number of bit parts and then major character leads I was privileged to play with those groups before I finally became a full-time professional (whatever that is) in 1968. It was all great stuff, often with more drama and comedy happening off stage than on.

In those far off days, Rowe Street always mounted its productions in the Sydney Conservatorium of Music, and the shows were always very well attended, the men almost always arriving dressed in dinner suits, their wives dripping with diamonds and furs. This was quite remarkable for an amateur company, for this was not always the attire for people attending the Theatre – amateur or professional – anywhere else, and is even more remarkable when looking at the attendees at Theatrical performances these days, for many of these people dress very sloppily indeed..

I started going to rehearsals with the company by hiking a ride on the back of Jim Brooks' 1949 Type B Lambretta scooter, which was then just on two years old. The bike was fitted with a 125cc two-stroke engine, employed shaft drive (!) and was adorned with a pair of single, sprung saddles. This was a bit of a joke because the engine was somewhat less than powerful – *powerless* might be a better description – and had trouble hauling the jockey-sized Jim about on his own. With **two** jockeys on board acceleration was very casual, or not in evidence at all. The suspension system was pretty much the same, and so was the handling, while that poor little scooter spent most of its time during that short journey in first or second gear. It could be slotted into top gear for the occasional downhill run, but then you couldn't stop the thing, because the brakes were not much better than anything else on the bike.

However, the brakes on the type B had been an improvement over the first model, which was made in 1946-7, because that model A Lambretta had a pair of plain alloy brake shoes in each drum, with the friction material bonded to **the inside of the drum itself!!** Oh, and the Type A had small, 7-inch wheels and no

1948-1954

> *"There were several girls in the company who I really fancied, but there was another girl with the most beautiful face and over-large figure who was very happy to return the compliment..."*

suspension of any sort! But I doubt if anyone who rode a Type A blindfolded could have picked the difference between the two once the scooters were underway, unless it was because the Model A employed a foot gear-change, while the later model B had a twist-grip-controlled gear-change – or unless the blindfolded rider ran into a bus he couldn't see long before he had had a chance to make any sort of comparison.

Fortunately Jim lived in Kings Cross and I lived in Woolloomooloo, so the poor little vehicle only had about four clicks to go before it finally arrived, at least as breathless as we were, at the rehearsal rooms in Rowe Street, just opposite what was then the Sydney GPO.

I bought my little 125cc James commuter at about that time, thanked Jim most profusely for his assistance in helping me get to the rehearsal rooms, but from then on I would ride that little bike to rehearsals two night s a week; usually in convoy with him or waiting patiently for him to catch up.

There were several girls in the company who I really fancied, but there was another girl with the most beautiful face and over-large figure who was very happy to return the compliment, much to my delight but to the dismay of another fellow in the company, who in turn fancied *her*. He told me he couldn't believe she had any interest in me and suggested that if she found **me** in any way attractive he was sure she must be very easy to please. I was forced to suggest to him that surely she couldn't have been *too* easily pleased because, if that was the case, then she may probably have found **him** attractive; which, quite clearly she did not. I couldn't understand why he took umbrage at this, but reacted to my suggestion by promising to drastically re-arrange my face sometime in the very future. In fact, if I wanted to accompany him outside, he would do that almost immediately. My friendly advice was to save the bother and possible serious injury, so he suddenly decided to withdraw the offer.

One of the company's major Patrons was a bloke called Sam Lands, at that time one of the largest jewellers in Sydney and, among other things, he was well known for mounting some very swish parties at his Double Bay mansion. I went to only one of those, and I rode the little James there. It was a bright and sunny day, with some heavy clouds forming in the west, but I didn't bother taking any special riding gear, probably because I didn't have any. Besides, I figured that if the weather should take a turn for the worst I could scramble home again in about 15 minutes before the worst arrived.

The bike looked a little out of place as I parked it on the footpath alongside a pair of jet black Austin A125 'Sheerline' luxury cars which were parked directly outside the mansion's tall gates. They shared the area with a maroon Bristol, a couple of Jaguars and other pose-worthy vehicles, while the most incongruous of the lot was a khaki WW2 Jeep, complete with Regimental insignia and large white numbers; there were a few of them running about in Double Bay, and they represented a kind of reverse snobbery, a fashion trend which was then just coming into vogue world-wide.

But it was the two Austin Sheerline cars with which I was utterly amazed and they attracted my attention because the only other luxury Austin I had ever seen belonged to the patriarch of Hazell and Moore, Joe Moore Senior, whose most imposing black A125 saloon car occasionally sat outside his motorcycle showroom in Sydney's Campbell Street. I was working there at the time and I often marvelled at its size, sleek lines, its beauty and indeed its extreme rareness. At that time I had never seen an Austin Sheerline in any Austin showroom anywhere, and it is no surprise to later discover that this fairly rare car was built only from 1947 to 1954 and that only about 8000 of them had ever been made. There must have been very, very few A125 Austin saloons which made their way to Australia, and even fewer into Sydney.

Austin was better known for its range of cheap and cheerful small cars, like the A30 and A40 models, the rare A90 'Atlantic' semi-sportster and some nondescript vans and utes, but the Sheerline was intended as a rival to the luxurious Bentley cars: the Austin was almost as well outfitted, hand built to some degree, beautifully detailed and listed at less than a third the price of the Bentley.

Joe Moore's car was adorned with the number plates 'JM-444', which was probably the first car I ever saw with personalised number plates.

Oh, I think I might have digressed again!

The air inside the grounds of the mansion was heavy with an almost overpowering fragrance and it was a surprise to see the source of this heady perfume, for the entire surface of the mansion's large swimming pool was covered several layers deep with many thousands of frangipani blooms, in both yellow and pink. Where they had come from, how they had been delivered and how much they had cost was anyone's guess, but they certainly made their presence felt!

A fellow sat posing at the water's edge engaged in loud and earnest conversation with one of the chorus girls, the rear legs of his wicker chair hanging tantalisingly over the lip of the pool. He was one of the company's soft ballet dancers and he was clearly monopolising the conversation as he occasionally sipped at a Mint Julep in a tall glass. I might say that, contrary to popular belief, not *all* male ballet dancers are soft, any more than all actors are, but there are some who could have that term applied to them, in the same manner as the term could be applied to some accountants, football players and Army personnel.

I scanned the visitors through the shimmering haze of the stifling, fragrant air and there, to my surprise, sat the large female chorus member, reposing – I nearly said imposing – on a groaning wicker chair which was buckling at the knees, while her ample figure bulged out in every direction possible from the confines of an overly small two-piece swimsuit. Well, perhaps it wasn't *really* overly small, but it certainly looked as though it was. She spotted me almost at once and heaved herself upright, to the enormous relief of the chair which straightened itself up again audibly and appeared to sigh with relief. She smiled her gorgeous smile and loped in my direction with outstretched arms, bowling the ballet dancer's chair (and him) straight over the side and into the pool, where they both swiftly vanished beneath the carpet of blooms as though they had never been there in the first place.

We all rushed to the poolside to see his horrified face suddenly re-emerge framed by a halo of beautiful flowers, the air around us filled with his shrill cries. He looked for the entire world like the Panto Dame Widow Twanky, whose (male) face was almost always framed by a flower-trimmed poke bonnet. At least it was whenever I played the part, which was often enough!

Sure enough some idiot shouted out "Oh look. It's Dame Widow Twanky!" I don't know who it was, but I wouldn't have been surprised had it been me. This taunt was greeted with hoots of laughter by everyone except the dancer, who had fallen in at the deep end and who, it transpires, couldn't swim a stroke. They managed to drag his bedraggled form out of the floral display before he went down for the third time, whereupon he curtly dismissed us all as 'a bunch of goats and cretins, with whom I shall never dance again' and swiftly departed the scene, muttering to himself as he minced wetly away, slammed the gilded gates behind him, fired up the Jeep and drove it away while rending the air with loud jarring blasts of an asthmatic groan elicited from several rude applications of his thumb upon the vehicle's little black horn button.

"Thank Christ *he's* gone!" someone shouted, and that might have been me as well.

After this dramatic – if somewhat comedic – farewell, we all tucked into the body of a large pig which was rotating slowly upon a large spit and fell upon a table packed high with an enormous mound of delectable foodstuffs. Thus sated, we then sat about belching and emitting a surprisingly large variety of other wind-induces sounds for some hours afterwards as the storm clouds slowly but surely began to stir ominously overhead. It started to look quite menacing, so I stood up and excused myself from the throng, explaining that I had ridden up on my motorcycle and had to make my escape before the approaching storm unloaded itself upon me.

The large chorus girl was swiftly on her feet as well "Can I come with you" she coyly twittered, "I'd love to go for a ride on your motorbike."

To a chorus of "yeah, go on", "that should be great", "good for you", "I'd like to see that", and similar cries I didn't really want to hear, she grabbed my hand and lead me away, stooping to pick up her small wicker basket and a throw-over shift, which she threw over her ample body as she smiled at me anew and hugged me to her ample bosom. She was actually a very nice girl; she looked great, was quite good company and laughed easily and well. Really chuffed that she was so eager to have me drop her off at her home (which was in Darlinghurst, on my way home) I didn't have the heart to tell her I doubted whether or not the bike, encumbered by both of us – but her in particular – would actually climb the steep hills out of Double Bay, much less the long Rushcutters Bay Road hill which was also on the run home.

"Gee, it's a little bike isn't it?" she trilled as she lowered herself into the tiny rubber pad which was all you could buy in those days as an after-market pillion seat, and one which I had thoughtfully fitted atop the rear mudguard, along with a set of pillion footrests which clipped on to the rear frame rails. That little seat was hardly big enough for a babe in arms to fit comfortably upon, and she overlapped it so much that the pillion seat disappeared, which meant it looked as though she was sitting directly on the rear guard itself, which she probably was.

It was a bit of a step up from the gutter to the top of the high crown on the road as we bumped down from the footpath. The bike landed with a crash, whereupon the rear axle snapped with a loud crack. It was hardly the fault of the rotund girl on the back, because the plunger-sprung James 125 was notorious for snapping rear axles at every opportunity when ridden over rough surfaces; which was all too often. For some unaccountable reason, this rarely happened with the rigid-frame models.

It took every ounce of the little James' power (?) to drag us to the crown of the road and this was achieved by a lot of paddling and the tangling of all four feet – and included a giggle or four – but we finally made it and then weaved away in first gear, the 125cc Villiers engine howling for mercy as I flat-changed (!) into second. It pulled that gear for about five meters as the engine died beneath us and I had to slip it back into first gear again, the rear wheel canting slightly to one side, the tyre chirping as it occasionally rubbed itself gently against a mudguard stay. There was a subtle smell of burning rubber in the air as the bike weaved up the steep hill at about walking pace, the wheel rims almost grinding along the road surface as the tyres were spread out to about twice their usual width and appeared to be almost flat.

A moist headwind had quickly sprung up and you could smell the rain in the air when suddenly the heavens opened up and the rain pelted down with such force it hurt just to be in the midst of it all. As the road levelled off a bit I managed to select second gear, but top (third) gear was out of the question. So was stopping, because there was nowhere to hide from the onslaught, and we couldn't know how long it was going to keep up. I felt it was better to keep going because we couldn't possibly be any wetter than we already were, and it wouldn't take long to get home from Double Bay, even at our very casual pace. So we battled blindly onwards, the rain beating mercilessly at us, the errant wind whipping around our bodies, but with not a sound coming from the girl imprisoned on the little pillion seat as we climbed – in first gear again – up the never-ending, steep Rushcutters Bay Road into Kings Cross.

I finally pulled up at the tram stops at the top of that long hill, and was at once quite glad, if sadly disappointed, when she leapt off the seat without a word and flounced across the road to the footpath. She looked back at me, shaking her head in either chagrin, disbelief or pity – I never found out which – her usually tightly curled ash-blonde hair now hanging down to her shoulders, giving her not only the build, but now the facial features, of an English sheep dog. Her Paisley-pattern shift, which had draped so decorously over her, now looked as though it had been haphazardly glued to her body by a first-day apprentice paper-hanger. She was quite clearly soaked to the bone, as indeed I was, for the rain continued to lash down mercilessly while the nigh hurricane strength wind howled through the funnelled intersection with unabated ferocity.

It was all too much to bear for suddenly, whether in relief, panic or a fit of high-speed hysteria, I burst out laughing at this absurd situation and couldn't stop no matter how hard I tried. I couldn't see her face because it remained masked by her bedraggled hair, but then she, as if prompted by my hysterics, began to shake from head to foot, then she doubled over and shook her head from side to side as she continued to shake with – I fervently hoped – uncontrollable laughter. Of course, she could have been crying, or about to be sick, but if she was laughing then I was pleased to note that so much of her was really having a good time. As she shook her head anew, she grasped a convenient signpost to support her, and waved me away with the back of her hand, so I rode off.

It took all of five minutes to ride home and I arrived still shrieking with laughter, although by no means oblivious to the rain which continued to beat down with renewed fury.

I didn't see here at the next couple of rehearsals, but she was there the following week, and she was as bright as button, which was quite a relief. I almost fearfully asked her how she was faring; she said she was fine, but thankfully didn't mention that frightful 'ride'

Hazell & Moore

home, for which I was grateful. In fact, her attitude towards me seemed to be unchanged, so I tentatively invited her to come to the movies with me. I had to point out, of course, that we would be going to the large Cinema in Kings Cross, which I could easily walk to, and from where I could just as easily walk her home again, and she happily accepted. We went out again several times again after that first date, but always travelled by public transport.

As if in some form of tacit agreement – for we certainly didn't discuss it – we never, ever, mentioned that unforgettable day I gave her a 'lift' home from the Sam Lands party. That parlous journey was certainly short, but it was far from sweet!

Skid lids

They used to call them battle bowlers, skid lids, crash hats, brain buckets and a variety of other odd and, you could say, derogatory names, but they all referred to the same thing: the once odd and at times rare, but now obligatory, safety helmet.

No, no, not crash helmet, I said *safety* helmet. The industry has always been a bit coy about the word crash, as in crash bars versus safety bars, and bent over backwards all those years ago when skid lids first appeared to push the safety image of the protective device rather than its assistance in the case of a... er... um.. well... *crash*.

Have you noticed how even the word, crash, hurts? No? Well, perhaps you haven't tried one yet, and if you have the time and opportunity to do so, take my advice (for what it's worth) – don't.

Incidentally, the word **crash** is a classic example of the Greek word '*onomatopoeia*', which is a word used to describe a sound associated with an action: other examples are 'tinkling' of bells, the 'bang' of an explosion, the 'boom' of thunder, the 'splash' of water, the 'splat' of falling flat on your face.

In the immediate post-War days let's say the early to mid '50s, folks, the only helmets to be seen in any numbers were Cromwell racing helmets, and the high dome – as distinct from the low crown – variety at that. The shell was made from many layers of laminated cheesecloth to a thickness of about six millimetres, your head held remote from the cork-lined shell by a webbed lining with an adjustable nylon lace. Riveted to the shell was a neat leather harness that incorporated a press-studded and buckled chin strap.

The helmets car racing drivers wore rejoiced in a trim white paint job and the addition of a stout peak, but were virtually identical to the motorcycle unit.

Those older helmets actually did a good job, for the padded harness provided a limited amount of protection if you skidded sideways down the road – which you usually did if you slipped off in a corner – but the shell, one suspected, would function best if you landed headfirst and perpendicular. Dunno about your neck, though!

One rider who will remain nameless, but who rode a very swift BSA twin, tested the Cromwell helmet to its limits on two occasions: once on the old Phillip Island track and once at the foot of Conrod Straight at Bathurst. Almost exactly the same thing occurred at both locations and with the same results.

I believe, though I am not certain, that the twin Beeza seized at high speed in the island and pelted him straight over the handlebars, where he landed upright... but upside down. The helmet split into four pieces and fanned out atop his head like a tiny, horizontal windmill. He walked away dazed and unsure of his name and address for several hours, but otherwise relatively injury free.

A matter of a few months later, and sporting a brand-new Cromwell, he shot down Conrod and sat up to brake hard for the left-hander into Pit Straight. He was , of course, unaware of the fact that his front tyre was as flat as a strap and, after rolling the tyre off the rim, executed another swan dive with vertical head landing (worth at least 9.5 in any competition) and split open yet another *crash* helmet!

This time, the Cromwell resembled a daisy, for it split neatly into several pieces, one of which refused to stay in place and dangled over his left shoulder. Other than speaking all day with a distinctly Romanian accent and claiming to be visiting clergy, he seemed to be all right and refused the entreaties of his wife, the ambulance officers and myself to have someone with a Degree in Strange Behaviour – other people's strange behaviour, that is – interview him.

That same man was taking his wife to the movies one night on foot when a VW driver lost control of the unwieldy device in tram lines and rolled over the top of him, breaking the man's right leg in three places!

From that day on, he always argued it was

more dangerous to take your wife to the pictures than it was to race a motorcycle. And he could prove his assertion, beyond the shadow of a reasonable doubt, to anybody!

Back in the early '50s, as a teenager, I was placed in charge of the accessories counter at Hazell and Moore when the first shipments of a new safety helmet arrived. It was an English Skulgarde, which was made of a laminated and heavily pressed material of unknown composition, lined with cork and covered with a fetching leather-like material in black, brown or white. A large rubber peak adorned the shell and there were a couple of rubber grommets either side to allow for ventilation.

A webbing material inside could be adjusted with a drawstring to keep your head off the shell and a leather harness with chin strap completed the ensemble.

The very first Skulgarde I ever sold proved to be a lifesaver, an absolute lifesaver!

As I recall, the rider had recently purchased a 600cc side-valve Norton (the fact that he had originally come in to buy the more popular Speed Twin Triumph is a story all its own!) and had swung by the counter on his way out.

He liked what he saw and bought a black helmet, remarking offhandedly that the thing would at the very least be warm and waterproof and would help shade his eyes when riding westwards. I cannot recall anything being said about the safety of the device.

He was back in about half an hour. I thought for a moment he had knocked off a few beers somewhere and become a sudden drunk, for he was not too steady on his feet and had some difficulty climbing the small step into the shop.

He stood in front of the counter with an odd, lopsided grin on his face as he swayed slowly from side to side and then back and forth. The top half of his body seemed to be executing a subtle figure of eight and moving in the opposite direction to the lower half. It looked as though one pupil was slightly larger than the other, and he seemed to be trying to focus on something just over my right shoulder, but there was no expression in his eyes.

He did not look well.

"Look at this, will ya?" he said by way of explanation, "I fell R over Z [I think that's what he said] and banged me 'ed on the gutter!"

With one hand on the counter to support himself, he slowly turned his head and pointed at the helmet. I was shocked to see the shell was crushed and flattened from just over his right

> *"The very first Skulgarde I ever sold proved to be a lifesaver, an absolute lifesaver!"*

ear and across the back where a large crack went up the side of the shell to end at one of the small ventilation holes. A small piece of the helmet shell material was sticking straight out one side and there was a large scuff mark around the base of the shell and on the leather harness.

I trotted out a chair for him to sit on and helped him slowly unbuckle the chin strap and remove the helmet. If I knew then what I know now (that should be in the Giant Book of Quotations along with "It seemed like a good idea at the time, Sir!") I wouldn't have touched the helmet at all. For all I knew the top of his head could have come off with the thing, like a hard-boiled breakfast egg you attack with a knife.

As it happened, the bloke's head was not among the best looking containers around, for there were a few lumps, bumps and dents on it, which he said had been there for years. Perhaps a phrenologist would have made something of them.

He thanked me profusely for having saved his life, which I thought a bit overly dramatic, and tottered off with a brand-new Skulgarde and the other near-new one as what he called a "trophy case souvenir".

You could argue, and with some justification, that a safety helmet is by no means a fashion statement, but there was a time when an odd attempt was made to make the things more acceptable to people who felt they should wear them even if they really didn't want to. Whether the manufacturers of these helmets were serious or whimsical I don't pretend to know!

I think it was the Corker helmet which tried to make an attempt at a more acceptable safety device London Police were sometimes mounted on the silent LE Velocette motorcycle as part of their patrol duties and their distinctive Bobbies' helmets were made to the safety standards embraced by the British Safety institute. They looked like Bobbies' helmets but were, in fact, safety helmets!

We can only assume the manufacturers were delighted with the acceptance of their new designs, for you could then buy a safety helmet which looked like a bowler hat, a floral *chapeau*, a deerstalker, a Homburg or – God save us, for this was one for the girls – helmets covered

Hazell & Moore

with a variety of different coloured WIGS! One or two arrived in Sydney as samples and were universally sneered at. Another object of memorabilia I (almost) wish I had spirited away...

Helmet design has changed radically over the years, for modern helmets have very thick shock-absorbing linings and your head rests directly on this lining instead of being held remote from the shell. I don't think there has been much debate over the benefits of one design feature over another, but part of the equation in helmet design relates to the series of small bones that hold our heads more or less upright. They, too, need to be protected.

Such brains as we may have are not glued to the inside of our skulls either, they are free to rattle around a bit as they float on a small sea of fluid, and can thus be injured even as our helmets perform their natural office if called upon to do so.

Quite some years ago I bought a French Roma helmet (not to be confused with the German Rohmer), which was a bit of an odd one. The shell was pressed aluminium (?) again lined with cork and, again, with a harness and drawstring adjustment, the chin strap riveted directly to the shell. It featured a tiny (and entirely useless) peak and a zip-off (?!) leather neck curtain – I assumed for summer riding, although I never unzipped the thing.

I was riding to Bathurst that same year with the Roma firmly in place and pushing my BSA single very briskly. I had just stamped the highly tuned single-cylinder "Iron Goldie" into top gear and breasted a rise, flat out with a mate's Vincent in close pursuit, when I spotted a pall of dust ahead and to my right.

It was the Portland turnoff and some oaf was howling along the dirt road, obviously unaware of the fact that the highway was just over the rise.

Before I could even see who or what it was, I had already slipped back a gear and slammed the brakes on as hard as road surface and good sense allowed. I cranked back another gear, the forks on full deflection, the rear tyre squealing in protest, as an old Ford ute sided onto the highway, its wheels locked up, to stop right in the middle of the road!

There was nowhere to go except into the gravel to the left of the stalled truck and I released the brakes as I swept (I thought safely) around the front of the vehicle. Of course, I endured a perfect tank-slapper and was speared over the handlebars at not much more than brisk running speed, to land headfirst in the waist-high grass at the side of the road.

From that position, and allowing for the parallax error, I saw Fred's Vincent flying through the air, apparently at treetop height. He had, it transpired, ducked off the road behind the offending truck, and at a speed much greater than mine, to encounter a metre-square drain with the lid off, the latter facing towards him and forming a perfect launching ramp for his astonishing leap.

I sat up and was suddenly aware of a great pain and enormous pressure on top of my head, while the helmet's chin strap was doing its best to strangle me. I tore at the chin strap's buckle, which shoved my eyes even further from their sockets, and managed to reef the lid off, to feel an enormous and immediate relief. Oddly, I didn't think for a second that the top of my head could have come off with the helmet!

When I examined the helmet I was amazed to see a huge dent stretching right across the crown of the aluminium shell, which had been pushed down and was resting firmly on the harness. Happily, the thick cork lining was still firmly in place. So, too, was the granite rock that had caused the damage, for it sat coyly in the grass with just a small graze on it as evidence of its collision with the alloy shell.

There is little doubt that my Roma was also a lifesaver, and it put me immediately in mind of the good fortune of the Skulgarde owner of some 10 years prior.

I was wearing helmets long before they were mandatory, if only because they were of course warm, waterproof and comfortable, and stayed in place much more readily than a cloth cap turned back to front and held in place by goggle elastic. They were also instrumental in correcting a sinus problem that had plagued me for years.

There have only been two other occasions where I have put helmets to the ultimate test, and it should be obvious that on each occasion they have performed their duties perfectly.

One of them was a thin-shelled, cork-lined helmet with its attendant webbing harness; the other, some 30-odd years later, a full-face design with thick inner lining and no harness.

The better of the two? Hey, who cares, it is much better not to put any of them to the ultimate test at all, but it's great to know the things work when they have to.

As someone once said, you pays your money and you takes your choice, and it doesn't really matter what you call the product.

Performing apes

It's been said that the other Great Apes out there, a category which includes gorillas, chimpanzees and orang-utans, are loaded with almost 95% of the Naked Ape's human DNA, which is of some concern to us all; or at least, it should be. It's also been stated that these furry critters are smarter than their naked cousins (that's us) in many ways, because they don't start wars and can subsist on just about anything they may stumble across which is bright green, sometimes yellow, or sometimes bright red. They don't need to fire up the family car, or their bike, to zip off to the local Supermarket and spend good money to collect their own bright green, yellow, red, or multi-coloured, often-packaged produce.

As far as is known, there is no written or oral examination of the Great Apes in existence which has been put in place to elicit their intellectual capacity in relation to ours – whether that matters to them or not, which I doubt – or to check their qualifications to be in control of any form of motor vehicle. This is without doubt a Very Good Thing Indeed, for the roads of this nation seem to be crammed with humans who – using the simple yardstick of driving (in)competence – apparently exhibit an IQ somewhat approaching that of the average (Celsius) room temperature of a balmy, autumnal evening; which I believe to be about 24 -26 or so. Our furry Fellow Apes are surely somewhat brighter than that – at least one would hope so!

Having said all that, I am just now reminded of a troupe of four or five chimpanzees who regularly appeared at Sydney's Tivoli Theatre back in the early fifties. The unintentionally-funny little critters were to be seen riding their under-powered, tiny fold-up Corgi machines (I won't call those things motorcycles!) about the Theatre's stage without running into each other – or at least only now and again, and then often with hilarious results. The shocking little 50cc one-geared Corgi was a half- baked civilian version of the Welbike, a machine which was dropped by parachute in some numbers to be used as very basic transport by paratroopers, who flung the frightful little things into nearby creeks or old barns in Europe whenever the unsprung, and equally under-braked, vehicles ran out of the fuel in their pre-filled tanks several kilometres after they were push-started. Oh, yes, naturally they employed no kick-starter and no clutch either!

Whenever they were in town, the performing chimpanzees' troupe's manager/trainer would have the little bikes serviced by the Triumph/Norton importers, Hazell and Moore, for whom I was working at the time. The company's store was almost directly opposite the Tivoli Theatre's stage door, so it enjoyed the priceless geographic advantage of being just a casual stroll away.

On one noteworthy occasion the manager, an odd, twitchy little man who spoke with an entirely unintelligible European accent, brought with him one of the larger chimps, who suddenly detached himself from his master's grasp and leapt, gibbering and screaming with ill-concealed delight, along and upon a large series of full-sized motorcycles which lined the large workshop, the size and shape of which he had probably never seen before. It seemed the little bloke(s) – both the chimp and his manager – couldn't be easily calmed, whereupon a large Police sergeant, who was having his near-new 1949 Triumph Tiger 100 pursuit motorcycle serviced, offered to quieten the little 'monkey' (as he so erroneously called the ape) by shooting the poor thing with his service revolver!

Suddenly the chimp settled himself down, which I thought – as a young kid at the time – might have been at the sight of the Policeman subtly unclipping the strap on his weapon's holster. Then again, it may simply have been the end of the novelty of jumping up and down on a large number of what would be by now several serried rows of Classic motorcycles. Then again, his master's screamed commands might have done the job: unhappily we will never know, but the chimp then shuffled shame-faced back to his handler and they quietly left the workshop, to the enormous relief of all of us; if not to the clearly disappointed, large Police officer, whose trigger finger appeared (at least me) to be twitching visibly!

Which brings me, after that long-winded pre-amble, to the three incidents which occurred within the space of about two hours in the same day, and which clearly indicated the lack of native intelligence which the three disparate car drivers displayed to all of us who were on the spot as 'innocent bystanders' whether we wanted to be there or not. No ape (licenced or not) would ever have been guilty of the terminally idiotic driving habits which were shown by the inept trio.

The great librettist, William Schwenk Gilbert probably summed their performances up perfectly when, in his Opera *'Princess Ida'*, he

Hazell & Moore

> *"If I had been a Magistrate and those two jackasses had been booked for the serious crime of Advanced Ridiculousness and arraigned to appear before me, I would have sentenced them both to a year's riding of a 1947 Type-A Lambretta scooter..."*

had one of his singers declare that "Darwinian Man, though well behaved, at best is only a monkey shaved"

The first, potentially disastrous incident occurred on Sydney's Seven Hills Road, where the elderly, flat-capped and scarfed driver of a near-new BMW sports convertible was driving along the inside lane of the four-lane road. He suddenly turned his left blinker on, clearly indicating that he was to turn into a driveway which he was approaching. I signalled to move into the 'fast' lane to overtake him, whereupon he swung the steering wheel hard to the right to ease his turn, the left flasher still on, the man clearly holding the switch in position to stop the self-cancelling device from cutting out. I am sure no well-trained, self-respecting chimpanzee would *ever* have attempted such a ridiculous manoeuvre, for fear of being kicked out of the show!

I was half into the near-vacant lane and had to brake to avoid the car, when a motorcyclist coming up astern swept past, crossed the 'dotted' centre-line for an instant and swept back again, continuing on his way, the while closely avoiding an un-laded semi-trailer which was coming the other way. The motorcycle rider was obviously very experienced, which was evident by the fact that he didn't look back, shrug his shoulders or angrily sound the bike's horn. I imagine he simply accepted the scenario as just another one of his daily 'close shaves.' But the trailer driver let loose with a deafening blast from the two, meter-long air horns which adorned the top of his cabin. He was rewarded for this indiscretion by receiving an arrogant road rage signal from the ageing imbecile in the BMW.

I wanted to go back and have a quiet chat with the errant BMW driver, but my wife Lyn forbade me from doing so, pointing out that the trailer driver had pulled up anyway, apparently to have an enlightening conversation with the man himself, for he was even now trotting across the road to give the BMW driver some much needed advice.

The second incident occurred in the parking lot of a nearby shopping centre, and only about a half-hour later. I had just parked the family Yaris, and alongside us was another narrow parking spot, which was clearly being approached by a car a level below us. The parking spot had also been spotted by the driver of a large Mercedes, who suddenly spurted violently along the parking lane, flashed his *left* blinker to indicate that he claimed the parking spot as his, then – just as the BMW driver had done so recently – he swung his steering wheel violently on full-lock to the *right* (his hand for a change wrapped round the normally self-cancelling blinker) then proceeded to slowly back into the confined space. It took him all of three attempts to do so, his mouth agape, his head swivelling about from window to rear mirror, just like one of those gaping clowns in the local country showground, down whose open mouths one rolls a series of ping-pong balls, hoping to score some game-winning points: and, hopefully, to be issued with a ten-cent, curly-haired celluloid Kewpie doll affixed by a twinkling ribbon to a short, thin walking cane with a curved handle.

That clown scored no points at all from the other car driver, who shook his head sadly and waited patiently for the bloke who had pinched his parking spot to finish buggerising about. It has always been beyond my limited grasp of consciousness to understand why any driver would **back** into a confined space when it would be easier to slot into a small parking space head-on and in one hit, which then leaves a great deal more room to back out into the much larger spaces outside the parking area. Perhaps that's just the way I am, which would be no surprise, because a lot of other people seem to park arse-about in exactly the same manner.

If I had been a Magistrate and those two jackasses had been booked for the serious crime of Advanced Ridiculousness and arraigned to appear before me, I would have sentenced them both to a year's riding of a 1947 Type-A Lambretta scooter – if anyone could find one, or a 1950 Douglas Vespa if they couldn't. The former was an unsprung little device with seven-inch (7") wheels, ultra-flexible handlebars and jam-

Vintage Morris

tin sized brakes, the latter featured short-travel, un-damped suspension, and an engine hanging out to the right-hand side some ten inches or more from the machine's centre line. The most enhancing feature of these immediate post-war scooters was that they wouldn't go, wouldn't stop, and they both handled like country farm gates with loose, worn-out hinges. Please don't ask me about their *worst* features!

After about two or three weeks of riding either of those grim two-wheeled devices about, these two buffoons would have learned more about road sense than they had learned in their entire lives while being ferreted about on *four* wheels, the while clearly avoiding accidents by the skill(s) of other road users.

And the third incident? I thought you'd never ask!

It was the worst of the lot, and it occurred just outside yet another narrow parking spot into which I had recently shoehorned the little Yaris. Lyn had at last made her purchases and we climbed into the car, fired it up and edged our way out of the spot, to turn broadside on before slotting into gear to drive happily away.

Suddenly we felt a fearful crunch, which turned out to be a large Prado SUV, whose inept owner had heartily backed the vehicle into us from a parking spot opposite where I had stopped. Lyn (very) forcefully told me to stay put (which is just as well!) and leapt out of the passenger's seat to confront the woman who had so efficiently backed into us, earnestly writing off our rear bumper, dinging the boot lid and plucking out the entire left-hand tail-light assembly. She also crunched over the shards of the light's plastic lenses as an encore, and shoved us half a meter sideways as well!

"I suppose she didn't see us?" I enquired pithily, and with no little sarcasm, to the closed window. I wound the window down as Lyn came back to the car to proffer the driver's excuse/explanation. "She says she didn't see us," she exclaimed. Why was I not surprised?

The Prado has two external rear vision mirrors fitted as standard ware, each of them about the size of tennis racquet heads, and one interior one the size of a business-letter envelope, so I venture to say that the dumbest nursing orang-utan, perhaps even while battling with a pair of squalling babes, could easily have seen us, if the orange ape had deigned to glance for a second into either (or better still all three!) of those huge mirrors. To make the absurd even more so, I noted a small hole just above the Prado's rear number plate, which was capped by a small, clear dome: evidence, no doubt, of a reversing camera which should have been utilised along with the mirrors – allied to that essential look over a right shoulder – to be sure no-one lurked within any of the large vehicle's rear blind-spots.

Clearly the driver had not looked into any of the safety features with which the over-sized vehicle was so cleverly endowed. Just as well we weren't seated upon a two-wheeled vehicle, I suggested to her through tightly clenched teeth, otherwise we would assuredly have had a series of deeply-studded tyre marks etched forever all over what was left of us.

Served her right, I say, that she had to pay a couple of thousand dollars to have our car effectively repaired; it would have been very much better for her than lurching about for twelve months being battered from pillar to post while fearfully riding a 70-year old, low-powered, ill-handling two-wheeler

I wish I had thought to mention that to her!

Harry Hinton

Australia has provided the world with some of the finest racing motorcyclists this planet has ever seen, long before our latter-day World Champion riders became world famous for their marvellous performances in International competition.

Just after the Second World War, even with no sponsorship and little money to splash about, the ACCA (the Auto Cycle Council of Australia) sent small teams of specially selected riders overseas to compete on the Isle of Man and other famous circuits, some of the great riders enjoying factory support. One of our greatest local riders, who went overseas only a couple of times, was a bloke called Harry Hinton; the 'Old Fox' as many were wont to call him. He didn't ride very often Internationally, so he didn't figure highly on the World Championship scene, but he was a force to be reckoned with any time he fronted the starting line on any of this Nation's racing circuits back in the '40s and '50s..

His sons, Eric and Harry Junior, who rode overseas more regularly, were not to be trifled with either: any time the Hinton name appeared on a programme in this or any other country, it assured those other entrants of a tough time in keeping any of them at bay. Except for Harry Senior's amazing little 'Blue Star' 250cc racer, and the BSA sidecar he raced pre-war, the

Hazell & Moore

Hintons were usually mounted upon Manx Norton racers, often with factory backing, but allied to some very smart home tuning. The machines were at once very fast and quite reliable, if not always pristine examples.

They called Harry the Old Fox because of his canny race strategy, whereby he often sat back in the field in about fourth or fifth place – but within sight of the leaders – until he would make his move to the front in the latter stages of an event, totally demoralising his opposition.

In the Good Old Days at Bathurst you could stand on Con-Rod Straight and watch in amazement at the speed these mere mortals were able to achieve as they sped down that long, undulating section of track. In those far-off days they were of course mounted on everything which came out of England, but with an odd sprinkling of a very, very few European machines.

Even as a kid I noted a couple of Harry's neat tricks he used to dislodge a competitor who may be tucked firmly into his slipstream as they dropped swiftly down that marvellous Conrod Straight prior to braking hard for the tight left hander that led onto the finishing Pit Straight. He used similar tactics on other circuits as well, and always with the same result.

He used one of two methods, both of which were very effective. In the first instance, he would sit up suddenly as he closed on the braking area, but keep the throttle wide open, then crouch down again and bury his chin onto the petrol tank rubber pad as his frantic pursuer braked several seconds too early and lost the best part the 100 meters or more he had fought so hard to gain. As they then accelerated hard along Pit Straight, his rival, with a greatly elevated heart rate, would lose even more distance as he tried to settle himself down again. Harry would then gleefully disappear into the distance.

His second method was even more cunning. On this occasion, as they approached the heavy braking area, he would have his chin buried deep into the tank pad then suddenly roll the throttle off, move into the centre of the track and slam the brakes on as hard as was prudent. His horrified opponent would shoot past, brake much later than he should have and then, whether he liked it or not, be forced to turn **right** and take the faster (escape) corner which lead off the track and towards Bathurst. By the time the furious rider was able to turn round and zoom back onto the Pit Straight, Harry would be on his way up Mountain Straight! So would about half the rest of the field. What a bugger that would have been.

The first time I saw Hinton the Elder was at Bathurst in 1948 when three of us stood goggle-eyed – we were just school kids at the time from Sydney, and therein lies another story! – at the foot of Conrod Straight during the practice day on Good Friday when Vince Darderi (I think it was Vince?) howled into the braking area on his 1000cc Vincent and sat up to brake. Tucked into his slipstream was an *un-streamlined* 250cc Blue Star BSA, with none other than Harry Hinton aboard. By rights that little BSA should never have been anywhere near that big, thundering Vincent, but there it was being sucked along by that big machine as though it was tied to it by an invisible string.

Then, as they both braked after that swift descent from the Mountain, a shower of small tools erupted from beneath the Vincent's large dual seat and flew everywhere. I have always fancied that I saw one of the gleaming tools ping off the top of Hinton's helmet, but it happened so quickly I could never be sure of that. But the rider on that little BSA was not amused and demonstrated this fact by shouting his displeasure at the other rider and shaking his fist at him, as well as making several gestures I later found would have been quite offensive. There were, I was later to learn, several words of a hostile nature bandied back and forth in the pit area later in the day.

For a change from his usual Norton, Harry was mounted on one of the new, but rare 500cc GP Triumph twins in 1948, which he rode to second place in the Senior event on Easter Saturday, behind Frank Mussett's even rarer ex-factory 500cc KTT Velocette. As a matter of interest, Mussett set a new lap record of 3min.5sec during the race, the open-wheeler (genuine) racing cars recording a new lap record of 3min.2sec on the following Easter Monday.

Harry owned a motorcycle store in Lidcombe, to which we despatched product almost on a daily basis. But he would often come into Hazell and Moore to purchase urgently needed spare parts for a repair job in his workshop. He arrived one day riding a 3T Triumph, that sadly unloved 350cc poor relation of the otherwise dominant 500cc Speed Twin and Tiger 100 models, and he was wearing nothing but a pair of sandshoes, swimming trunks, an old gasmask bag and one of those large, ex US Air Force Polaroid goggles everyone seemed to be wearing at the time.

> *"What an honour! What a monumental privilege! To be allowed to ride on a motorcycle operated by one of the finest riders this nation has ever seen!"*

Amazingly, 60 years later these goggles are still to be seen on the helmets of US soldiers in Iraq and Afghanistan! Either they made too many millions of them for WW2, or they are still (justifiably) very effective. They are certainly very popular.

As it happens, I had to take a few small parcels to the air freight office of ANA in Phillip Street and time was going to beat me to have the vital spare parts catch the last flight out of Sydney, and this fact was made known to Harry by the beaming spare parts manager.

"Hop on the back," he exclaimed enthusiastically, "I'll take you down town and wait for you."

What an honour! What a monumental privilege! To be allowed to ride on a motorcycle operated by one of the finest riders this nation has ever seen! I could not have jumped onto that motorcycle any quicker had I been jet propelled.

Gawd, if I had known; if I had only known!!

Had I any idea of what that terrifying trip would be like I would have resigned my very newly acquired job on the spot and retired, sobbing, into oblivion. Or, more likely, have hidden away somewhere until someone else was forced to risk life and limb in the service of getting the mails through at all costs. (**Bugle call, please**)

I sat on that tiny – about 5 inch x 9 inch – rubber pad which was referred to as a 'pillion seat' and smirked at the passing peasantry as Harry swung on the 3T Triumph kick-starter and then with no warning at all, we leapt from the gutter and flew along Campbell Street to the adverse-cambered left hander into Castlereagh Street.

A tram had just left its stop and was halfway across our path as, with its bell clanging like a funereal dirge we slid sideways across its bows, missing the thing by a coat of paint and then hurled ourselves up the steep climb which followed. Of course I was desperately trying to juggle three small parcels and hang on for dear life, while unintentionally leaning back at about forty-five degrees and on the very lip of that tiny rubber pad.

Thankfully, an ultra-swift gear-change allowed me to bury my nose into Harry's bony spine and to slide forward about a tissue paper's thickness, the while stuffing those parcels down the front of my shirt and grabbing hold of the base of the bike's single saddle. How that somewhat agricultural engine managed to hold itself together during that frightful journey I will never know, for it was wrung out to nearly peak engine revs before it was mercifully allowed the temporary relief of the occasional selection of a higher gear.

We roared up that narrow one-way street as though it was an open road race circuit, swooping in and out amongst the fleeing pedestrians, sliding along those slippery tram lines and howling past horn-blowing cars, that tiny pillion seat – perched on the rear guard and atop an unsprung rear wheel – kicking me up the backside, and the *front-side* as well, at very regular intervals.

Minutes later (which seemed like hours), we screeched to a halt outside the air freight office and I slid limply from that absurd pillion seat and stumbled towards the counter inside, heart pounding like a jack hammer, my knees turned to water, my red-rimmed, streaming eyes sticking out of their sockets like organ stops, my tenor voice assuming the *tessitura* of a high soprano.

"I'll wait for you, mate." Harry shouted as he unslung his goggles and draped them round his neck

"There's a big queue here" I croaked in my new-found high *timbre,* which was a lie for there wasn't a soul to be seen other than the bloke behind the counter. "You better take off, I'll be a while." I furtively checked the front of my trousers, fully expecting to find a damp patch there, and was relieved in an entirely different fashion as he nodded, re-adjusted his goggles and shot off like a rocket to joust once more with those poor, innocent fools who were unintentionally in his path.

I would have to say that Harry seemed to be pretty relaxed about it all, but I had to sit down for a minute or so before I was able to shuffle silently to the counter, the bloke standing behind it eyeing me off the while. It suddenly dawned on me that I had probably not taken a single breath from the time I slid onto that too-short rubber pad until I slid limply off it again some minutes later!

Hazell & Moore

Early days Bathurst

It was a Saturday night at Sydney's Showground Speedway way back in 1948 which changed it all, and it was very much for the better. It was, as usual, almost a packed house, but one of the unexpected items on the programme was the addition of several promotional laps by a large number of motorcycles which differed radically from the skinny, ultra-lightweight Speedway bikes. They were in fact highly-specialised, un-streamlined road-racing machines, which looked extremely impressive, although they were naturally ridden on the slick dirt surface at much slower speeds than the nigh-frantic pace of the many races we had already witnessed.

The loud-barking machines, with their trumpet-like open megaphone exhausts, were there to promote the forthcoming road race meeting at Bathurst, which was to be held in a few weeks' time over the Easter break, from practice on the Thursday prior to several races on Good Friday, with the major events listed for Easter Saturday. Nobody said it at the time, but the open-wheeler GP car racing events were then scheduled for Easter Sunday and the following Monday, the motorcycles expected to leave the Pit area immediately after Easter Saturday's races were finished.

As the 'poor relations' in motor sport – at least they were in those far-off days – anyone who might have been a bit tardy in packing up and leaving at once on Easter Saturday afternoon was almost hounded out of the dirt-surfaced Pit area by the clearly toffee-nosed car types, who appeared to think they were God's Gift to Motor Racing. As it happened, of course, in view of some very close motorcycle racing for two full days, followed by two days of the high-speed procession which often typifies GP car racing, the car-types were nowhere near as spectacular. In this regard, nothing much has changed over the last sixty and more years, although it must be said that the later, V8 Taxi-Cab races do have their own drama, and can be quite a spectacle.

My brothers and I, all of whom were still at school, along with a great school mate of mine, were so smitten by the sights and sounds of those gleaming road race machines that we hot-footed it to Central Station the following day to book our train tickets for the journey over the Blue Mountains to Bathurst. We had a faint idea where/what Bathurst was, but no blind idea what to expect when we finally arrived there. We booked our hired, four-man tent and our pushbikes into the Guard's Van, because we thought that to have our bikes on hand for basic transport might be a Good Idea. In fact it was a smart move which proved to be – for a pleasant change – a *Very* Good Idea!

We noted the fact that there were two motorcycles stashed in the Van which were sporting racing number plates, so we reckoned the track might be near the station, and that the owner(s) of the two bikes had doubtless arranged for them to be conveyed to the track by a truck of some sort, with us following in their wake. As we were later to discover, one of the bikes was a pre-war 250cc single-cylinder Triumph Tiger 70, which had made an amazingly long, long journey from Western Australia entirely by public transport (!), the other, from Sydney, was a rigid-framed 350cc MAC Velocette.

Naturally, we were not to know (how could we?) that the train we were to catch at 7pm on the Thursday prior to Good Friday was the *'Paper Train'*, which always took its own sweet time on the journey as it dropped off bundles of newspapers here and there, as well as the odd one or two papers which were hand-delivered to individuals representing householders and who lived close enough to the railroad tracks to trot across the paddock to pick them up. True!

But what was infinitely worse was the fact that a Migrant Hostel had been built in Bathurst to accommodate the burgeoning Migrant population which was even then beginning to make its presence felt. We were also not to know that an influx of new migrants were (was?) to catch the same train as us, and that there were a great many of them as well!

We became very well aware of this as soon as we approached the platform from which the Bathurst train was to depart, because we could hear the loud, excited babble long before we got there to see what the noise was all about. When we arrived at our platform we were horrified to see it was absolutely jam-packed with a great variety of swarthy looking men, who seemed to be arguing loudly with each other because there were arms and legs flying about all over the place, the men speaking in rapid, stentorian tones, often almost face-to-face. There was not one female to be seen anywhere on that platform.

Of course we couldn't understand one word any of them were saying, but the men all seemed to know what they were on about, because they were to be seen nodding to one another, occasionally laughing, or gesturing as if to draw imaginary pictures in the air around them. I remember one large, florid looking bloke who said something like "Sidderknee" while his mate made an utterance which sounded a bit like "Suddenly", and which could have meant 'Sydney', but the rest was lost in the loud hubbub, as well as in the odd range of foreign languages in which they all spoke.

The air around that platform was a bit on the thick side, and seemed to be rent with cigarette smoke allied to a garlic, and cheap, plonk-induced Halitosis, while many of these men were to be heard loudly venting their other digestive problems *via* an alarming array of faintly-amusing, wind-induced sounds. Deep bass belches and loudly-trumpeted, wet farts seemed to be going off everywhere, mixed with some tenor-like (and infinitely more polite) burps from the more civilized of their number.

An astonishingly large number of vastly differing keys could be heard, which would probably be declared 'musical' by today's very poor standard of 'pop vocalising', but most of those odd keys were never in evidence on any sheet music of any song I have ever sung.

Suddenly, there was a loud shuffling of feet, abetted by a series of strangled cheers and foreign curses, as the steam-train – for thus it was, because the electric railway line extended only to Parramatta until 1955, believe it or not – slowly backed into view. Try as we might (or as dumb as we were), we could not get within a bull's roar of the edge of the platform, while those who were clever enough to have placed themselves at the far end were opening carriage doors and windows, and launching themselves recklessly inside.

Many of the men were pelting bulging briefcases and small portmanteau into the train as well, with some of their number assisting those who were half-way aboard by belting them across their various backsides with sticks, umbrellas or rolled-up newspapers. One bloke who tried to jump aboard just in front of me had a .22 rifle strapped sideways across his shoulders for some incomprehensible reason, which severely inhibited his access. He had shoved me brusquely aside as he tried to climb through the narrow window, so I was delighted to see the rifle slip from his shoulder and clatter to the tracks below as he struggled to get aboard. Happily, there was no way known he could have retraced his steps to retrieve the offending firearm, although I did wonder why he had it with him, and what he thought he was going to do with it when he arrived at his destination.

So there we were, jammed in like sardines in a can far too small for them, standing upright, face-to-face and with nowhere to go. The man I was jammed up against seemed to be pleasant enough, but his nicotine-stained, moth-eaten, lop-sided, moustache was of some concern, as his garlic-and- curried prawn breath was. It wasn't his fault, of course, and he seemed to be apologetic enough, but it was in no way a comfortable experience. Perhaps, as in Shakespeare's 'comic relief', his funny moustache was enough to have me giggling like a schoolgirl not long after we moved slowly away, and it was some time before I was able to settle myself down again. My companion looked at me very sadly, and tried to make soothing noises, which didn't help at all – in fact, it only succeeded in making it a whole lot worse.

But it was to become much worse as the small steam engine struggled to move away with its huge cargo of oddly-assorted human beings. It fairly crept out of the station, which brought the thought to mind that it was never, ever going to have enough grunt to carry us safely over the Blue Mountains.

To make matters even worse – if that was possible – it seemed to pull up at every platform and whistle stop from Central to Parramatta, and then, ever slower, to Blacktown and finally into Penrith. I'm sure it stopped, or slowed down, at least ten times during that short journey to drop off bundles of papers.

But at Penrith we stayed, stayed, and stayed some more, as we were shunted off into an unused siding while we waited for another engine to be hitched to the one we were in, hopefully providing enough impetus for us to creep over the Mountains.

We lurched on anew, and still at a snail's pace, the two engines puffing like mad while struggling to heave a train with its over-loaded human cargo over the ever-steepening rails ahead. Even then, the train stopped at tiny, narrow platforms on very regular occasions over the Mountains, which meant it had to shuffle painfully away from a standstill many times o'er. On three occasions, as dawn was breaking, the train slowed down as people – one of whom, a woman in a pink dressing gown, was obscenely shouted at in a variety of languages and obvious gestures – trotted across open fields to dodge rolled-up papers which were hurled at them by the train driver and/or his coal shoveling off-sider.

I wondered aloud into the face of my friendly passenger why they didn't think to deliver the papers by truck, but he just raised his eyebrows, blinked in my face and said nothing. Of course he couldn't understand any more of what I said to him than I could of what his friends were saying to him. Even with that enormous number of men jam-packed into the carriage it was a lonely ride, because I couldn't see my brothers or school-mate anywhere and thus had no-one to speak (English) to.

I did hear them on one occasion, as some foreign jackass opened a train window and hung half-out of it to relieve himself, for my brother was heard to shout. "Christ, it's cold. Hey, sit down here where there is a natural windbreak." To which my chum from school drily remarked "Oh, and who broke it?"

A small procession of other men began, as best they could, to noisily relieve themselves out of that train window, while a couple of other windows were coldly opened nearby to allow others to gleefully indulge in the same pursuit. For the most part they seemed to be fairly successful, except for the occasional lurch round unexpected corners or over rough level crossings; it's called 'getting your own back', while accidentally anointing several others.

At long last that shocking train journey ended when we pulled into Bathurst station at 8am on Good Friday, that awful journey taking more than twelve (12) grim hours! The doors quickly burst open and everyone fell out of the carriages; one or two flat on their backs, one or two face down, where they were naturally trodden upon or stumbled over, but all of us at last able to flex cramped arms and legs and to gulp in the life-enhancing, freezing, crystal clear air.

The train's engine was enveloped in clouds of steam, but then so were most of us as everyone – that's **everyone** – noisily relieved themselves from positions between the carriages, up against the sides of the carriages, or even where they stood. It was a grossly awful spectacle, if an absolutely essential one, which seemed to raise the ire of the busy station master who was running about all over the place, shouting hopelessly at everyone.

We repaired to the Guard's Van to collect our bikes, to discover that the owners of the two race machines had enjoyed a far more leisurely trip, sleeping for most of that long journey within the confines of the van, one of them settling very comfortably upon our tent.

The strangest thing about those two men was that neither of them had arranged for anyone to meet them, which meant they had to wheel their motorcycles the two miles or so out to the track, which we of course helped them to do. The Velocette owner – whose name, from memory, was Robertson – had a large suitcase and smaller toolbox perched upon the bike's single saddle and rubber rear-guard pad. But the rider of the Tiger 70 (who carried everything he needed within a large ex-Army haversack) was to tell us a marvelous story about his journey across the continent from Perth by train(s) as we walked along, as each of us proudly took turns in wheeling one or the other of the machines; our own bikes held by other pushbike riders.

We marveled at the incredible story of the man who booked himself and his bike across the Nation many, many years before the one-gauge line from Perth to Sydney, being conveyed for much of his trip in a variety of Guards Vans. He and his bike went from Perth to Kalgoorlie, to change trains for Port Augusta, to join another train into Adelaide, yet another train to Melbourne, another to Albury, to change yet again for the journey to Sydney, and again from Sydney to Bathurst!

That was a total of seven (7) trains he had to catch on his lomg, long journey from Perth to Bathurst, and he had to do the same thing all over again to get back home!! If ever there was a Gold Medal on hand to be awarded for Sheer Guts and Rampant Enthusiasm, that bloke should have been given a sugar-bag full of them!

As it happened, he rode to a very high place in the 250cc Lightweight event – fourth or fifth from memory – and finished high in the placings in the 350cc Junior Clubman's event as well.

I trust it made his arduous trip well worth-while – he said afterward that it did, as he made the journey back to Sydney with us within the relative comfort of a half-empty, second-class carriage. I foolishly asked him how he might have felt had his engine blown up within five minutes of firing it up for practice, but he said nothing as he smiled and stared dreamily out of the carriage window.

Clearly, he had enjoyed the whole exercise, and what a wonderful adventure that parlous journey must have been; what skill and ingenuity he showed in organizing it, and what enormous courage, not to mention determination, he displayed in bringing it all to fruition! I often wonder what his friends, family and neighbours thought of him when he told them what he had planned to do.

Pillion riders

A few years ago I was cast as the leading character in a TV commercial for Praise Mayonnaise, the final shot of which saw me riding briskly out of shot while mounted upon a 1200C BMW Cruiser, a mature, but slim and quite attractive female pillion passenger grinning over my right shoulder. We were supposedly enjoying a new lease on life after consuming a few dollops of the delicious product, the commercial apparently shot within the confines of the retirement village in which we were supposed to be living. It was in fact shot in what was once a busy Naval establishment on one of Sydney's headlands.

The pillion passenger was a tall, well-known character actress who looked like the comedienne Lucille Ball, and behaved very much like her as well. I had met her some years previously, during the filming of a TV play for the ABC, wherein I was supposed to be a little more than half-tanked as she was almost carrying me home for some obscure reason which was never fully explained. They were playing that old short man/tall woman gag which I have often used on stage to great effect for as far back as I can remember – which is a long, long time!

Before the final scene was to be filmed later in the day she confided to me that she had never so much as *sat* upon a motorcycle before, much less upon anything as tiny as that little rubber pad which sat forlornly upon the fat rear guard while masquerading as a pillion seat; the device, as she said 'obviously intended only for emergency accommodation.'

It was an odd little pillion seat, for it would usually be employed as a sort of small, if welcoming, lumbar 'backrest' to augment the rider's deeply padded, large and low-slung **single saddle** when locked into an upright position, but could then be unlocked and folded down upon the rear guard to then assume the role of a slightly tapered and tiny, if softly-padded 'pillion seat', very much, as the girl had so pithily maintained, for use only as an emergency pillion if a change in one's luck was apparent.

I checked with the director to see if it was OK to take her for a short burst up the road and around a large roundabout which I had circumnavigated several time earlier as I familiarised myself with this over-large Cruiser, if only to see if she was comfortable enough with *me*, even if she might not have been too comfortable upon that small, 25cm x 20cm x 10cm deep (approx.) rubber pad.

As usual they were forever buggerising about with the lighting so he was quite happy with my suggestion, so I borrowed another helmet from the fellow who brought the bike to us and she plonked it on, complaining that her ears would by now be resting somewhere upon her shoulders. I then had to gently explain two simple procedures to her as I lifted it off again. Firstly, I announced, she would need to grasp the chinstraps and pull them apart to 'spring' the sides of the helmet a little to allow the thing to slide more comfortably over her ears, and secondly she would need to have it sit on her head square-on, instead of on the *back* of her head, where she had initially placed it.

For a reason which always amazed me, all women to whom I ever sold a helmet (and there were lots of them over too many years) always – that is, *always* – perched the helmet on the very back of their heads, where they might normally wear a hat to the Spring Carnival at a horse racing event. I always knew it was going to happen, and I always found it faintly amusing, but I could never work out the *rationale* for them doing such an odd thing. I would invariably have to straighten the helmet up and check it for size. This was always done by the simple insertion of the little finger at a client's temple and then the forehead area. There was no other way to do this, but no-one, regardless of gender or preference thereof, ever complained because it was done swiftly and without pre-amble but simply as part of the process of ensuring a perfect fit.

Her helmet, it turned out, was a perfect fit and she looked radiant with the thing on as she sidled up to the bike. "All right love," she said, "You're the boss, what do you want me to do?"

"What I want you to do" I pontificated, as I had told many a 'new' female passenger before we ever went anywhere, "is to sit as close to me as you can. And don't fight either me or the bike. Go where I go; I repeat, don't fight either me or the bike. When I lean the bike into a corner you must know it is not going to fall over. So go with the flow and there will be no problems at all. Just sit there as comfortably and as quietly as you can. Remember, you go where I go. Look over my right shoulder in right hand corners and over the other one when we are turning left. So you can see where we are going. But whatever else you may do, *don't close your eyes*. You should be able to see everything ahead just as easily as I can. That way there won't be any surprises. OK?"

Hazell & Moore

"Okay, love," she said, and then, as all women before her have done since the Year Dot, she stepped onto the left pillion footrest and stood upon it in preparation for settling herself upon the 'pillion seat.' Of course I was half ready for that, but even then the bike canted over so alarmingly to the left that I very nearly dropped the thing before we had even moved off the spot. So help me, it took every ounce of the strength born of the desperation we all possess in such emergency situations for me to hold the bike upright.

I was almost on the brink of popping a hernia by the time I was finally able to heave the large bike upright again, slotting the thing into gear and moving *gently* away. Almost immediately she wrapped her arms around my waist and buried her nose into the back of my neck, from where I knew she couldn't hope to see where we were going, but she soon relaxed a little and in fact obviously began to peer over one shoulder or the other as the occasion arose. But every time I changed gear, or backed off and braked for something she would bang her nose into the back of my neck and thump me with her helmet.

It was a nuisance, but not nearly as bad as the girl to whom I offered a ride around the Albert Park road in Melbourne in the early '70s, who spent almost the entire ride pecking at me with the peak of her old-fashioned helmet any time I rolled the throttle back to change gear or apply the brakes. How she couldn't hear the engine running, or even watch my hands at work on the control levers was a mystery, until she explained at the end of several laps that she had seen nothing because her eyes were tightly shut for the entire time. Not very confidence inspiring, I would have thought!

So the actress and I rolled up to the large roundabout and swept majestically through it, rode off again and then, just for fun, I executed a tight U-turn to go back and go through the roundabout again. She then uttered the words any young and virile lover would be chuffed to hear from his new and surprisingly eager girl-friend.

"That was fantastic," she cooed into my right ear. "What a great buzz! Let's go back and do it all over again."

I should have known better I suppose, but I peeled over into an even quicker U-turn and made our way back to the roundabout; this time somewhat quicker than before. I was just lining the bike up to crank it over when she unaccountably grabbed me around the waist and flung herself (and with her not only me but the Bee-Emm as well) into the right hander. The bike flopped over of course, the footrest dug in and the bike propped a bit, but the motorcycle was blessed with wide swept-back handlebars – which would probably have measured all of 1.5 meters in length had they been straightened out – so it was no problem controlling the bike, which was naturally still driving out of the corner. I then lifted the bike up again as she wriggled about with ill-concealed delight upon that little seat which so ably supported her trim little backside. I didn't say much to her, except to remind her to go where I went and not to (ever) try to control the bike from the back seat. I certainly didn't explain to her that we could just as easily have come unstuck, and I didn't lecture her (again) on the fact that a pillion passenger must be as one with the machine's rider, and must in no way attempt to do anything which might jeopardise the inherent stability of a machine once underway.

Even moving the chewing gum from one cheek to another should be avoided by a pillion passenger, unless the rider is advised of this manoeuvre prior to its execution, for this sudden shift of weight might also compromise the stability of a machine being ridden at speed.

I am suddenly reminded of an accessory which I sold at one time at Omodeis, that long gone, but thankfully never to be forgotten accessory store in Sydney. It was a very handy device which consisted of no more than a wide leather belt to which was attached a pair of neat, leather-covered 'handles' near the rider's hips; the perfect position for maximum stability in providing a firm and reassuring hand-hold for pillion passengers. I wonder how many of these belts– if any! – might still be Out There?

While they were not an overly successful accessory, they were nonetheless a Very Good Idea, and certainly far, far better than some of the simple handles with which many of the newer machines are fitted: and probably as an after-thought. Most of these so-called 'grab rails' are mounted either between the rider and passenger, alongside the dual seat or, even worse, in entirely the wrong position **behind** (?) the pillion passenger who, in this situation, is thus forced to reach around and hang on for dear life, while leaning back at about 30 degrees from the vertical and with much too much weight placed too far back (not to mention too high) upon the machine.

It should be self-evident that a machine thus equipped has its stability at speed seriously compromised, particularly with a heavy passenger, or even a much lighter one while a machine is traversing uneven road surfaces or zooming through a succession of great corners.

There is never a better example of this than the one which occurred when I was asked to pick up a previous sister-in-law from the local railway station and transfer her home. This happened during the early-fifties, when the fashion was for full 'ballerina' skirts and tight blouses, the skirts held out at about arm's length by a series of voluminous *tulle* petticoats. Oh, and she was also carrying a very fashionable small wicker basket, the device which, for some inexplicable reason, replaced the inevitable handbag for a mercifully short period of time in those days.

Naturally, there was no room at all for her and the basket – and the skirt! -on the tiny pillion seat of the little James, but she settled down as best she could, half on the seat, and half on the mudguard, that confounded basket of hers sitting proudly between us. And so we took off, her weight too far to the rear as we wobbled alarmingly away. All went well enough until I approached a favourite right hander, the bike pulling hard in second gear at about 45 Km/h in modern terms.

I cranked the bike hard over as we wallowed into the corner, but she wasn't having a bar of this and, almost screaming at me as she suddenly sat bolt upright, at the same time finding the strength to heave the bike upright as well!

What a surprise that was, but by now, totally out of control, we ran wide on the corner and onto a stand a high paspalum grass which grew with some enthusiasm upon a thin bed of moist earth adjacent to a large drain. The bike ploughed two deep furrows sideways into the soft earth and banged against the gutter, then it sprang out again as the brand new muffler I had recently purchased from Hazell and Moore leapt out of the bag it was in and vanished down the drain to then be carried away by the swiftly flowing water gurgling therein.

She howled at me all the way home – which was not far away, but still too far off! – and refused point blank to ever be seen sitting on the pillion seat again. I fervently thanked a local Deity for that, because I had already decided that she was never again to adorn the pillion seat of any machine I ever owned. I should have made the same decision about her sitting in a sidecar as well, had I known I was going to be driving one of those things around in only a few years' time!

Near misses

Everyone who has ever flung a leg over a motorcycle or scooter of any size and then ridden the device any distance will probably have had the odd altercation with one or more objects on the road. These objects may be stationary or moving, may employ two, three, four or more wheels or be some arboreal nuisance which your local Council may have planted in entirely the wrong place; or at least the wrong place on the occasion when you might happen to have come across it – or them.

It might have been an unmissable, shapeless bundle which had fallen from a truck right in front, an errant spare wheel which had escaped from underneath a semi-trailer (don't shake your head like that, it happened to me once, and it was far too close for comfort) while it might, on very, very rare occasions, have even been a person. It is more likely, however, that any animal which strays across your path would be either a yapping dog, or at night a wombat or kangaroo; assuming you might happen to be in the wrong place...?

This isn't a subject for any of us to dwell upon for long, but most of us have either run into something at some time or – worse still! – allowed something to run into us, which is of course quite different from slipping off in the wet or running wide in a corner and spearing off into the scrub. Some are accidents, others are incidents. Some are very much our own fault, others very definitely the fault of others.

Along with the occasional bingle – some of which may hurt while others are just bloody annoying, or the least embarrassing – are also some *very close calls*, but for me to be still kicking along more or less in one piece after more than half a century of blasting about this nation's Third World roads points to a clear combination of some luck, a modicum of skill, keen observation and a vivid imagination. Oh, and no doubt more than a little Divine Intervention!

I have endured just two Big Ones (which is at least 2 too many), a few which were little more than a bloody nuisance and a whole bunch of Near Misses, the latter no doubt aided by the above-mentioned Celestial Intervention. One or two have been little more than pulse-raising incidents, but there have been several others which reside at various levels on the sliding scale of Much Too Close For Comfort.

Hazell & Moore

> "*I assumed he was suffering no more than an elevated heart rate and damp knickers so I very quickly removed myself from the scene.*"

At the top of the scale of Near Misses was the occasion when I was riding my little 125cc James along at a fair clip in Sydney's CBD when a brand-new Jag suddenly pulled out from the gutter in front of me – yes, the classic right-hand turn in front of the rapidly approaching motorcyclist – and screeched to a stop side-on leaving me with nowhere to go but to crank the bike over and run wide into on-coming traffic.

As the footrest dug in I reefed the little bike upright again just as a Council truck whooshed past in the opposite direction with its accompanying blast of fetid air, stinging grains of sand and little bits of paper, the truck's horn blaring. The little bike was fitted with a (useless) rectangular mirror on the right side of the handlebar in which, because of high-frequency vibration, everything was always heavily blurred .When I pulled into the gutter to settle myself down I glanced down to discover that the mirror head was **gone** and that its mounting arm was pointing straight back at me like an accusing finger!!

You can't get much closer than that and expect to get away with it!

On another occasion I was riding the same little bike up William Street in Sydney one night when the car in front suddenly pulled up and I (again) had nowhere to go, except between the car and the tram which was rattling along at my right elbow. I can clearly remember touching the tram's running board as I leaned against the vehicle, but that was not the only thing I touched.

There, in the wan glow of the little bike's headlight, stood a sailor facing the wrong way while clutching a tapering brown paper bag in an outstretched hand. As I nudged the tram on one side so, too, did I nudge the highly-inebriated sailor on the other.

Because the traffic had by now stopped, I rode into the gutter and looked back, to see the top half of the sailor spun round through about 185 degrees, his legs well and truly crossed and his feet apparently facing in the opposite direction!

I remember thinking it was a neat trick which perhaps he should take on tour around the licenced Clubs when his days at sea were over, but then he slowly unwound himself and glared about, finally focussing on me.

I must say I had half expected to see him sprawled on the roadway when I looked around, and was relieved to see him still upright but then he shouted something at me and began to totter in my direction waving a large fist in the air. I assumed he was suffering no more than an elevated heart rate and damp knickers so I very quickly removed myself from the scene. That was another incident which was much too close for comfort.

On another occasion I was riding the little James home and carrying a workmate on the pillion (we weren't travelling very quickly, as you can imagine!) when a near-new Austin A30 panel van suddenly leapt from the gutter to our left, executing a U-turn as we were nearly level with him. It was impossible to avoid the collision but I heaved my left leg off the footrest to almost shoulder-height – I confess I was attending Ballet classes at the time as part of my training for a career in theatre, which I have successfully pursued for many years – just as I hit the side of the driver's door.

When I jumped to my feet again I strode back to the driver to advise him of his room-temperature IQ, I saw with horror that his side mirror was gone, the radio aerial was dangling limply by the driver's door and that the outside of his chromed front bumper was sticking out ahead of the van at an extremely rude ninety-degree angle!

My pillion rider was picking the bike up as the driver emerged to inform me that it was all my fault and that in fact he had not seen me coming, anyway. There's nothing new about that, is there? I was forced to advise him that I would smack him in the mouth first and then explain that a recently passed law dictated that, as he was the one making the manoeuvre and we were simply riding past, he was clearly at fault.

After I settled him down with his split lip I strode back to the bike and I, too, was gob-smacked, but for me the smack was painless except to see that the left footrest was entirely missing and that the rear brake lever was bent double and was pointing *rearwards!!* Only the Good Lord himself would know how that leg would have been had it stayed where it was supposed to be.

Vintage Morris

Even odder than that is the fact that the brake pedal was cast iron and it should have snapped clean off, because any attempt to bend it under any other circumstances would have simply broken it. Who knows what energy is generated under an impact such as that? In fact, when I tried to straighten the lever out again in our garage, the thing snapped off almost immediately and without any hint of apology.

Even later, when working for a suburban motorcycle dealer I pulled up at work just as the throttle cable broke. The only throttle cables I had in stock before my next delivery were cables for the 30" ape-hanger handlebars we still see Harley riders use for some unaccountable reason. My handlebars were flat and quite low, but of course the longer cable I was forced to use worked perfectly for the time being, even though it hung out some distance to the right of the old BSA.

I was giving my brother Andy a lift home that afternoon, the cable flapping about in the breeze, when a large V8 Ford barge loomed up alongside and suddenly dived in front of us to sweep hard left into a side street we were just passing.

So help me, the car's rear bumper bar hooked the cable and dragged the throttle wide open as the car swept into the side street and dragged us along with it. Naturally, the cable snapped again, but not before Andy, the BSA and I were wedged somewhere under the car's boot!

The driver pulled up and stepped out, shouting abuse at us even before we could see him.

He came round the side of the car with one hand leaning on the car to support himself and glared at us, bleery-eyed.

"What the Hell do you think you're doing," he slurred, wiping his leaking mouth with the back of the other, somewhat grimy hand. "Why don't you learn to ride that thing before you get out on the road."

"You're pissed mate," Andy advised him through gritted teeth, as we struggled to extricate ourselves. "Now get back into that bait bucket of yours and get it off our bike. Get into it!"

Without a word the man staggered into the car and graunched into gear as we crawled from under the rear overhang and inspected our moveable parts, then turned our attention to the softer bits.

Suddenly the car lurched backwards and bowled Andy over to drag him underneath it again. The fool had slipped the thing into reverse gear! The car stopped with a lurch and the engine cut out.

Andy leapt up and immediately bent over in front of me at ninety degrees, grimacing over his shoulder at me. "Look at me brand new strides," he bellowed. "The arse is out of them!"

Sure enough there was a large patch on his backside where some of his new trousers used to be, and a tattered piece of multi-coloured underpants could clearly be seen. You could also see a hand-sized piece of pink cheek with a red gravel-rash at its centre, from which several small globules of a bright red fluid were beginning to erupt.

Andy could no doubt see the slack-jawed look of fascination on my face as I dabbed an exploratory index finger on one of the larger globules.

"What's wrong with me Khyber?" he howled, "It's sore as buggery!"

"For a start you can see half of it hanging out," I said, desperately trying, and without much success, to stifle a giggle. "There's a big hole in your strides." Suddenly, I burst into a shout of unrestrained laughter, though I tried – I really tried hard – not to. I almost bit my bottom lip off, but I couldn't hold it back.

"You'll laugh on the other side of your face in a minute, mate," he said, as he dabbed gently at his backside and removed his hand to stare morbidly at his reddened fingertips, "Look at this, I'm bleedin'"

By this time the driver who had nearly driven over us had re-appeared to apologise for backing over us again. "How's it goin', you two?" he lisped drunkenly. "Need a hand?"

Andy was less than impressed with the offer and made his feelings clear; as only he can.

"Piss off, you," he growled, "Or I'll nail ya to the floor."

As he was well into his second year of the study of a 'new' sport called Karate, I knew from my own experience that Andy could easily nail anyone, or anything from the animal kingdom, and he could do it with ease and very little effort.

Suitably chastened, the driver slid behind the wheel of the barge and drove slowly away, leaving me to heave the bike up un-aided and check it for damage. Luckily for us, if not for him, Andy had landed underneath the bike in the bingle so it was less damaged than *he* was except for the newly busted throttle cable.

While Andy minced about on tip-toe muttering to himself, while craning over first shoulder then the other in a vain bid to glimpse his damaged posterior I turned my attention to the throttle cable. It was useless so I removed the carburettor air-slide cable from its small lever (similar to a lawnmower throttle control lever, and similar

Hazell & Moore

to the type used on very early motorcycles) and tried to fit it to the twist-grip but the grip was locked wide open and I couldn't budge it.

I was forced to re-fit the throttle cable to the little lever on the right handlebar and attach the other end to the throttle slide for the ride home. This was a very daunting ride with Andy standing on the pillion footrests and complaining about the cold breeze whistling around him while I wrestled with that tricky little lever when changing gears or backing-off in traffic.

These are some of the unalloyed joys of scampering about the countryside while mounted upon two wheels, but we still do this, regardless of the dangers which may be ever-present – which is, perhaps, part of the challenge – and we do this whether it is hot, cold, wet or dry.

These incidents which were so annoying at the time, and potentially disastrous, are so often amusing stories to tell as the mists of time dull our memories of just how grim those incidents could have been when they occurred. Ah, yes, such are (some of) the joys of motorcycling.

We could smother ourselves in cotton wool, as our mums tried to do without much success, or should we never have experienced the delights of zipping about in the open air upon two wheels, assuming there is a questionable 'safety' of commuting on four wheels instead? Most serious motorcyclists would say that, while there may be an element of danger in riding the devices about, then there is an element of danger in almost everything else which surrounds us anyway.

Mudgee trip

Why we decided to do it I still don't know, perhaps it was the girl we were both more than a little keen on that decided us, but if we had had the brains we were born with we either would never have contemplated it, taken a different route entirely, or chosen a pair of motorcycles which would have been very much better suited for the job. It was way back in 1952 when a mate and I decided to ride from Sydney to Mudgee to attend the birthday party of the girl upon whom we were both rather keen. We had, at various times, lavished no little attention upon her, but with the same negative results. I was, at the time, ignorant of his lecherous intentions towards her, as he was of mine.

There was nothing unusual about riding off into the sunset for a few days, except that we were not mounted upon the sort of machinery which was intended for this type of pursuit. It was certainly not the type of motorcycle most people would choose for such a journey these days.

My mount was the year-old 125cc James of happy memory, Jim Brooks' was a 125cc Model B Lambretta scooter, of 1949 vintage. My commuter was fitted with plunger rear suspension and a spring saddle, which allowed a degree of comfort, while the telescopic front forks were unique in having long rubber tubes in each leg instead of steel springs and they were located by an equally long threaded rod down the centre to control the shape and stop the rubbers from collapsing. The front forks were thus of long travel and very effective, crude thought the suspension medium would *appear* to be.

Naturally the rubber was self-damping, but there was oil in the forks to allow for even smoother operation, and I thought it a good idea to drain the old oil and replace it before the trip.

How was I to know way back then that the rubber 'spring' required a **vegetable** based oil for the job, instead of the **mineral** oil with which it was replaced? The rubber 'spring' naturally swelled and became slimy as well, which rendered the once-great front suspension almost useless as the fork legs seized and only allowed about 50mm of movement. As a result of this stupidity – or let's say lack of knowledge, to be kinder – it was not much fun over corrugations and the numerous potholes hidden in the bulldust we were to encounter. No, not the bulldust in this story, which is almost entirely true, the bulldust on the dirt track we were to discover on that long and arduous journey.

On the other hand, the little Lambretta scooter was almost entirely naked, except for a small front apron and platform for the rider's feet and two sprung saddles, with the entire power-plant exposed for all the world to see, and very little in the way of weather protection. The leading-link front suspension seemed to be entirely undamped, with the heavily valanced front mudguard attached to a large floating metal pressing which jazzed up and down frantically in harmony with the errant front wheel movement.

Most unusually for a scooter from that era, and even more unusual today, the final drive was by *shaft* contained within a solid casting on the machine's right side. There was a tiny crown-wheel-and-pinion to provide the right-angle drive to the wheel's stub axle, and the rear suspension was assisted by a wrist-like joint just ahead of the pinion which allowed the wheel to move over bumps while the engine/gearbox unit remained firmly mounted. There had to be a universal joint in the casting somewhere but we never bothered with it because it never bothered us.

In fact the little Lambretta was in many ways very advanced for its day, and was a far better design in the forties than the rival Vespa, which was a bit lop-sided with its engine hanging well out to the right allied to its small 8" wheels and undamped suspension. Tiny 8-inch wheels were also fitted to that early Lambretta, which did it no favours at all.

However, it was quite odd to watch the little scooter as it took off from rest, because as soon as the power was applied and the clutch released, the rear end would raise itself daintily like an eager chicken when a rooster was abroad (I nearly said **aboard**!) and it would dump itself again when backing off to change gears. How this would have affected the rear suspension I have no idea, but it's fair to say it would have been compromised to at least some degree.

As a point of interest Vespa has of course survived, whereas Lambretta – which made hundreds of thousands of units in Italy alone, quite apart from those made in several other factories in other countries – has, quite sadly, all but disappeared; at least in Australia, and excepting the occasional new model which springs up overseas, and which are probably still made in India. or Taiwan; or Outer Mongolia?

We two fools had taken the advice of some other fool who suggested the best way to get to Mudgee was to ride almost into Bathurst, and then take the turn-off to Sofala, it being quicker (we were assured) than turning off the old Great Western Highway at Wallerawang.

This we duly did, my only recollection of the ride through the Blue Mountains one of being overtaken by everything with a set of wheels underneath it. The little James ran well and smoothly enough, and would occasionally see some 55mph-plus on its optimistic speedo, but it was not the most powerful of open road cruisers. In comparison, however, it left the struggling Lambretta for dead up hills, on the flat and downhill as well.

The little scooter had a set of handlebars which sprang from just above the top of the front mudguard and were about the same size as the high-rise handlebars we see on some of the big Harleys. They were also just as flexible and compromised the handling to the same degree as well. You could hold the Lambretta front wheel between your ankles and move the bars several degrees in each direction even with everything nipped up as tight as possible up front. I imagine the Harleys are the same.

So we turned off to the right at the Sofala sign on the Kelso Flats and lurched onwards towards Mudgee. After several clicks, and some alarming bangs and rattles from both machines, the poorly-sealed road suddenly became a badly rutted and deeply pot-holed dirt track with more than a few bush rocks shyly peering out of the rippled surface.

I could see my travelling companion glaring at me as we rode two abreast, the little 8-inch wheels leaping and gyrating about underneath him, that sliding front panel banging noisily away as the wheels dropped into even the smallest of potholes or launched themselves over the ever-larger rock outcroppings which were becoming more and more frequent. It was, I felt sure, even worse than riding over the roughest of French cobblestones.

He was not amused, and mentioned this on several occasions. Neither was I for that matter, with very little movement from the front forks and even less from the plunger rear end. It was all neck snapping, shoulder popping, kidney floating, tooth loosening stuff, and remains far and away the worst road surface I have ever been forced to traverse.

As it happened, it was also rear axle snapping stuff, for one of the James motorcycle's weak points was a rear axle which would snap on irregular intervals after some time over uncertain road surfaces. I knew the axle was broken, because the signs were unmistakable. The machine could still be ridden, for the axle was well supported, but the rear wheel could wobble about alarmingly and would occasionally rub against a rear mudguard stay. For some odd reason, however, the rear chain would not shed itself and may have played its part in keeping the wheel in some reasonable alignment.

The other odd quirk was for the James to shed its front mudguard as several of its mounting stays fatigued through a high-frequency vibration I could never feel. Happily, this did not happen on the trip, for this time the front guard had been rubber-mounted for safety

That frightful road seemed never to end, as each hill and corner showed even more of the track which was simply carved out of hillsides and across otherwise-open fields.

Vintage Morris

Hazell & Moore

> *"Suddenly, as we dropped down a steep incline a STOP sign appeared out of nowhere and thus heralded the approach to the tiny village of Sofala."*

Suddenly, as we dropped down a steep incline a STOP sign appeared out of nowhere and thus heralded the approach to the tiny village of Sofala. We stopped at the sign of course even though there was nothing to be seen on the move anywhere, and then took the left turn onto the main drag of the sleepy little hamlet. It was simply a long badly tarred track masquerading as a main street with old-fashioned shops bordering it and the odd –very odd – Pub dotted here and there, but it was like riding along a billiard table in comparison to what we had so recently endured.

A few locals stopped and stared at us as we rode along the welcome stretch with its infinitely smoother surface and we were also assailed by a small group of ragged urchins who trotted alongside us. They rewarded our presence with a series of rude gestures, cat-calls and other forms of offensive behaviour; including the discharge in our direction of several missiles of a substantial composition.

One of their number displayed a substantial limp generated by a flaccid left leg demonstrably shorter than the one on the other side. He appeared to have no teeth and was by far the most vocal. I would like to have added that he was cross-eyed as well, but alas he was not.

Thankfully the young predators soon departed the scene and we thus trickled through the tiny settlement to be confronted, just as we left civilisation, with a steep climb up a hillside which appeared to be a solid brick wall! Not only was it the steepest climb I have ever encountered, it was full of brick-sized bush rocks as well.

We climbed the cliff face in first gear to be confronted near the top by the urchins, who had obviously taken a short-cut across a paddock somewhere and were soon strolling alongside us as we fought to stay upright over this shocking surface. Their legs handled a whole lot better than out bikes did – I did notice that the limper was not amongst them – but we ditched them at the top as the road suddenly took a change for the better.

At that time I was wearing a cloth cap and ex-USA Army Polaroid goggles with amber lenses and I was surprised to feel the surface underneath me to be very, very much smoother than it had been, even though the bike's rear end was pivoting around the steering head like some giant windscreen wiper. Busted back axle of course, or so I thought.

I looked round for my mate but he was nowhere in sight, so I pulled over to stop and promptly slipped off, albeit at about walking speed.

When I lifted the tinted goggles off I could then see the cause of the machine's errant ways. The road surface was in fact well saturated and covered by a thin film of butter-like clay. The Lambretta's little wheels didn't like this at all, and had decided not to grip, pelting my friend off with no warning whatsoever.

The little James was leaned against a roadside tree and I walked back along the grass verge to find the hapless pair struggling through the morass, churning up the gluey mud and leaving a trail of long, sweeping lazy Ess streaks behind them, dotted here and there providing proof of the rider's efforts in keeping more or less upright by dabbing his feet onto the slick surface.

As it happened the little scooter's gear-change was operated from the left handlebar twist-grip by a single, thick flexible cable and the mechanism had been damaged in the fall, and was stuck in first gear. We fiddled round with it for some time but could do no better than have the choice between first and third gears or second gear on its own. We chose the latter and pressed on as before but obviously at a somewhat more sedate pace.

Several clicks further on we discovered the cause of our woes, because there they were, casually parked at the side of the road: a huge grader and its side-kick water truck. The duo had just finished some bottled refreshments and were in fact climbing back into their respective vehicles as we skidded sideway to a stop. We were well splattered with mud from AH to BT, and were very happy indeed to have the guy with the water truck hose us off and I was even more happy to find that, covered in baked-on mud though the engine and my trouser legs were, the front mudguard was still firmly in place!

We very happily followed that grader into town, as it laid down a much more acceptable surface for us, the huge fountain from the water truck which followed *us* laying down a thin film of butter for anyone else who happened along. I asked the grader driver why they hadn't graded that grim stretch of God-awful track we had ridden over when we had left Sofala, but he said that was the responsibility of 'someone else.'

That ride, above all others, was simply the worst long-distance ride I have ever experienced. But it remains an adventure which becomes part of the things we do which "seemed like a good idea at the time". It may be a well worn cliché, but we have all been there. And probably will be there again.

I don't know how he managed it, but a local mechanic fixed the gear-change free of charge and the party was great, so was the girl who seemed more than enthusiastic that we had made the trip and rewarded me handsomely. I never asked Jim whether he was similarly rewarded. I simply didn't want to know.

Big Fred, Bathurst

Nobody had much money at the time, and nobody knew anyone with a large pantechnicon, or even a reasonable sized truck of *any* description. There was not even a three-bike trailer to be had, because everyone who owned one had it already filled with three bikes, along with the necessary tools, several large cans of racing fuel, Castor oil, extra spare parts, leathers, helmets, camping gear, grog, and all the other *accoutrement* needed for a solid three days of practice and very serious road racing.

You see, it was Easter in the early fifties, and the three-day road-race carnival was soon to be conducted on that great, world-famous Mt Panorama circuit at Bathurst, and everyone, but everyone, was going to be there. So when the apparently insurmountable problem of transporting a serious bunch of impecunious racing motorcyclists safely across Sydney's forbidding Blue Mountains for the road-race carnival at Bathurst was to be planned, someone's organisational prowess would need to be put well and truly to the ultimate test.

As usual, practice was to begin on the Thursday, with more practice and some 'minor' qualifying events on Good Friday, before the really busy programme of serious racing was to be conducted all day on Easter Saturday. Back in those days it was not unusual each day to see a huge queue of enthusiastic motorcyclists stretching almost from the centre of the town to the demountable ticket office at the track itself, and it was often said at the time that there were more than 30,000 people in attendance *every day* at most Easter meetings at Bathurst.

Some competitors came from as far away as Queensland and even Western Australia, so this was a meeting never to be missed by any genuine enthusiast – unless hospitalised and possibly heavily anaesthetised – and it mattered not how difficult it might be to arrange some form of transport to get there.

So here was the dilemma of which I had absolutely no knowledge at the time. How to transport four solo racing motorcycles, one race outfit, the six riders who would pilot these machines, all the material they would need for the full week-end, and to deliver the lot safely from Sydney to Bathurst, when there seemed to be no way in which this could be done. Their mates would probably ride along later with some extra gear, but practice started on the Thursday (if they could make it) so all the material necessary for this pursuit would have to be taken along with the first wave of rabid Club members.

Somebody had a Very Bright Idea to overcome this problem, and it was an idea of such utter simplicity and in fact stupendous brilliance that it should go down in the annals somewhere as a prime example of the resourcefulness which is no much part and parcel of the Australian character. The fact that the solution might have been on the far side of illegal must have been looked upon as of little consequence.

When needs must?

So there I was, riding through the Mountains to Bathurst in 1953, and about to meet a bloke who was to become something of a great riding mate, even though we didn't mix much on other social occasions. It was Big Fred, that Long Distance thrasher of a very swift Black Shadow Vincent, the man with whom I spent many a long and hard-charging weekend belting the old highly-tuned 500cc single-cylinder 'Iron Gold Star' BSA along as hard as it would go to keep up with him, and sometimes to actually have him chasing me for a change.

I had left Sydney much later in the day than usual that Easter and it was somewhat before dawn on Good Friday; that early morn as usual cold and frosty. The fog was very thick and so was anyone who rode a motorcycle at any speed above a brisk trot when the visibility was so poor. I was making reasonably good time, the borrowed Triumph Speed Twin's engine singing smoothly beneath me and the sprung hub soaking up the bumps with contemptuous ease.... that shows how capricious one's memory can become, for

Hazell & Moore

the Triumph engine was usually anything but smooth, while that evil sprung hub (the subject of an Edward Turner patent application which the British Patent Office should have flung out instantly) was a diabolical device at best and near-suicidal at its worst.

If you never rode upon that rear sprung hub and were forced to endure its odd machinations you may consider yourselves fortunate. The device was a peculiar invention intended to provide the bike with a form of rear suspension in disguise. The device was fitted to a Triumph motorcycle by the simple ploy of removing a standard rear wheel and replacing it with a wheel containing that odd suspension unit.

Rather than adopt the plunger-type rear suspension which was good enough for other manufacturers to adopt – or even the infinitely better swing-arm type which a couple of other manufacturers used – the Triumph's optional rear suspension from 1947 to 1954 consisted of that odd rear wheel with a large-diameter full-width hub which was equipped internally with a banana-shaped alloy box containing a pair of slightly curved, and entirely undamped, springs.

The oddly-shaped rear axle slotted into the box with a double-sided boss machined on to the axle to locate the springs, which were of course under tension and locked in place inside the alloy banana. Thus the axle was free to move up and down inside the box to provide some 30mm of rear suspension, at the risk of some very strange handling problems.

Sometimes it was bit too free to move within the confines of the box, with the result that a very heavy bump or a really savage pot-hole could sometimes result in a spring punching its way out of the end of the banana and locking itself against the inside of the swiftly rotating hub, with the inevitable result that the wheel would then swiftly lock solid and you would probably fall over. And, even if entirely un-injured, you would not be able to ride the bike home, or even to wheel it away. Oh, and as for handling, the sprung hub imbued the bike with precisely the same feeling you would get if the rear tyre was as flat as a flounder!

So help me, if you were mounted upon a Triumph which was equipped with a sprung hub you seemed to spend half your riding time looking down at the back-end of the bike to check the condition of the rear tyre. One could always tell the Triumph owners in Bathurst restaurants; they were the fellows who suffered from what I called "Sprung-Hubbers' Twitch" as they frowned every few seconds and glanced fitfully under their seats to see if they were sitting on a set of four flat chair legs. That odd, 'phantom flat tyre' feeling must have taken an age to dissipate.

Triumph tried manfully to overcome the serious problem of the springs punching their way our of their tightly bound container by introducing an 'after-market' modification, which was simply a pair of steel condoms which slotted over the ends of the alloy banana and were locked securely in place by the six bolts which closed the banana and locked the springs in place.

It was a suicide mission to ever attempt to either replace the springs or to open the alloy box for fun just to see what was inside it. The strong springs were under heavy tension and would fly out and sprong about all over the place, so if you happened to be closely peering inside the box as you forced it open the springs would swiftly escape from their bondage and you would probably need a surgical operation to remove at least one of them from the front of your amazed face. Oh, and just to complicate your recovery thereafter, those heavy springs were always covered with a liberal smearing of graphite grease as well. There was, of course, a special clamping tool to be used in servicing that strange device.

I digress, for which I apologise.

So, there I was on the way to Bathurst and making reasonably good time – particularly in view of the sprung hub and the bike's *apparent* flat tyre – as I lined up the tight, twisty corners at Yetholme, that once- notoriously pot-holed and corrugated stretch of road which has thankfully been greatly improved over the years, when I perceived a great and ever-increasing noise coming up fairly briskly astern. It sounded like an extremely low-flying aircraft, and it seemed certain it may crash very close by at any moment as it rapidly approached.

As I dropped into a tightening left-hander the noise became a great deal louder and then louder again, and I felt the plane (for I was certain it had to be an aircraft) was about to fall out of the sky, and to fall right on top of me! The sound of the open exhausts was bloody near deafening, because helmets weren't worn much in those days, and, while my cloth cap wasn't much help in keeping my frozen ears glued in place, they were still there and were entirely functional, and they still allowed for a great deal of wind – and other – noises to be clearly heard.

Vintage Morris

1948-1954

> *"To my amazement, the first thing that flashed into sight was a Triumph outfit, with a Triumph racer perched where the sidecar body would normally be, the racing machine strapped securely to a timber platform."*

I was nearly off the road on the inside of the corner as the frightful sound drew level with me and I had to dart a quick look over my right shoulder to see what the hell was about to either rapidly overtake me, or to flatten me like a bug. Of course it was the briefest of brief glances, so I looked front again as the sound came blasting right alongside me.

To my amazement, the first thing that flashed into sight was a Triumph outfit, with a Triumph racer perched where the sidecar body would normally be, the racing machine strapped securely to a timber platform. The gigantic driver of the sidecar (who was bereft of balaclava, cap or goggles, but was wearing a khaki Army greatcoat) hung his huge frame into the corner to help keep the outfit on an even keel, while the front wheel chattered and crabbed across the road. A pillion passenger hung likewise, one palsied hand gripping the rear guard of the racing bike, the other trying to hold his leather cap in place.

But that wasn't all there was to it, as I marvelled at the apparent expertise of a sidecar driver who seemed to know more about the roadway ahead than I did, or who may have possessed a form of supersonic eyesight, because the visibility ahead was down to almost zero!

As the outfit rushed past me, it disclosed another outfit it seemed to be towing – another Triumph outfit, but this one was an out and out racing machine – with a man steering it, and with *another racing Triumph solo on the sidecar platform*!! But rather than a tow-rope between them, or even a chain, a solid bar was mounted between them, the racing outfit's engine howling on full song as it provided its own power, the open megaphone exhausts bellowing frightfully. Far from simply being towed, the second engine was actually *helping* the road-going outfit to haul its heavy load over the Mountains!

A forlorn passenger sat, humped shapelessly behind the driver of the second outfit, which was an even greater surprise, but the greatest shock of all arrived moments later when the two heavily-laden outfits thundered past to display yet another pair of racing solos being towed from the chassis rails of the rear outfit by stout ropes! Two grim-visaged riders clung to the handlebars of the two machines for their very lives, exerting little control over their respective fates as they alternatively banged together and sprang apart, the two ropes twanging like violin strings.

This group of desperates surged past while the outfits listing dangerously first left and then to the right as they weaved drunkenly about before the whole lot was swallowed up in the seemingly-impenetrable mists which roiled ahead of us. They disappeared as though they had been nothing but a passing nightmare, only the sounds of the bellowing exhaust betraying the fact that the high-speed caravan had actually been there at all.

For some reason, the driver of the first outfit executed a rapid series of rude gestures as he shot past, which must have been very hard to do as he was then fighting an errant front wheel one-handed. Frankly, I thought it was uncalled for, particularly as I had all but run off the road on the inside of the corner to let whatever it was pass me without some sort of carnage occurring. That is assuming the gestures were meant for me, and not intended for the bloke behind him who was pushing him hard and fast through the murk ahead whether he wanted to be shoved about like that or not.

My stomach suddenly churned as, just seconds later, a large semi-trailer loomed out of the mist ahead and roared past, clearly avoiding by a hair's breadth the head-on collision which would have been inevitable had the timing of their passage been even slightly awry. That fearsome group of hard-charging motorcyclists was heard, seen very briefly at my right shoulder, upon me and gone again in about 20 seconds, but it was more than long enough to imprint itself forever on my mind as *The World's Most Illegal Road Train!* How they had survived at all remains remarkable, and the fact that the road-train had gone so far into the night was either a tribute to the expertise of the two drivers, a testimonial to the alertness of other road-users or a judgement on the inefficiency of the local police force.

Hazell & Moore

Having said that, it may well be that any member of the local Constabulary who actually witnessed the thing might be afraid to report it, for fear of being charged with – at the very least – being Terminally Drunk or possibly suffering from a sudden fit of Advanced Ridiculousness, compounded by Gross Absurdity; any of which mental aberrations being clearly indictable offences.

I might say that the sport of motorcycle racing was very much an amateur sport in those long gone days, with an impecunious band of riders, mechanics and enthusiasts like this lot making the annual pilgrimage to Bathurst by whatever means may have been at their disposal.

Obviously, this small band of serious enthusiasts had pooled whatever resources they had and made the trip by that dangerous and illegal road-train, ferrying four racing solos, one race outfit and six riders in one swoop – and for not much more money than it would have cost to ride one well-laden outfit over the Mountains. Legal or not, it was at the very least a most ingenious solution to their problem and was certainly done in the true Aussie spirit of "making do."

The next 40km or so into Bathurst was a sober ride indeed, with many a fearful glance over my shoulder to see what else might be coming out of the murk, but I arrived in the chill of an early morning as the half-frozen people lying about in damp Army greatcoats or inside frost-encrusted sleeping bags in the open were stirring themselves (?) and blinking owlishly at the dawning of a new day. Though the years rolled on, that was a sight which greeted me every time I made that Pilgrimage to Bathurst.

I'd slept in the open at Bathurst before – and a few times *since*, as it happens – but that year I was staying in one of the old hotels in the town, so I set about finding the place, hoping to unload some of the small mountain of gear I was carrying and get stuck into a large, hot breakfast.

The pub was off the main drag a bit, but easy enough to find. As I turned into the typical, dirt parking area I found an innocent-looking group of machines parked quietly inside the fence or leaning against the wall of the Gent's outhouse. Oddly enough they were all Triumphs. There was a road outfit with some stout planks bolted to the chassis where a sidecar would normally be, there was also a racing outfit and four solo racers sitting there as though they had been there for days, and there was no evidence to the casual observer to even suggest they had made the 200km trip from Sydney to Bathurst *in toto*.

The front wheel of the road outfit was muddy and had some grass wrapped round the spokes, while the race outfit's engine was still warm and close examination revealed several black scuff marks on the platform where both towed solos had tried to climb into the chair on several occasions. It was very certainly the group that scared hell out of me in the fog not very long before. I looked about, but there was only one person to be seen, a huge bald-headed guy propping himself against the wall of the outside convenience with one hand, half-invisible in a huge cloud of steam as he noisily relieved himself into the dirt.

He looked up with a grin. "Silly buggers have locked the door," he said by way of explanation, as he nodded at the wire-mesh gate. "I'm just splashin' me boots before I go inside. I've been boilin' for a leak for hours."

He leaned his oddly pointed head against the brick wall, and held out the hand with which he had recently supported himself as he peed on.

"I'm Fred," he said, "I've seen you behind the counter at Hazell's haven't I?"

I wished he had waited a bit longer before introducing himself, and fervently hoped he didn't shake hands too briskly as I was standing a bit too close to him, and was thus well within range. I said yes I was working in the spares department at Hazell and Moore, the agents for Triumph and Norton motorcycles at the time. In fact it was they who had lent me the Triumph to ride to Bathurst, and I'd managed to get the hotel room in a very roundabout way through the same firm.

I shook hands tentatively and backed away as he straightened up and made the necessary adjustments. "Coming up the street for breakfast?" he asked, "Leave your gear here and the others will take care of it." I told him I ought to check in first, but he seemed to know what was going on and assured me that we'd all be staying together anyway, because that's how they do it at Bathurst every year. Nothing changes.

Over breakfast in the White Rose (now the Panorama Café, for those who've eaten there) I mentioned that he and the entourage had zapped me in the fog outside of town earlier that morning and given me a hell of a fright in the process.

"Hey, keep it dark," said Fred, holding up a conspiratorial hand, "Christ knows we were lucky to get here without being spotted in the first place. Don't broadcast it around. It was an arsehole of an idea in the first place – you're not supposed to flat-tow anything, not even on a bar." Gawd, it's all a blur," he went on, "I needed to pull over and strain the spuds on the way up here, but every time I slowed down for anything that turd behind me cranked up the race engine and gave it a squirt.

"You reckon it startled *you*, Jees you should have been driving the bloody thing. I've never even driven an outfit before this trip. Stuff 'em, they can go home on their own."

He went on to tell me how he'd been conned into driving the bike up to Bathurst, towing that wretched caravan of racing machinery along behind him. It seems the guy who was going to do the job in the first place chickened out (wonder why he did that?) and suggested Fred step into the breach. Fred wanted to make the journey and promised to help them out, though he *claimed* he didn't know what the job entailed and couldn't back out at the last minute.

Driving a three-wheeler is an acquired art and usually takes some little time to get used to, but Fred was big and very strong, finding little difficulty because of the weight of the racing bike on the sidecar platform and the agility of his 'passenger' through corners.

He decided to make the trip and they left in the wee small hours so as not to attract attention, which I thought logical enough under the circumstances. The 650 Triumph twin found the going very tough over the steep climb up Kurrajong Heights because of the monumental weight it was carrying. Apparently, the driver of the race outfit, without warning, kicked the engine over, warmed it up for a bit and then proceeded to add the engine's not-inconsiderable power to the towing bike.

"I never asked him to do it," Fred said with a long sigh, "And I kept signalling him to slow the bloody thing down. He bloody ignored me, and we ran off the road a dozen times in the fog. I could hardly see most of the time. Christ, here they are, look at 'em."

I looked up to espy a quintet of bedraggled motorcyclists shuffling morosely into the café, making their way through the crowd and moving in our general direction. They each wore the nigh-universal Army greatcoat, crumpled jeans and wool-lined flying boots, their eyes were still more than a little red-rimmed and their hair was, for the most part, matted and unkempt. Fred stood up, dominating the room with his bulk.

"Over here," he shouted, and everyone in the café and on the footpath outside looked around.

The quintet flopped into vacant chairs by us, their khaki coats already beginning to steam softly in the heat of the little café.

Fred introduced us all round, and I found out that the sidecar racer's first name was Tommy, though I cannot remember his last name for the life of me. He was small and wizened, with a thread-bare Hitler moustache, around four days' stubble of beard and about six yellow teeth. He had the smallest eyes I've ever seen, and I wondered how he could see anything out of them.

"Owyergoin' mate," he said, extending a hand like a brown chicken claw, "Can you ride an outfit?"

"No he can't," said Fred, before I could answer. "And he doesn't bloody want to, neither."

For the first and last time the fellow grinned, his eyes disappearing in perfectly formed crows' feet, his yellow, horse teeth on display. That was probably the longest sentence he uttered all week-end.

I ran an eye over the other characters, and they certainly looked a rough bunch, just as desperate as you'd expect them to be if they were capable of planning and executing the trip they had so recently accomplished. Fred was very certainly out of place in that company, and as for genteel little me....

A small Greek girl appeared with a tea trolley upon which reposed about 30 cups and saucers and the huge aluminium teapot which was, for so many years, almost the trade-mark of the old White Rose Café. The teapot was about the size of a four-gallon drum and was used to entirely fill the teacups of a restaurant-full of people in one pass. Fred, who could be surprisingly gallant when the occasion arose, decided to help the waif and descended on the trolley with arms and ham-like hands extended.

"Tea, anyone?" he roared, and several people passing the café door fell about in surprise, whereupon Fred hoisted the huge teapot out of the trolley and proceeded to pour out the tea for the multitude. He did it in one move, swiftly revolving the enormous container over the top of the tea trolley.

There was probably more tea in the trolley and in the saucers than there was in the cups, while the Arnott's 'Nice' biscuits which had been neatly placed upon the various saucers were now floating about and slowly disintegrating. It's a fair bet the tea was never poured with such speed. Fred beamed and sat down again,

Hazell & Moore

> "*Watch this," he said, "Hup!" So saying, he flicked the shorts to the ceiling, and ducked under them when they descended, catching them on top of his head.*"

while the red-faced little Greek girl mumbled her thanks and fled for the kitchen as patrons descended *en masse* upon the trolley.

As I learned later, Fred was always something of an enigma, for he could be charming on occasion, possessed of a searing wit on others, apparently shrewder than most and yet capable of absurd acts when the whim took him, and for no apparent reason. A great guy as a touring partner, but I'll bet he was a hard man to live with!

Back in the pub I found myself closeted with those characters in a lounge room which had been converted into an eight-bed dormitory for the week-end, and to find my bed next to Fred's. I assumed it was my bed simply because someone had taken my gear upstairs and flung it under one of the beds, where it reposed against one of the three enamel chamber-pots with which the room had been thoughtfully supplied.

There were a couple of tired chests of drawers and an ancient wardrobe, but otherwise the airy room contained nothing but the eight beds and the three dented chamber-pots

Fred dropped on the bed next to mine and shook some of his gear out of an old haversack he produced from somewhere. He dropped a huge, well-used jar of Vaseline on the floor alongside the bed and then, with a flourish, proceeded to climb out of his trousers.

"Off with your strides," he said to the room in general, and stood up as his own trousers fell to his ankles. I was startled by his behaviour, and even more so when he bent to the Vaseline jar.

"I use this when me cheeks get chafed," he said, which instantly horrified me, and I was just beginning to wonder what the hell I had got myself into when he slipped the lid off and smeared a handful of the stuff over his face. "I shove some on me nose as well," he added unnecessarily, as he rubbed the lubricant vigorously all over his face, round the back of his neck and over the top of his shaved head.

"You getting changed?" he asked, "Practice soon, and we got a few bugs to sort out. He towelled the excess material off his head, stomping on his trousers as he did so, till first one leg, then the other was freed. He bent down and whipped his undershorts onto the toe of one huge boot.

"Watch this," he said, "Hup!" So saying, he flicked the shorts to the ceiling, and ducked under them when they descended, catching them on top of his head.

"Betcha don't know anyone who can do that," he grinned, only half his face visible.

I agreed that I didn't know anyone on this earth who would even think of executing such a neat trick, and with such practiced ease, but excused myself and made an exit before the rest of the performance got underway. I promised to see them at the track, but I was not interested in helping them find their way there. Practice was the mixed bag it always is, with some people falling off here and there, the occasional engine blow-up, and some inflated top speed claims and deflated lap times. Again, nothing changes.

We were back at the pub that evening, and there were glum faces all around.

"Look, mate, I wouldn't bloody ride a rigid frame over that bloody mountain track if they paid me," one of the solo riders was sounding off at no-one in particular. "The ripples at MacPhillamy, and the bloody rough straight. It's bad enough on me sprung hub."

"It's a bloody sight better than riding the meeting with a flat tyre." The voice preceded that of the other solo rider as he entered the room.

"They're not like that at all," the first rider said defensively "What do you think of them, Herb?"

"Hey, Herb, what do you think of sprung hubs?" The guy was looking straight at me, and it took a few seconds for the penny to drop.

"Your mate's right," I told him, "They all feel the same. Just like a flat back tyre."

"Crap! How long have you been at Hazells anyway, Herb?" He called everyone, but everyone, Herb. I never knew why.

"Five years," I said.

"Oh, well you oughta know better, Herb." He never mentioned the 'superiority' of the Triumph Sprung Hub again, but fell to brooding. "Frank fell off," he said, apropos of nothing at all. I looked across and sure enough his mate was tending to a graze on his right elbow and dabbing at a small, skin-less patch in the small of his back.

"Stepped off in the Cutting," he said, "It's a bit sore but it's alright."

Fred entered with the tiny guy who drove the race outfit; he came straight to the point. "Can he have your crankshaft?" he asked.

"Eh?"

"Your crankshaft. He blew it in the Esses and he wants to use your cranks to get it going for tomorrow."

I pointed out that I would have liked to help the guy, but the bike I was riding wasn't mine, in fact had been loaned to me just for the weekend. I could hardly take the remains back in a wheelbarrow and tell them I'd lent half an engine to a guy I had met a matter of hours before, and may never see again! It put me on the spot a bit, however there was no way I would make that sort of decision and I told them so in just so many words.

"That's alright," said Tommy, "I'll see you around." He shuffled forlornly away, leaving an unspoken question hanging in the air.

If the bike was irreparable, how would they get home again with the road-train? For that matter, how would I get home again if I gave them half the guts of the bike I had ridden to Bathurst upon?

Of course they could easily have removed the engine from one of the solos and fitted it to the race outfit for the return journey.

"I'm sorry about that, you guys," I told them, "I don't own the bike, so the decision isn't mine to make. You can change engines to get home again if you need to."

"I'm goin' home on the train." Frank said "There's no way I'm goin' to do a trip like that one again."

"I'll join you," his mate put in, "I couldn't do that again, meself."

"That's okay," said Fred, "We'll make out. Shove your bikes in the Guard's van, Freight On, and we'll pick 'em up in Sydney later on."

"We'll tow that outfit home with its engine dead," he added, "Thank Christ I won't have to contend with being rammed up the arse every time I back off for a corner or something."

I spent the day with Fred, wandering up and down Conrod Straight and criss-crossing the track on the inside, which of course no-one was allowed to do in later years. The other members of that odd party of characters were left to their own devices, but I exchanged phone numbers with Fred and promised to join him for the odd foray 'into the scrub' (as he called it) on the odd long week-end.

I was hardly to know it then, but we spent many years covering many, many thousands of kilometres in touring and attending race meetings in various States. Bathurst 1953 had seen the beginning of a long – if distinctly odd – friendship.

Arthur Nutt, supersalesman

It would hardly be fair to say that we have too-often fallen as willing victims to super-sales people, but we have all met them at one time or another; those immensely charming sales people who could sell a substantial, gleaming white refrigerator to a wary Eskimo, or a bunch of worn-out camels to well-heeled Sheiks in Abu Darby; perhaps even a *fine-printed* life insurance policy to someone who is about to be dragged through Death's Door.

Often we eagerly hand over our hard-earned money to these eminently trust-worthy people, assured that they have our best interests at heart, while assuming that the product we have so joyously purchased had indeed been the very article we wanted to purchase in the first place. This is not to say for a moment that we may have been ripped off by a clever sales person, but there are certainly those out there who might not be quite as up-front with us as we would have hoped they would be.

There was a bloke in Sydney who was employed as a salesman on the showroom floor at Hazell and Moore, and he was very, very good at his job. He was a short Englishman, a Cockney who always wore a trim little moustache, starched white shirt with broad tie, beautifully pressed trousers and a crisp, spotless white dustcoat. He could, and did, sell almost anything to almost anyone, often regardless of what a customer had come into the showroom to purchase in the first place.

He was by no means a con-merchant, but he did admit to me that he was often to be seen on Blackpool or Brighton Piers much earlier in his life during what he called 'the season' and he made a good living out of flogging Irish Gold watches to happy, if unsuspecting, holiday makers. He said he would set up his folding suitcase, pull his Trilby hat over his sparkling eyes and waylay any of the passing peasantry who happened to pass too close to his mobile retail outlet. I once asked him what an 'Irish Gold' watch was, and he told me it was a gold watch which turned green on the new owners' wrist within about a fortnight!

There was a character in the series of the St Trinian's School movies from England in the fifties called "Flash Harry", a genuine spiv who could have easily been the prototype for that bloke and I mentioned it to him at one time. "Where do you think they got that character from?" he asked with a wink and a nod. Whether he was joking or not I had no idea, but Flash Harry looked, and behaved, more like Arthur Nutt than Arthur Nutt ever did.

Arthur was a great little bloke, full of first-rate, scrupulously clean jokes, and with many a tale to tell about his earlier days on the Piers, "dodging the Bobbies" and often pretending to be a tourist or an earnest holidaymaker instead of the slightly off-colour (if not entirely 'shady') itinerant unloader of dodgy merchandise he was. He made it all sound like a great life, which I am quite sure he lived to the full and which he greatly enjoyed.

The new Norton twin, the Model 7 "Dominator" with its 500cc engine and plunger rear suspension had arrived in Sydney in 1949 and, quick though it was, it was not amongst the best handling machines of its era; it vibrated more than most and its low-slung centre stand displayed an alarming tendency to dig into the road surface on left hander corners. For some inexplicable reason, a cheaper Norton twin arrived some months later with no rear suspension, its rigid frame augmented by the traditional sprung saddle, and it had no other name than its Model 7 designation.

"What are you going to call this one?" I asked him, as one of the many dumb questions I was known to ask. "I fink I will call it the Norton *Exterminator,* vat's not unlike Dominator, you know" he nodded sagely. "It won't take long for me to shift 'em orf, wiv a nickname like vat. Not long at orl"

He was of course quite right, and that small shipment of machines vanished off the showroom floor in no time, that rigid-framed model never to be seen again.

At that time there were two other rigid-frame Norton motorcycles on the floor which probably had no right to be there. They were the 16H, and 500cc side-valve plodder, and the larger, 600cc side-valve Big 4, the latter, even more of a plodder, intended mostly for sidecar use. As it happens, nobody seemed to want either of them, which was no surprise for the inefficient side-valve engine was well past its use-by date and the bikes smattered very much of the mid-twenties when their original design was a little more acceptable. I might add that the 600cc side-valve Norton single was a great sidecar machine because of the engine's prodigious low-speed pulling power.

The small range of Panther singles from 250, 350 and the stolid 600cc were part of the range on display, and they were similarly hard to shift, in particular the smaller-capacity models, but there were other motorcycles on that showroom floor which were very much more acceptable to eager enthusiasts, including the 500cc Triumph twins (which sold by the boatload) a couple of rare 250cc OHC NSU singles, and a very few Motobecane mopeds. A lone side-valve, Vee-twin 1200cc Indian, in fetching blue with deeply valanced mudguards, plunger rear suspension and lashings of chrome, stood proudly, head and shoulders above the rest, upon its imposing plinth.

An unsuspecting sailor swept into the showroom one bright morning and gleefully announced his intention of departing later in the day upon a new Triumph Speed Twin, that delectable, Amaranth Red 500cc twin which was even then, with its stable mate the sportier Tiger 100, well into the job of establishing Triumph as the number one motorcycle on this – and just about every other Nation's – want list.

He was of course set upon with some haste by Arthur who was rubbing his hands together with such enthusiasm I expected them to burst into flames at any second. "May I assist you sir," he said in that charming, oily tone he had perfected, which was probably the first time that Able Seaman had been addressed as 'sir' since he had joined the Navy. He was thus won over in an instant.

Arthur was, as usual, all eyes and teeth, and I reckon he shone so brightly he would have glowed in the dark if there had been a sudden blackout, as he cupped the man's elbow into his hand and lead him to his sales centre. It is fair to say he may well have been outshone by the sailor, who was lit up like a beacon with his face shining like a well polished Jonathan apple. If he knew what fate awaited him, that sailor's face would probably have been much more like the colour of a Granny Smith apple.

I didn't stand and watch the arch-salesman at work of course, but I did note that not long after they had been closetted at the sales desk one of the staff rode off to the Phillip Street Motor Registry perched on one of the more-ordinary side-valve single-cylinder Nortons.

I had several other things which took my attention during the day, but I watched with a mixture of horror, amazement and sheer admiration as the young sailor proudly rode off in the mid-afternoon upon his newly purchased, rigid-framed, side-valve 500cc Norton single. Note that it wasn't even the 600, which was (very) occasionally sold to an enthusiast for sidecar use, and was thus a better performer ridden as a solo, but it was the smaller capacity machine nobody wanted. Well, perhaps the sailor did, but then again...?

I sidled up to the spiv later in the day to admonish him upon the irksome pursuit of unloading an unwanted (and distinctly second-rate) machine on the innocent matelot, instead of the Triumph twin he had so earnestly wanted. "What did you do to that bloke," I said, "he didn't want that Norton clunker when he came in here."

"I know," he nodded wistfully, "but he sure as Hell wanted it when he left."

Make a note of that when next you desire to change your current steed, or replace the ailing family saloon. Arthur has surely long since met his Maker, and I imagine he would then have been duly chastised for his lifetime of dubious sins. To his eternal credit, Arthur was not a rip-off merchant, at least not when I knew him during the late forties and into the early sixties, but he was able to exercise a polished charm which he used to great effect in shifting off machinery which was a bit slow to move of the showroom floor.

> *We should all be able to pay our money and take our choice, but that may not always be the case.*

For all I know, that 500cc side-valve Norton might well have been a far better, more ideal machine for that young sailor's needs than the much more sporting Triumph Speed Twin might ever have been. After all, many a good salesman is also a good advisor, probably more in touch with what we may *need*, rather than what we may *want*, even if it does mean shifting off to us a product we didn't come in to buy in the first place.

As I've suggested, there are probably one or two Arthurs – or Arthurettes – in every sales yard or showroom across this nation, and they may have entirely the same charm and whimsical nature enjoyed by that great character. We should all be able to pay our money and take our choice, but that may not always be the case. It is fervently to be hoped however that, good though those latter-day sales people may be, they are as essentially honest in their dealings with the public as that trim little bloke was on Hazell's showroom floor.

Old Indian

There is a long, long strip of sand at the very tip of New Zealand's North Island called Ninety Mile Beach, which is actually just on 55 miles long. It got its name, so legend has it, from travelling Missionaries who were in the job of trying to save the indigenous Maoris from themselves. These zealous people always travelled by horse in those far off days and were well aware that a horse could cover 30 miles per day before conking out, and that it took them all of three days to traverse that long sandy beach. But in sand –even the firm sand which formed the beach's surface – a horse could not travel 30 miles per day; hence the miscalculation of the length of the beach.

Although the beach continues to be called Ninety Mile Beach, that 55-mile long beach, by a strange con-incidence, measures just on 90 **kilometres** long!

Back in the thirties, the beach sand was so hard packed that it was routinely used as a landing strip for aircraft which delivered Air Mail into the sparsely-populated area, but it also provided the perfect surface for motor racing, both on four wheels and, far more often, on two wheels.

My dad once told me the story of a motorcycle race he had seen on the sands of Ninety-Mile Beach back in the mid-twenties when he was a young man courting my mum. When he walked along the beach surface earlier in the day, he found it to almost as firm as 'soft concrete' – whatever that might be! As usual with these rather informal 'circuits', the track consisted of two long straights connected by a fast, sweeping corner at each end, the track some mile or so in length.

He told me that the race leader in the feature event later in the day was a Kiwi champion who was riding a Vee-twin Indian, a machine which I was later to assume was one of the 42½ degree, eight-valve, pushrod engine racing motorcycles designed for the board and/or dirt tracks so beloved by Americans back in the 1920's.

The race he described was the final event on the programme he said, and several laps into the event the race leader was well clear of the pack when, as he backed off and cranked the Indian into the open corner which lead onto the back straight, the front tyre suddenly deflated and rolled off the rim, taking the pink inner tube with it. Of course the rider slipped off, but took little time in heaving the bike upright and climbing back on again.

Then, to everyone's amazement, the rider yanked the tyre over his shoulder (the lower fork crown no doubt holding the tyre well clear of the front wheel) and sped off in earnest pursuit of the new leaders. My dad reckoned the bike seemed to be just as fast with no front tyre, the rim skimming along the surface and spitting the sand out to the side like a bow-wave. That bike was clearly faster than anything else on the day, he said, and the bike seemed to actually corner faster on the rim than it did with the tyre in place! This could well be so, for I imagine the rim would dig into the sand and possibly allow more grip than a rubber tyre skimming across the surface would be able to do.

Be that as it may it was a fascinating story and it sat with many others festering in the memory banks for many years until – like many other stories which are suddenly stirred up by a chance remark – they are dredged out of the deep, dim recesses to enjoy the enveloping beam of a bright and blinding spotlight, the incidents almost as fresh and detailed as if they had been recorded on DVD. Or, at the very least, on VHS tape. This was one such story.

It was back in 1949 where, as a young kid not too long out of school, I was working at Hazell and Moore, the NSW agents for Indian motorcycles (among several other marques) and on this occasion I was engaged in casual conversation with a fellow who had just stepped into the store. He was from New Zealand he told me and he was to go upstairs and talk to the spare parts manager about a box of old 'Power-Plus' Indian parts he had heard about. I had seen that box of course, I told him, and had wondered what the brand new (but as it happened, quite old) parts were, and why they were not on the shelves with all the other bits and pieces.

I had been told they were not of much value, because the machines they were intended for were old bikes made just prior to, or just after, the First World War, and were to be taken to the tip somewhere.

That box contained a large number of brake blocks, several valves and some tattered boxes of valve springs, with a few sets of gears and number of cast-iron cylinder barrels – the much earlier type with non-detachable cylinder heads and large screw-in plugs which covered the heads of the valves. Those Power Plus parts were for the 1000cc side-valve Vee-twin engine, not nearly as efficient as the overhead valve models which were also available back then, and by now so very old-fashioned.

The man to whom I spoke in 1949 told me he raced an Indian motorcycle in NZ and suggested he was something of a star performer on the bike, particularly in beach racing, and that he held a number of National speed records on sand as well.

This was hair-raising stuff because it transpired that, when I told him about my father's story of the bloke who hefted that front tyre over his shoulder and zoomed back into the race on the sands of NZ over 20 years earlier, **he was the rider who had done that!!** It was, and remains, on the far side of co-incidence and almost defies credibility. I clean forgot to ask him the result of that heroic effort, or what his name was, because it was such a shock to have my father's tale repeated by a man I had never seen before; indeed, the man who actually carried out that extraordinary feat.

As it happens my recollection of briefly meeting that motorcyclist from NZ was awakened when I recently read a small, potted history of the Legendary Bert Munro and it mentioned the fact that he was in Sydney in the *'late forties'* to visit a friend who had some Power Plus Indian spares in which Bert was interested. Could it be that his friend mentioned there was a small box full of old Indian parts lurking in a dim corner at the local Indian agent's store?

It must be understood that I can't lay any claim to having met the late Bert Munro, although I have been well aware of his existence for many years, but I do begin to wonder if this bloke was in fact that fabled character.

It all seems to fit together too smoothly, but as I said I didn't ask the man's name and may well have forgotten it even if I had done so. I can clearly recall the earlier US 'Cycle World' magazines of the mid-sixties – back then it was the A5 size of a Readers Digest – which often carried photos and stories of the 'old codger from New Zealand' who had turned up unheralded and unannounced at Bonneville Salt Flats at that time and was originally not allowed to compete, at least not officially.

I recall an early photo in Cycle World of Bert at the Salt Flats as he was standing alongside the streamliner while wearing a jet helmet and goggles, an open-neck chequered shirt and a pair of crumpled trousers the cuffs of which were tucked firmly into his socks. The story mentioned this was an early appearance at Bonneville, and it may well have been prior to his famous first outing on the salt.

One thing is for sure, other than a composite of several runs on his so-called Indian Scout, which the film suggested was 201mph, his slowest run through the electronic timing was 161 miles per hour, his fastest one-way trip was 205mph, and he once threw the bike down on its side at 195mph when his goggles were whipped off as he sat up out of the streamlined shell and simply couldn't see where he was going!

When we realise the original 1920, 600cc side-valve Indian Scout was capable of no more than 60mph in its original form those figures are highly impressive indeed.

Why did that Kiwi rider want the old Power Plus Indian spares, have you wondered? The Power Plus was listed as a **1000cc** side-valve twin (though a very few were listed with overhead valves), and those bigger bore cylinders would have been very handy indeed once the cylinder heads had been sawed off and were probably used to increase the engine size as Bert worked his magic on that old engine. The larger valves would also have saved some time in machining new ones from valve blanks, but would probably have needed to be reduced from the original as Bert developed his own cylinder head design with four valves in each of them.

Regardless of how that 1920 Indian Scout performed during the incredible 57 years of Bert's ownership that final, eight-valve Vee-twin, which looked not unlike a 1000cc, eight-valve board track racer engine, was very assuredly a Munro Special with, we may be well assured, none of the original components still installed.

That Munro Special suffered numerous blow-ups over the decades and was entirely re-built each time with radical engine modifications which were very much of the man's own design and making, then finally machined under fairly primitive conditions. It was said that Munro brewed his own entirely suspicious fuels, and many of the engine internals were either beaten into shape and then finished by hand, or extensively modified by using whatever materials were available or could be scrounged from scrap metal dealers. Of such things are legends made.

It has been suggested that there was a time when he cast his own pistons in thick beach sand before he made his own moulds, and then carefully finished them by hand. We can only guess at what other metals were added to the basic aluminium to create several different types of Munro alloys. Some pistons would no doubt have gone off like hand grenades, others may well have lasted for extended periods of time.

Thanks to the film "The World's Fastest Indian" – for 'Indian' read 'Munro Special' – the name of one of the greatest of all (amateur?) engineering geniuses will be forever remembered. If this was indeed the bloke I met all those years ago, then I consider it to be a retrospective privilege.

Here in Australia we have enjoyed more than our fair share of mostly self-taught engineering geniuses, many of whom I have met over the years, and some of these men continue to service a large number of Classic racing motorcycles to keep them at the top of their game. By race regulations, they are sometimes allowed to fit engine parts from later model motorcycles where these components can be fitted with ease – or altered to fit, more likely – with many of these engine components made from scratch within a modern engineering workshop somewhere.

But it is much more likely that, just like Bert Munro himself did, that most of these highly-stressed engine components would be all-but hand-made in any one of a number of small suburban garages; probably in the wee small hours of the morn at that, and by brilliant, self-taught engineers who remain more or less anonymous

Oh, and just as a footnote to the story, the Indian factory was the largest motorcycle factory in the world back in the 1920s and the designs were sometimes years ahead of the several other US manufacturers. For example, a 1914 "Electric Special" Indian could be purchased with an electric starter, a 1000cc engine and a crude form of suspension by quarter-elliptic leaf springs front and rear, surmounted by a pair of well-sprung single saddles. It has been said there were not many 'E.S' models made but they were listed in the local catalogue, so were available to eager buyers.

A major advance for motorcycling in general was Indian's invention of the twist-grip throttle control, albeit on the *left* handlebar. This finally did away with the lawnmower-like control lever which was in use by other manufacturers until this invention. As we are well aware, the twist-grip throttle control is in universal use on motorcycles to this day, and will probably remain so forever.

Hazell & Moore

Parcels

The accent these days is very much on safety. For example, you can't work on somebody's roof without wearing an approved safety harness; our cars are all fitted with seatbelts and airbags; the design of safety scaffolding for roof tilers and high-rise building workers is more stringently controlled than ever; you aren't even supposed to ride in the back of a utility truck anymore, or a caravan when it's being towed.

There are, in fact, a thousand and one regulations that control what you can and cannot do and they are tailored as much towards possible litigation as they are towards our personal safety. It is called Health and Safety, or Personal Liability Insurance.

It was not ever thus, as we shall observe.

One of my earliest jobs in the motorcycle trade way back in 1948 was packing parcels to be dispatched by mail or freight train, then to deliver them to Central Station in Sydney or the main post office in Railway Square, which was almost on the same site.

After packing the parcels we would wait at the store's side entrance to be transported to the dispatch depots by the delivery vehicle, an ex-Army 10/12 Indian outfit. In place of a sidecar, the machine was fitted with a large box into which we piled the parcels and then found whatever space we could to sit in there ourselves – sometimes on top of the pile, sometimes wedged into a tight space and hanging on by our fingernails as though our very lives depended on it. Which, of course, they did!

In those far-off days, over 60 years ago, nobody outside the confines of a racing circuit ever thought of seatbelts or safety harnesses, even for innocents like us!

If the sidecar driver had enjoyed a heavy and somewhat liquid lunch, which was by no means unknown, the 15-minute journey probably took about five minutes but seemed to take an hour and a half, the outfit leaping over tramlines, potholes, bumps and silent cops with equal abandon, while we – the two terrified incumbents – were tossed about in the side-box like a pair of hapless peas in a referee's whistle.

The return journey in the empty side-box could be even more hazardous, because we often encountered the 200cc Villiers-engined Ambassador outfit (fitted with Tilbrook's little 'Tom Thumb' side-box) from Bill Mahler's motorcycle store which was directly opposite. Its driver was one Jim Crombie, a happy and somewhat cheeky character, well known and well respected in later years in Sydney as the proprietor of London Trading Company.

These meetings would usually result in a harem-scarem race back to the store with nothing for us to hang on to but our various appendages. We often arrived back at the store with bits of bark missing from elbows or knees, having been planed away by our sliding about within the confines of the large side-box. Try getting away with that these days; you would find the Heavy Hand of the Law on your shoulder before you could lurch into second gear.

For what this is worth, the little Ambassador outfit won those illegal events as often as it was defeated, for it could slip through smaller spaces than the much wider Indian could, particularly when the two-stroke's sidecar wheel was more than waist high in the air – a feat that its driver managed to achieve, with great enthusiasm, through every left-hand corner on the circuit!

They called those delivery outfits "bun-trucks" for some reason, Hazell and Moore employing yet another bun-truck from time to time: the rare ex-Army 600cc side-valve Norton with its long steel side-box which was so much smaller than the one on the big Indian and so very much more uncomfortable. The Norton outfit was used during the War as a delivery vehicles mostly for arms and ammunition, not for personal transport.

I only rode in that bun-truck once and found the steel box so tight a fit that I had to wedge myself into the thing while the strengthening lip atop the box dug into, and separated, the third and fourth rib on either side of the cage. Painful though it was, I felt safe enough because – even though I could hardly breathe – I was wedged firmly in place.

For some obscure reason the bun-truck driver decided to return to the store via the large Centennial Park after we has delivered our cargo of parcels to the depot – a route several of us were wont to illicitly take if the machine we happened to be riding took our fancy. We were zipping along at a fair clip when the driver unaccountably decided to quickly return to home base by wrenching the handlebars to full right lock, which of course spun the outfit around almost in its own length.

It was a near-disaster, for the Norton's chassis featured a large rail with a knob on the end which poked out just above ground level and inboard of the sidecar wheel but which seemed to serve no useful purpose – except, on this occasion, to dig

1948-1954

itself firmly into the road and instantly flip the motorcycle over the side-box!

Yes, I did say he flipped the motorcycle over the side-box: it was **not** the other way around!

As I would discover later, the driver was pelted onto the grass verge, but I was flung out of the side-box and trapped under the motorcycle itself.

There I lay, flat on my back, ribs aching and twanging like harp strings, my feet unaccountably on the petrol tank and my kneecaps doing their best to gouge my eyes out of their sockets. Did you know that your kneecaps are a perfect fit in your eye sockets? Well, they are, though I suggest you don't try this at home, unless you like attempting that sort of thing, of course. I must say I imagine some young couples might have discovered this anatomical fact very early in their married lives.

Of course you can't see anything if you attempt this exercise, but – try as I might – I have never been able to achieve that feat again. I have remarked upon the fact the our Creator obviously found an ideal location in our knee-joints for the waste material he had left over when He gouged out the holes for our eyes from the front of our skulls when we were originally designed! Waste, not, want not.

No, my past life didn't flash before my eyes (and I couldn't have focused on it even if it had) but it occurred to me at the time that my dad had always said, "The only things you should ever put inside your eye sockets are your own elbows."

The crushing weight of the bike was forcing the air out of my lungs – and several other orifices as well – and I was on the verge of panic, for it took some time before the imbecile who executed that absurd flip showed his hideous face over the top of the bike. By then the situation was made a great deal more serious by the thin stream of petrol piddling out of the tank cap's tiny breather hole and dispersing itself all over the front of my trousers.

Although it was so dark I couldn't see the clown's smirking face over the top of the upturned motorcycle, and my ears were ringing like Village church bells at Harvest Festival time his voice, though somewhat shaken, was clear enough.

"'Ow are ya?" he asked, without a trace of concern in his voice. "Ang on a minute, I'll drag the bike off ya!" he suggested helpfully.

'Ang on a minute', did he say? Where the Hell did he think I was going to go? And if I was in any hurry to go anywhere, why did he think I was lying there in the middle of the road balancing a motorcycle on the soles of my feet? Wouldn't I have crawled out of there if I could and rushed over to kick him soundly up the backside, or better still, up the *front side*, injured though he might have been?

Without further drama he lifted the motorcycle well clear of me and I was able to roll out, scramble more or less upright, and then quit the scene on the double as he, and he alone, heaved the bike right side up, sidecar over bike this time instead of the other way round. There was no way I wanted to be within a bull's roar of the area if there were going to be any sparks around, because the front of my trousers were by now freezing cold and more than a little damp. Mostly from the petrol, I hoped!

I didn't know at the time if I was injured or not, but I wasn't going to wait around to find out – or run the risk of being barbequed.

Then suddenly the cold at the front of my trousers was replaced by a slight tingling, then a full-blown burning sensation. No, my strides were not on fire but it was almost as bad. Ever been in hospital when a friendly nurse offers you a backrub with methylated spirits and then accidentally slurps some of it down your Builders' Cleavage? If you have, you know how it feels. If not, let me tell you here and now, it burns like fire, that's what it does, and it does your wedding-tackle no favours at all!

In any event, and with the pain increasing like compound interest, I rushed down to the nearby Duck Pond, whipped my pants and knickers down to my ankles then, with legs well spread, splashed as much water as I could over the area. It was Panic Stations, let me tell you, for there was no other way to ease the frightful burning sensation that had me almost gibbering with pain.

At the time I couldn't have cared less if a small group of Carmelite nuns had been enjoying a vigorous game of shuttlecock with some friendly, local Priests at the water's edge, nor if it was the annual Pornographers' and Perverts' Picnic with revelers rushing nakedly about. I couldn't have cared less if a group of giggling Girl Guides had been busily involved in a frantic tug-of-war with a bunch of tooth-baring, moaning choir boys. I had to put the invisible fire out at once, that's all there was to it, and I didn't give a hoot who was there to witness the spectacle. I must say I wondered later what anyone who could have been there might have thought of my strange performance. Fortunately, there was nobody about.

The odd thing was that there was no flame, but my loins were at once burning, freezing cold and soaking wet. This would account for the fact that I didn't disappear in a cloud of steam when

— Vintage Morris —

Hazell & Moore

I frantically applied many soothing handfuls of water to the pain.

The area was as red as a boiled lobster. As the searing pain subsided somewhat, I glanced down to assess any damage only to be confronted with a well-camouflaged secondary navel which had never been in evidence before, no matter how cold the weather! How odd was that?

I confess I had to sit down for a bit because my heart was banging away like crazy and I was a bit lightheaded, the pain by no means a thing of the past, although it was still slowly subsiding. I could hear my companion fiddling around with the bike, which he had by now righted. He announced that the battery was loose in its bracket and some oil had escaped from the tank but everything else seemed OK. He didn't ask how I was, I noted, but he must have assumed I was more or less in one piece if I could have escaped the scene as quickly as I did.

"What are ya doin' over there?" he asked, "havin' a leak or somethin'?"

"Quite the reverse!" I snapped back at him. "I'm recovering. What are you doing?"

"I'm lookin' at the bike," he said, with a touch of awe in his voice. "Thank Christ there's hardly a mark on it!"

"Of course there isn't, you fool," I informed him, "because I was underneath the bloody thing!"

"Yeah," he said. "We're lucky though, we won't have to tell anyone about this."

Actually *he* was the lucky one, because I could have been badly injured (and so could he for that matter) and he would have been hard-pressed to explain what we were doing in the park in the first place. I was the innocent party after all, being simply the bun-truck's passenger.

Fortunately, there was little or no traffic through the park in the middle of the week way back then – no one was there to offer any assistance or ask us what had happened – so we checked the bike over as best we could and fired it up again. There was a cloud of smoke from the exhaust for several seconds and a few coughing noises from the engine, but the bullet-proof old Norton soon settled down to idle as reliably as it ever did. That bike had survived the drama a bloody sight better than I did.

We made our way back to the store, with me sitting sidesaddle on the unyielding rear mudguard – and we returned at a much more sedate pace, let me assure you!

When we arrived back at the store the driver made some half-baked excuse about things being very busy at the Freight Office, which accounted for our lateness, but nobody mentioned the outfit at all as it sat innocently near the workshop door, waiting to be called into action again. It had several dents and bruises from its already hard life so there was little or no evidence of the dramatic turn of events we had so recently endured.

Happily, I had been wearing an issue dustcoat when the accident occurred, which now bore several scuff marks on the back, but I buttoned the thing up to cover the stains so obvious on the front of my strides from the water I had so carelessly doused upon myself. I didn't want to have to explain *that* little lot away!

British rear stands

One of the most essential items of equipment attached to your favourite motorcycle might be its simple prop-stand, which is clearly essential when there may be nothing close by upon which your bike may be leaned when you leap off it. But an even more essential item is surely the machine's centre stand, which is safer if the ground may be soggy and is certainly safer if the bike has to be left unattended for long periods of time.

Most off-road bikes come equipped with prop-stands, as do most roadsters, but the centre stand is a standard fitment to nearly all road-going machines, while it remains an oddity with machines intended for more rugged use.

True, many off-road machines are equipped with just a prop stand these days, whereas in days of yore, the few machines fitted with prop stands as standard equipment were AMC models, those AJS and Matchless singles and twins, and the Velocette range. Prop stands were listed as an *optional extra* (?) on Triumph machines from 1954 on, when the range was first outfitted with swing-arm rear suspension; they were also listed as an extra on some Ariel and BSA machines, where the device was simply bolted to a lug which was brazed onto the lower frame rail.

There was also a locally-made, after-market prop stand which was designed to clamp upon one of the lower frame rails if this trim little lug was not there; which was the case with earlier rigid frame or sprung-hub equipped Triumphs and plunger sprung Norton and BSA machines. But for some odd reason, no matter how tight its mounting clamp was nipped up, the bike's weight leaning on this stand would often result in the clamp not having sufficient grip with the inevitable result that your well-loved bike – earlier Triumphs were a good example – would slowly subside and then lie down quietly, waiting patiently for your horrified return.

You would then sorrowfully note that battery acid had leaked onto your left hand muffler, wrecking a patch of chrome plate in the process and scarring the muffler for life. It would also have left a tell-trail track of ruined paint along the outside of your toolbox which traced the path the acid had taken as it departed the confines on the now near-empty battery.

Having come to grips with this grim situation you would then need to push that prop stand back from its extremely rude, erect angle. Naturally, it would need to assume its designated position before you could ride off again, that is unless all the corners on the way home happened to be right handers.

This was easier said than done, for your short list of choices would be very plain. Firstly, you could loosen off the clamp and re-align the prop-stand (or pelt it into the river or over someone's fence to save the same thing happening again); that is assuming you could get a spanner to the nuts which would by now be hidden away underneath the primary chain case and impossible to reach. You could belt it with a hammer if you happened to have one with you – which wouldn't be very likely – or you could attempt to saw the blasted thing off if you happened to have a hacksaw with you, which would be even more unlikely.

There would be little point in jumping up and down on the stand to try to move it, which I have tried to do in the dim dark ages, and with no success at all, or you could ask a Very Large Passer-By to do likewise, which still wouldn't budge the thing. If you belted it hard enough with a hammer and were lucky enough, the thing might snap off and then you could ride home again. However, were this the case you might need to bear in mind that your favourite left hand corner would need to be negotiated with a little more caution in case the little bit of stand which was still sticking out, and had been forgotten about, might dig in and happily high-side you.

Ah, yes, how times have changed. But the ubiquitous centre stand could also be a source of great woe for us all, because these have sometimes been more than a little difficult to come to grips with. The centre stand fitted to single-cylinder BSA's, along with most other singles, was a good one, and always easy to use, but its opposite number fitted to BSA *twins*, while almost exactly the same unit, was something else again. In a similar fashion to earlier Norton twins, the little arm with which the stand could be engaged was wrapped around the outside of the left-side exhaust pipe.

The lower position of the stand, by now forced upon it by the small engaging bracket outside the exhaust pipe, seriously compromised cornering speeds through left-hand corners, with the result that the centre stand would dig into the roadway with some enthusiasm and either jack the rear wheel slightly clear of the road or bend the stand itself. Occasionally, you could wear the little clip away to razor's edge and then couldn't use the thing at all, because it would dig a hole in your favourite boots.

When – not if, but when – you actually *bent* the stand it was then almost impossible to heave the bike onto it. This was because you had to heave the entire weight of the bike almost vertically and then have it flop back onto the stand, which meant you had to do the same thing in reverse to get it **off** the stand again. The latter manouvre was really hard work, folks, hard work.

Because of my short legs, and a certain degree of puniness, I learned a neat trick all by myself, and I learned it the hard way, a simple trick I hereby pass on to all you motorcyclists out there who may be having trouble lifting your machines onto a centre stand, for almost everybody tries to do it in precisely the **wrong way**!

The way it *should* be done is as follows:– Push the centre stand lever down with your **left foot** – that's your left foot (not the **right** foot as almost everybody seems to do, but which results in them being hopelessly off balance!), and when the two stand lugs are on the ground, you face your bike, take your hands off the 'bars, and, by now perfectly balanced and not splay-footed, grasp a convenient frame rail, bracket or dual seat base and lift the bike easily onto the centre stand. Try it for yourselves and be prepared to be amazed at how much easier it is.

If for some strange reason you had decided to buy a Panther back in the early fifties, you were greeted with a great roll-on **rear** stand with heavily curved legs which would allow the bike to be rolled onto the spring-loaded rear stand with ease; assuming you had legs right up to your armpits, that is! The bikes were always a bit long in the wheelbase, which meant the rear stand, which logically hung out behind the rear mudguard, was all but out of reach to most people of below average height, unless you were prepared to migrate, hand-over-hand, down the full length of the machine to reach it with a fully out-stretched leg.

Again, if you happened to easily park your Panther on a steep hill and then strode off downhill on your longer-than-average legs, the bike could often demonstrate how easy it was to roll **off** its stand again and race you to the bottom of the hill.

The Vincent motorcycles had a rear stand as well, but which nobody could use – at least not on a daily basis. The stand was not spring loaded, but was held in place by a small spring clip and a T-shaped Tommy-bar, which locked it up against the rear guard so you couldn't hope to loosen it off when you parked your bike, no matter how hard you tried. But the bike came with not one, but *two* prop stands, which, when used as they were designed to be used, would either support the bike on one side, or jack the front wheel clear of the ground for maintenance when using both prop stands.

It was then that the strange Vincent rear stand made sense, because it was there primarily to lift the wheel well clear of the ground so the wheel could be easily removed if necessary. It wasn't quite as odd as it seemed at first glance.

But the oddest, if not one of the worst, was the rear stand fitted to all Triumph motorcycles prior to the introduction of swing-arm rear suspension on Triumphs from 1954 on.

In precisely the same manner as that employed with the Panther motorcycle, you (or at least me) when putting the bike onto its rear stand, would need to let go of the handlebars and sidle along the length of the bike, hanging on to whatever frame rails you could find – or under the excellent single sprung saddle, with the first-rate barrel shaped springs upon which it was attached to the frame – and *reeeeaach* back to push the rear stand downwards with right foot. Then, having shuffled along half the length of the bike and then changed feet, so your right foot could by then contact the opposite leg of the stand, while you left leg held the other side of the stand to the ground, you would stand *behind* the bike, lean back at about 45 degrees, take a deep breath, and heave the machine onto its stand.

Or bugger it. Do what nearly everyone else ever did who owned a motorcycle in those days, lean the footrest onto the footpath or a convenient lamp-post and just stroll nonchalantly away.

It must be noted that Triumph did its best to help because there was a curved, chrome-plated handle just aft of the saddle, with a corresponding one on the right side which was intended for the pillion passenger to hang on to. If you were smart enough to use this, it eased your passage somewhat on the journey, but it got even better from there on.

The rear number plate holder was designed with a neatly rolled-in section atop the holder and just where its single bolt connected it to the rear guard, the component shaped quite deliberately to allow you to grab it with both hands as you hefted the bike onto its rear stand. Wasn't that very thoughtful of them? But the very worst was yet to come, because almost as soon as the rear stand had assumed a vertical position, with the bike about to be propped upright, the heavy springs which located it in the 'closed' position to stop it bouncing about were suddenly tired of being stretched almost beyond endurance.

They suddenly decided to assume their original, relaxed condition, and they did this very quickly indeed. The result was that the bike would suddenly, and without warning, violently flop backwards onto the stand with the result that you would either be (a) found sitting on your backside just behind the machine, or (b) rubbing at your aching legs because the tail pipes on your mufflers had suddenly pretended to be a pair of large, high-speed wad-punchers and had slammed into your (often unprotected) shins.

You didn't need to ask, because you could always tell who the owners of those early Triumph motorcycles were, and you knew this at first glance. They either wore heavy, knee-high boots and/or dark trousers, or had the clear evidence of ownership emblazoned upon their lighter toned pants by a series of black circles about two inches (50mm) in diameter half way up their shins. These abstract designs were of course imprinted upon their strides by carbon in the ends of the twin tailpipes of their motorcycles because the riders were usually nowhere near quick enough to swiftly depart the scene as soon as the rear stands began to be lifted over centre.

On one or two noteworthy occasions, I have actually witnessed the owners of these otherwise first-rate machines drop their bikes on their sides as they tried to scrabble clear almost as the stand was at its apogee, but not *quite* there yet. Naturally, the bike would then roll forward again, the stand snap back into position, and the bike would then just flop over on its side.

Ah, yes, the centre stand is a very essential item of equipment, but can be hard work to use. Try operating it the correct way around for change, and let your highly steamed writer know what you think of *that* half-fast idea!

A P North

1954

Motor Show 1

The first Sydney Motor Show was held in 1911, but no-one seems to remember much about it, which should be no surprise, because, as far as I know, no-one who was there at the time is still with us. But a recent discovery of an old catalogue from the show mentions that there were no fewer than 200 vehicles on display at the show, from a staggering number of 89 manufacturers! We can only imagine what some of those motor vehicles on two, three or four wheels looked like, but we don't know how popular that first Motor Show may have been. It is understood, however, that the Show came and went several times during the many years since its inception. For most of those many years, the Motor Show – now called the 'Australian International Motor Show (AIMS) – was mounted at the old Sydney Showgrounds. These days the AIMS alternates between Sydney and Melbourne on a bi-annual basis.

My involvement with a Sydney Motor Show began and ended in just two days; Opening Day and the day which swiftly followed. On opening day of the 1954 Motor Show at the Sydney Showground I accompanied the spare parts manager of the Matchless motorcycle importers A.P. North to the Showground on the pillion seat of a motorcycle, which I was then to ride back to the store. Either he was not the most skilful of riders or there was something radically wrong with the bike, because it was not the smoothest of journeys, fairly short though the journey was. The bike was a *rigid-frame*, 1948 500cc single-cylinder AJS which had recently been traded-in on a new Matchless twin. The manager mentioned to me, in passing, as I slid forward onto the single, sprung saddle, that the bike had not yet been checked through the workshop and that there were '*a few things wrong with it.*'

Delighted to escape the pile-making sponge-rubber pillion 'seat'- which was about the same size, shape and consistency of a house brick and was attached directly to the rear mudguard – I didn't take much notice of what he said, until I tried to kick-start the engine. A few things wrong with it, did he say? Only a *few* things, did he say? In fact, the ride back to the store on that dangerous bike was an unmitigated disaster, as I was very shortly to discover.

Firstly, the little valve lifter lever – which was used to lift the exhaust valve off its seat to make starting easier – was loose and flopping about, for its clamp, which was attached to the left side handlebar just under the clutch lever, was loosely held in place by only one of its two mounting screws. This made starting the engine very difficult, but when the engine finally fired up it wouldn't idle slowly and raced badly, because the carburettor flange which mounted the carburettor to the cylinder head was visibly warped, allowing it to suck air through the gap, which always resulted in a lean mixture and a very fast idle speed. This could often be a problem with Amal carburettors when they were mounted directly to the cylinder head without a heat-insulating 'composite' block being interpolated.

To make matters worse, when I lifted the right-side mounted lever into first gear the bike leapt forth with neck-snapping eagerness, because the clutch was grabbing badly and would not fully release. This potentially serious problem, allied to the very fast idling speed, meant that the bike's progress through heavy traffic was about to be effectively beyond my control.

Oh, and there was very much more to come, so don't relax just yet!

The rear brake didn't work very well, even with the left-mounted lever almost dragging along the ground, but the front brake was great, except that it would lock up almost instantly, even if you merely touched the handlebar lever. It was a real one-finger front brake that one, and the little finger at that! I must say that I had never before, nor have I since, experienced a small-diameter drum brake which exhibited that strange feat.

And so off we lurched, the AJS much more in control of my destiny than I was, you may rest well assured of that.

There weren't many pedestrian crossings about in 1954, but there were many trams, and there were many tramlines. There were also many tram *stops*, and there was a Law

Vintage Morris

A P North

which demanded that you stopped whenever a tram did, thereby allowing the passengers who alighted to be able to make their way to the safety of the nearby footpath. I was quite happy with that arrangement, but clearly the AJS was not, because each tram stop we encountered saw the Law shamelessly flouted as I slipped through the abusing throng, sawing the gear lever back-and-forth, back-and-forth; first gear, then into second, then slotting the lever up again into first, then back down again into second gear, with no sign anywhere of the neutral 'gear' for which I was so frantically searching. Of course the rear brake pedal was almost dragging along the ground at the same time, the front end dipping as the tyre yelped before springing back up again as I eased that confounded front brake lever on and off again.

It was all frightful stuff, but the worst, as they say in the Classics, was yet to come!

By some miracle I managed to select neutral gear at the very busy Taylor Square multi-intersection as a 'point-duty' police officer stopped our traffic stream, and I thankfully hid behind a very large lady bowler in her Morris Minor as the engine spun loudly beneath me.

When we were allowed to continue I gave her a couple of lengths' start, steeled myself for the flying start and leapt after her.... just as she kangarooed off and stalled her car right in front of me, while we were halfway to the intersection!

So help me that blasted AJS shoved the hapless Morris Minor into the centre of that intersection, the clutch lever to the handlebars, the rear brake lever dragging along the ground, the woman frantically gesturing and screaming at me from her driver's-side window, while blowing a shrill series of stirring blasts by enthusiastically engaging the little vehicle's stentorian warning device.

I wasn't brave enough to look at the police officer, besides which, I was too busy to do that, anyway, and it was only the front wheel sliding along her rear bumper – well, the *car's* rear bumper – and a quick shove with my foot that cannoned the bike clear and allowed us to careen along the busy Oxford Street, then down the steep Wentworth Avenue to finally arrive at the A.P. North showroom.

By then, I had hatched a cunning plan to stop the wayward motorcycle. I practiced finding neutral a couple of times on the descent, and managed to do so just once, but just in case it was missing again and I was still in gear at the showroom door I decided I would stop the errant machine by pulling the little valve lifter lever up to slow the engine and then slam the front brake on. Yeah, that's what I would do; how clever of me. I would soon show that bloody awful motorcycle who was boss. In hindsight, I knew I should have *coasted* down Wentworth Avenue when I finally found that elusive neutral, but I didn't think to do that.

The showroom's sliding door was open by about half-a-meter as I rode up the layback and shot onto the footpath while trying to reach for the valve lifter lever, my right hand poised over the front brake lever. The clutch lever had of course been earlier pulled in to the handlebars with my right foot sawing the gear lever up and down, up and down, first-to-second gear, second-to-first, first-to-second and back again, and yet again, but with no neutral to be found anywhere. I released the clutch lever and groped for that little valve lifter lever, but there was no lever to be found, either!

I was later to discover that the thing had loosened off even more and had slid all the way down the handlebars until it came to rest against the handlebar's clamp atop the head stock, where it was by then well out of reach.

A split second later we flew through that narrow gap with scant millimetres to spare and ran – well, at least we moved at a slow jogging speed – onto the highly polished floor of the spare parts department.

A.P. North's store had two double-window frontages, the spares department on the upper level with a few bikes on display, while its main motorcycle showroom was somewhat lower and was accessed by several steep, linoleum-covered stairs, with its access to the street by its own windowed sliding doors, which were of course closed at the time.

I had once witnessed the great Observed Trials ace Bill Mayes make an ill-fated attempt at riding a near-new Competition Matchless gently down those stairs with his huge feet still on the footrests, only to end up underneath the machine, while someone went away looking for the Vintage First Aid Kit which had never before been used.

Naturally, a directive was issued thereafter which forbade anyone from riding a motorcycle into either of the showrooms: a rider was supposed to stop the engine on a machine he was riding and then, as instructed 'disengage himself from the machine', and heave the bike up the slope and into one or the other of the two showrooms. This applied to everyone, and no-one ever rode a bike into the shop again.

Well, not until I arrived with that AJS in October, 1954, that is!

With the clutch lever pulled to the handlebar again and the rear brake pedal still dragging on the ground, we trotted to those four steps, whereupon I bounced the front wheel off a convenient handrail (Bill Mayes hadn't thought of that, but then, neither had I!) and rode that rigid-frame shocker down them with great aplomb to start the first of what was to be three laps of the showroom. I was of course still sawing that blasted gear lever up and down, down and up, up and down, and then down and up again, desperately searching for that damned neutral gear...

All I could hear over the engine was shouted abuse where I had half expected to hear some generous applause or perhaps even a stifled cheer, but I still couldn't stop the bike and couldn't find that elusive neutral. By now, though almost out of my focus, several spectators had magically appeared, including one or two heads that sprang from windows 'upstairs' where the Oracles sat.

I was absolutely terrified because there was clearly no escape, but why some clown didn't swiftly materialise to open that lower showroom door to allow me to escape onto the street again I still don't know.

There was nowhere to go and I was clearly in desperate straits as I made another circuit of the showroom, knowing all too well that if I applied the front brake the bike would slip from under me on the highly polished floor and crash into one of the second-hand bikes on display or, if I was lucky enough, a softer onlooker – should one suddenly emerge.

On the last lap, sobbing in horror and still playing a tune on that confounded gear lever, I noticed a strip of roughened concrete about half a meter wide and a couple of meters long against a wall where there once stood a small display cabinet. That small area just might allow enough bite to stop the machine without losing control of the front end. I headed for the strip and jammed the front brake on.

The front forks went onto full compression, the tyre yelped – so did someone else, and it might have been me! – the engine was on the point of stalling, when suddenly, and with impeccable timing, the nipple pulled straight off the handlebar-end of the brake cable!

The bike launched itself forward again, to plough side-on into a plunger-frame Dominator Norton we had recently traded. As the Norton fell to one side it leaned on another second-hand bike, which leaned on another, which fell onto yet another, the AJS almost climbing onto the Norton as it finally stalled.

I can clearly remember throwing the bloody thing away, almost in tears, as the Sales Manager grabbed me and shouted something incomprehensible into my ear.

Naturally, I was carpeted in the Oracle's office, but I stood my ground as I explained in some detail a few home truths about that awful AJS. I expected to be sacked on the spot, but Perce North was, to my surprise, quite sympathetic, which shouldn't have been such a surprise in view of the report he had so recently received on the condition of the bike. He also made some comments to me about the mental capacity of the guy who gave that God-awful motorcycle to someone he saw, for some inexplicable reason, as a fairly inexperienced rider. No-one thought to query why that dangerous bike was ridden to the Showgrounds in the first place, and I must say it didn't occur to me to ask that question either.

As it happens, the very next day I was on the company's stand at the Motor Show with Perce North himself, and that is yet another story replete with some more high comedy, and more than a little drama. But I must say that neither of those two momentous days in October, 1954 were in any way comical or dramatic at the time, let me make that very clear!

Motor Show 2

As I pointed out in the previous piece, my introduction to Sydney's Motor Show, which has nearly always featured a long list of motorcycles as well as passenger cars and light commercial vehicles, was on Day One in 1954, the event a very popular one which thoroughly established its place in history and which continues to be very successful in its new Darling Harbour home and elsewhere. It may well continue as long as motor vehicles abound. As it happens, I attended the Matchless stand at the 1954 Show for just one day only, but that was more than enough!

As I noted, I was working for A. P. North at the time, the NSW importers and distributors of Matchless and Francis-Barnett motorcycles and – thankfully for a very short period – the frightful three-wheeled Messerschmitt (which I nick-named the *Mess-o-schitt*) cabin-scooter.

Their stand gloried in the range of 350 and 500cc Matchless singles, the 500cc ohv vertical

A P North

twin, which enjoyed one of the most beautiful-looking engines ever fitted to an English motorcycle, and a couple of Competition 500 singles, with their tiny petrol tanks and huge alloy heads and barrels. All these models employed swing-arm rear suspension to augment the telescopic forks on the front, that type of rear suspension by no means a standard fitment in those days, although becoming much more so.

Prominently on display were two of the rare – and today rarer still – G45 racing versions of the 500cc ohv twins, beautiful-looking all-black machines with fat alloy heads and barrels and even fatter fuel and oil tanks. The bikes were imported to be ridden by Keith Stewart and Keith Conley, both of whom were later to enjoy some success with these machines.

The showpiece was a 500cc G80S single mounted upon a large packing crate, which featured a pair of big wooden 'cams' which were driven by an electric motor via belts and pulleys. The wooden cams were intended to push the bike's wheels up and down at odd times to ably demonstrate the unquestioned superiority of the Matchless suspension system.

Of that, more anon!

After the disaster of Day One with that awful AJS, and which I felt at the time might have seen my instant dismissal from the company, I was *very* surprised to have been asked to be on the stand on the Second Day, a chore I shared with no less a personage than Perce North himself, which, I was assured by those who should know better, was something of a signal honour.

On Day Two my mount was a far more acceptable machine than that dangerous AJS, for it was a near-new 500cc Matchless G80S single, the machine which had just finished second – behind a 500cc Matchless *twin*, it should be noted – in the inaugural 1954 'Round-Australia' Redex Trial for motorcycles.

The bike I rode was still well-muddied and shod with thick, knobbly tyres; great for loose or muddy surfaces but hopeless on sealed surfaces, and even worse on Sydney's slick tramlines. Why this bike was not featured as part of the AP North display only Perce himself could answer, and for some reason I didn't think to ask him. As it happens we were very busy with other things!

I had never ridden a bike fitted with these heavily-studded, off-road tyres before but I jumped on the bike and rode it very briskly it up Campbell Street to the very busy Taylor Square intersection with little drama, except for the odd twitch or two over the tramlines which were there at the time. The bike was very well sprung, comfortable in the extreme, and handled very well, in spite of the chunky off-road tyres.

It was a very different story at the busy Taylor Square intersection!

In those days, the tramlines in that area which led to the Showground curved gently to the right at the top of the hill, which made it difficult to cross them at anything like the ideal ninety-degrees, and this was the direction in which I was headed. They also crossed several other sets of tramlines which went straight on or curved in the opposite direction – a bit like the old St. Kilda intersection in Melbourne although, thankfully, not quite as bad.

Knobbly tyres were never meant to cross highly polished steel tramlines at all, much less at a nigh-parallel angle, a fact demonstrated to me (and a small army of casual bystanders), when the rear-end of the bike suddenly swung into a full-lock broadside when the bike was stupidly cranked over almost onto the right footrest.

Instinctively, I dabbed the sole of a highly-polished wall-toed brogue to the ground in an attempt to correct the errant machine, to be rewarded for my pains by a tearing sound, which could have been a newly-popped hernia but which was, thankfully, merely the centre seam of my newly-acquired suit trousers opening obscenely and displaying my brand-new knickers for the world to sneer at. I was, after all, representing the company at the Show, so was very smartly dressed in a fetching dark grey suit of clothes I had recently purchased and I hadn't bothered wearing specialised protective clothing; besides which, I didn't have any to speak of in the first place!

In those far-off days you could buy matching nylon knickers, socks, tie and suit-pocket hankie in the most bizarre fluorescent colours, from lime green, through canary yellow, sky blue and nipple pink to a more subdued burgundy.

Mine were, of course, glow-in-the-dark lime green, which the whole world could have seen had I bent over on the **moon**, trouser-less, and grinning over my shoulder, the wide split which gaped in my new strides going all the way from the base of the trouser flies to the rear waistband. Had that happened, it may well have been the first example of 'mooning' to be witnessed anywhere, while the sudden, unexpected cold draught which was suddenly manifest was worth a fortnight of cold showers.

The bike corrected itself, as many had before, and some have done since, so we continued

1954

> *"Turn it off, turn it off!" I demanded. Perce quickly obliged as another shot of lubricant pelted itself with great enthusiasm over the suede-covered single race-seat of the Stewart G45.*

to the Sydney Showground without further incident, me throbbing with embarrasment, the bike throbbing along as all 500 singles were wont to do.

I flashed my pass – pass! – at the guy on the gate and tried desperately to find a quiet place to dismount, but when I did so some fool laughed out loud and a few others were seen giggling into their hands and pointing the finger of scorn at the gleaming, lime-green crescent which was seen to suddenly adorn the crotch of my new suit's trousers.

Holding my too-short coat down at the back, I sidled, crab-like and almost on the tips of my toes, to the AP North stand and borrowed a Sellotape dispenser which I took to the toilet to make some repairs. It wasn't too successful, but it *was* better than nothing!

Perce was talking to someone when I returned to the stand and I was horrified to see that the display's showpiece was not working nearly as well as it should have been. In fact, it was a bloody disaster.

Far from demonstrating the Matchless' smooth-running – and very comfortable – front suspension, the wooden cams were moaning loudly as they turned, the whole bike shuddering and rocking about violently on its centre-stand. The rear suspension was working perfectly, the front forks were not!

"Hey, look at this!" I shouted to Perce and the world at large as I found the power-point and turned the device off.

The wooden lumps sighed with relief and ground silently to a halt, a wisp of smoke curling up from the small electric motor which by now was glowing in a soft pink and from which the subtle whiff of burning rubber made its presence known.

"What the hell's wrong with this thing?" Perce demanded of me.

"I dunno," I said. "I've only just arrived. Let's have a look at it!"

The bike on display was a brand-new 500 single, and I felt that the fork legs may not have been correctly oiled, so I scrounged around to the BSA stand, borrowed a small screwdriver and removed the small drain plug at the base of the lower fork tube.

Nothing happened! Not a drop of oil emerged, which seemed to confirm my suspicion that there was no oil in the fork leg. Let's not mention that I forgot the air-lock which existed because the top filler-plug was still in place!

"Turn the motor on again," I commanded, "We'll see if that has made any difference."

Perce was nothing if not obedient, so he flicked the switch on again and the `cams' swung into action with renewed vigour, allowing the front forks to sigh as they reached the bottom of their stroke.

As the forks were forced upwards again they emitted a deep, asthmatic groan, then an horrific flatulent sound, which was immediately accompanied by the gastric emission of a cupful of oil, which squirted with great enthusiasm onto the front of my brand-new suit coat. This was followed a second later by a giant belch as the forks readied themselves to repeat the performance on the downward stroke.

I swung aside and ducked under the next onslaught, noting, in that fraction of a second, that the forks were by now performing almost perfectly, and that the cold draught had suddenly re-asserted itself.

"Turn it off, turn it off!" I demanded. Perce quickly obliged as another shot of lubricant pelted itself with great enthusiasm over the suede-covered single race-seat of the Stewart G45.

"I'll pay the dry cleaning bill," Perce said, almost matter-of-factly, "and – er– the repairs."

"Repairs?" He nodded, looking down at the remains of my suit trousers. In those days, the flies in men's trousers were still buttoned, and the clutch lever on the G45 Matchless had neatly flipped the flies open as it dug in when I ducked away from the spray of oil. This meant that the hastily-repaired tear in the seam of the pants appeared to be gaping even more obscenely than before, accompanied by the equally-obscene gaping at the front as well.

For some reason, the small crowd which had quickly gathered – amazing how that happens, isn't it? – was highly amused by the proceedings and rent the air with loud guffaws, spontaneous applause and a short series of ironic cheering.

We searched the single drawer in a small desk on the stand and found a couple of paper clips, a

A P North

large ball of fluff, a chunk of an unknown brown substance which was pliable and extremely heavy and – of all things – a pair of long, white shoelaces. We used everything but the pliable, brown substance and the fluff to attempt a repair, but I was not terribly happy about the stark white bow which was now to be clearly seen hanging obscenely from the front of my wrecked trousers. Naturally, I had to remove my badly-stained, oil-soaked coat because I couldn't wear it on the stand, which meant that the large bow I then had on lewd display couldn't effectively be disguised.

> *I was also not happy to subsequently learn that the problem with the forks was that some fool had filled the right leg with oil twice, while there was none at all in the left leg!*

I was also not happy to subsequently learn that the problem with the forks was that some fool had filled the right leg with oil twice, while there was none at all in the left leg!

Naturally, I had to ride the Matchless home after the event, my brand-new trousers rent again as I flung my leg over the dual-seat and kicked the engine into life. I wore my suit coat home as well, of course, not only in a forlorn attempt to cover the gaping tear in my strides, but because that was the easiest way to carry it. In the end I was forced to pelt the whole lot out, including my lime green knickers, matching socks, tie and breast-pocket handkerchief. To his eternal credit old Perce North happily paid for a new suit, which I might add cost quite a bit more than the ruined one I hastily – if sadly – consigned to our household garbage bin.

Yes, my first experience at a great Motor Show was very daunting, attended by almost total disaster, some of it by my own making, I must say, but most of it entirely accidental and by no means through any fault of mine. I left A. P. North several months thereafter for greener pastures, but it had nothing at all to do with the shenanigans at that 1954 Sydney Motor Show. I was to re-appear in the motorcycle trade a couple of years later at the suburban dealership, Ryde Motorcycles, and therein lies a series of similarly odd experiences!

James to work

It was somewhat more than half century ago that I was first married and at the time the three of us, my wife and I, with our small babe, were living in a small week-ender at Palm Beach, a good hour's ride from the centre of Sydney, where I was working in the spares department of A.P. North, the importer for many years of the small range of Matchless and Francis-Barnett motorcycles. My bike at that time, if for some time thereafter, it should be noted, was my little 125cc, three-speed James commuter, which was not very quick but which delighted in being flung about with gusto through the great curves above Bilgola Beach and other medium-paced corners I traversed around the Neutral Bay area on my way to work every day.

The little bike was strictly a commuter machine and was nearly always ridden absolutely flat-out, which meant it could be quite entertaining through tight corners when away from the traffic with its inhibiting factors. The drop down to Spit Bridge in those days was a tortuous series of tight Ess-bands, all of which were a joy to negotiate. To ride that little bike was certainly a faster way to get into the city than either the bus or a car could ever hope to be, and was far more enjoyable. This fact was proved beyond doubt when I twice had to catch the fearfully slow double-deck bus into the city, which took all of two hours for the trip, and again on the one occasion in which I was offered a lift into town by my next-door neighbour.

My neighbour was no less a personage that the legendary 'Scotty' Allan, a former ace pilot from WW1, who also flew with the even more legendary Charles Kingsford-Smith and Charles Ulm. Scotty was a head honcho with Qantas at the time, and he proved to be one of the dourest, and unintentionally funniest, characters I have ever known.

While we were strolling down the bus stop one morning, another neighbour and I were invited to 'climb aboard' as Scotty eased his luxury Jaguar sedan car out of the garage and proceeded to reverse down his drive.

We 'climbed aboard' the Jag and settled ourselves comfortably as his young daughter ran out of the house to bid a fond farewell to us. Scotty shoved his head out of the car window and waved to her as he moved off, but ran off the drive and nudged the overhanging frond of a large tree-fern, which responded by swinging back at him, knocking his tartan cap into a rakish angle and dislodging his glasses, which hung off one ear and the end of his prominent nose at a very amusing angle.

She burst out laughing – she could hardly be blamed for this, because the Scot's two passengers strove manfully, but with little success, not to do the same thing – whereupon Scotty shouted at her "Now look what ya've dun, ya little booger!" and glared back at us balefully with his specs still at that absurd angle, and his cap, with its bright red bobble on top, hanging on by a thread. I thought we might be ordered out, forcing us to make that terminally-boring trip into the city by bus after all, but he continued to back out of his narrow driveway, his tam-o'-shanter at a rakish angle, his specs still hanging off the end of his nose.

"Will ya stop yarr gigglun?" he shouted at us as he adjusted his cap and dropped his glasses into his lap, " Ye'll ornly encourage herrr, un she's baird enough as it is!"

That ride into town was one of the finest comedy turns I have ever been privileged to witness, and all of it was entirely unintentional, although at the time it seemed to have been a carefully rehearsed performance.

He delighted in (too) often overtaking several cars at once and shoving the car's nose back into the traffic stream where there was not room for even a tyre lever to be inserted. "Did ye see thut?" he would shout with unbounded enthusiasm, "we took fourrrr of 'em in wun hit thut time!"

"Salmon pink!" he shouted at the driver of a dun-coloured Sunbeam Talbot 'Alpine' sports car we had just cut off, "It's the colourrr of yerrr brrrairns, no doot aboot it."

What a trip that was, and it ended with a ride like a merry-go-round when we speared into the basement garage of the Qantas office in the city and shot onto a turntable which began to rotate at some speed when Scotty drove quickly onto it and slammed the brakes on. "There goes me parkin' space," he gleefully announced as an empty space slid over our collective shoulders, "and we'll slip into it after a couple of rounds," he added, as he drummed his fingers on the rim of the steering wheel.

The turntable began to slow after about four revolutions and Scotty shot off the device with a squeal of tyres and passengers, as he drove into his designated spot. "Here we arrrre again, luds," he brogued, "thunks for the guid company." So saying he left us without so much as a backward glance and nodded at the attendant while removing his string-back pigskin driving gloves as he fairly galloped towards the exit sign.

Ah yes, what a trip that was, but I must say I missed my 'accidental' travelling companion whom I met without any form of announcement, or indeed acknowledgment, almost every morning on the way to work when I was riding that little James. It was great stuff, indeed!

Those meetings seemed to be quite unintentional, as we appeared to totally ignore one another, but just as I would drop off the main drag at Mosman to descend the switchback corners through Cremorne and down to Neutral Bay, a 200cc LE Velocette, ridden by an employee of P & R Williams, the company which imported the marque, would suddenly be manifest at my right elbow. We shamelessly raced one another down the hill and through the great collection of fast, slow, off-camber and sweeping bends which were so much a highlight of that odd stretch of road.

Of course nobody but us would have had any idea that we were racing each other, because the performance of both machines was a bit on the light side, so we must have appeared to be just two simple commuters riding in very close company. We were, in fact, hammering one another mercilessly, for we were at it tooth-and-nail as soon as we came across each other.

I would lead into a couple of corners, he would lead into a couple more and it was all very heady stuff for a couple of simple, ultra-light motorcycles which were ridden by a couple of simple, ultra-light riders intent on emerging onto the Harbour Bridge first. We would then play cat-and-mouse in the heavier traffic until we at last reached our respective venues, which stood almost next door to each other in Wentworth Avenue, the very hub of the motorcycle trade in Sydney in the fifties and into the late sixties.

There was a motorcycle store just on the exit of that sweeping left-hander at Neutral Bay, which was owned and operated by that late, great character Ern McCredie. It sat against a rockface directly across the road from that corner, and it could almost certainly have laid claim to being the smallest store on the planet, for it seemed to be about the size of someone's double bedroom. Ern would sometimes be outside the place and he would occasionally hold up a hand in greeting, which we could not return for we were hanging onto our respective steeds for all we were worth.

I shall never forget one morning when we were really scratching through that corner, the LE Velocette on the inside, and the little James trying desperately to overtake round the outside, the skinny tyres scrabbling on the uneven road surface and threatening to slip away from underneath me.

I could hear the sound of another motorcycle coming up from behind and suddenly there was Ern himself right alongside me on a 200cc Ambassador, the rider still just inboard of the double yellow lines. As he drew level to pass both of us – which he did with a consummate and annoying ease, he grinned over his shoulder and took a hand off the bars to remove the pipe he was (apparently) smoking.

"Morning boys," he said with a studied, casual air which was at once sickening, embarrassing and entirely deflating. He then shot straight across the road to slide sideways up a small driveway outside his shop, which left me – and I have to assume, both of us – feeling more than a little crestfallen.

I am quite sure Ern's manoeuvre was as carefully planned as it was brilliantly executed, and I must say that, if I was that way inclined (and at least a meter taller) I would have ridden back, doubled Ern over till his chin was at the level of his knees, and then kicked his arse round the block several times. I doubt if he would have allowed that to happen, of course, for he was a fairly tall person and I was not.

I am still not a tall person, which should surprise no-one, and it is probably just as well that I never was, because that poor little James would have been hard-pressed to have handled that daily trip to the city with such alacrity, or anywhere else for that matter, if its owner had been any bigger than I was/am.

Moving

The Editor of a major magazine for which I have written many and many an article sometimes looks at me a bit sideways, for which, be it understood, he can hardly be blamed. On this occasion he stroked his greying beard in an upwards motion with the back of his hand, which is always a good sign that he has something to impart: sometimes a gem of wisdom, on other occasions a searching question. He then slowly stroked the fuzz at the sides of his mouth and pursed his lips before slowly coming at last to the point.

"You've scratched around this country's roads for many a long moon, Morris, and on many a forlorn motorcycle, have you not?" he intoned, while pretending to riffle through a small pile of notes he had placed on his desk-top.

It was my turn for a change to look at *him* a bit sideways, because I knew something was coming, but of course I had no idea what he was about to ladle upon me. He leaned forward conspiratorially and finally asked "What was the worst trip you ever had on a motorcycle?"

With more than a little relief I told him that there were several, but the one which was probably the most difficult, and probably the worst, was a trip I made in 1954 when I moved house from Palm Beach to Fairfield by motorcycle. Well, it wasn't the entire contents, because my wife and I had rented a house which was fully furnished, but I moved all our belongings in one hit... and I did it all by motorcycle, and a small one at that!

No, it wasn't an outfit, I hadn't learned to ride one of those things yet; it was, believe it or not (sometimes I don't believe it myself) my tiny, three year old, plunger-sprung 125cc James commuter!

We couldn't afford to hire a furniture removalist, and there wasn't enough property to warrant the expense even if we could, because all my wife and I possessed in those days was a bunch of bed linen, pillows, several sheets, blankets, a canteen of cutlery, a dinner set and our wardrobe. Of clothes, that is, certainly not the wardrobe itself.

It was raining of course as we packed my wife's (and the baby's) clothes into two large ex-WW2 Army haversacks which were draped securely over the small rubber pillion seat on the rear guard of the little bike. The two webbing straps were a very snug fit over the pillion seat assuring us that, whatever else may happen on the trip, the bags would stay precisely where they were.

When they were tightly packed, the backpacks were nearly round and about as big as a pair of medium-sized steel garbage bins. They were also nearly dragging on the ground!

I owned three Army gas-mask bags, two of which we filled to capacity – if not beyond – and hung either side of the steering head, where they were sure to flap about all over the place. The third one I shoved on my head over a cloth cap because the bag was waterproof.

I wore my entire wardrobe of several shirts, some jumpers and around five pairs of trousers, the outer couple unzipped and gaping open.

Fortunately, we owned a large wicker laundry basket which we filled with all the bed linen, the canteen of cutlery, dinner set and some shoes; it was to sit across my back and be held in place by two trouser belts looped through the handles and buckled tightly together.

A large briefcase which held the balance of our few possessions was to sit on the petrol tank and be held in place by thighs and inner arms. This is a trick, may I say, largely forgotten by modern riders who wear haversacks on their backs instead of back-to-front on their chests, where the pack is then weightless and allows a tiring rider to lean on it from time to time on a long ride.

Try it some time, it is surprisingly comfortable and entirely secure!

Luckily I could fire up the little engine by coasting down a steep driveway, because there was no kick-starter on the bike at the time. The crank had a tendency to loosen on the shaft: it had fallen off the bike only days before, and had not yet been replaced.

Oh, and the engine would not idle reliably for some reason and a run-and-bump start (followed by the process of heaving the heavy basket over my head while trying the keep the engine running) didn't enthuse me as an option.

Thus equipped, and no doubt looking like a hermit crab on steroids, I sat and waited on the driveway for the bus to come along. My wife and baby son were to be picked up in the city and taken to my mum's house at Fairfield while I rode the bike there by a somewhat more circuitous route. I would of course arrive before them and have a meal and bath ready for them when they arrived.

When the double-deck bus came along and they were safely ensconced therein, I trickled down the drive, fired the bike up and wobbled off in pursuit of the rapidly departing vehicle, the dull amber glow of the flywheel lighting rig – which only worked while the engine was running – almost lighting the way ahead.

I followed the bus for a couple of stops, concerned that the jam-tin-sized brakes didn't seem to be working terribly well and there were odd grinding noises from the wheels as the bike weaved about. It was under control, but only just!

The reason for the grinding noises became clear when I looked down at the wheels whilst stopped under a street light. Because of the extra weight the bike was carrying the wheel rims were almost on the road, in spite of the fact that I had inflated the tyres to the hardness of house bricks earlier in the day.

In those days service stations closed at 5pm, and, incidentally, weren't allowed to open on weekends, so I had to press on regardless of the marshmallow feel of the tyres. At least I wasn't likely to fall off the bike, the haversacks, which also scraped through corners – and over bumps! – would have prevented that!

It was hardly eventful, the climb out of Avalon in first gear and the sweeping corners above Bilgola Beach – such a joy on a solo motorcycle – less than inspiring as the bike weaved drunkenly about on what were two nearly flat tyres.

But it was more eventful just before Manly League's Brookvale Oval when a Police Patrol motorcycle waved me over as he cut across my bow and made his way to the kerb. I nearly ran over him simply because I couldn't stop the bike and I pulled up a matter of about 30 meters down the road.

He then pulled up alongside me and, despite my protestations, demanded I stop the engine – which naturally included the lights.

"What the Hell have you got there?" he wanted to know.

"A 125 James." I told him.

"Don't be smart with me," he said, as he began to pull a gauntlet glove off slowly, one finger at a time, "What's all this stuff you've got here?"

"My mum takes in washing," I lied outrageously, pointing to the basket and the bulging bags.

"Washing?" he was clearly astounded, "Where are you going to?"

"Fairfield."

"FAIRFIELD? Where have you come from?"

"Palm Beach."

"PALM BEACH??" he said, even more amazed, "You tell me that....."

Thankfully another Police Officer pulled up on his sprung-hub Triumph Thunderbird. "What have you got here?" he asked rhetorically.

Before his mate could answer an Angel, disguised as a Village Idiot, roared past in a Plus 4 Morgan sports car and disappeared sideways around the left-hand corner several meters away as the first cop slammed the glove back on, fired his bike up and shot off, siren howling, in pursuit.

Mercifully his mate, shaking his head sadly at the mess before him, took off in the opposite direction executing a neat, illegal U-turn over the double yellow lines.

I didn't know what to do: I had just been pulled over by a Police Officer for some reason and I thought it prudent to wait till he returned. I certainly didn't want to go through the drama of starting the bike up again only to be pulled over further down the road. And perhaps not quite so politely next time!

The first cop suddenly came back, cutting the corner outrageously and riding down the wrong side of the road for several meters, though he

A P North — 1954

had no legal right, or reason, to do so. I was not about to acquaint him with that fact!

"Where's my mate?" he asked, without pre-amble.

"Gone back," I said, "He told me he's going to put the jug on."

"The jug? What jug?"

"I dunno," I answered, getting deeper and deeper into it with every falsehood. "He just said... the JUG! P'raps it's for a cuppa tea at the station?"

"Take off mate," he said, gesturing with his thumb in the direction in which I was heading, "and think yourself thankful."

With that he flung the throttle to the stop, slipped the clutch for a few seconds and speared off, the rear-end of the bike fish-tailing about as the bike slipped across the wet double yellow lines.

It was suddenly very quiet and I was alone! It was dark and again beginning to rain lightly, there were no cars parked anywhere and almost no traffic to be seen in any direction. Why had I been pulled up in the first place? I couldn't think of any law I could have broken (unless there was a law concerning ill-treating an Ultra-lightweight motorcycle) and pondered upon the thought that the Police Officer himself should have been booked – if only for causing a nuisance to me or endangering non-existent traffic as he cut the corner so dangerously.

Naturally, I tried to paddle-start the bike while still astride it and, just as naturally, it refused to start. I flung the briefcase to the footpath and heaved the heavy wicker basket over my head, nearly dislodging the head protection as I did so, then trotted alongside the bike to run-and-bump start, the basket sitting in the gutter.

It was a nightmare, kicking a gasmask bag along in front of me while shuffling my feet frantically as a fully packed haversack nudged me behind the knees at every step. Whether through panic or the absurdity of the situation I can't say, I was giggling like a schoolgirl!

Mercifully, the engine fired after about six faltering steps – thank God for the ever-reliable Villiers flywheel magneto unit – A Wico-Pacey-equipped BSA Bantam would never have done that! – so I carefully wheeled the bike backwards to try and heave the basket over my head and settle it in place again.

I opened the throttle fully and reached for the basket, then revved the engine again with the load halfway over my (fat) head but it was stuck halfway when the engine conked out!

This happened, as I recall, at least twice but on the next try I managed to heave the basket into place and replace the briefcase on my lap and wobbled off into the night, ignoring the fact that at least one dinner plate and a couple of knives had fallen to the ground with a clatter.

They could stay there forever as far as I was concerned!

Most of that awful trip remains a blur, but I can clearly recall the clutch beginning to slip; not badly, but full throttle couldn't be used on anything but downhill runs, which was fine for that descent of the switchback S-bends which used to lead down to the Spit Bridge and up most of the other side.

Downhill was pretty awful, because the brakes weren't working as they should and the bags were dragging on the road through corners, but I caught up to a double-deck bus over Spit Bridge and blew the thing off along the flat.

How embarrassing to see the passengers inside grinning at me as the bus overtook me up the other side, while the bike crept up the steep climb in first gear and on about half throttle.

I whipped into the slipstream hoping for a tow, but of course there is no assistance at that speed, even from a Juggernaut that size. And it was no fun at all to watch the bus conductor leaning off the back platform and making 'whip-the-thing-along' gestures as he shoved his backside at me.

He thought it highly amusing: I did not!

Of course my wife had been home long before I arrived, and it was a giant relief to be assisted off the little bike and almost carried indoors. I peeled of the various layers of damp clothes and left them in a steaming heap as I leapt (for leapt read crept!) into a warming and oh-so-welcome bath.

The family was frankly amazed that so much equipment could be carried so far by such a small bike, and that a fool would have attempted such a feat in the first place!

I did remark that it would have been helpful if someone could have come to Palm Beach to help remove our belongings, and that stopped them all... except for my older brother Don, who remarked that he couldn't help, as there was no way he could have fitted everything I had just transported into his Vauxhall Wyvern sedan!

He went outside and had a long look at the amazing little James, a machine he had seen many, many times before, but a bike he was clearly amazed to note had transported all the household items of an impecunious couple half-way across Sydney. He shook his head in admiration at the little bike, which sat there so innocently, showing no outward sign that it had made such an epic 40km journey while loaded down with such a mountain of goods.

Vintage Morris

Indian Outfit

1955

Auction

There is no doubt this has happened to most, if not all, of us, but I wonder if a casual reader has ever flung a motorcycle into a nice looking left hand corner somewhat quicker than they should to scratch around half-terrified with the bike's right footrest scraping along the ground on the exit and the bike heading straight on? Hang on; negotiating a *left*-hand corner, with the *right* foot scraping along the ground, did I say; surely that's impossible? Not really, it's a whole lot easier to do than you might fondly imagine!

Of course you'd need to have a sidecar fitted to the bike to be able to do that, and any rider (including this article's highly-steamed writer) who has entered his first left hand corner a little too quickly with no-one in the chair can tell you what a daunting – not to say terrifying – feeling it is to find the sidecar wheel a metre in the air, the bike cranked over to the *right* and the bike running very, very wide on the exit. Oh, and into the on-coming traffic as well!

All your years of experience of riding a solo motorcycle mean absolutely nothing in this situation, and in fact the longer you have ridden a solo machine the worse it is. For a start you can try to crank the outfit into the corner as hard as you like and it makes no difference at all: you have to turn the handlebars like a tiller to round the bend because the bike naturally refuses to do anything but remain well and truly upright.

Until you scratch your way out of the corner cranked over in the *opposite* direction, that is – and that feeling is stranger than anything you are ever likely to experience on any solo motorcycle, you may be well assured of that.

With practice comes skill, and one day you find you can terrify the peasantry by hurling your outfit quickly into a left hand corner with no-one in the sidecar and the third wheel waving about in mid-air. There is a technique involved in this exercise and I'll explain what this technique is soon, but – as they say – Do Not Try That At Home!

I will *never* forget the disaster of my first passenger-less left-hander, and, again, anybody who has ventured into the traffic in a similar situation will tell you a tall and harrowing – but true – tale of how grim that experience was!

The year was 1955, I had left A.P. North for a job closer to home and I was forced (by she who was dominant) to seriously consider disposing of my hard-ridden, four-year-old 125cc James solo in favour of some family transport. I was able to strike a compromise in suggesting a motorcycle outfit, instead of the four-wheeler which was the stated preference, and I duly sallied forth in search of such a device, happy to still call myself a motorcyclist, albeit a family one.

A friend had recently purchased an Indian

Pressing on briskly into an 80Km/h left-hand corner with no-one in the un-weighted sidecar and the power full-on, in effect driving the bike round the sidecar. The outfit's wheel is still on the road surface, with a degree of opposite lock. Do not try this at home, please!

Same corner, same speed, same line, but with throttle rolled back. Immediately the sidecar wheel is on its way to being almost a meter in the air, the bike's right footrest finally near the road surface. Managed to scratch around, but too dangerous to ever do this again. Slow but sure? Oh, yes!

Indian Outfit

outfit which was disposed of by the Police force, and the thing looked to be just the ticket for me as well. We set forth to University Motor Auctions in Glebe, opposite Sydney University, one bright Saturday morning to see if I could pick up a similar machine for myself.

The plan was simple; as simple in fact as the four Crackpots who hatched the plan from scratch. We were to be conveyed to the auction house by my brother in his Vauxhall Wyvern car, whereupon he would tow us home with the agency of a stout rope and the able assistance of two large mates in the sidecar. Their job was in fact two-fold; to act as ballast in keeping the third wheel on the ground through corners and to hold onto the tail-end of the rope in readiness to jettison the device if – or more likely when – disaster threatened. In effect, they were safety officers as well, so then perhaps their job was probably *three*-fold, or *four*-fold if you included keeping an eye open for the Police. After all, the latter might explain to us the evils of (illegal) flat-towing, or might even assume we had pinched one of their pursuit (?) vehicles. As it transpired, the outfit I bought was registered for a couple of months, so no-one could book us for that offence,

I was head of the idiotic plotting committee, as I had read somewhere that the best way to tow a motorcycle outfit was to run a turn of rope round a convenient chassis rail and have an incumbent hold onto the end as a half-baked safety measure. I relayed the intelligence to my ballast that a suggestion in the learned article was that a tow-rope thus secured could be very easily flung out of harm's way should an occurrence demand its sudden removal.

At the auction I bought a 1944 1200cc Indian 344B outfit which had only had two previous owners, the Army and the Police, and I bought it for thirty-five pounds, with some rego still on it and (apparently) quite road-worthy. In view of the fact that these machines were fetching an extra hundred on showroom floors the price was a bargain, with the bonus of some months rego thrown in, even though the car-sized battery was as flat as a flounder.

No matter, thought I, was I not to be towed home at the end of that stout rope; was I not to be accompanied by the two stalwarts in the sidecar; was I not in total command of the adventure which awaited us all during the next hour? As it happened, the answers were variously yes, yes and..... **no,** not by a long shot!

Anyone who has been on the wrong end of a tow-rope will tell you that you are at the mercy of the person who is towing you, even though you *think* you have the advantage of a readily detachable towing device.

My brother Don began the tow well aware of the fact that we were being dragged along at his pleasure and we moved off with surprisingly little drama. I had not supervised the attachment of the rope to the front chassis tube, but was assured all was well by the smiles and up-thrust thumbs of the two clowns in the sidecar. At the time, they were shouting words of praise to the *tower* and proffering unsolicited advice to the *towee*, while nodding happily at each other and delivering words of encouragement to unattached females who leapt screaming out of our path.

Almost imperceptibly, our speed increased – along with my concern – and the two incumbents fell to silence, glancing from time to time in my direction as I tried to pretend I was in some control of the escapade. I noticed my brother drumming his fingers on the car door in time to a tune he assumedly had somewhere in his head (there were no car radios in those days) as the speed crept up a little more.

Perhaps unconsciously, the two sidecar passengers were beginning to shift in their seat and lean into left hand corners, while I followed suit by cranking myself towards the chair as well, the meter-wide handlebars turned into the corners with a new skill I had discovered earlier at a much more sedate pace. Faster and faster we went, our shouted pleas for mercy blown to the four winds or lost in the tune hummed by a driver by now beating time on the side of the car door with the open palm of his hand, nodding violently the while.

We three victims saw at once a tight left-hander arriving all too quickly, the driver with enough presence of mind to apply both hands to the wheel as we swept into the ever-tightening corner. "Drop the rope! Drop the rope!!" I clearly remember shouting out as I all but leapt into the sidecar, suddenly evacuated by its two passengers who now hung fearfully over the sidecar mudguard.

I can remember one of them: he was nearly invisible except for two boot soles (one with a large hole in it) framed, as in parenthesis, by eight glaringly white knuckles and tightly-clasped fingers with recently-chewed fingernails, surmounted by a terrified face, his mouth agape with a Gargoyle's grimace. His red-rimmed, bloodshot eyes were almost hanging out of his

1955

head like spring-loaded ping-pong balls as he stared directly at me. The other, poor sod, had embraced the sidecar mudguard, which – he was to suddenly learn – was sprung with the sidecar wheel and leapt up and down with unrestrained glee over bump and into pothole alike.

We swept majestically outwards like a trio of hapless water-skiers to be almost parallel to the car driver's door before he saw us and slammed the brakes on to screech to a stop as we swung past and were suddenly jerked into a full one-eighty degree spin. Luckily, there was no traffic coming in the opposite direction or there would have been a monumental disaster, for, among other things, the rope was stretched tightly across the road and would have certainly wound itself round the front suspension of anything which happened by.

I jumped off the bike and ran round to help one passenger back into the sidecar while the Mudguard Embracer trotted (tottered?) over to render the air a purple hue as he cast aspersions on the marital state of our parents at the time of my older brother's birth. Don at least had the presence of mind to wind his window up and he sat, grinning like the oaf he was, with a hand cupped to his ear and a questing expression of his smirking face.

We then wheeled the outfit back to the correct side of the road and I noticed the Embracer (who had attached the tow rope) had initially applied a tight, double-hitch to the rope, which negated any benefit we *might* have obtained when flinging the rope to its fate.

To make matters worse, the rope had slipped along the chassis rail until it met the resistance of another tube clamped onto it, which allowed the rope to be too close to the motorcycle, interfering with the amount of movement of the handlebars and thus the degree of cornering ability of the outfit's driver.

I have to say the rest of the trip home was devoid of drama and at a much reduced speed, owing, in some degree, to the machinations of the Mudguard Embracer who completed the trip firmly ensconced within the passenger seat of the ageing Vauxhall. I could see – by much gesturing and shaking of heads – he was apparently busy discussing the absurdity of the whole exercise with brother Don. Not to mention, I daresay, comparing the mental capacity of both drivers

The outfit sat for a day or so in the garage until I decided to take it for a practice run all on my own. It was then that near-disaster struck!

Think of this: a motorcycle outfit is probably the most unwieldy device known to Civilised Man. All the power and braking effort is generated by the motorcycle, and that is where most of the weight is. The weight of the sidecar itself cannot be lifted clear of the ground by mortal man, but a Newtonian Theory becomes fact when it enters a left-hand corner too quickly with no-one in it and the driver unaware of what is certain to happen.

In the Newtonian effect, the sidecar then becomes weightless and floats into mid-air with great enthusiasm, cranking the left-turning outfit hard over until the right footrest digs into the ground. The trick is this; you come into your corner fairly briskly and change down a gear, tweaking the throttle open at the same time as you turn the handlebars. The bike actually drives itself round the sidecar, the third wheel lightly skimming the road, the tail-end stepping out a little with a few degrees of opposite lock applied. Go into the same left-hander with the power *off* briefly and you terrify the natives as you exit under full power while waving the wheel about in the air.

I didn't know all this at the time when I ventured out alone, but I was very soon to learn all about it. I came down the dirt road in early 1955 which is now Cumberland Highway to turn hard left opposite the 17th green on the long-gone Smithfield Golf Course, and I did this at a fair clip.

The corner was an adverse camber with a steep bank leading to the Golf Course and I swung into the left-hander with more enthusiasm than sense. Suddenly that sidecar wheel was shoulder-high in the air (admittedly that's my shoulder, but still well clear of the ground!) and the outfit ploughed straight on, to fly down the bank and demolish a three-strand barbed wire fence as though it had been made of string!

In second gear, not quite in control and with the throttle by now wide open, we leapt onto the 17th green with clods of earth flying everywhere, where I executed an unintentional sweeping arc – to the right, by a stroke of good fortune – and shot off the course again through the newly-formed gap in the fence! The bike flew up the short slope and in fact became airborne for a second as I hung onto the thing as if my life depended upon it. No doubt it did, for a group of rapidly-approaching golfers were shouting hoarsely and waving a variety of fairway irons – and, for all I knew, the occasional *shotgun* – as they closed in on the scene of utter devastation.

I remember graunching into third (top) gear

Vintage Morris

Indian Outfit

without the agency of the clutch and lurching back up the hill in what I hoped would be a large cloud of dust. Happily, I resumed a form of control shortly thereafter and neatly turned the right-hander onto Bruce Street, the dirt road in which I lived, but I confess I hid the outfit in the back shed for several weeks thereafter.

There is little doubt the golfers would have sworn my display was an act of rabid vandalism, but I never ventured down that road again, whether to find out how they felt or for any other reason! I did, however, spend many more years riding a variety of outfits around this nation's roads, this time well and truly under full control and enjoying, well, *most* of it.

Bathurst

The Easter motor cycle races at Bathurst way back in 1956 were a mixture of good and bad: the racing was good, in fact very good, the weather was bad, in fact very bad and so were our experiences of the weekend itself. It started out well enough, because my mate and I were to ride our Indian outfits through the Mountains and camp out for three days away and we came, I thought, very well prepared for the exercise. I had a passenger with me, a mate who rode his bike to my house and left it there while we were away, while Wally had the other outfit well-filled with all our camping gear.

We had camped out with the Indians at Bathurst in 1955, but with somewhat mixed results, occasionally awakening, half-frozen, in the pre-dawn, to find our sleeping bags half-full of ants or a back out of plumb after sleeping on a small stone which was not discovered until it had apparently assumed the size of a large grapefruit.

Back in the late forties and fifties you could camp in the grounds halfway up Con-rod Straight and it was quite a sight to see in the early morning a small army of officials moving through the area with their open bookmakers' bags collecting admission from all and sundry. They were at once very quick and very efficient and I doubt if they missed anybody.

One could also camp at Bathurst Showgrounds, among many other choice camping spots, but I had had enough of that rubbish and decided we would camp in the most inviting and comfortable spot in all of Bathurst – in the soft and yielding sands in the river bed just under the bridge at the town's entrance.

We were going to pitch our small tent there and snuggle down to a comfortable night's rest away from all the hazards we had been unfortunate enough to have endured on previous occasions. It was to be, I felt sure, a memorable weekend. Oh, yes, it was to be all of that and more, much more!

When we arrived in Bathurst in the early morn after a mainly uneventful squirt through the mountains (except for a bunch of a ten or more pigs which trotted casually across our path at Yetholm) we rode our respective outfits down a small, grassy incline just short of the soft sand and parked there while we joyfully pitched our tent in the middle of the river bed. Then, for it could be cold in Bathurst at Easter, we piled sand high around the sides of the tent to make the interior completely draught-free and thus, was assumed (or at least I did) somewhat warmer.

We spread our trio of sleeping bags out late in the evening after a good feed at Heath's Café and settled ourselves down for what was certain to be a quiet and restful night's sleep. The deep, soft sand was all-embracing and comfortably conforming, there was absolutely no draught through the tent and, after humbly accepting congratulations on a brilliant selection for our camping site, we all slipped quietly into Morphia's warming arms.

After sleeping the sleep of the only-just, I awoke in the first light of an early dawn to the sounds of running water. For a second I thought it was a bunch of unfeeling drunks relieving themselves against the sides of our tent, but with ever-mounting alarm I realised that this was not so, for we were in fact under water! Well, p'raps not quite I *under* water but it was getting on for it, because there was running water all round us. It had obviously crept upon us from somewhere upstream while we were blissfully asleep and entirely unaware!

The tent was leaning over at a crazy angle but it was dry inside, except for a trickle of water which was running through the trough down the centre of the tent and in which my only pair of socks lay completely immersed! My sidecar passenger was also sleeping in the trough and I wondered idly what the movement was inside his sleeping bag until I could see that the entire bag and its incumbent were actually being buffeted about by an ever-swelling stream of water.

Quite obviously, the heavily piled sand around the periphery of the tent had diverted most of the water, but even then it was beginning to rush upon us with unbridled enthusiasm.

1955

> *"He was shivering like a jellyfish and gibbering with the cold, which was not an unreasonable reaction to such an extremely rude awakening."*

Suddenly Wally sat up, blinking owlishly and looking fearfully about. "What the Hell's going on?" he demanded of nobody in particular. "Where are we?" he shouted in panic, his staring eyes by now the size of a pair of luminous saucers.

Having said that, and with no warning at all, he leapt up and – still in his sleeping bag and his brain not yet in gear – reached down and reefed one of the tent walls free of its sandy fortification. He was rewarded for this oafish behaviour with a wall of water which almost bowled him over and which swept into the third party's sleeping bag, filling it to the brim.

I grabbed my socks before they were swept away by the torrent and fearfully peeped through a – thankfully downstream – tent flap to see what the heck was going on, while the sleeping bag's incumbent sat up coughing and spluttering and demanding that the Good Lord's Son explain to him quickly and in some detail what was happening to him.

He was shivering like a jellyfish and gibbering with the cold, which was not an unreasonable reaction to such an extremely rude awakening.

I stuck my fat head out the tent flap to be greeted by a rousing, ironic cheer which erupted from the throats of what looked like hundreds of fellow-campers who had had the good sense to camp on the riverbank instead of the middle of what by now was a swiftly flowing stream.

For some reason the audience on both sides of the riverbank had begun to dramatically increase (as they are wont to do at the scene of a grim accident) and there were many howls of laughter, interspersed with cat-calls, whistling and much shouted advice, the lot augmented, as usual, with lewd comments on our/my choice of a suitable campsite, and my/our mental capacity.

As it happened, we were atop a small island only just above most of the water, but we were stranded well clear of the bank and would obviously have to wade out of there. Though clear of the stream, both outfits had water lapping up to almost a third the height of the wheels, with footboards just underwater. Ah, yes, footboards, much more comfortable than those tiny foot-pegs will ever be!

So we struck the tent after carefully removing the three sleeping bags and pelting them onto the riverbank – funny how much further you can fling a soaking-wet sleeping bag than you can a dry, or even damp, one – then waded ashore with pants rolled up while dragging the now-limp tent behind us by some of its ropes. We were of course heartily encouraged in our endeavours by the ever-swelling ranks of amused onlookers who were very free indeed with their advice, but curiously shy of providing any assistance.

I don't know about the others but I felt as though I was red as a beetroot and was throbbing with embarrassment, wishing the entire audience of scoffers would flop head-first into the broiling water as the riverbanks collapsed under their weight. Those things don't happen often enough, of course, and they certainly didn't happen this time.

OK, so how was I to know there had been heavy falls of rain overnight well upstream, which had then resulted in a wall of water happily rushing *downstream* to where we were innocently awaiting its arrival? Common sense should have dictated that we sleep anywhere but in the centre of a riverbed in case just such a thing occurred, particularly as we were warned that rain was expected on the Easter weekend. As we all know, common sense is an uncommon virtue and was never one of my strong points: then or now.

Ah, yes, what a weekend! I wrung out my socks and hung them on a stick to dry over a fire Wally had started very suddenly with a liberal dose of petrol, but they promptly fell into the flames while we weren't looking. They were rapidly dried in the event, but were too crisp to wear and in fact fell into a powder when I tried to pull them on.

Vintage Morris

Indian Outfit

Wally had begun to tip a small mug of fuel onto some wet sticks we scrounged for the fire, but he pelted his mug into the middle of the river when a shaft of flame leapt from the fire to the receptacle he grasped when our shivering mate thoughtlessly flung a lighted match into the pile.

The mug looked very spectacular as it arched into the stream trailing a comet-like tail of flame behind it. The cheers and yelps of laughter which followed the performance would have been very heartening had this been a stage production, but in the event it proved to be no more than bloody annoying. Particularly for Wally, who had brought the mug with him from Poland for some religious or other obscure reason, and was thereupon forced to wade swiftly downstream in pursuit of his precious talisman as it bobbed merrily along with the swirling current. He was heartily encouraged in this endeavour from the banks of the river.

What a trio of idiots! Or at least one of them was.

With the fire crackling well, Wally dropped a small can of LBDs (small, uncircumcised red frankfurts, known universally as Little Boys' Dicks) into the flames after thoughtfully punching a hole in the lid with a greasy screwdriver. He had asked me to bend over while he cleaned the screwdriver, but I explained that not all actors were like that, and even the few who were..! What we didn't know at the time was that our shivering mate had dropped a larger can of LBDs into the fire but had neglected to punch holes in it to relieve the build-up of pressure as the thing heated up.

Wally was just in the act of retrieving his can as it started whistling at us and bubbling enthusiastically when there was an almighty bang from the fire and a crescent of steaming LBD's shot unfettered into the air. The fire went out in an instant.

Almost at once I saw that one LBD had glued itself to Wally's cheek, while at least three others were seen to plop into the centre of the river. Oddly, something seemed to come up from the depths and grabbed one of them, but whether it was a fish, a yabby or some poor bugger who had been swept downstream and was looking for some nourishment I never did find out.

Wally of course yelped and whipped the LBD off his cheek but it took a lump of skin with it and left in its wake a glaring red spot, which looked very angry indeed. Not quite as angry as Wally, I might add, who was leaping from one leg to the other and threatening to pelt the guilty party into the middle of the torrent.

With our fire well and truly wrecked and the rain beginning to fall, we decided to strike out for the riverbank, which of course meant firing up the bikes and riding them to higher ground. Easier said than done because the last few degrees of the kick starters' swing ended underwater, which meant that wet though we were about to get a whole lot wetter.

Fortunately, both engines fired up in a couple of kicks (what would we have given back then for press button starting!) and we briskly exited the scene pursued by twin rooster tails of sand-filled water and the jeers, cheers and cat-calls of the multitude of highly-amused onlookers.

Later that morning, we slithered up the unsealed, buttery-clay road to the top of Mount Panorama where we watched a stunning day's racing from McPhillamy Park, the weather closing in through most of the day with heavy wind squalls and even heavier rain.

There were several cloudbursts during the day, in particular at the start of the Junior (350cc) race, which resulted in more than half the field coming to grief in the very first corner, necessitating a re-start. Ken Rumble rode the incredible Walsh Bantam to a win in the 125 race, while the legendary Jack Forrest won the 250 race on the swift NSU and rode the race of his life – with a broken right ankle and no front brake – to win the rain-soaked Senior event by half a lap on the unwieldy, un-streamlined 500cc Rennsport BMW.

If we were not entirely dry during the day, Wally and I were at least warm in our heavy-duty, war surplus ex-army waterproofs, which was more than could be said for the poor bugger at our feet, who spent the entire day covered in an old tarp while he shivered uncontrollably. I slipped a hot dog or a cold pie under the tarp from time to time and the food seemed to disappear so I assume he ate it up, but he didn't surface all day even though we nudged him with a boot occasionally to remind him a race was imminent.

Perhaps he would have known that from the noise, anyway.

As we crossed the bridge on our way home from Bathurst I was shocked to see the placid stream had become a raging torrent lapping at its banks, with no sign that there was ever a small island in the middle. We were chastened to realise we could so easily have become the victims of a flash-flood, had the rain been much heavier or more intense upstream. It was bad enough, but it could have been a great deal worse!

Vintage Morris

As it happened, my workmate spent almost 10 days off work, more dead than alive after his grim experience.

"What did you think of the races?" I asked him when he finally turned up. He said nothing, but fixed me with a baleful glare as he clenched and unclenched his fists.

I didn't mention it again, but I'm sure his recollection of Bathurst 1956 (if he hasn't expunged it entirely from the memory banks!) is quite different from mine!

Teaching the wife

As you zip up behind the family car in front which is emblazoned with a couple of L plates, have you ever noticed that, for some obscure reason, the entire family seems to be riding with the young son – or, rarely, the young daughter – who is being patiently taught all his dad's bad driving habits as he is finally on the road for an early driving lesson.

They say one should never attempt to teach a close family descendant how to drive a car, and the reasons for this are all too obvious; and as for trying to teach a *wife* how to drive? Therein lay the seeds of near total disaster: I know this all too well, because I have attempted to this on more than one occasion, and always with very similar, and entirely inevitable, consequences.

To attempt to teach any of them to drive a car can be grim enough, but to try and teach a loved one how to drive a motorcycle outfit is tantamount to enduring a serious attack of the Sudden Death-Wish Syndrome; and I don't mean in saying it that any form of accident would be involved. Perhaps with auto gearboxes, power steering, ABS and other goodies to be seen everywhere these days, it may not be quite as grim to learn to drive a car as it once was. I don't know about that, for I am never again going to make the mistake of trying to teach my nearest and dearest how to control anything – except perhaps herself, and that would never work.

It was in the early winter of 1956 that I had a sudden and entirely inexplicable rush of blood to the brain (for a change) and rashly decided I would teach my then-wife how to ride/drive my old Indian outfit.

As I would normally do at a later stage when indulged in this pursuit at Ryde Motorcycles when some-one purchased a motorcycle from the store and then blithely announced he had absolutely no idea of how to ride the thing, I first explained in some detail where the various controls were and how they all worked.

Her sister and I pushed her around the (flat surfaced) backyard several times as she steered the outfit round a small obstacle course I had patiently laid our, and she seemed to be able to steer the outfit with some accuracy, even though a high degree of strength and manual dexterity was obviously called for. The Indian steering was always a bit on the heavy side, because, unlike Dotty and me, the engine was not running at that time. It was always much less of an effort if the rear wheel was actually under power at the time, but we weren't ready for that. At least not yet!

If the engine was not running at that time, then Dottie and I certainly were, so this meant several pit stops for refreshments, and some degree of resuscitation, as we shoved my wife about the yard, with Florence shouting encouragement to us from the saddle of the Behemoth.

I next fired the engine up and she practiced moving off, steering the device (to the *right*, naturally) braking and throttle control. For some inexplicable reason she didn't stall the bike once, was seemingly quite relaxed and apparently enjoyed the experience, which I thought was quite remarkable. But she seemed to be a bit throttle- happy at the time, which should have been noted by me. It wasn't, but perhaps it should have been!

It was then time to seriously attack the narrow, little-used road on which we lived at that time, so we took off with me on the rear end of the large full-pan (and, they claimed, anatomically correct) saddle, while her sister was firmly ensconced in the sidecar and grinning at us for all she was worth.

From my position immediately behind her I was nowhere near the handlebars or foot pedals and so I had no control over the machine, but I felt that, should it come to pass, perhaps I could fling her off the thing (or even into the sidecar with sister Dottie) then slide forward on the large saddle and assume at least *some* control of the outfit should disaster look like finally catching up it with us. I was thus as relaxed as you could expect any imbecile to be when he had placed himself in this absurd situation.

At the bottom of the steeply descending track – it was tar-sealed but hardly a road – was a small rural all-wooden bridge, which was approached down a steep 'blind' dip after negotiating a tight left-hander, and an ess-bend – which Florence took a bit too quickly for

Indian Outfit

my liking, but still more-or-less OK – and she seemed to line it up quite well. Inevitably, it was a very narrow bridge which sported a faded sign upon which was emblazoned the legend **"NARROW BRIDGE: NO PASSING OR OVERTAKING. GIVE WAY TO VEHICLES ALREADY ON BRIDGE."**

We certainly didn't need this reminder, for any half-baked jackass could clearly see there was little room to manoeuvre on the bridge, and certainly no room at all for anything other than two slim pushbikes to pass one another while crossing over it.. It was probably the narrowest bridge I have ever seen just about anywhere.

The three of us dropped down that steep approach much too quickly for my liking, with my shouted advice, entreaties, prayers and general abuse obviously shouted to the winds for all the good it did, or was more likely ignored as usual, even though it was shouted with ever-increasing volume and more than a hint of panic. Florence was in control of the Indian outfit and anyone else on the thing could go and get thoroughly stuffed as far as she was concerned. Either that or jump off the thing.

Naturally there was a small car just mounting the small rise which led onto the other side of the bridge, its front wheels now claiming an inalienable right to be first across, for the sign clearly stated that this Ford Defect – er, Prefect – had now claimed right-of-way; after all, it had crossed that invisible barrier and was now about to move unsteadily across that rickety old bridge. We would simply have to wait until it had passed us by.

I noted with some alarm that the Defect's driver was in an advanced state of Fossilisation, the shuddering car not a whole lot better, while a snowy-headed lady could just be seen peeping over the car's dashboard.

We might have been able to stop in time, if only just, but suddenly Florence slammed the throttle wide open and the outfit fairly leapt onto the bridge at ever increasing speed, the wide Indian seemingly taking up every inch of the available space. The Fossil, apparently more in control than we were, then jammed the Defect into reverse and shot backwards to try to climb a small grass hummock on the roadside, before slipping backwards down a small, grassy slope. We shot along that narrow bridge at undiminished pace, the timbers rattling as usual while they rose and fell beneath us.

The poor bloke in the Defect didn't look behind him at all, for there was no time to do so, but he stared straight through the windscreen directly at us, his mouth wide open in disbelief or a silent scream. There was no sign of the little white head which had been right beside him only moments before.

But far from silently screaming, the sounds from the sidecar's incumbent could be heard on the moon as we weaved across that bridge to the near-certain doom we were closing on so rapidly. There was nowhere to go, and we were going

there very quickly indeed, for the tight, and ever-moist, slippery left-hander off that bridge was only a few seconds away. I could already feel the pain and anguish of the crash which seemed to me to be inevitable, so I believe I bowed my head to Fate and clung on and I think I may have turned my head away as Doom rapidly closed upon us.

I have no idea how we avoided the disaster, and I had absolutely no hand whatsoever in what Fate was soon to have in store for us. There was no time to pelt Florence over the railings and into the stream which flowed swiftly beneath, or even to heave her into the sidecar with the hysterical Dottie, but for some entirely unfathomable reason she was well in control of the situation. She moved the bike as far to the right as the bridge would allow to give as much room as possible for the fast entrance onto that slow left-hander, and then as we dropped off the bridge with a bang she wrenched the left handlebar through almost ninety degrees, applied whatever movement was left in the twist-grip, and attacked the corner with an expertise she should never have known.

We must have all but clipped that little car as we shot past it, but the sidecar wheel then slammed onto a grass berm on the inside of the corner, pelting the sidecar body well clear of the high grass verge and opening up at least a meter or more of road which was certainly not available to us a second or so earlier. Florence instantly took advantage of this and moved the motorcycle almost against the grass bank as the sidecar was waving about in the breeze. The sudden jolt all but pelted me off the back of the seat, but my wife then compounded this drama by leaning over her right shoulder and shouting "silly ole bugger!" to the elderly driver of the now-silent Prefect.

At least I think she shouted this at *him*, but in hindsight it might have been shouted at *me*, and if so, I must say it was probably with some justification.

It wasn't all over yet, because we were still almost flat-out in second gear, while sliding sideways across the slippery road surface and I had to spend an interminable time for many meters almost in the sidecar, as that left-hander kept left-handing, trying to get that errant sidecar wheel back down to earth, while trying to calm my hysterical sister-in-law at the same time. Florence stopped the outfit a little further up the road and, to my eternal relief, climbed calmly off the front of the large saddle. She slipped into the sidecar beside her sobbing sister, sharing the single seat, Dottie on her lap.

"It's all right Dottie," she said, "no harm done!"

No harm done? No harm done, what the hell was she talking about "no harm done?" I was all but a gibbering mess, Dottie wasn't much better and the old bloke was red-faced and shuffling painfully up the road, his tiny wife several paces behind, and he was waving about an implement which looked like a crank handle from an old steam tractor!

Dottie was by now trying to climb out of the sidecar, probably for fear that Florence was going to drive us home again – which was never going to happen! – and the old bloke was slowly gaining on us, so I had a swift look at the grass covered sidecar wheel, saw that nothing was out of whack, then I fired the engine up and rode home very, very soberly indeed.

The most astonishing thing about the whole exercise was that here was a woman who, to my certain knowledge, had never driven a motor vehicle before (much less a motorcycle outfit) but who displayed an expertise in handling an unwieldy vehicle which should have been – and indeed was – well beyond her experience. It was, as it will ever remain, an unbelievable chain of events, which took only a few long seconds to unfurl, but which can never be forgotten. Had I been of a Religious bent, I would have strongly suggested that someone above us had been pulling a few strings at that time, for all three of us would have been at the very least seriously injured in no time flat had she not been able (or 'allowed?') to do what she did.

I never offered to teach her to drive the bike again, and I must say she never asked, but I did suggest if she wanted to consider a career in sidecar racing on the Sydney Showground, I felt our financial problems would disappear forever, because I remain certain that no-one would have been able to get anywhere near her on any Speedway track in the country. How she managed to ride that outfit as she did and escape what could have been a really ghastly accident, is still a mystery to me.

I did ask her once, not long after the incident, how she was able to do what she did, and her only answer was that she had watched me at work many and many a time from her position in the sidecar, and that as a result of this she knew exactly what to do. I couldn't buy that, because I never would have pulled off anything quite like the manoeuvre she executed with such apparent skill on that unforgettable day all those years ago.

Indian Outfit

Sidecar trials

It was a combination of nostalgia and lost riches which I didn't know I had at the time that brought a tear to my eye when I beheld an advertisement for a 1944 Indian Chief outfit which was for sale in one of those 'Motorcycles For Sale' comics.

It was the same model as my old Indian 344B outfit which had served me faithfully for a couple of years from late 1954 to early 1956, the machine powered by a side-vale Vee-twin engine of 1200cc capacity. The engine vibrated more than a little, and was on the noisy side, for as it ran it sounded like a metal bucket half full of old tin cans, added to by a large handful of nuts and bolts, the bucket being shaken violently from side to side to elicit some alarming grinding, clanging and banging sounds.

The exhaust was on the fruity side, the slim 'muffler' with a small split in it (every one of the few I ever saw were like that, for some reason) which meant that a form of 'after-burner' would elicit a sharp back-fire and other mumbling sounds, once the throttle was closed off for short periods of time when descending hills.

An odd front suspension consisted of a quarter-elliptic leaf spring which hung over the rear half of a heavy front mudguard, its movement controlled by a pivoting, leading–link system. It appeared to be a very crude form of suspension, if only because it was, but it was effective enough. Rear suspension was by the popular, short-travel plunger type, with pairs of heavy springs located in metal shrouds above and below the rear axle: they usually allowed about 80mm of movement. However, while there never seemed to be much movement in the Indian rear wheel springs, it probably took the edge off the worst of pot-holes and/or bumps.

Whatever road shocks were not absorbed by that short-travel rear-end were very well accommodated by the large-deep-pan single saddle, which was supported upon a vertical, sprung pillar, the seat pivoting from its nose.

As you can see from the recitation of some of the bike's specs, the outfit which was advertised for sale was of greater interest to me than to the casual reader. This is because the Indian Chief outfit I owned was bought at auction for some 35 pounds in the mid-fifties – that's $70 in the current money, folks – while the machine advertised for sale was offered at $20,000! That's right: *Twenty thousand dollars!*

Somebody pinched my Indian outfit just down the road from my house after it point-blank refused to start one foggy winter's morning in 1956, not long after I had returned from Bathurst Easter motorcycle race meeting and had stupidly attempted to teach my wife how to drive the thing. I had kicked that engine over until we were both exhausted before I coasted down the road for a clutch start, but there was nary a sound from the engine. That's more than I can say about myself, for I must have uttered a large variety of sounds --- most of them noisy and none of them complimentary. I left the bike at the bottom of the hill, but when I came home that afternoon it had vanished! A very neat trick, when one thinks of the size and weight of the outfit. Perhaps it was towed away?

That Indian had few serious vices to speak of, but its primary fault lay in the ignition/light switch, which was mounted in a panel on top of the large petrol tank. It was a rotating tumbler switch and apparently there was some wear at the points where various spring-loaded electrical contacts were made, because the engine and/or lights would occasionally cut out entirely, with no hint of its intention to do so and always at the most inopportune moments.

For what it's worth, the engine only conked out about five or six times during the two or three years I owned the thing but on those rare occasions a swift jiggle side-to-side of the mischievous switch usually had the thing suddenly behaving itself again. Usually, I said, but not always. No, not always.

On one occasion, as I squirted the throttle open to sweep majestically past a bus, then crossed (legally) to the wrong side of the road for an instant, the power deliberately switched itself off as if by some unseen and unfeeling hand. It then refused to fire up again no matter how much I wriggled and jiggled that blasted switch, all the while trying to ignore the tooting horns of motorists who had swung out immediately behind me or, even more urgently, those that were rapidly approaching on a head-on collision course.

Naturally the engine burst into song again as I was frantically looking for an escape route and, of course, just as the bus had rumbled past again, so I tweaked the throttle and leapt (?) away while my sidecar passenger crept under the small tarpaulin cover and pretended not to be there. So help me, the bloody thing conked out again at a set of lights further down the road as the bus crept alongside for a closer look, its uncaring passengers grimacing out the windows

Vintage Morris

at me or feigning total indifference, the vehicle's oafish driver grinning from ear to there.

The traffic lights had turned green again as I leapt to the kick-starter and it was some few seconds before the engine inexplicably chimed in and settled down to the rough, dot-and-carry-one idle that was always part of the charm of the big punchy Vee-twin engine.

With the traffic very heavy around us, I slammed the thing into first gear, opened the throttle almost to the stop, then, in a fit of pique, dropped the clutch and leapt away from the head of the queue to screech to a stop in the middle of the intersection as traffic, with horns blaring and voices raised in anger, struggled to filter around us.

I should have checked, of course, but 'my' green light had gone red in my face for several seconds, with just enough time to allow cross-traffic to move away and I had stupidly run the red light at exactly the right time to be a total menace to everyone within shouting range. It could have been a disaster but fortune smiled, the engine ran sweetly beneath me and the lights changed a matter of a few seconds later, allowing me – with never a backward glance – to flee the scene as briskly as possible.

The Indian agents had an absolute warehouse of spare parts (bought by the company at auction in large crates, most of which had been opened by me some years previously) but there were very few ignition switches to be found, and there was not one of those switches left when I needed to buy one. Could it be, you may wonder – as I did – that the offending device had an inbuilt design fault that resulted in demand well exceeding supply?

On another occasion, at night this time, I was winging my way home at a good clip while ignoring the derisive comments shouted at me from the sidecar by a half-frozen spouse who was soon to be carried off by my best friend – actually, I don't know who he was, but he was my best friend from then on, let me assure you of that.

It was a dark and moonless night as we sped into a great, fast left-hand corner outside the St Ives Showground in Sydney's French's Forest. On the very apex of the corner, halfway into the chair and rapidly accelerating downhill, the engine – and with it the entire lighting system – suddenly died.

In those days, there were no street lights in that area, so we were suddenly plunged headlong into a blackness of Stygian proportions. It was as black as the inside of a ginger cat and I could

> *"My heart was pounding like a bass drum and my mouth was suddenly so dry my tongue was glued to the roof of the aperture."*

see absolutely nothing as I reefed the front brake lever to the handlebars and stood on the rear brake pedal. It seemed like an eternity before the bike screeched to a stop, while it felt at any second as though we could have speared off into the heavy timbers on one side of the road or been launched over the edge of the embankment on the other. My heart was pounding like a bass drum and my mouth was suddenly so dry my tongue was glued to the roof of the aperture.

Unhappily, this could not be said from the other side of the three-wheeler. The monumental relief when we finally pulled up some 100 meters down the hill was suddenly tempered by shouts of outrage, interspersed with advice as to where I should go, and sooner rather than later, with advice on what would be gleefully done to me when I arrived. But the cruncher came when the tirade subsided and a chill voice from the sidecar I could not even see finished the dressing down with the question: "and why don't you grease your bloody brakes?"

It was all too much! So the brakes squealed a bit when they were working, so what? If I had greased the brake *shoes* as she suggested, it's a fair bet we would still be trying to pull the outfit up to this very day!

But there we sat, with not a soul in sight, and I couldn't see the side of the road to know whether we were in the middle of it, poised on the brink of a small cliff or about to slam into a tall gum tree.

It was an awful feeling and not at all helped by the less than friendly advice I was still being offered by the sidecar's incumbent, who had been my wife for a little too long. Who cared, at that time, whether she should have heeded her sister's friendly advice about the charming radio announcer; or run away with the local Preacher; or married the randy butcher, all of whom, I was advise anew, having been candidates for her affections at one time or another? Why did she think I was trying to kill the both of us? Why on earth would she think it was my fault everything went black so suddenly? Why did I turn out to be an idiot some Village was out there looking for? Why didn't I buy her Uncle's tattered old Vanguard motor car?

Indian Outfit

OK, so maybe I should have looked for a small car instead of the outfit just like her cousin Marty had done. If he could afford to run a car and support four kids as well why couldn't I do that with only the three of us to look after? If I had decided to pursue a career as an actor at some later date, she was stuck with that just as I was. Besides, who told her all actors were poofs? Surely I had proved to her – and her hare-brained sister before her, of fond memory – that this was certainly not so in my case.

Boy, did I cop both barrels that night. And there was, I felt sure, much more, and much worse, to come. I heard a sharp intake of breath and readied myself for yet another blast when the Cavalry suddenly arrived. *"Tutta Turrat Turrah! Tutta Turrat Tarrrrahhhhh!"* Thank Gawd for the Cavalry, I remember muttering to myself.

Yes, the tirade suddenly ceased when a car swept round the corner behind us just as another came towards us in the opposite direction, which at least allowed me to see where we were. As it happened, and through no skill on my part, the outfit was on the correct side of the road but with the sidecar wheel almost on the narrow strip of dirt at the roadside. It was a very close call and on the far side of terrifying as well.

When the two cars had swept past, without apparently acknowledging our presence, we were once more plunged into total darkness, the vehicles taking with them the quick flash of night vision we had begun to generate.

"What now, may I ask?" chimed the invisible spouse, revving herself up again, "I'm not gonna sit here half-frozen in this mobile bathtub any longer than I have to. The next car that comes along, I'm going to jump in front of it and hitch a ride home. You can make your own arrangements". I silently hoped that whatever motor vehicle she jumped in front of would keep right on going, or at the very least have its driver abuse her savagely as it screamed to a stop, tyres smoking and possibly side-on as well.

I felt miserable enough as it was, without the threat of being left alone to possibly be spirited away by someone from another Galaxy, but the lights suddenly, and for no reason at all, flickered on again. With a hoarse cry I swung to the kick-starter and was rewarded for my pains by a loud back-fire and a vicious kickback that swung me almost at arm's length high above the handlebars. When I landed I tried again, this time remembering to roll back the left twist grip, thus retarding the ignition timing to make starting the bike easier. The engine fired up halfway through the kick and then idled innocently as though nothing had happened.

Retard the ignition timing, did I say, what am I talking about? Hey, this was a 1944 model motorcycle, remember. Half of you don't know how well off you are with modern motorcycles, while the other, more elderly half, will probably recall and nod their collective heads in sympathy.

We had a much more leisurely trip home, be assured, and the engine never missed a beat nor did the lights waver for the entire journey. Along the way, I was rewarded by a sullen silence from the sidecar, which was a relief at the time, but I confess I was in no hurry to arrive home. It was a safe bet I would (again) be kicked out of the Big Bed.

Besides riding that bike to Bathurst twice, I used the outfit to take my wife to several pristine wilderness areas, to secret blackberry patches in Blue Mountain valleys that are now well underwater, to the beach on many a summer's weekend, and used the thing mostly as daily transport.

I must say that, for the most part, I enjoyed the lumpy roughness of the venerable old warhorse – the outfit, that is, not my wife, poor thing, who was one of the badly abused, Stolen Generation, and for whom I must say I *always* felt a great deal of empathy. This, I felt, when I was advised of her earlier life after we had been married, was surely responsible (at least in part) for some of her sudden outbursts of vitriolic anger. I, on the other hand, was just as surely responsible for all the others!

Some people have suggested that the old 1944 10-12 Indian outfit was some sort of Classic machine? Perhaps, in the current climate, it might be considered to be a Classic motorcycle now, if that is one's feeling, but it certainly was no Classic way back when, and it would hardly have improved with time.

But if that blasted switch had performed its natural office without playing games with me, I might have been able to pick up a cool twenty grand for that outfit today, assuming I still had the thing of course. That wouldn't be likely after all this time, because three wives, some dalliances and countless changes of address – with its inevitable loss of reams of paper warfare and some valuable possessions – would have seen to that.

After all, I bought that outfit just over 60 years ago as a solid old workhorse and a lot of water has been passed since then, folks, while many, many things have changed. And, it must be a said, nearly all of them for the better.

Ryde Motorcycles

1956-1960

Gear changes

We don't really need to be reminded of this, but it is a fact that the right arm and left leg move in concert whenever we are walking, running about the place, or generally engaged in ambulatory pursuits. There are some odd dance moves, both balletic and more sedate, in which, say, a right arm and right leg might momentarily move together, but this remains a rarity, because it can look awkward, is clearly unbalanced, and goes against one of the more simplistic of Nature's laws. In swimming, both arms work alternatively, unless one is an exponent of that distinctly odd 'butterfly' stroke, but in all other situations in which one moves about the countryside on two legs, Nature dictates that arms and legs move in opposite directions to complement each other, both for balance and because it simply feels better that way.

Ever since foot gear changes became the norm, which is from around 1929 with Velocette, and some years later with most other manufacturers, the Brits – and for many years the Italians as well – correctly argued that, as the left leg and right arm naturally move in close relationship to one another, then it would make perfect sense to have a motorcycle's clutch lever attached to the **left** side of the handlebar, with the gear lever naturally operated by the **right** foot.

To test this conviction try it for yourself some time and you may note – if you haven't already done so, which most of us have – that when you move your *right* foot forward, your *left* arm moves back in a complementary manner, and vice versa. This of course is entirely normal, unless you are striving for the comedic affect which Benny Hill, the noted British comic, so often did to great effect. This is the simple reason why all the great and (once) famous British motorcycles were designed with the entirely logical layout of a clutch lever where it still remains, but the gear lever firmly attached to the right – which is, arguably, the *correct* – side of the gearbox.

In this simple context, they also made a fuss over the inescapable fact that the front brake lever should be on the **right-hand** side of handlebar, with the rear brake pedal perfectly in accord by being applied by the **left foot**, again using the same logic. That's fair enough, because this makes the same sort of sense that was once applied to the positioning of the two foot controls on British and some European motorcycles.

There were very, very few European motorcycles, and none at all from the Orient, when British motorcycles were King of the road in Australia just after the war, so all of us who rode those machines became used to the 'normal' manner with which we withdrew the clutch, changed gears and applied the brakes. In those far off days, the extremely rare 500cc single-cylinder Moto Guzzi Falcone and the rarer-still 175cc and 250cc Lodola machines from Italy had a gear change lever, which was operated by heel and toe on both models, on the machine's right hand side, which was, as we have noted, fairly common practice. The rear brake was of course controlled on the left side, the occasional Falcone model having the rear brake applied by *heel,* the foot removed from the footrest, which made riding over rough surfaces a bit of a chore.

However, the not-quite-so-rare 250 ohc NSU single, the nippy little Zundapp 250cc two-stroke, and the vicious DKW 350cc two-stroke twin, along with the BMW machines, the latter slowly coming into its own in the late-fifties in Australia, had their gear levers mounted on the **left** side for some unaccountable reason. All of these machines came from Germany, which seemed to have a mind of its own, for what a King-sized pain the placement of those control levers was; at least initially.

In 1960 the NSW Police helped BMW from bankruptcy by purchasing a string of R60 BMW machines – their small orders added to much more substantial orders the factory received from Brazil and India, which then allowed BMW to apply for a substantial loan from the German banks to save their bacon – and soon some members of the local constabulary were to be seen mounted on these machines. They were also to be seen muttering to themselves or shouting to the winds in frustration as they rode these German machines about, because these riders were just as often mounted on British BSA or Triumph motorcycles, either solo or with a sidecar attached; in the latter case with a large, and somewhat embarrassed, Police Sergeant usually occupying the sidecar. The very first

Ryde Motorcycles

Mini-Minors soon put a stop to that pursuit!

Obviously, these Police riders had become accustomed to riding British motorcycles every day, and changing gears by using the right foot, but had to then concentrate on using the opposite number, and then often having to go back to the more 'logical' gear lever of the right hand side when they were riding a machine built in England.

The motorcycle store in which I worked in Ryde at the time was almost opposite the local Police station so we serviced their machines, and many a tale of woe was recited to me by many a Police officer who would be waiting patiently for a chain-driven BSA or Triumph or be serviced, or then, on another occasion, the same rider would be waiting on a shaft-drive BMW with its gear-change lever on the 'wrong' side.

These riders complained that the new BMW motorcycles were not quick enough to operate as pursuit machines, but I hadn't the heart (then) to point out to any of them that the R60 models they were riding were in fact the BMW models intended for sidecar use, because these engines were equipped with heavier flywheels, slightly smaller bore carburettors, 'soft' cam profiles and employed somewhat lower gearing.

It was unkindly suggested at the time that the rare, sporty R69S BMW, had had its distinctive rocker-box covers replaced by the more pedestrian R60 covers, the thinly-disguised bike then trialled by the Police Sergeant whose job it was to recommend various machines to the purchasing officer in the State Government. The R69S was very much faster, and also more expensive, than the plebeian R60, but it was said that the price of the R60 was acceptable enough to the authorities, and the machine was thus acceptable for purchase by the local Police force.

History has not recorded whether or not the Sergeant rode one of the new acquisitions, but he would surely have been disappointed had he done so. History has not recorded whether or not the above story is true, either, but it was certainly doing the rounds in the early sixties. The story was quite probably one of those urban myths which spring up all over the place because, had the switch of machines taken place and been discovered somewhere down the track the repercussions would have been dire indeed, for the pois*ed* hawk of retribution would then have swooped down upon the wrong-does and savaged them severely.

My first experience of a motorcycle with its gear lever on the 'wrong' side was when I rode a trim little 250 NSU up the narrow side lane adjacent to the Ryde store just prior to the bike being serviced. As I rode away I was concentrating hard on the strange, left-foot gear change, but at the top of the lane, with its tight right hander over loose gravel and broken bitumen, I braked lightly for the corner but the bike wouldn't stop! Naturally there was a car using much of the roadway as it was coming around the corner and this captured some of my attention, while I was somewhat gently cranked over at the time, so I wasn't about to use the front brake on the loose surface. I was of course expecting the normal retardation which would happen when applying the brakes, and so the bike actually seemed to *accelerate*!

The car slipped past with very little room to spare and the only thing to do then was to swiftly lift the bike up again and grab a handful of front brake, while trying desperately to bend the gear lever to the ground in the fond hope that it would help stop the bike. Of course it didn't help at all, but the front wheel was all but locked up, and I had almost come to a stop when I nudged a convenient telegraph pole head on at less than walking pace, came to an instant stop and unintentionally kissed the top of the bike's headlamp! Be assured, I coasted back down that little hill in neutral at less then walking speed, my right foot gently caressing the rear brake pedal all the way down.

By then Japanese motorcycles had begun to arrive, and they all had their gear levers on the machine's left side. But as a sop to the earlier British machines which had once abounded but were slowly disappearing, most of these new models had long, serrated shafts emerging from the opposite side of the gearbox with a corresponding long shaft on the brake pedal pivot. This was to allow anyone who couldn't yet come to grips with the control pedals on the opposite side to which they were accustomed to actually switch the two control levers around.

Very many riders did just that, particularly those who were beginning to race some of the very high performance racing machines which were emerging from Japan. It was felt, and with very good reason, that in the heat of battle a rider who had made his name riding a British motorcycle might come unstuck if he hadn't done so. It was felt that at the end of a long, fast straight a hard-charging rider, no matter how clever, might try to pull up by using a lever which was supposed to be employed in changing gears. That lever would be less than useless in trying

1956-1960

> *"He should have thanked his lucky stars that he didn't have a left-foot gear lever to concern himself with at the same time!"*

to slow down a very swift racing motorcycle, for a top rider in those days usually had one good stab at his old drum brakes, whether on the front or the rear, and losing even a second or two could see him into the fence, over the embankment or to be blown into the weeds by his opposition.

But we should be forever grateful for the fact that the only controls which were radically changed were the two levers which were used to change gear or to apply the rear brake. Can you, for instance, get your various heads around a Japanese – or, for that matter European, or even American – motorcycle which would come to this country with a left-hand twist-grip, which opened up the wrong way round? The Indian motorcycle was the first to ever employ a twist-grip control, and it was on the left handlebar (but worked the correct way), a twist-grip on the right side being used to advance or retard the ignition timing. Indian claimed the left grip allowed a frantic Police officer in earnest pursuit of a miscreant to be able to fire his revolver with his right hand, while controlling the speed of his machine with his left hand.

I once owned a large 1300cc Indian motorcycle, and rode the thing everywhere, so I have often been left wondering how anyone on this earth could hope to effectively control one of those monsters with just one hand on the tiller! Take one hand off the 'bars to change gear by hand and the front end would shake itself violently about like a Jack Russell which had just taught a swift lesson to a rat it had discovered eating the dog's dinner. Opening the throttle stopped all that nonsense at once, but what if you happened to be flat-out at the time, and trying to take a pot-shot at someone?

There is, however, at least one occasion I know of in which a twist-grip had to be located on the left handlebar, and which then had to be operated entirely the wrong way round. Most British motorcycles employed handlebars of ⅞" diameter, but Triumph 'bars were always one-inch in diameter, the right side swaged down to $^{15}/_{16}$" so that the two handlebar rubbers were then the same thickness.

Long before I knew him Ernie dal Santo had to deliver a Triumph motorcycle to the store at Top Ryde, and it had to be ridden there from the smaller store which was being closed in Burwood. The Triumph twist-grip on the bike was badly damaged for some reason, and was entirely beyond repair, with no other stock available for several days, and the normal ⅞" twist-grip couldn't be used because it was too small in diameter.

There happened to be a one-inch twist-grip lying about which was once fitted to an unknown pre-war motorcycle, and this was very easily screwed to the left side of the handlebars, but which then of course worked in precisely the wrong way. Roll it forward to go, and back again to slow down.

Nothing to it, you would think.... forward to go, roll back to back-off. Oh, if it were only that simple, because he had ridden motorcycles on the road, and had raced them as well for years, with a twist-grip on the right side which opened the way they still do to this day. Oh, and there was also a clutch lever on the left handlebar to think of, the operation of which made it impossible to ride the bike with any degree of smoothness. Can you imagine rolling the throttle forward, then back again as you grab at the clutch lever, and then trying to ease the clutch out gain while rolling the twist-grip forward? No? Neither can I. As for moving off from a standing start??

Ernie told me once it was the most perilous ride he had ever undertaken, for the traffic even in the early fifties was very heavy on Parramatta Road, and he was forever rolling the throttle off (that is, opening the throttle *up*) when traffic was slowing, and opening the throttle to the stop to get out of trouble and finding himself in even more trouble as the bike would suddenly slow dramatically.

He should have thanked his lucky stars that he didn't have a left-foot gear lever to concern himself with at the same time!

I have asked this question many, many times, to many, many people, but nobody can yet explain to me why it is that every motorcycle for sale anywhere in the world which has manually selected gears has a left side gear-change lever, with the rear brake lever on the opposite side. There may be very good reason for this, but nobody knows what the reason is. I must say I have long since come to grips with these arse-about controls, while still enjoying the occasional ride on a 'Classic' British or Italian machine which has these levers in the position in which they perhaps should still be were Nature's 'normal' dictates to be observed.

Ryde Motorcycles Sharpies

It has been my great pleasure over more than half a century to be heavily involved with motorcycles in every conceivable manner, from the purchase of my very first machine, a clapped-out old 1929 ES2 Norton which I bought in 1947 when I was still in school, to my many years employed in a variety of motorcycle dealerships.

On any given day I could be seen riding up to a dozen motorcycles of various shapes and sizes, from old bangers someone wanted to trade in on something a little better, a little newer, to brand new machines ridden off to be registered, or machines which had been recently serviced and then double-checked by a swift road-test. Among those many hundreds of machines were some of the best ever built, and indeed some of them were amongst the worst ever built. Most of them were solo machines, but more than a few of them employed a third wheel and chassis, with a sidecar body perched thereupon.

Sometimes, machines which someone might want to trade-in would arrive with frames which were slightly bent due to minor accidents but whose owners were ignorant of the fact until someone else rode the machine for the first time and discovered this. A machine might arrive which had brakes somewhat less effective than they should be, with an owner making the necessary mental adjustments as to braking distances, but which might not equate to stopping in time in an emergency situation.

For instance, a bike may fly around left-hand corners but have to be forcibly held down and eased through right-handers, or a brake lever might almost be pulled into the handlebars before it worked at all, or a foot lever be almost dragging on the ground before there was any indication of the bike slowing down, much less actually stopping! This became evident on many occasions when somebody would offer a machine as a trade-in on a later, or brand new, machine.

An example which springs to mind was on otherwise clean example of a 1953 Red Hunter Ariel, the rare VHA model with all-alloy head and barrel and probably the best of all the plunger rear suspension units. A fellow rode the bike to the Ryde store, offering to 'trade up' to a pristine 500cc AJS 'Spring-twin' we had on the showroom floor

For some odd reason, that Sports model Ariel – still referred to as the *Red* Hunter – employed a fetching powder-blue paint job (the same colour scheme at that time as featured on their unique, Wedgwood-blue 1000cc Square Four) and, amazingly and for no apparent reason, employed *cast-iron* flywheels, in place of the usual, stronger forged-steel components. Perhaps it was just one more example of some of the odd British thinking of the time?

I could feel straight away that the Ariel was not tracking true, and the first left-hander saw me having to heave the bike off its footrest as it dived into the corner with unbounded enthusiasm, while a following, sweeping right-hander was attacked as though it was one side of a giant hexagon instead of a nice parabolic arc.

We traded the bike in anyway, straightened the frame at the steering head and gave it our standard 'pre-sale' check-and-tune-up in the workshop. It ran very sweetly as a punchy 500 single, and virtually sold itself a couple of days later.

On another occasion, another 500cc AJS twin was offered to be traded which proved to have no effective rear brake at all. The lever had to be pushed down so far that the brake cam actually went over-centre, and that brake had to be applied by heaving it *up* with my heel, which hurt like hell and was in no way more efficient than operating in the right direction. With the brake pedal almost dragging along the ground, it might have made emergency braking an interesting experience during some serious cornering.

On more than one occasion, I came across the occasional *sharpie,* adept at playing strange games with us, which could be manifest in any one of several ways. One character came into the Top Ryde dealership and plonked down a twenty-five pound deposit on a Speed Twin Triumph which we had for sale at Eighty Pounds. After the financial papers were dealt with, he joyously rode the bike off into the sunset. He bought it back just two days later and said it was not quite suitable for his purposes even though he could find no fault with the machine.

I told him we would take it back, but he would of course forfeit his deposit. We then tore up his contract, with which he agreed, but upon sending it to the workshop for a check-up before we put it back on the floor it was discovered that the bike had covered just over **645 Miles** since he rode it away! He had hailed a Taxi and disappeared before we discovered this, but we put the bike back into the showroom at the original price and sold it with no problems. I suppose he was happy with his cheap 'loan' of the bike for Twenty-Five Pounds and we picked up some extra profit as well, so you could argue that everyone was happy with the deal.

On another occasion, we allowed a customer to take a BSA Bantam on a demo ride and he was away for some little time, which was a concern because we thought he might have pinched the thing. He duly returned, to tell us the front fork bushes were shot, the rear chain was not up to scratch and that the brakes were badly in need of repair. I knew this was patently untrue because it had gone through the usual workshop check-up and was not a bad little unit. I asked him how he came upon this information.

"I just took it into Gladesville to your opposition," he smirked, "and offered to trade it in on a 350cc Velocette. They went over it and told me what was wrong with it."

Knowing the way some dealers would often find fault with a machine an owner wanted to trade-in – and probably being more than a little guilty of this ourselves – I explained what in fact had happened and he agreed the bike was not bad 'considering it was what it was(?)' He bought the little bike, anyway.

I must say it was often up to my boss to take a trade-in for a squirt after I had ridden it, and usually advised an owner what a crap heap the thing was in comparison to the pristine example we had on offer. I was never, ever, asked to do this myself, and I was happy enough about that.

A bane of most dealers occurred when a potential customer asked a family 'expert' to come and look over a machine, and it was obvious the party concerned had no idea what he was talking about. Unlike the situation rampant in car sales yards, I never saw anyone kick a motorcycle tyre, but a machine 'examiner' would invariably give the throttle grip a couple of twists and then (always) heave on the clutch lever. No-one I spoke to about this could ever give a logical reason for the exercise. I wonder does this odd, if prevalent, behaviour apply to tyre-kickers as well?

We had a nice 500cc Velocette outfit on the floor on another occasion, which a fellow offered to buy, but he admitted he had never ridden an outfit before, so I took him up the road while he sat, happily enough, in the Murphy sidecar. When he got out he grabbed a couple of the bike's frame rails and gave then a bit of a shake, then did the same with the sidecar chassis, and then bounced the sidecar a couple of times on its leaf-springs for some odd reason.

Amply demonstrating that he had no idea what he was doing, he wrapped his hand round the still extremely exhaust pipe, and removed it very quickly indeed as the sound – and smell! – of sizzling skin filled the air. I could only assume he thought the exhaust pipe was another of the bike's frame rails! Through gritted teeth, which he flashed at me in what he felt was a smile, but was very much a grimace, he said he would take the outfit and I took him up the well-worn side lane to show him how to ride one of those exceedingly difficult devices.

He rode away very slowly after some time practicing; firstly with me trotting alongside him shouting advice, and then on his own. He came back a couple of days later with a subtle flesh-coloured bandage on his right hand and asked us could we order a new exhaust pipe and silencer for him. That was a bit odd, or so I thought, but when I went out to look at the bike, I discovered the exhaust pipe was almost ground away from about the gearbox to where it entered the badly-dented muffler.

It happens, he told me, that he had become a little over-enthusiastic and had speared into a left-hander much too quickly with no-one in the sidecar, shot across to the wrong side of the road with the sidecar wheel reaching for the moon and had slithered to a shuddering halt with the exhaust system well and truly ground away by the heavy kerbstone in the right-hand gutter.

Luckily no traffic was approaching from the opposite direction at the time, otherwise who knows what could have happened. As it happened, it was lunch time and I was about to zip down to the Station on the double-adult Panther outfit we had on display, so I took him with me and gave him a quiet lesson on the way. With me in the chair and shouting friendly advice at him – no, not *to* him, *at* him! – he rode the thing back to the shop, declaring himself happy with the trip and promising to shove a heavy sandbag in the sidecar whenever there was no-one he could con into going for a ride with him.

That was simply part of any old day's work in the motorcycle trade, folks, just part of the job. And a bloody good job at that!

Skiing

He was an insurance assessor for one of Sydney's biggest insurance companies, his job being to call into a variety of suburban motorcycle stores, big or small, to inspect machines which had been involved in accidents which were serious enough for the machines to need major repairs. That is not to say that the riders of those damaged machines would need

Ryde Motorcycles

major repair work carried out on them as well, although this was sometimes – I could say rarely – the case, but he always viewed those of us who got most of our jollies from riding motorcycles as people who were somewhat removed from the norm.

He called into Ryde on a more or less regular basis, and his name was Something Williams. 'Something' was not really his first name; I just can't remember what it was, but I remember he was some sort of distant relative of the P and R.Williams clan, the Sydney company which imported AJS and Velocette motorcycles. The company also had something to do with MG cars as well, but no-one I knew seemed to have any idea what that connection was.

The assessor always seemed to me to be very aloof as he looked down his nose at the trade and feigned a very superior attitude whenever he visited the place. In fact, he had a bit of a snout on motorcycles in general, and motorcyclists in particular. I found this fact quite odd because, as I often mentioned to him, he would have been out of a job if we weren't there at all, or if we weren't falling off the things – or bouncing off other vehicles – on a fairly regular basis.

His passion was skiing (or she-ing, as he so rightly called it) and I never tired of telling him how dangerous skiing could be, while pointing out I could ride uphill as fast, in fact a whole lot faster, in *summer* than he could going downhill in the middle of winter. I didn't have to wait for winter time, and an expensive weekend in some remote chalet, to be half-frozen and half-soaked most of the time while swishing downhill and wishing I could easily swish back up again. Oh, and I could indulge in this entirely delightful pursuit every day for all of twelve months every year; I didn't have to spend half a day getting from home to the snow fields to do that, either.

Further, I often suggested, I could corner on a solo motorcycle in the same manner as he would on his skis, and I suggested he had never felt the buzz of cranking a hard-ridden 500 single into a tightening uphill left-hander, a pot-holed or rippled road surface smoothed out – at least to some extent – by a suspension system which worked a whole lot better than the knee-action shock-absorbers he was forced to use, absorbers which were a bit on the flimsy side and with which he came equipped from birth.

Of course he didn't want to hear this waffle (you mightn't either) and couldn't be convinced of the arguments I put forth. No, she-ing was very much the pursuit of the well-heeled, he would bray, while motorcycling was for the less fortunate majority who couldn't afford the equipment or the high cost of the odd week-end in the fridge. How wrong that poor bugger was, but I could never convince his of that simple fact.

He could keep it, as far as I was concerned, because I would ride to work day-in and day-out, uphill and downhill, hot, cold, wet or dry, while he only had about three months or less of odd weekends to enjoy the same buzz I enjoyed every single day. He obviously thought I was a bit sad, while I knew more about what he was missing than he ever would.

Imagine my surprise – and, I confess, my delight – when he fronted at the store one wintry Monday with an arm in a sling, a subtle limp he tried manfully to conceal, half a tooth missing and a large, yellowing bruise in the middle of his forehead.

Although I had a fair idea of what had happened to him, it was with ill-concealed glee that I enquired about his injuries, and had to bite my lip almost till it bled as he shyly told me his sorry tale of a weekend which had gone horribly wrong.

He had finally persuaded a girl he had admired from afar to accompany him to the snow for what he thought was to be a dirty weekend, only to wreck their relationship when she disappeared with an Austrian ski-instructor after he crashed out of contention while waving to her on a high-speed descent while showing her how clever he was.

It transpired he had run into a hidden rock just off the defined ski-run and had then been pelted into a small pine sapling. The tree bent to the ground and then whipped upright again, cracking several ribs, busting the arm and doing no end of damage to the Jewels at the same time, as he was straddling the tree trunk when it decided to assume its normal, upright position.

I suggested it may be some time before he could emulate the pine tree's normal, upright position, which was probably the reason the Austrian enjoyed a more invigorating weekend with the nubile secretary than the poor assessor did. He fixed me with a baleful glare and said nothing, as he limped off to assess several machines while I had a quiet snigger at his expense.

I apologised to him later, because it really wasn't a funny situation. That tree would probably have written him off had it been any bigger, but at least it brought him down to earth a bit and demonstrated – more than words ever could – that our daily pursuits were no more dangerous than his occasional weekends in the snow. To his credit, he finally agreed.

He was going to enjoy a she-ing weekend in more ways than one, I suggested, and I thought it was all a bit sad when a promising sojourn into the freezer would end up so disastrously. Perhaps, I asked him, tongue in cheek, he would never again refer to his passion as she-ing? For some reason, he never mentioned the word again. Nor did he look quite so far down his nose at us mere motorcyclists, but conceded that one had to be on the far side of careful no matter what the pursuit. She-ing, he was forced to agree, had its dangers, and left it at that.

If, I said, as I allowed myself a parting sally, he had taken his girlfriend away on the pillion of a motorcycle for the weekend, and anywhere but the snow, he would have enjoyed the time away more, a promise would have thus been fulfilled and the Austrian would have had to look elsewhere for his jollies. I suggested that he could easily have borrowed a motorcycle from P and R. Williams showroom if he had wanted to, but I think I went too far over the edge in mentioning that.

This odd attitude to motorcycles and their inherent dangers was displayed on a later occasion, according to German production machine racer Helmut Dhane (the spelling is probably wrong, for which I apologise) who was visiting Australia for a series of races back in the early eighties.

It seems he was enjoying a holiday in the snow at an Austrian ski resort and slipped off his BMW motorcycle in the parking lot one cold and frosty morning. He busted an ankle in the tumble, and was taken to the local Hospital for repairs.

The Hospital ward in which he found himself was filled with ski enthusiasts in various states of disrepair. There were some with their necks in braces, some had legs sticking rudely into the air with heavy weights attached thereto, while others had their arms plastered from shoulder to wrist, their arms held in a salutary position at right angles to their bodies by a stick from elbow to waist.

One bloke, he assured me, looked like an escapee from a horror movie, his upper body (including his fat head) encased in plaster with a metal frame covering his face, which was being pulled back into shape by a series of jigs, dies and long threaded bolts which stuck out of his mouth, cheekbones and nose.

It was said this unfortunate skier was forced to consume his din-din in the form of a hearty soup, slurping it loudly through a thick straw which often collapsed if the mixture was too hot. The poor sod had gleefully leapt over a snow crest and lost an argument with a small pine tree which had suddenly sprung up in front of him, flattening his face in the process.

A couple of patients had their heads swathed in bandages and sat staring gloomily about with slack jaws and drooling mouths, one of them apparently shooing away non-existent blowflies which were bothering no-one but him. One or two patients lay moaning in bed, their injuries either not yet apparent, or yet to be addressed.

A Doctor, attended by a pair of mincing, pneumatic nurses who – according to Helmut – flaunted their charms shamelessly at a bunch of losers who could do nothing about it, was tut-tutting at the patients' charts as he did his rounds.

The good Doctor was apparently quite sympathetic to his charges, enquiring as to their well-being and discussing the various ski runs, and the skills required to negotiate them, thus displaying, as he did so, an intimate knowledge of the Chalet's various challenges.

When he reached Helmut's bed he placed a sympathetic hand on the newly-plastered ankle and gently asked how he was feeling.

"Tis der angle, hein?" he asked.

"Ja, tis der angle," Helmut confirmed, "und eet iz nut too bed." *You can now polish up your stage-German accent if you read this lot phonetically.*

"Und, er, vich off der rrruns dit you hev tze full on?" he asked kindly, "Vus it der Slallum, or tze Caratzel, or.." he half closed one eye and clenched a fist as he leaned forward, to whisper, "Der Viddowmeker!!"

"It vus der pukkink lut."

"Tze pukkink lut," he shouted as he stepped back in amazement, "Vere iss der pukkink lut?"

"Utside der Chalet, vere der karrzar."

"Tze Karrzar! Vus iss dass, tze Karzarr?"

One of the nubile nurses cupped a hand to his ear and explained what, and where, the car park was.

"You full offer in tze pukkink lut," he asked somewhat incredulously, "How dit you do tzat, eggsackly?"

"I full orf der mutterzycle,"

"Nein, das mottorrad?" the doctor stumbled back a pace, a hand flying to his throat. "You min you vos rrridink vun of zose dengarus tzings?"

"Nein, you cud hav bin kilt." he shouted

Ryde Motorcycles

disapprovingly, "Zose tzinks are dess trups, desss trups. Oohh, dir, you wus luggy to excape vis your live."

"Vot aboud tzis lot?" Helmut asked, "Loog at tze brrrokin buddies efferyvair. Tze are luggier tzan I am. I zlipped orf at vokkink spid."

"Ja. But tzeze are der scki zlopes," the doctor explained not unkindly, "Vun expecks tze ockazional exxedent on der scki zlopes. But mutterzycles? Nein," he shook his head as he moved on to his next victim. "Tzey are dess trups."

I cannot vouch for the accuracy of the previous dialogue, for there is no transcript of the proceedings, and no minutes were taken, but the good Doctor's philosophy is almost universal, I'm afraid.

Be that as it may, you will excuse me I'm sure. I'm off for a hard squirt along the Bells Line of Road; I'm going to attack that glorious series of corners in the Blue Mountains yet again while perched upon my motorcycle, for it is now the middle of summer and the road ahead beckons. Ah yes, the middle of summer, or spring, autumn, or even *winter* in this glorious country. I don't have to wait until winter's blast to arrive and then have to spend all day finding my way to the distant snow fields. I don't spend a couple of days in the freezing snow while only being able to slide downhill, then wait half a day to be conducted *uphill* again, at high expense, just so that I can slide downhill once more. I can to do all of that, uphill and down again, on just two wheels, and I can it from the moment I leave home!

Vicky

By 1948, just three short years after the war ended, the motorcycle trade in this country was booming as never before, with Australia still the world's largest importers of British motorcycles, but with only a very small sprinkling of the odd European machines to be seen here and there. By 1958, just ten short years later, it was almost as dead as a dodo, with the trade – not only here, but world-wide as well – hanging on by its fingernails, or sliding down the gurgler while many great and famous factories were soon to disappear or to severely curtail their operations.

With motorcycling almost at its lowest ebb, on the floor of Ryde Motorcycles in 1957 sat a forlorn assortment of about twenty or so second-hand British motorcycles and a lone plunger-sprung BMW. There was also a brand-new 500cc MSS Velocette we couldn't sell, while one of the last all-alloy 500cc OHC International Nortons was enjoying its happy birthday with us, having sat on that floor for all of 12 long months. They are both eagerly sought-after Classics today but unwanted when they were new more than half a century ago!

In desperation we had two new motor-scooters on the floor as well, a 125cc Vespa and a 150cc ISO, the latter machine built in some numbers – also in desperation, I have always felt – by *Iso-Rivolta*, one of the great Italian Classic car makers. We also had a trio of new pushbike-like Mopeds (MOtor assisted PEDal cycles) on the floor, all 50cc two-strokes – an NSU Quickly, the beautiful Austrian Puch, a three-speeder with telescopic forks, fan-cooled engine and neat swing-arm rear suspension, and a mid-blue, two-speed Victoria Vicky.

The Vicky`s tiny, 50cc two-stroke engine was almost hidden behind a pair of knee-high leg shields made from thin, cast aluminium – yes, *CAST* aluminium, the same material we see as fragile *cylinder barrel fins*!! The leg-shields were apparently listed as extras because, in the odd photo of the little machine I saw in later years, that Vicky was the only one which was fitted with leg-shields. The deeply-valanced front and rear mudguards featuring side panels attached to the front axle, and were also made from cast aluminium. The machine's forks were also cast alloy, while an unusual, large centre tube, which formed all of its tiny frame, contained the in-built fuel tank as well and from which the engine was hung.

The main casting was a long, slightly curved single component, made from cast aluminium alloy as well. It curved down from the steering head stem – which was cast integrally with the curved-tube 'frame' – and it swept up to form the pillar from which the cantilever-sprung seat was hung, while a small 'handle' was also a trim part of the large alloy casting, where it was sited between the two pedals.

The handle's purpose was clearly to allow the machine to be lifted bodily and carried away, should an owner ever wish to take it for a walk, or for some other obscure reason. It would have been easy to carry the Vicky about, because the little machine was certainly light enough, for *all* of the main structural components of the little Vicky on that showroom floor were made entirely from cast aluminium, including the bike's rear chain cover.

Front forks were leading-link, similar to the

type as fitted to the NSU, and as copied faithfully by the new, bright-red Honda step-thru, which was featured on that same showroom floor a year or so later. Rear suspension was, again like the NSU, not in evidence, with a single saddle which hung, cantilever-like, from its nose to take the edge off road shocks. The Vicky's centre-stand was made of thick 12mm wire, neatly bent to a tortuous shape and apparently sturdy enough – at least for the simple job it was supposed to do.

I must say that I have seen photos of the Vicky moped of around that period with a much more substantial centre-stand, and what is said to be a frame made from welded, steel pressings, with thin steel mudguards and other components, but the one of which I make mention was very different. It may well have been an unsuccessful, all-alloy, pre-production prototype orphan which might have been found to be too fragile. That could then account for the large, 'one-off' alloy leg-shields and lightweight, 'wire' centre stand, among other things.

The little bike could have been a fizzer as an early prototype and may have been 'dumped' in far-off Australia, where no-one would be likely to ever hear of it again. It remains the only Vicky moped I have ever seen – other than in old photos – and it was clearly a very early example, for later, more substantial versions employed rear suspension and steel components.

The Vicky importer's rep arrived one day and proudly announced that he could spin the pedals on the machine so quickly that the rear wheel would actually drive the bike and thus rev the engine much higher than it could ever rev on its own.

I didn't ask him to do so, for my boss was a bit touchy about anything he hadn't himself organised (you know the type), but the rep sprang to the bike and flicked the pedals to fire the engine up with the bike still on its centre-stand.

As the little engine burst into life, he opened the throttle wide and leapt on the pedals as the engine began howling beneath him, both he and the Vicky slowly disappearing in a cloud of pale-blue two-stroke smoke.

"Listen to this," he shouted as he bent to his task, head down and arse up, his legs whirling so quickly they vanished like humming-bird wings, his toes almost rubbing against the alloy leg-shields. Sure enough the engine revs rose higher and ever higher as he grimaced over his shoulder at me, his eyes bulging as though thrust out by little springs, his teeth firmly clenched, with a fleck of white foam at the corners of his mouth and his brow furrowed with effort, his face as red as the Vicky's tail-light.

His dustcoat had blown open, the tin belt-buckle pinging onto the spinning rear wheel and being flung out again at arm's length. I stood slack-jawed in amazement and/or admiration at the display before me, the while wondering what he could possibly do for an *encore* – if an encore was ever going to be called for.

"Watch this" he bellowed, as he snatched second gear with the left twist-grip, still pedalling frantically as the little bike rocked back and forth on its flimsy centre-stand, its engine howling frantically like a Banshee in torment.

Suddenly the door to the shop owner's office flew open and he stormed out. He stood in front of the bike and shouted something none of could hear, although his gestures were plain enough. He displayed impeccable timing, for in that instant the centre-stand collapsed and the bike flopped to the ground with a loud bang. The sequence which followed was awe-inspiring and was over in about seven seconds.

The bike was of course stationary when it hit the floor, but the rear wheel was doing about 70 Km/hour as it chirped loudly, spun for a second then bit hard and launched the little moped into its first ever – albeit unintentional, and entirely unrehearsed – wheelie. Sadly, it was also its last wheelie!

The 'rider', his arms by now forced over his head as if in surrender, virtually threw the Vicky at my boss and stood, open-mouthed, as the blue streak bounded vertically across the showroom floor like a large, unoccupied, and entirely out-of-control pogo stick. It spun the boss on his heels as it clipped him on the way past and he toppled against a large stand of Castrol oil bottles some of which fell to the floor with a crash and several odd tinkling sounds. The little bike, its throttle obviously jammed wide open, climbed a small step and slammed, still vertical, into the showroom's double-brick wall.

With a horrendous sound the moped exploded upon impact, alloy shrapnel flying in all directions. So help me, it went off like a giant, bright blue hand grenade. The bike's remains fell to the floor, spun around a couple of times, sobbed loudly and shuddered to a halt. A very small spattering of petrol/oil mix was splashed upon the wall, but fortunately it didn't burst into flames.

I leapt over the boss, who was writhing and shouting under one or two swiftly-emptying oil

Ryde Motorcycles

bottles and dashed to what was left of the Vicky, the bike clearly dead and bent in half with the front end located only by its control cables, its two wheels buckled into Ess-shapes.

Perhaps the alloy leg-shields formed part of the frame's structure as well; I never did find out, but I literally swept up three-quarters of the little blue machine with a dustpan and brush and shoved it into a cardboard box. The alloy castings were by now smashed to small granules, many of them for all the world like a broken windscreen.

It was amazing, I had never seen anything explode like it before nor since – except for the occasional piston, that is– for the little bike had virtually disappeared, leaving behind it nothing more than a huge scattering of small pieces of alloy castings, a couple of pretzel-shaped, wrecked wheels, a few drooping control cables and a pair of badly-bent handlebars! The poor little engine looked a bit the worse for wear as it lay on its side some distance away, as though someone had carefully removed it from the alloy castings and had then savagely flung it aside in a fit of pique.

I dunno what happened to the bike, or who paid for what, but I do remember its remains departing the scene in a Harley-Davidson side-box with the cardboard box securely strapped in place, the Figure-Eight shaped wheels stashed alongside it.

The German Victoria factory was famous for many excellent and innovative machines made during its 54-year history from 1912-66. I suggest the 50cc Victoria Vicky was not amongst them! The bike's small engine, it has been said, was quite powerful for its size, but the rest of the all-aluminium machine was assuredly fragile in the extreme.

As a postscript to this absurdity, a fellow called in a few days after the explosion and expressed an interest in the similarly-sized, 50cc NSU Quickly – *Quickly?* – but we couldn't get the engine to fire up. I cleaned the spark plug and replaced it, but the thing still wouldn't fire.

"Gimme the thing here," instructed the boss, still smarting from the previous day's events, as he took the little bike outside and pedalled it up and down for a while until, with a couple of loud belches and some rude flatulent sounds – from the bike as well – the thing suddenly took off like a rocket after the boss had jumped off and was trotting alongside it while bouncing the rear wheel to keep the engine turning over. In passing, I noticed that both tyres would benefit from the

> *"He used to be with the circus." I told him and he nodded a couple of times in acceptance of my asinine reply.*

heavy application of a large air hose, or at least a small tyre pump, for they were more than a little on the flat side.

With yet another throttle stuck wide open – thanks to some white-powdered verdigris-like residue inside the top of the carburettor body from standing around too long – the NSU executed the classic '*Lazy-S*' with the rider by this time belly-down on the single saddle, his arms at full stretch, with legs trailing behind, scuffing the toecaps off his precious, highly polished wall-toed brogues.

They disappeared down the steep Ryde Hill on the wrong side of the road weaving drunkenly about from lane to lane while entirely out of control and facing the streams of on-coming traffic, a trail of blue smoke in their wake, the un-attended pedals whirling around at an alarming rate, the incumbent (you couldn't call him a rider, at least not at that time!) clinging onto the handlebars for dear life.

I wonder what the other road-users thought, for he was very much in the company of late peak-hour traffic...... and about to meet a large number of them head-on, a very daunting task at the best of times for any machine, and no mean feat for an out of control moped, let me tell you! The tortured scream of many locked wheels and the angry blast of more than a few car horns announced his progress to us as he sped out of our sight; if not our hearing!

The would-be owner turned to me with a quizzical look and no little alarm on his face. "Does he know what he's doing?" he said, blinking once or twice.

"He used to be with the circus." I told him and he nodded a couple of times in acceptance of my asinine reply.

I didn't know whether to call an ambulance or not, because it was a full five minutes before they re-appeared – to my enormous relief – the boss riding the machine quite sedately, but out of the saddle and standing on the pedals while applying LPA (Light Pedal Assistance, they used to call it) as they breasted the rise.

He hopped off and tried to pretend nothing was awry, but a small tear on a trouser cuff and most of the toecap shredded off his left shoe bore mute testimony to the earlier drama as no words ever would. I noted a piece of grey sock peeping shyly through the toe cap and the merest hint of a pink toe-nail as well with a little red dot in its centre, but of course said nothing. I also noted that tyres on the illegal (for it was of course not registered at the time) NSU 'Quickly' had been magically inflated.

"Merely a stuck throttle slide, sir," said the boss by way of explanation for his performance. "We'll soon take care of that." Smiling wanly and displaying a subtle limp, he cradled the man's elbow in the cup of his hand as he man-handled him into his office. "Goes well, doesn't it?" he said rhetorically, favouring me with a sly wink as they disappeared inside.

Had I been his clearly-amazed client, I would surely have disappeared long before the duo ever breasted the rise on the way back to the store, but if the store's owner was surprised to see his client still there he showed no sign of this as he coasted casually to the footpath and handed the little bike over to me. The man bought the NSU moped, but I couldn't imagine why. Perhaps he was impressed with its impeccable handling (?) or its surprisingly spirited performance (??). Of course it may have been that the boss was a far better salesman than I had ever given him credit for being.

Model J Tinfield

The 1936 Harley-Davidson and side-box we used for deliveries was always a bit of a handful, even if it could quite easily pull more than its own weight of man and machine over a wide range of road surfaces and gradients. The outfit belonged to Ryde Motorcycles and it was used at the very least on a weekly basis, if now and again as a daily conveyance. The old outfit was un-registered, of course, because it would never have been able to be registered as it was anyway, for its lights didn't work any better than its brakes, clutch or gear-change mechanism did, and its tyres were a bit on the bald side when tyres back then needed all the tread they could get. But it was sort-of legit because it bore an entirely legal trade plate on the rear number plate bracket and was used in this guise quite often for the transportation of a large variety of motorcycles, or their associated parts, to various areas within the precincts

Many years ago, when British motorcycles were to be seen everywhere, the occasional European machine a novelty and no sign (yet) of the Japanese 'invaders', I was banging along with the old Harley and side-box (the device called a 'bun-truck' to most of us in the motorcycle trade, but for some unfathomable reason) when we came across that one-lane goat-track which was called the Prospect Highway (?) in those days.

I had borrowed the outfit for the weekend to carry home the complete frame, tin ware and running gear of a 175cc engine-less Gilera motorcycle, along with the peculiar, 'split-single', two-piston, one con-rod, one big-end, 125cc Puch engine (the twin-single, or 'twingle' to many of us) I was going to fine-tune and fit into the Gilera frame by fabricating a trim set of alloy engine plates. The completed bike, which I rode at Oran Park several months later, was called the 125MPG – for Morris-Puch-Gilera – the initials having nothing at all to do with its fuel consumption figures. I was on my way to a mate's place at the time with a near-new three-in-one entertainment unit he had just purchased and which was being carried – while being well secured – in the bun truck. My mate was also seated in the wide side-box and seemed to be comfortable enough even if he might have been illegally accommodated; the law being more than a bit grey in that area in the fifties.

As we came across the lumpy old Prospect Highway I beheld a motorcycle slowly approaching us, which turned out to be an eight-year-old 1948 500cc single-cylinder J-type Royal Enfield, a Very Ordinary Motorcycle which was very much the sadly underpowered 'cooking' version of the much more sporty Enfield Bullet. As a point of interest, a version of the Bullet Enfield is still faithfully reproduced to this day in far off India. The model J was a very much maligned machine, nick-named the Royal *Tinfield*, but it employed the same bore and stroke (84x90mm) as the Bullet sports model, and the same 'fully-floating' white metal big-end bearing, but there the similarity mostly ended.

The Model J bore an oddly-shaped cast-iron head and barrel, and a compression ratio of a miniscule 5.5:1, with a very small bore carburettor, and no rear suspension, a deeply-valanced, unsprung front mudguard was bolted in place just under the steering head, while the front forks were a spindly telescopic number. The earlier machines were fitted with the Dowty Oleomatic fork internals which were similar to the forks fitted as standard equipment to early Velocette, Panther, Scott, EMC and a few other motorcycles.

Ryde Motorcycles

Dowty were world famous for their substantial landing gear and undercarriages fitted to large commercial aircraft, but their telescopic front forks for motorcycles left much to be desired – particularly if your primary desire was for an efficient, trouble-free, comfortable and reliable suspension system on the front end of your machine.

If the dull Model J had little going for it, other than cheap utility transport, then the much more acceptable 350 and 500cc Bullet models were something else again. The sporty Bullet Enfield enjoyed a much smarter colour scheme and employed a very much more shapely cylinder head and barrel, the cylinder head in light alloy, with a higher compression ratio piston, larger carburettor, slightly more sporty cam profiles and was one of the very first British production motorcycles (if not the first) to be fitted with swing-arm rear suspension, the system adopted in 1948, not long after the awful Model J had appeared. The Bullet later employed its own design for a much more substantial front fork, the fully-sprung machine a fairly nippy performer with very fine handling thrown in for good measure.

The extremely plump Model J rider was creeping up to the intersection, and seemed to be paddling the bike along, with both legs out-thrust like a pair of bony outriggers. As I pulled up, for he was on my right and was thus guilty of the once-sacrosanct 'right of way' rule, I noted that his entirely round face was like a large tomato which someone had trodden on. His face was the same colour as that fruit we use as a vegetable, the face apparently squashed and somewhat out of shape, with odd, non-standard creases here and there and rough wrinkles randomly scattered about it. I also noted, as he came closer to us, that his eyes appeared to be firmly closed! He was also vigorously nodding his head – I assumed at me – as though giving us the go-ahead to shoot across the intersection, so I gunned the engine and made to lurch across his bows.

Suddenly, his red-rimmed, bloodshot eyes flew open and his neck stiffened up as he made to dive underneath us and then he slammed the front brake on while still cranked over and was of course neatly pelted over the handlebars. He was wearing little more than a thin sports shirt and grey trousers, his feet slipped into a pair of Roman sandals, with a pair of red-and-white football socks worn inside them. Because he was wearing socks-and-sandals I was thus forced to assume he was either an Englishman or someone from New Zealand: it turned out that he was neither one thing nor the other, for he was from some indescribable area in Ireland, with an accent you couldn't slice through with a carving knife.

I did a swift full-lock turn to the right – thankfully, for all its faults, the most redeeming feature of the old Harley was its effortless steering, for it could slice through corners with consummate ease, the light steering as though power assisted – and pulled up at the man's right elbow. He began to sit up and looked dazedly about him, the Tinfield lying alongside him on its left side with the engine plonking quietly away, the rear wheel still spinning. Royal Enfield motorcycles in those days were fitted with an Albion gearbox, the box's main feature being a very handy little lever above the right-side mounted gear-lever which could be depressed to allow neutral to be selected in any gear other than first. I shoved the lever down to select neutral, and ran around to the other side and heaved the bike upright, while my erstwhile passenger heaved the rider upright at the same time.

As he was held upright, but then slowly subsided again into a sitting position, the Tinfield owner said something which I could hear quite clearly, but which I couldn't understand at all. Firstly, there was the man's thick unintelligible accent, allied to the fact that he was as drunk as it was possible to be and still be alive, while his lips were flapping about all over the place and his unrestrained tongue was darting in and out of his slack mouth like a chameleon on ultra-fast motion. This was clearly because there wasn't a tooth in his head! As it happens, he *did* have a full set of teeth, but they were entirely detachable, and they were grinning wanly at us from within the confines of his top shirt pocket, where they had managed to accomplish something which would have been physically impossible had they been safely carried where they should have been carried all along. As a result of him landing almost face down on the roadside, he had somehow managed to bite himself deeply on the left breast! Surprisingly, this appeared to be his only injury.

He sat up and peered b(l)eerily about him and said something else which I managed to make some sense of, for I was just coming to grips with the strong accent. "Could ya tairl me where de bloody 'Ell oyam?" he croaked, his breath savage enough to blister the paint on his bike, which was by then on its stand close by. I told him he was sitting on the roadway beside the Prospect Highway. "Dat's a foony ting," he said, "Oi kin remember tournin' left frahm Paddy Royan's sharp oon Charch Strit, boot Oi cairnt remember nuttin' else. Oi musta dozed orf, of soomtin', Oi tink. Oi bin norn ta doo dat narn agin."

Quite apart from the fact that a right turn – yes, that's a *right* turn, not a *left* turn- from Ryan's Motorcycles on Church Street Parramatta onto the Great Western Highway on the way to Prospect was entirely illegal, but to have a giant skinful of grog on board as well was really looking for trouble, because the bloke was far too drunk to be able to stand upright, much less ride a motorcycle. How he had managed to ride his Tinfield as far as he had – it was all of about 6-8 Kilometers – was beyond me. Clearly, he had been asleep at the time we met him, which was why his eyes were closed as his head was nodding at us.

"Har's me boik?" he suddenly asked, "tis naht smushed oop, is it?" "Well, it's nothing like as smashed as you are, mate" I told him, "where were you headed anyway?" "Waddya min, smushed oop. Oi even't broarkin nuttin ahn meself, have Oi?"

"Look mate, all you've done is bitten yourself on the left tit!" My friend suddenly exclaimed, and with some annoyance in his voice. "You had your teeth in your shirt pocket, you fool, while they should still have been in your mouth."

The bloke managed to get the message across to us that he had brought up his lunch outside Paddy's shop and had forcefully ejected the teeth at the same time, so he had (he thought prudently) placed them in the top pocket of his shirt in case he had shoved them back into his mouth again and lost them if he repeated the performance. He then took his teeth out and wiped them on his shirt, and spent several seconds trying to focus on them before he placed them back inside the receptacle in which they would normally reside. It made his utterances even more difficult to understand, because those teeth surely belonged to someone else, for they were a terrible fit and were so loose that they were jumping about all over the place as he strove to be understood, and they threatened to fly out of his mouth at any time. He had to clamp his jaws tightly closed to stop them from being ejected again, which meant we were back *beyond* square one, because we simply couldn't understand him at all!

We couldn't leave him where he was because he was likely to fire up the Tinfield again and attempt to ride it home, so we managed to finally understand that he lived in Blacktown – which was only about another ten clicks or so up the road – so we bundled him and the bike into the bun-truck and trickled away, the side-box by now jam-packed with *two* passengers, the three-in-one sound system and bike as well. There were several conveniently placed eye-bolts located in the box along with some lengths of rope which were there to secure up to two motorcycles at a time, so there was some little room, but it was still a tight squeeze.

The man was asleep again when we dropped him off at his home. We banged on the door but no-one answered, so we woke him up again and made him comfortable on an old settee which was on his veranda then wheeled the bike down the driveway and into the small garage. I removed the spark plug – in case he wanted to ride away again – and sat it on the top of a small bench where he could find it easily enough when he was wide awake, then we rode away and left him to it.

To fall asleep while riding a motorcycle must be a rare event indeed, and to do so would surely be a very, very dangerous thing, but I have heard of one – just one – other instance in which someone fell asleep while riding a bike. The man (who shall of course remain nameless, but who was *very* well known in motorcycle circles at the time) was working for Bennet and Wood in Sydney and was riding home on a brand new 1948 500cc shaft-drive S7 Sunbeam. For some unaccountable reason there remained for a great many years a monument right in the middle of the road at an intersection of two major arterial roads in Summer Hill, a Sydney suburb, and it was into the base of this monument that our rider turned his attentions one early evening while wending/weaving his way home.

He was known to enjoy a cleansing ale or two – or three, or four, or maybe more – but the question of his state of consciousness at the time of the accident has never been established. But he rode that bike head-on into the monument and had no recollection at all of how he managed to get where he was and how he managed to run into the thing. He was not injured, and the bike was not damaged so badly that he couldn't ride it home from there, but he always claimed he must have been asleep at the time of the prang, because the first time he was aware that he had crashed the new bike was when he was picking the thing up from the roadway. To make matters

Ryde Motorcycles

even stranger, he never rode a motorcycle through that area on his way home for he always followed a totally different route.

Now then, let's look at some of the information which we heard, and some info which we either made up, or had assumed: was the Sunbeam rider in fact asleep, and if so, for how long? Was he actually sober or did he have a skin-full of grog earlier in the evening? The facts at this time and in this place are very clear – and that is no-one knows, and no-one ever will.

But surely there must be a Deity somewhere, and of some description, whose task it is to keep a caring eye on most, if not *some*, of us, because it remains a mystery how *anyone* could ride a motorcycle any distance at all while asleep at the bars instead of being in total in possession of **all** their faculties, allied to more than a little luck as well.

After hours mechanic

The sole mechanic at Ryde Motorcycle, the suburban dealership for whom I worked for some six years prior to 1961, was a bloke called Ernie Dal Santo, a very clever, mostly self-taught engineer, who was later to make quite a name for himself as a very successful tuner of Classic racing motorcycles. His job, as ever in those small, if essential establishments, was to carry out any and every type of repair imaginable – along with some which were not! – and it varied widely on a daily basis.

He might be involved in the first 1000 mile servicing of a brand new machine at one point, then dismantling an engine which needed major repairs at another time; perhaps straightening a frame which had been bent in a minor accident, possibly panel-beating a dented fuel tank; welding a mudguard stay which had come adrift… it could be the most interesting job for someone with the passion for those things, for each day brought its own challenges, to which he always provided his own solutions.

He sometimes worked for a couple of hours at night if he couldn't finish a job off in time and on those occasions I would sit with him while he worked. One evening we were sitting on a couple of four-gallon oil drums in the workshop, discussing nothing in particular as Ernie worked on somebody's bike which had been promised to be finished first thing next morning. It was about 7 o'clock, the place having been closed since 5.30pm.

There was a pair of tri-fold doors at the workshop entrance in the side lane and these had been closed, their three shot-bolts locked, but with the large wooden bar which secured the entrance not yet in place. There was thus some springiness in the overlap where the two doors met, though they were by no means easy to pry apart; assuming we would ever want to do that. In the normal course of events we would simply remove the wooden beam, lift the shot-bolts from their holes drilled in the concrete floor and slide the doors open in their well-oiled tracks.

As we chatted quietly that evening, we could hear some scraping sounds outside, the scuffing of boots on the rough gravel surface and a couple of muffled curses followed by a long sigh of what sounded like a combination of exhaustion, frustration and relief.

Then, with no announcement of any sort, the doors began to bang and rattle, while the back of a hand, its attendant wrist and then a fully extended arm, slid through the gap between the doors. We sat transfixed as this was followed shortly thereafter by the appearance of an oil-stained, wool-lined right boot with the right leg of a pair of paint be-spattered trousers tucked into it.

I remember we glanced at each other for a second as a shoulder was then slid painfully into view, and then a head bearing a face with a purplish tinge, bulging eyes and jaws a-gape made its appearance, its owner straining mightily to gain admittance through an opening which a cockroach might have found too daunting to attempt.

The head then withdrew, to be replaced much lower down by a large backside and then with a large crack and some rending sounds the rest of the body magically appeared. The vision which confronted our frankly amazed eyes was then complete, except for the left boot, which was to be seen ensnared within the still-narrow gap of the tightly closed doors. There was much muttering and cursing as the complete person bent to retrieve the boot by wriggling it about, and then slipped it on over a naked left foot.

He then turned to face us as though it was the most natural thing in the world to do, grinning the while as he displayed some well-gapped teeth which looked like a series of badly maintained, stained and lichen encrusted tombstones in a very old cemetery. He grasped the front of his tattered trousers and made an extremely personal adjustment as he executed a grotesque burlesque of a balletic curtsy, the while rolling his eyes and pursing his lips. It was a remarkable performance.

Vintage Morris

1956-1960

> *"Hang on a minute," he said as he went back to the narrow opening through which he so recently squeezed himself. "I'll go and get me chain."*

"You blokes still open?" he asked, favouring us with what he fondly imagined was a smile, but which indicated to us that he knew very well we were not.

"No," I said, not unkindly. "We closed a couple of hours ago."

"Great," he replied, ignoring what I had just told him, "Have ya gotta con-link for me chain? I just snapped it. I had to push me bike here from Gladesville." I might add that Gladesville was the next suburb along, but was about four kilometers away and he would have pushed his bike mostly uphill to get to where we were. No wonder he was so relieved to find us 'open', or at least still on the premises.

"Hang on a minute," he said as he went back to the narrow opening through which he so recently squeezed himself. "I'll go and get me chain."

As we were quite obviously going nowhere I obligingly slid one of the shot-bolts up and opened the door for him while he briskly trotted over to his bike and brought the limp chain inside. And what a sad looking chain it was at that. It was bone dry, covered with a fine powder of brown iron oxide and it rattled badly when I took it and laid it on the its side on the floor.

I bent the ends of the chain and the ends almost met in a perfect circle, the pins all loose in their side plates.

"This chain has long since had the claw," I told him, "It's eaten away by red oxide and all the plates are loose. It'll go off like a hand grenade at any time. If your chain's like this what the hell are your sprockets like?"

I knew this guy very well because he was one of our customers and he was as tight-fisted as it was possible to be.

Whenever he needed work done on his AJS single he would always ask for a quote first. I would have to give him a vague idea of what it would cost and I always erred on the high side, and explained it was by no means a firm figure, but it made no difference to him whenever he came to pick the bike up.

"What are ya gonna stiff me for this time?" he would invariably ask. No matter what the job cost he would always complain about the price. "That's a bit steep, isn't it?" was his stock reply, and on one occasion I stared him in the face and uttered those very words at the same time as he did, while he (again) politely asked if I could "take the edge off it a bit."

On another occasion when he asked the cost of servicing I said softly "Funchburble."

"That's a bit steep isn't it?" he asked, for the umpteenth time.

"What is?" I innocently replied.

"The price you just quoted" he said.

"I didn't mention a price," I gloated, "I said Funchburble."

"Funchburble?" he queried, with an upward inflection, "What's Funchburble got to do with it?"

"Nothing" I replied, more than a little tersely, and sick of his attitude ."You caught yourself out that time. You complained about the price of the job – again! – without being given a price to begin with." He was not amused at the jibe and paid up with a bad grace then stamped briskly out of the place.

I hadn't seen him for months, except for the occasions in which he rode stiffly past the shop, and here he was back again, after we had 'officially' closed and having gained access through an almost impregnable door.

I felt sorry for the poor bugger, because it appeared no-one had laid a spanner on his bike since we last saw him and it was badly in need of some TLC. So, too, was he, I thought.

"Wheel your bike in," I said, "and we'll have a look at your sprockets while you are here."

He meekly wheeled the AJS in and there was no surprise to see the "teeth" on the rear wheel sprocket were not much more than small humps, while a torch shone on the countershaft sprocket showed it looked like a disc with a series of thick fish hooks on it.

"As I expected, your sprockets have gone as well." I told him, "We have an exchange re-banded rear brake drum in stock with new teeth shrunk on and brazed into position. That will save you heaps on a new one." Not surprisingly he seemed to like the sound of that, but when I mentioned he would then need a new countershaft sprocket **and** chain he turned a pale shade of green, which deepened when I explained that the entire clutch assembly would need to be dismantled to reach the smaller sprocket and then re-assembled to finish the job.

"Gawd, how much is that gonna set me back?" he gasped.

"Dunno," I said triumphantly, "But it has to be done. You won't get home with what you've got here, mate. Let me assure you of that."

"By the way," I added, "how do you think your

Ryde Motorcycles

primary drive chain from engine to gearbox is, or the generator drive chain, which is right next to it? It's a safe they aren't much better than the rear one. In fact, I'll bet they're a bloody sight worse. Oh, and you would probably have to replace the cast-iron clutch centre while it is removed because the thin splines are probably nearly cactus as well. It's a bit of a weak link in Burman gearboxes."

I escorted the bloke to my then-vacant oil drum and assisted him into a semi-prone position as the bad news sank in.

"I can't afford to do all that!" he exclaimed, "It's worth more than me bike is."

"I know," I countered, "But you can't afford *not* to do it either."

He stood up and wandered about muttering to himself, wiping his brow and dabbing at his face with a filthy oil rag he found on top of one of the benches.

"Look," he said finally, as he turned to face us looking for all the world like an Al Jolson impersonator, "Can I leave me bike here while I go away and think about this?"

I assured him we would take good care of the AJS and he tottered off into the night.

We never saw him again, and his bike – which would now be looked upon as a very acceptable Classic motorcycle – sat with about a dozen or more off-casts of similar vintage which sat in the darkened corner of the shop for many months.

It was still there when I left the store for greener pastures and was, I have been assured, placed with several others into a shallow depression as fill for a large concrete slab which was initially used as a parking lot.

Unhappily, Ryde Motorcycles is long gone, the once-dominating, two storey, double-brick building long since demolished to make way for an additional lane on the widened Devlin Street site. But beneath that inner, third lane there still lie several old motorcycles which might be revered Classics today. If I refer to them as buried treasure, but treasure which will probably never be unearthed in any of our lifetimes, I reckon it might describe the final resting place of those once-proud old British motorcycles very well.

I could draw a mud-map of the area and mark their grave with a large X to mark the spot, should anyone be interested, but that section of roadway is far too busy to ever be torn up, so those bikes will probably remain there until some archaeologist digs them out several centuries from now. I wonder what scientists of that era would make of that exciting discovery?

Chlorophyll

One occasionally sees it on the shelves of dedicated Health Food Stores, for its attractions are little known today, but back in the fifties to early sixties the manufacturers of a large range of deodorants, toothpaste, breath fresheners and highly-specialised, boiled lollies were loudly extolling the unquestioned virtues of a brand-new compound called *Chlorophyll*. For a very good reason the material seems to exist mainly in toothpaste these days. This magic material was claimed to provide the answer to *all* the ills associated with a wide variety of offensive body odours, which is the reason it had suddenly been applied to almost everything to do with personal hygiene. One either chewed on a green tablet or two, fizzed some stuff under one's armpits or cleaned the teeth with any one of a large number of bright green toothpastes.

Here was a newly-discovered material, the publicity enthused, which was made from some component found in the green, green grass of home, and its extraction and subsequent use was certain to make one, among many other things, at once attractive to members of either sex. It was insisted upon that the use of this miraculous ingredient would assure one's sudden acceptance in all areas of Polite Society, regardless of how much one may have been on the nose prior to the adoption of this universal *panacea*.

It was stated that the material was, in effect, a type of 'plant blood' with a startling similarity to human blood, and that the refinement of the plant material would naturally be of great benefit to us all, and not only in the manner in which it would greatly reduce the entirely normal odours to which all bodies are prone. However, more recent studies have indicated that, by the time the material had been heavily processed into a wide variety of products, it no more resembled the original chlorophyll than methylated spirits resembled the sugarcane from which it was derived. Arguably, its benefits may therefore have been of little, or no, use at all.

There were plastic models of both genders grinning into TV cameras, their faces aglow, their teeth white enough to glow in the dark, while they prattled on about the virtues of this wonderful, newly-discovered cure-all. Chlorophyll was the buzz word in those days, and it was used in almost everything you could think of. It was never said to be used as a fuel additive to freshen the exhaust gasses, or to remove carbon dioxide from the atmosphere; but that is probably because nobody thought we would accept that.

The publicity blurb was not always accepted, because I well remember a piece of doggerel written by a frankly-disbelieving poet who once wrote "Why reeks that goat on yonder hill, who eats his fill of chlorophyll?" How dare he fly in the face of what everybody was expected to believe was the new Saviour of Us All? Whoever this bloke was he seems to have disappeared without trace. Perhaps the Chlorophyll Purveyors shot him, or otherwise shut him up, for as far as I know he was never heard from again; unless of course he had then pursued a career with Hallmark, or someone else who would appreciate his obvious talents as a poet.

We all know that cows, goats and sheep are smarter than our most brilliant scientists, because these creatures seem to have no trouble at all in converting grass into milk, and they appear to do this with contemptuous ease. But having been closely associated with a number of these critters on more than one occasion, I have to state categorically that chlorophyll has *never* freshened the breath of **any** of them! The best examples by far are the various species of goats, whose ripe breath has often been known to actually blister the paint on red-hot furnace doors. Or so I have been advised.

I confess I have been known to shout "Goat's Breath" out of the window of the large touring bus I drove for many years while taking one or another of my production shows on the road, but this only happened if some myopic oaf who happened to stuff my approach to a long, steep mountain pass which I had been preparing to attack while building up a good head of speed long before I arrived at its foot. "Here comes a rattly old bus," I can hear this idiot intone, " I'll just kangaroo out of this side track and lope along casually as I ease my way up this gradient. He won't be anywhere near me for a while yet."

Little would this jackass know that the 32-seater Toyota Coaster he had so recently vilified had been fitted with a 3-odd litre six-cylinder Holden 186 motor to replace the asthmatic 2-Litre four originally specified, allied to a higher-ratio diff and several detailed engine modifications, not to mention a specially modified suspension, Bilstein double-acting gas shocks and rally seats. All this was done not so much for speed as for the ability to climb steep hills with alacrity and to allow the cast (some of whom were amongst the finest performers this country has ever seen, or will ever see) to remain as relaxed and comfortable as possible.

That errant driver would also be unaware of the fact that I would be closing on him at a very rapid rate of knots, and he was very soon about to know all about it! Therefore the shout "Goat's Breath", I suggest, would be entirely appropriate to that situation.

I have no wish to insult any goats which may be reading this piece – or their owners, for that matter – but there have been several examples of the absurdity of claiming that chlorophyll, that element contained within green things like grass, broccoli and stinging nettles and which purportedly removes the pong from those of us who don't know the trouble we are in, actually works. In a word, my experience of the stuff indicates that it doesn't bloody work at all! Or if it does work, then it's pretty subtle about it.

The BSA was being punted along with some enthusiasm and I had just flung the thing into a tightening left hander under power and with the footrest skimming the ground, when I suddenly beheld a convoy of about 40 large bullocks strolling casually along the grass verge on the left-hand side of the road, a hundred meters or more up ahead. Even from that distance I noted that they seemed to be perched on the tips of their hoofs, with their backsides tightly clenched.

I have always entered these types of corners with some caution, simply because you don't know what is just out of sight around the bend, but I wasn't prepared for what was soon to befall me, even though the sight of that group of bulls was by no means unexpected. But what was unexpected was that the air was suddenly filled with a throat-tightening stench of monumental proportions as I suddenly noticed that these apparently amiable creatures had just enthusiastically fertilised the roadway ahead.

But far from being the usual small piles of cow-cakes, most of which one can manage to avoid, the roadway was liberally coated with a thick film of gunk which looked like the Army had been past and spilled a large 44-gallon drum of khaki camouflage paint, which now coated the road ahead with a heavy, oil-like film. I was shortly to discover the gunk covered the rear legs of those hapless beasts as well. To make matters worse, the bulls had not strolled directly across the road, but had casually loped along the tar-sealed roadway for quite some distance and gleefully sprayed the remains of their lunch all over the surface.

So help me there was more BS on that stretch of

road than you would sweep up after a week-long session in Canberra's Lower House, or within the confines of the Annual General meeting of the Dodgy Used Car Salesmen's Association.

Of course it got worse and worse again, because my BSA was shod with a frightful 3.25 x 19" Olympic Patrol tyre on the front and an even worse 3.50 x 19" *Black Spot* Patrol on the rear. These tyres were almost square in section when viewed head-on, so that when cornering one was always on a knife-edge of hard rubber which in itself was bad enough, but that material had about the same co-efficient of friction on a road surface as a house-brick might have. In those days, it must be noted, there was very little choice in the rim-protectors which were available, but those shockers were perhaps the best of a pretty poor lot.

There was nobody coming in the opposite direction, so I could at least heave the bike up a little as I swiftly entered the minefield, but I dropped it over a touch further before I did that, to allow for quite a bit more room on the exit. My Polaroid goggles were fogging up and my eyes were watering as the air around me was filled with that frightful stench. I couldn't touch the brakes, of course, but I eased myself off the single saddle to await the onslaught as I shot into the stuff.

So help me, I didn't know which way was up! I felt the handlebars see-saw from lock to lock several times, the bike side-on to the left and then to the right as I felt the muck being flung up against the old Belstaff greasies, the air around me not so much ripe as rotten. I had to flop onto the seat and drop a foot to the roadway once or twice because the road surface, I swear, was as slick as if it had recently been oiled.

The bike was pretty well out of control as we swung wide on the exit and onto the grass verge at the side of the road, where fortunately there was a little more grip, and I remain uncertain whether or not I rode along the foot-wide parapet of cast concrete which reinforced the roof of the small brick bridge which we suddenly flew over. I was able to slip back a gear, and then try the front brake, which scrubbed a bit off, but there was still a bit of that pungent stuff here and there along the roadway ahead and the bike by now was under a measure of control so I slowed to a trickle on that grass verge and tried to clear my head.

The sinuses were clearer than they had been for years, but my eyes were watering and the pulse rate, I'm sure, was well elevated.

I rode gingerly up to the man who seemed to be looking after these creatures. "What's wrong with them?" I asked him. "What's wrong with what?" he replied. "Those cows, what's wrong with them?"

"For a start, mate" he said, "they're not cows, they're bulls, and I dunno what's wrong with them. That's why I'm taking them all to the vet. They've been like that for a week. But don't come any closer, I smell like a bloody vintage glue factory" That last piece of information was unnecessary, because the stench was all-enveloping and I couldn't get away from there fast enough, particularly as a couple of the bulls were coming back to hear what I had to say. One of them appeared to be pawing at the ground, while several of them were emitting a large variety of wind-induced noises which were not helping the situation in the slightest. I must say though, that some of these sounds, wet as they were, seemed to be almost harmonious.

Fortunately, there was a small rustic stream a few clicks further on, in which I was shortly to be seen paddling about to wash most of the muck of boots and greasies, but of course the engine, and in particular the hot exhaust pipe, had managed to have a liberal coating of fetid fertiliser baked on. It took several days, and the application of a stiff wire brush, portable grinder and a cold chisel to get most of it off. Not *all* of it mind, so for some little time thereafter I was reminded anew of the 'Episode of the Loose-Bowelled Wandering Livestock' whenever I fired up that old BSA to take it for a squirt.

Perhaps I should have taken those con-merchants to court for flogging the virtues of chlorophyll as a natural cure-all for all unsavoury body odours, for I suggest they may have been obtaining money under false pretences. I could have produced clear evidence that a group of young bulls had consumed large quantities of fodder which must have contained enormous amounts of their much-lauded chlorophyll material. I would be there to say that no self-respecting cow would have come within a bull's roar – bull's roar? – of those stench-ridden blokes.

There could be little doubt that any self-respecting jurist who would be involved in any litigation would agree with my submission, were they to be invited to have a quick sniff at the hot exhaust pipe of the old BSA; provided it was able to be presented as evidence in Court. I feel the jury would immediately have sent those chlorophyll-flogging charlatans to gaol for life; that is, assuming there was any justice in this world.

Foul weather at Ryde

It was one of those frightful days which often bode ill for the casual traveller, whether 'safe' within the confines of a four-wheeled metal cocoon, or riding a motorcycle while being lashed by heavy rain and being pelted about by blustering, high winds. The weather was on the far side of foul on that day, the imposing building which sat atop two major intersecting roads entirely open to the elements, thus bearing the brunt of the high winds which howled about the structure. The rain was heavy and unrelenting as it flung its deluge of water against the three showroom windows, the glass panes rattling alarmingly in their metal sockets as though they threatened to burst in upon us at any moment.

We had watched the rain and swirling winds as they slowly crept up the valley from Rhodes and Meadowbank, so its arrival at the Ryde Motorcycles dealership was no surprise, but the ferocity of it when it *did* arrive was certainly surprising. It's an ill wind, we have often been advised, and though it was not the ideal day to be selling a motorcycle to someone, at least we could take care of some of the paper warfare which had piled up for a while.

You can't make much money shuffling papers around (unless you are a Bank CEO, or an overpaid Bureaucrat) but attending to this most boring of enterprises is all too often as much part and parcel of earning a crust in any business as flogging your product might be.

So we sat there, scratching about in several legers, counting stock and making out orders, sucking on the odd cup of tea, and generally not looking forward to a damp ride home later in the day, when a Taxi pulled up outside, and a very welcome person emerged from it. The person was indeed ***most*** welcome, not so much because we knew him, for none of us had ever clapped eyes on him before, but he was very welcome because he emerged from the comfort of that Taxi wearing a complete outfit of specialised, waterproof motorcycle clothing! I thought that was a Very Good Omen.

As he emerged he unfolded a small cloth cap and stuck it on his head as he approached, smiling the while, and banged upon the firmly locked front door. In those days the few people around who wore helmets on the road were people like me, and I only wore one because helmets were warm, waterproof to some degree, and were easier to keep in place than the odd cloth cap – or fashionable ski-cap, with its fold-down flaps and chinstrap – which most of us used to wear: with goggles, of course.

There were road race helmets and touring safety helmets for sale even in the late forties and mid-fifties, but they were not yet obligatory, and I had sold many of them some years earlier, but helmets were mostly looked upon as a bit poofy, if not downright sissy, so most riders still rode about wearing cloth caps. Occasionally, there were to be seen the odd – very odd – Disposal Store leather helmets pressed into service, the type which had been worn by fighter pilots during the war, but for some reason they were usually looked upon with some disdain, very practical though they were. At one time I had sold a bunch of those leather helmets as well.

My meagre base salary in those days was augmented by the sum of ten shillings (that's one dollar in the *new* money, folks!) each time I sold a second hand motorcycle, and a full pound if the bike was new, and the money was paid at the end of each four week period. Doesn't sound like a lot, I know, but I could sometimes end up with more than an additional week's wage at the end of each month, if it was a good month, and this was very handy money indeed all those years ago.

And so as chief motorcycle salesman, clerical assistant, spare parts manager, floor sweeper, road tester, oil changer, tea man, caretaker, (sometime) workshop organiser, window cleaner, bike polisher and all-round dogsbody I duly trotted to the front door, quickly whipped it open and swiftly dragged the grinning client inside, slamming the door behind him, in fact almost leaving him on the *outside* in my haste to do so.

"I've come to buy a motorbike," he announced un-necessarily, "I like the look of that Royal Enfield." He pointed directly to a trim, and spotlessly clean, 500cc twin-cylinder machine of about 1953 vintage, the bike by then about four years old, and well looked after by its previous owner. I could only admire his choice of motorcycle, and his undoubted wisdom in doing so.

To my mind, the Royal Enfield twins never achieved the fame they certainly deserved, for they were always first rate motorcycles which, quite unhappily, were thoroughly up-staged by Triumph twins, the AJS and /Matchless models, BSA and Norton.

Royal Enfield was one of the very first British motorcycles to feature the now-ubiquitous swing-arm rear suspension, which they introduced on their sports single-cylinder models as early as 1948 (the twin appeared in 1949), while Norton

Ryde Motorcycles

and BSA continued to use the old-fashioned plunger-type rear set up for several years, and Triumph had either a rigid frame or that odd, and deservedly denigrated, sprung hub. The AMC machines, AJS and its badge-engineered Matchless counterpart, were the only other British marques to employ swing-arm rear suspension back in the late forties.

But the Royal Enfield 500 twin, sometimes called the 5T by the company – a designation already used by Triumph for its Speed Twin – also enjoyed one of the nicest looking engines of them all. It employed deeply-spigotted separate cylinder barrels and heavily finned alloy heads, with very attractive, highly polished alloy rocker-box covers, timing cases and large alloy primary drive chain-case, a deep, ribbed wet sump to carry oil, and enjoyed a road performance equalling any of the other, much more favoured, vertical twins. Enfield was more comfortable, and handled much better than most of them, which may well explain why the Royal Enfield frame was eagerly sought after in those days by many riders who rode on dirt surfaces in short-circuit and Scrambles (read Motocross) racing.

The Enfield had been sold to me only a day previously, had been quickly checked over in the workshop, had had the oil changed and a detailed, if un-necessary, service carried out, then ridden home by me that night, after it had spent most of the previous afternoon standing proudly on display in one of the garden beds (?) outside the store. That bike was as sweet as a song, and if I hadn't already owned my long-suffering BSA single, I might have seriously considered buying the thing for myself.

The fellow who sold it was a whinging Pom headed home again because it was too hot, with our very bad car drivers out to get him, and he had naturally agreed Enfield was not a very popular brand, so I bought it for peanuts, and the mark-up was very acceptable. The more so because it was going to be sold again on the following day, wet and miserable though the weather was.

I was so excited I could hardly contain myself, because I was just about to make another ten shillings, a whole dollar, and with no effort involved at all. That miserable day was not going to be quite so miserable after all!

Of course I asked him how he could have known we had the Enfield on display because we hadn't seen him before, but he said he had driven past in his dad's car a day before when the sun was on high and the bikes were on display on the footpath outside, and – he said – he had spotted

> *"During our discussion he revealed he had never ridden a motorcycle in his life, but always wanted to do so..."*

me scratching myself as I stood framed within the doorway. It must be said I was probably looking for a customer like him, because surely there was no way the sight of me in that doorway would have brought *anyone* into the store.

Fortunately, it was the bike which interested him most, and he agreed the trim little twin looked great and further agreed that the Royal Enfield marque deserved a better fate in this country. During our discussion he revealed he had never ridden a motorcycle in his life, but always wanted to do so, and admitted that he seemed to spend much of his time while training for that day by falling off his father's pushbike! Suddenly the bubble burst, because it then meant that as usual, hot or cold, wet or dry, part of my job was to patiently teach a new owner how to ride his very first motorcycle... and today it was pelting with rain!

Naturally, I suggested he pay for the bike on the spot but to come back again when it had stopped raining. This way, I stoutly maintained, I could devote more time to his training, and in much more acceptable circumstances, with benefits to him and, more selfishly perhaps, to me as well. Would he like to do that? Didn't he think that was in fact a Good Idea? In short, no he did not. He wanted to ride home on the Royal Enfield, and he wanted to ride it home *today*. Not tomorrow, or the day after, but today.

And so, with the very occasional trip indoors to gratefully attend to a few clients who refused to stay indoors on such a foul day as that one was, I spent much of the day in my waterproofs, sweating like a pig, and a damn sight wetter than if I had been stark naked, trotting up and down the lane outside showing this frankly not terribly good rider how to ride a two-wheeler with grace and elegance, and some safety as well. It was an extra dollar well earned. I was never happier to see someone ride away, the man crouched upon his new bike like a badly-stuffed bag of spuds, into what remained of that blustering day, than I was to see the rear of that bloke. It would seem I was successful in my lectures and practical demonstrations, because the man wobbled off uncertainly into the gloom but returned several days later unscathed, and became a regular customer for some time thereafter.

But I had also suggested to him before he rode off that our brand new range of frankly awful Roma helmets – with their pressed aluminium shell and miniscule leather peak – would be a darned sight better in the wet than his little cloth cap could hope to be, so he bought one of those before he departed.

Until I bought one for myself, I could hardly have been aware that it was very difficult to see where you were going after you had ridden in the rain for a couple of days while wearing a Roma helmet.

That little leather peak, so useless for its intended job of keeping the sun out of your eyes, would fold up like a wet hanky after it had been seriously rained upon for a couple of days, and would thereafter proceed to lovingly drape itself across your eyes. But you only needed to put up with that for a while, with head tilted back and looking down your nose at other road users, because not too long afterwards, with no warning, or apparent reason, the peak would suddenly detach itself from the helmet and fly off like a brown dickey bird.

A detailed inspection of the area on my own helmet from which an erstwhile leather peak had recently been projected proved it had been attached to the helmet shell only by some form of foul-smelling glue. The adhesive was probably like that used on the postage stamps and envelopes of yore; a mixture of boiled down old horses and cows! The material was well adapted to the task of sealing letters and allowing postage stamps to remain in place, but was less than useful when it came to holding in its position a non-compatible material which was subject to the vagaries of water, heat, and the winds that blow.

It should go without saying that helmet design has improved very dramatically since 1957, the time of which I write, so much so that direct comparisons with modern-day helmets are, to say the least, odious. That awful, Roma helmet with its aluminium shell, along with several others which did the job just a little better than not wearing a helmet at all, has certainly gone to God, but it is interesting to note that Roma still manufactures fully-accredited motorcycle helmets, and in a large range at that, which must make the company one of the oldest manufacturers of specialised safety helmets just about anywhere on earth!...

Road rage

Human nature being what it is, you can bet there has always been a serious problem for anyone, anywhere, who operated any form of wheeled transport, whether it be a semi-trailer driver, the driver of any form of public transport, the rider of a pushbike or, more importantly to us, a motorcyclist. The problem, quite simply, relates to the vast number of absolute jackasses with whom we are forced to share space on this – or any other – Nation's roads.

If we were able to check the history of Egyptian or Roman chariots, and the records of their version of the Road and Transport Authority records, assuming there were any records of traffic infringements in those far off days, it would be a safe bet that Road Rage was just as alive and well in heavy traffic in those days, as it is today.

For all we know, those charioteers were probably just as belligerent in traffic jams outside the Coliseum or the Cheops Pyramid thousands of years ago as they are to this day. Perhaps even more so, because those brave souls would have been very easily accessible to verbal and physical abuse, simply because of the design of their vehicles: a bit like motorcyclists are!

I have been the innocent victim – and, I hereby confess, very occasionally the perpetrator – of Modern Road Rage, even before it was so recently christened. (N.B., do you wonder, had the offence been called road-rage back then in ancient Rome, would it have been Christened, or Pilated?) I know, I know, and I'm sorry about that!

Be that as it may, I was innocently involved in a Gold Medal example of World Championship Road Rage when I was tootling home one bright summer's day back in the late fifties, the trusty old BSA outfit humming along, lurching and shuddering over the tarred MX circuit which was – and still is! – Concord Road, when I espied a barge-like, near-new Bel Air Chevrolet convertible tucked in behind a bus ahead of us, while a Holden was in the process of overtaking both of them.

The bus pulled over to ease into its designated stop and the Chevy swept out to pass it just as the Holden was level with the driver's door. Of course the Chevy's driver glanced neither to the left nor right as he did so, apparently ignored his twin rear view mirrors , and graced us with neither nod nor hand signal to notify us of his intent.

As few blinkers were about in those far-off days, the Law required us to signal our intent by a series of quaint hand-signals, but – though most of the Chevy driver's arm hung out of the car as he gripped the top of his door – this may have been beneath his dignity. He simply swung the Power-assisted steering wheel hard right with the pressure of the inside of his wrist, his flaccid hand draped atop the wheel, as though he had recently fractured it. His hand, that is.

Perhaps he thought he was a local version of America's Joe Cool, but the Holden driver called him something else as he swung the car almost across to the wrong side of the roadway to escape the Chevy.

As they passed the bus the Holden driver suddenly swung his car back onto the correct side of the road, which of course caused the driver of the Chevy to reef the wheel hard left again to avoid the so-obvious, and clearly imminent, collision.

Amazingly, the Chevy driver swung his car violently to the right *again*, this time signalling his intent by shaking his fist at the other driver, who by now had swung back to the wrong side of the road again. I sat about 50 meters behind the debacle, and watched goggle-eyed (sorry about the pun, there were very few helmets, and certainly no vizors, in those days) as the two swung their cars violently at each other several times and sprang apart again without actually making contact, the while glaring and shouting at one another, apparently quite oblivious to other road-users.

Both drivers were frantically using a series of lurid hand signals which were not in any Traffic Handbook I had ever read (although everyone knew what they meant) but they sped on with some vigour as they approached the blind left-hander approaching the turn-off to Concord Hospital.

Amazingly, they kept the charade up even as they entered the corner, the Chevy driver swinging his large car out and forcing the Holden almost into some cars parked on the opposite side of the roadway as they exited the corner.

The amazing thing is that, even though it was getting on for six o'clock (that's a guess, but, as I was on the way home from work at the motorbike shop, I reckon the time to be pretty right) there was little traffic about, but there was one car on the road at that time.... and the Holden was headed straight for it!!

It was a pale-green Morris Minor driven – I was soon to learn – by a Member of the Cloth, possibly on a visit to a member of his flock, or to open the Church for Evensong, and he was in nigh-mortal danger, as he was about the discover.

The Holden driver, intent on shoving the Chevy into the left-hand gutter again, hadn't spotted the Morris Minor as the latter disappeared behind one of the parked cars and suddenly shot out again, the Vicar craning back to look over his right shoulder, with his head and waving arm shoved out the window, the Morris missing the Holden by a coat of paint but by now headed straight for me!

I recall seeing three things happening almost simultaneously: The Vicar trying to drag his head and arm back into the car but being trapped by one of those fashionable, nigh-useless, door-mounted wind deflectors which were all the fashion in those days; the Holden finally forcing the Chevy into the gutter in a cloud of dust, detaching a hub-cap the size of a large garbage-bin lid; the Morris Minor rapidly closing on me, with no escape which I could then detect. I was, for several seconds, in dire trouble, for the Village Vicar was still looking back at the two cars and had not seen me at all! He was also playing a brisk fanfare upon the car's horn

These things, as we are all aware, happen in a matter of a few seconds, and all too often separate disaster from triumph, and all too often, more by good luck or bad luck allied to good and/or bad management.

There was a narrow street to the left off Concord Road which was my only escape, so I whipped back into second gear and cranked the throttle wide open, hung myself over the sidecar body and speared off Concord Road, the engine howling, the sidecar wheel half a meter in the air, the rear-end stepping out.

Narrow as the street was, there were cars parked on both sides which narrowed it even more, the situation not helped by the fact that a group of four or five people were in the middle of the road not far around the corner, accompanying a girl hobbling painfully up the small hill on a pair of crutches. Thankfully, they quickly dispersed between the parked cars as I shot past, but I knew I had incurred their wrath and would soon have to face them as I turned up somebody's driveway and trickled back to apologise to them.

The girl waved her crutch at me as I returned (which isn't as rude as it sounds) and her father was not amused until I explained what had happened. He wasn't amused then, either, but at least grudgingly admitted I was lucky, the while pointing out that they were just about to open the car door when I suddenly appeared.

A few seconds later and I would have either have worn that car door, or they would have all joined me in the sidecar, and, not much later, in the Casualty Ward just down the road to which I could so easily, however unintentionally, have conveyed them.

When I returned to Concord Road, the Chevy owner was ruefully contemplating his graunched hub-cap and a large graze on the front guard, while the Vicar was either administering a solemn Benediction or about to smack him in the mouth. They joined me in reflecting on how grim it could all have been and tut-tutting at the behaviour of the Holden driver, who had shown the good sense to disappear.

I didn't bother to remind the driver of the Yank Tank that much of the fault was his, but considered myself lucky to have escaped what could have a been a multiple disaster.

Fortunately, I had driven sidecars for some years by then, and had often waved a sidecar wheel in the air for fun or to terrify, or delight, the natives, but I would have preferred not to be put to the test in this way.

As we have noted, there is probably nothing new about Road Rage, and it certainly takes many forms. We have too often seen serious footage of dangerous road rage on our TV screens and have occasionally been involved in it, however innocent we may well have been. It has been said that there are no winners when a serious episode of Road Rage occurs, although it could be argued that the Chevy driver may have got his just desserts.

But there was one clear winner on that day, for that tight little left- hand corner sprang up at almost exactly the right time for me to make an undignified exit from the scene, just managing to avoid the head-one collision with the Vicar's Morris Minor which seemed to me to be only a few seconds away.

Vespa

Whether we like it or not, there are occasions in all our lives where an event, or perhaps a person, suddenly crops up, with no bidding and from absolutely nowhere, to haunt us or to disturb us anew. Sometimes it is a very pleasant surprise, but sometimes – and more often than not – it can be more than a little unpleasant. Again, sometimes it is a shock to the system to suddenly come almost face to face with someone we thought we had long forgotten, but whose antics way-back-when suddenly stir up a range of memories and/or emotions which we had no idea had been swiftly consigned to the brain's dustbin of history.

Well, one of those people, whom I had long forgotten, though the occasion was clearly hidden away in the files forever, cropped up several months ago while Lyn and I were enjoying a quiet repast at a local Maccas.

We were on display in a large picture window when a man rode into the car-park on one of those neat 250cc Honda Lead scooters – that's Lead as in ahead of the bunch, not Lead as in base metal! – and weaved through a tight bunch of clearly terrified clients. He nearly clipped a car backing out of its parking spot and dived into a vacant space just under our noses. He beat a car to the space by a scant meter or so.

He sat up, nodding and smiling to everyone around as he unbolted an ill-fitting helmet which perched, pimple-like, upon his pumpkin head. He looked directly at me, nodding and smiling. I nodded back, a half-handful of French Fries midway between packet and slack jaw.

I thought he was a Ghost! A genuine Ghost!!

He had to be a ghost, because there is no way known he could have survived the many, many years which had passed since I last laid eyes on him. But there he was, large as life and twice as ugly: by now sporting a thatch of near-white hair, he had apparently aged no more than about five minutes in all that time! In a word, I was Stunned.

Naturally, he didn't recognise me, he simply smiled at everyone around him whether he knew them or not, but I recognised him instantly and at once the memory of our first meeting came flying back – as I said, from nowhere and with no prompting at all!

It was in the Ryde Motorcycles shop in the late fifties, the man a local PMG Postman coming in to buy his first – and damn near his last! – motor scooter. I was the eager sales person who was (initially) delighted to look after him.

There were a couple of those fiendish devices on the floor; a new ISO – one of the better motor scooters, made in Italy by one of the great luxury car manufacturers – and a second-hand Douglas-Vespa. The ISO was a cross between the fine Lambretta and the distinctly odd Vespa, the near-defunct Douglas made in England under licence to the Italian firm, both of whom should have known better.

The Italian Vespa was an odd design, the 125cc two-stroke engine hanging well off to

Ryde Motorcycles

the right-hand side of the rear wheel, which it drove directly through a cruciform-ended shaft via a three-speed gearbox. The latter was controlled through the left twist-grip, a pair of push-me-pull-you cables running to the external gear selector plate at the rear of the engine. You rotated the grip back for first gear, centrally for second and, with the clutch lever pointing earthward, forward again for third gear. It was a strange set-up, but it was nonetheless very effective.

The Vespa glorified in tiny 350x8" wheels front and rear (which loved to drop into potholes!) the wheels located on one side only, with front suspension by a leading-link with single, naked spring and a separate damper unit which worked to some degree. Drum brakes were about the same size as jam tins, though not nearly as deep, and were about as effective.

The British-Built Douglas-Vespa was something else again!

Dispensing with the Italian twin-cable gearchange, the Douglas version used a series of rods, bell-cranks and little levers which pursued a tortuous path from the left handlebar, down the inside of the front weather shield, under the metal floor, across to the right and rear of the engine to the selector mechanism which sat out in the breeze: and the mud; and the slush; and the water; and the wee-wees of passing dogs.

What a disaster that English design was! As wear occurred in the various linkages gear changing became an absolute lottery, the left twist-grip having to be rotated through nearly 360-degrees. The only indication of a positive response was a loud clunk and alarming grinding noises as each gear was selected.

As for the suspension! Let it suffice to say that the front damper didn't work at all, the front end bobbing up and down like a horse's head at full gallop, the rear swivelling around the steering head like the tail-end of a happy dog! Would you like to dance the Cha Cha, and the Rhumba at the same time? Don't bother, we'll buy a used Douglas-Vespa instead! Let's not mention the handling at all, except to say that there was no sign of it.

Oh, and when you applied the front brake it dipped to full compression and your arms appeared to finish at the wrists, as your hands disappeared in a haze of shimmering vibration.

Now where was I? Oh, yes, the guy came in looking for a cheap scooter to ride to work. They didn't come much cheaper than the Douglas-Vespa, so I put him on the back and lurched up the road to show him its performance... although it didn't have much of that to boast about, either.

He jumped off when we returned and surprised me by hanging around instead of running away. He wanted to buy the thing and asked could I teach him how to ride it! You couldn't teach anyone how to ride one of those things, the skill had to be acquired – and the hard way at that! – but part of the deal was teaching new riders how to get home in one piece, so we ran through the well-ordered basics.

The trick was to push the scooter to the top of the lane which ran alongside the shop, and then have your client wheel the device about to get the feel of it, discover the various controls and how they worked. He would then trickle it slowly down hill again several times without the engine running. He would by then have learned how the brakes worked, how to apply them properly and how the bike felt without someone else hanging onto it – or so you hoped!

Of course it was pretty exhausting stuff, firstly helping shove the thing uphill then running alongside it on the way down again shouting advice or prayers, whichever was the most appropriate.

The next step was to fire the engine up and have the proud owner ride the bike uphill and coast back down again. This he would do several times over, as you gleefully trotted into the shop from time to time to attend to other clients.

He seemed to be doing well so the next manouvre was to ride *downhill* under power and turn – feet up, please! – at the bottom to ride up the hill again while changing into second gear.

I left him at it for awhile and he seemed to have nearly mastered the strange handling – noone ever fully mastered an early model Vespa's strange handling, rest assured! – so I suggested he do a slow lap of the block. Down the lane, left into the traffic stream, and a series of left hand turns would bring him back into the lane again, just outside the shop.

The rule was that if a client came back again in one piece, with no dents on the machine, and no scratches upon himself, you could send him home on his own. If not, you'd have to fire up the old 1936 Harley and side-box and deliver the bike, the client sitting illegally in the side-box; which was very much the last card in the pack!

He reckoned he was OK, so he took off down the lane while I trotted alongside patting him on the pack, advising him to lift the soles of his shoes off the ground for a change.

As he retracted his undercarriage and planted

them on the footboard he changed into second gear and then, for some reason – or no reason at all! – opened the throttle to the stop!!

The smile had gone as he took off, bug-eyed and grim-visaged, towards the three-lane Victoria Road at ninety degrees to the traffic stream. I caught him almost as he burst out of the side lane, grabbed the tail of the scooter and leaned back to dig my heels in, while shouting loudly "Brakes! Brakes!

He dragged me towards the middle of the road and planted his own feet hard down as he heaved on the front of the scooter to gain extra purchase. Over my right shoulder I caught a flash of green as the lights changed. Oh, Gawd!

We pulled up almost at the median strip as a phalanx of cars leaped away from the lights and bore down on us, both of the scooter's wheels clear of the ground, its engine screaming like a Banshee, the rear wheel spinning crazily inches away from the Jewels.

With feet tangled and tripping over one another, we shuffled, sobbing with terror, onto the median strip as traffic zoomed by in both directions, the Vespa engine still on full song, but the bike now miraculously in neutral.

I dragged the clutch lever in and strained to roll the throttle back as we waited for a month till everything on four wheels sped by. Chastened, he apologised as I wheeled the scooter back to the curb, only then discovering that the sole of my left boot had been peeled back and was laughing at me as I walked.

He practiced for an hour or so up and down the lane and then called in to say he was going to ride home. I waved him away as he wobbled off, to execute an illegal U-turn at a break in the concrete and come back on the opposite side past the shop again.

He gave the scooter a squirt, changing up as he passed us and looked over to wave... just as the traffic in front stopped at the red light!!

I rushed to the kerb, boot-sole flapping, pointing ahead and shouting "Brakes! Brakes!" anew, but he had already seen the truck as he turned to face where he was going, and he reefed the front brake lever to the handlebars.

For the first, and I'm sure the last time ever, the front end locked up and the bars swung through ninety degrees as the scooter and its new owner slid under the back of the truck and all but disappeared!

The shop's owner rushed over to pull them out as I went to check the fuel level in the Harley tank, but by the time I nipped back to the scene he had departed – by all accounts not much the worse for wear – and the boss was back inside the store, grinning wanly at me.

The fellow came back a few months later and bought the ISO – yes, it was still there, which was no surprise – having written off the Vespa under the wheels of a near-new Mark Two Jaguar, the owner of which paid cash for the bike as an admission of guilt. The ISO was a sweet scooter, and the guy rode it away one day never to be seen again.

Except for a few months ago, when he suddenly re-appeared!

He didn't show much expertise in that side lane, and he didn't seem to have improved at all over the years. He was riding a near-new, and vastly improved machine, but only the Good Lord Himself – who must have watched over him for nearly four decades – could tell how on earth that man had survived on this nation's roads for as long as he had!

The moonlight mechanics

There have been many illicit, or at worst illegal, nocturnal activities carried out for eons by law-abiding citizens, or those of a criminal bent, in every Nation on earth, at every darkened hour of every day, from the first minutes of darkness to the few minutes prior to the dawn of a new day. This practice has probably been part of our ancestors' activities since those far-off days when they were living fearfully in their caves. In much later years, after-hours dumpers of rubbish have sometimes been apprehended by Police, which happened to one bloke who was nabbed one night by the Police while he was dumping a bin full of household scraps underneath a sign which clearly forbade him from doing so.

"Didn't you see that sign, mate?" the constable sternly demanded, as he unfurled his well-thumbed, dog-eared notebook.

"Course I did," the man replied, "that's why I'm dumping the stuff here. The sign clearly says 'Fine for Dumping Rubbish', so if it was *fine* to do so, then I reckoned it was OK."

Now that you've asked.... no, he didn't get away with it!

There were also contractors of local Councils who have been more than a little wayward when it came to discharging their various duties, as evidenced by one or two sly contractors who were employed in the grim pursuit of servicing the out-houses of an outer Sydney suburb, in which some areas were not yet connected to a sewerage system.

Vintage Morris

Ryde Motorcycles

These men gleefully discharged the contents of their over-ripe pans onto the surface of a large paddock which sat alongside a long stretch of road called Fairfield Street, in, naturally, the Sydney suburb of Fairfield. It is still there, of course, but has undergone enormous changes over the last sixty years or so.

In the time of which I speak – in the early to mid-fifties – on that road from Merrylands to Fairfield that long, flat grassed area of some 200 and more meters in length and about the same depth, just before a pot-holed right-angled corner which dropped onto the narrow, wooden Loscoe Street Bridge was attended by an all-pervading stench. This eye-watering, throat-clutching stink was for some years the legacy of the emptying of their many tar-encrusted tins of raw sewage dumped – I presume entirely illegally – by the local Moonlight Mechanic(s).

In those days, there was no such a thing as an *en-suite* bathroom, with much of the area not yet fully connected to a sewer system, while most homes which rejoiced in the 'luxury' of a very basic sewerage system were still attended by the traditional outhouse, known colloquially then, as now, as The Dunny.

There are several stories from the era of the so-called 'pan service' – read Moonlight Mechanic – one of which concerns a lady of some substance who approached the mother of a little boy and asked her, very politely, from whence he had inherited his highly freckled face. Was it his father, she enquired?

"They ain't freckles, lady" she is said to have remarked, "He's been flingin' stones into the dunny again!" Phew!!

On another occasion – it is said – the local Mechanic had flipped his fetid truck on its side into a sodden ditch as he had entered the illicit "Moonlight Mechanic's Stretch" and had, as a result, unintentionally emptied several tins of their over-ripe contents into a large, festering pond.

He was seen fishing about in the stinking mess in the early morn with a long stick, and was queried as to why he was engaged in this odd quest. "Me jacket's in there somewhere, mate." he is said to have remarked. "But what do you want your jacket back for?" he was asked, "it's no use to you now."

"I know," he is said to have replied as he prodded about, "but me lunch is in the pocket!" Phew again!!

On a dark and moonless night, when a light fog drifted across that ill-lit road, the stench was all-embracing, and even the most powerful of 'modern' motor cycles, which were not all that powerful back then, would need to attack that stretch of road in a lower gear than normal, just to provide enough grunt to burst though a pungent wall which hit the unsuspecting motorcyclist like an almost immovable object.

The trick to riding this awful stretch of road was simplicity itself. One would take the deepest of deep breaths about 100 meters or so before the Dumping Ground, then change back a gear and accelerate as hard as possible to drive swiftly through the murk, and then brake desperately for the tight right-hander which dropped onto the one-lane Loscoe Street bridge. Draught-free goggles were, of course, invariably worn because helmets, and their attendant visors, were unheard of in those far-off days.

Nor did your troubles end as you dropped onto that ricketty structure, for the bridge was made of long, thick planks which were bolted **longitudinally** to stout supporting joists.

Unfortunately, the planks had weathered almost a century of misuse since they had been originally bolted in place. The passage of numerous vehicles, including the Mechanics' trucks with their dribbling pans, had resulted in a series of loose planks which rose and fell under one, while long, rusting – and, I assume, nut-less – coach-bolts, with their tinkling washers, would leap out of well-worn holes and brush the toes of one's boots or scrape against the sides of those thin, bullet-proof and highly polished tyres which existed at that time.

A small, and almost illegible, sign on either end of the short – but altogether too long – wooden bridge warned it was very much a one-way bridge with "No Passing or Overtaking" anywhere on its dangerous surface. Though a short trip, the ride over that tiny bridge was always an adventure. To make matters worse, the daunting "road" surface on the other end of that awful bridge was unsealed clay, with numerous, water-and-sewage filled, bone-jarring potholes, tooth-rattling corrugations, numerous highly-polished stones and the occasional large rock to trap the unwary; along with everyone else who chose the adventure of riding a motorcycle over this stretch of forbidding road.

About 100 meters later, a tight left-hander (which often meant a quick dab with a well-shod foot to negate the unintentional slide which almost inevitably occurred) was followed by an equally arduous 200 or so meters to the welcoming tar-sealed Horsley Drive, itself a

1956-1960

> *"I clearly recall two occasions in which I was unable to slow down my little James motorcycle in time for that tight corner..."*

pretty awful stretch of road, but a feather bed in comparison.

Oh, and just to make the trip down that road a little more exciting there existed, just past that frightful Dumping Ground, at the very end of that long straight before the tight corner onto the rustic bridge, a large, and entirely illegal, garbage tip used with some enthusiasm by local residents who would creep out at night and empty their bins, or deposit their deceased farm animals, onto an ever-growing heap which confronted the speeding rider head-on like an impenetrable brick wall.

In those far off days, I might add, there were no plastic bags, so garbage bins were usually lined with paper, into which household scraps were scraped without benefit of any other form of enclosure. This too, was more than a little on the nose as the refuse rotted noisily, the while aided and abetted by a large army of gleeful blowflies, and some well-fed, thoroughly obese, cat-sized rats!

I clearly recall two occasions in which I was unable to slow down my little James motorcycle in time for that tight corner, and then spent the next several minutes in extricating myself from the middle of the morass into which I had unintentionally flung us. It was hard work escaping from the tip, because I had to get off the bike and heave it over the rubbish, aided, now and again, by careful throttle control and a gentle caress of the clutch lever.

It was tough going the first time, at night, but on the other occasion, during the day, with blowflies trying to get up my nose, and, I assumed, rats nipping at my heels, I couldn't get out of there quickly enough, but of course 'more haste, less speed' meant it took half as long again to extricate our selves that it did the first time. Or, perhaps, it just seemed that way?

It could be argued that 'less speed' in the first place would have meant I could have spared myself the trip into the scunge in the first place.

My brother Andy tells an entirely true story about one of the many, many occasions in which he sped down that road one night, his lungs swiftly filled with fresh, clean air, his nose and mouth clenched tight, back in third gear with the throttle wound against the stop, the bike pulling hard into the greenish mist which swirled across the road over his right shoulder.

He beheld a large horse on the left shoulder of the road, apparently firmly tethered to the adjacent fence and munching contentedly at the grass verge. He was almost alongside the horse when it lifted its head slightly to display a stout (and thus far unseen) chain which was actually tethered to the **other side** of the road! He said the chain was almost level with the road when the animal momentarily lifted its head, and he was able to swerve into the centre of the road and bump over the lower run of chain, averting a disaster. For both he and the horse!

There was no way he could hope to negotiate the corner onto the bridge, and he says he was side-on, with both brakes locked up, when he pitched headlong into the illicit garbage tip. He said he was pelted onto a large mattress which of course scrubbed off quite some speed, but the surface of the bedding bore the marks of a large, and possibly nocturnal, emission of a still-moist and noisome bodily fluid!

He said he had to drag the bike bodily, and sometimes *sideways,* out of the filth into which he had all but disappeared, and when he came home some time later he was well and truly on the nose! He took most of his gear off in the dirt-floored humpy which passed for our garage, and you could hear him clanging about in his boxer shorts as he trotted briskly inside, trailed by a less than subtle pong from the noisily ripening gear he had left standing on its own in the garage.

Fairfield Street now runs straight on where once the garbage tip flourished, the Loscoe Street Bridge long forgotten – or, more likely, unknown – by local residents. There now stands a sports ground where once the Unofficial Sewerage Dump lay, and it is no surprise that the general lushness of vegetation in the immediate area is so stunning, and remarked upon so often by visiting football teams. I often wonder whether players who are unceremoniously tackled on that ground endure various open injuries which quickly fester and, quite likely, take an age to heal.

Were there homes built on the Dump instead of a playing field, the various flowers and/or vegetables which would thereby spring up might well be listed Internationally as one of the New Wonders of the World. The Chinese *deliberately* used this method of sewage disposal as a form of fertilisation for centuries (they still do!!) so if it works for them, why should it not work equally as well for everyone else?

Vintage Morris

Ryde Motorcycles Safety

Someone once asked me what the most dangerous thing was about riding an 'invisible' motorcycle back in the fifties. *He* didn't say invisible, I did, because most of the rear vision mirrors around in those days were the small mirrors inside cars (mirrors were rarely to be seen mounted on car exteriors and were not compulsory on motorcycles, believe it or not) and you had to be well aware of the fact that you simply couldn't be seen unless you made a deliberate effort to sit directly in a driver's line of vision.

This didn't help much either, because the tiny mirrors which were about in those days were more often than not out of focus, and very few people ever looked into them in the first place! Nothing much has changed today, people still don't always use the battery of mirrors they have while the most dangerous manoeuvre a car driver will ever execute is still the quick right-hand U-turn across the bow of a rapidly approaching motorcyclist.

It's true to say they simply didn't look, either behind, alongside or in front in those far-off days, and I suggest that even with the "Motorcyclist Aware" campaign occasionally waged in Australia today, the situation is not a whole lot better. We now have clowns chatting on mobile phones in air-conditioned comfort, enclosed within sealed off vehicles which have little contact with the outside world.

Their inner peace is often soothed (or jangled) by various forms of musical, and other sounds, piped through several powerful Hi-Fi speakers. Little wonder, then, that the world outside most four-wheeled vehicles can often be somewhat remote.

Yet this is a very real world, and one inhabited by a large number of more adventurous souls who prefer zipping about on two wheels and enjoying the freedom their choice of alternative transport allows.

There were very few turn indicator lights on cars way back when (Citroen was the notable exception, but then they are always ahead of the game) with the result that all drive-side windows were wound down to allow for hand signals to be employed. These signals were not always reliable, because for every well-executed, obvious hand-signal there were thousands of sloppy variations which in the end were meaningless. Or, at the very least, confusing

One leaps readily to mind: I was riding a brand-new Honda Dream to Parramatta Motor Registry back in 1958 when a Vanguard driver in front of me thrust his hand out at arm's length to indicate a right turn. He of course veered in that direction, then, just as I was cranking over to dive underneath him, he snapped a left-turn/ stop signal (which was a bit like Adolph Hitler's half-masted, patronising salute to his closest Henchmen) and reefed the steering wheel to the **left** to lurch up his driveway.

With nowhere to go, I bounced up the layback which led to his driveway, shaved the inevitable telegraph pole with my right shoulder and shot down the footpath for several yards: the distance would have measured in yards at the time, because Australia had not yet adopted the metric system.

It was a very close shave indeed, but had we collided it could have made history, and been a disaster in more ways than one, because there were probably no spare parts available at the time to affect any major repairs to the new bike. That C71 Honda was a very rare bike indeed in early 1958, and quite probably the first of its type to be sold and registered outside of Japan. It was one of a batch of just twelve which had only just been imported into Sydney 'on-spec', the New South Wales distributor of BSA and Sunbeam motorcycles the first company on earth to import Honda motorcycles, and it was one of that batch which I was riding at the time.

I leapt off the bike and trotted back to acquaint the errant driver with my opinion of his prowess, or lack thereof, to be greeted with the words you have all heard before, and I'm sure you'll repeat after me – on the count of three: 'one, two, three' – "Sorry mate, I didn't see you!" My repost was as short as I am, "Sorry mate," I bellowed, "You didn't bloody look!!"

Now then, I hear you ask, in reply to my friend's enquiry about 'what was one of the most dangerous aspects of riding motorcycles about in those far off days?' The answer, simply put, is (male) car drivers clearing their various throats and spitting through the car's open window!!

It's true! With the now- universal acceptance of Kleenex tissues and no further need to flash hand signals (except the occasional road-rage finger, which has all but superseded the two-finger salute) 'wogging' out the car window is now becoming a dying art. A bit like making waggon wheels, or wooden wine and beer kegs, although *draining* the latter is a culture which continues unabated.

Window wogging hasn't altogether disappeared, be aware, for there are still enough trucks, vans and light commercials around for the practice to continue. Usually, these vehicles have the driver's side window wound down, while the seemingly-inevitable elbow still rests (illegally) atop the door sill.

A friend of mine who shall remain nameless, but whose name was Big Fred, carried with him what he called his 'wogging deterrent' which was always hanging out of his war-surplus gasmask bag. It was a large tyre lever and so common was the practice of 'voiding one's rhume,' as Shakespeare himself put it, that Fred became quite adept at the art of whipping the tyre lever out of his bag, waving it about and then fetching the offender a swift clout on the not-so funny bone as Fred's big Vincent thundered past.

A split second later the tyre lever was back in the bag as Fred sped on, apparently innocent of any wrongdoing. It's fair to say that a sudden, searing pain in the right elbow, allied to an extremely short time-frame and highly elevated heart rate meant that errant drivers could have no blind idea what the hell had just happened to them – except for the fact that, whatever it was, it hurt like blazes!

As I've remarked, most drivers in those days – as some still do today, for some strange reason – drove around with an illegal elbow resting on the door sill: an irresistible and – though I didn't altogether agree with the harsh punishment – deserving target for the vengeful person who has so recently been enthusiastically spat upon.

By the time the pain had subsided a little and the tears had been wiped away, the *spitter*, one would hope, had learned a hard and lasting lesson. Only the dumbest of the dumb could fail to associate a sudden and searing pain with the cleansing of one's sinuses and the swift disposal of the residue therefrom.

As the offending driver would have suddenly lost touch with reality and, if Fortune smiled, unwittingly voided his loins as a cleansing encore, he may well have assumed the assault was from On High as a form of Divine Intervention. By now, Fred would have been long gone and the driver's sudden and all-consuming pain may have erased the memory of him ever having been there at all!

Let us all hope the memory of those swift and painful interludes would remain with the victims of Fred's vengeance forever. The practice of window-wogging (a strange expression, if ever there was one) has all but died out, and sometimes I wonder how much Fred's one-man crusade had to do with that.

I was once nearly the unwitting victim of one of Fred's assaults, as I was once chasing him on my old (which wasn't quite so old then!) BSA single, when some ill-advised moron spat out of the car window in his direction. Quick as a flash the instrument of torture appeared, was held aloft for a brief moment and swooped with a resounding crack onto the driver's exposed elbow.

In an instant I was accelerating past the car's open window and I heard him screech his Saviour's name as he began sawing the steering wheel about, apparently almost out of control. So, I might add, was the car!

Happily, I was clear of the vehicle in an instant but it was as close a shave as I've had in many years.

I remonstrated with Fred when we stopped for a coffee some time later, pointing out that he had initiated a physical attack with an offensive weapon in the first place, it was a dangerous ploy in the second place, and was probably rewarded by a stiff fine, if not a short time in the slammer. Someone who was the receipt of such a sudden attack could cark it from a heart attack, I mentioned, or lose control of the vehicle and spear into something else, or – as in my case – leave tyre marks all over an innocent motorcyclist!

"Listen mate," he said gratingly, his head cocked to one side and an eye half-closed, as he pointed a finger at me the size of a plump German sausage, "If some turd thinks he's going to wog an oyster out of his car window in my direction and get away with it....?" He shook his head slowly as he drew a breath to continue the speech, "Then my boy he has got another think coming." He winked and pulled a wry face as he slurped his coffee.

"Served him right, the filthy bastard," he continued as he almost sighed, "and that goes for all the others as well!" You may not agree with his philosophy, any more than I did, but it would be hard to argue against it.

Ah, Fred, what a character he was! I haven't seen him in many years, but I do hope he is still out there somewhere (he would have to be comfortably into his eighties by now, if he is still with us), but he always seemed to me to be bullet-proof and I like to think he is still as once he was.

It isn't likely of course, even though he was as tough as nails and enjoyed a robust good health, because *none* of us oldies are quite as once we were. But when I remember Big Fred I like to remember him as someone well removed from

Ryde Motorcycles

the norm, a timeless character who was in almost every way – quite apart from his enormous bulk – larger than life.

Happy days, Big Fred; happy days, lad!!

Honda's arrival

One balmy day way back in 1958 I was lurking behind the spare parts counter of Ryde Motorcycles, the suburban motorcycle store in which I spent several happy years, idly re-adjusting a balled-up sock which had been sucked under my foot by an ill-fitting wool-lined 'flying' boot. I straightened up to behold a black Ford Mercury pulling into the gutter outside the front door, which seemed strangely ominous, but which in fact was to be the portent of monumental things to come.

The car disgorged a trio of short Orientals, one of whom, a step or so ahead of his fellows, reached back into the car and removed a small stack of what appeared to be colour brochures of some sort. He moved with measured steps to the front door and then, following a guttural command from one of his off-siders, climbed up the steps to the front door then into the lower of the two showrooms and suddenly shoved his arms out in front of him like wheelbarrow handles as he bowed his head towards the floor.

He stumbled up the step to the upper showroom where the parts counter stood, and I noted he was nodding his perfectly tonsured head like a pigeon as he approached, his slim fingers and perfectly manicured nails clamped in a death-grip on the pile of brochures he carried.

He was emitting odd hissing sounds and I wondered idly if there was something radically wrong with him; perhaps there was a fault in his breathing equipment, or an extra hole in his head where one had no right to be. Perhaps he was flatulently disposing of the remains of a bad Caucasian meal where something he ate disagreed with him, or could he simply be boiling for a leak after having spent too long within the confines of the Merc? I was not about to ask, and I imagined he wasn't about to tell me.

All three were immaculately dressed in matching dark suits with crisp white shirts and dark ties. I felt, at the time, that they might have been cold canvassing for an Asian funeral fund of some sort, perhaps flogging grave plots, or Bibles; maybe looking to lure people into some obscure religious sect? They arrived unheralded and un-announced, so they could have been there for any number of reasons.

Happily, it was none of these, I was soon to discover, as the trio filtered through the two showrooms, which featured twenty or so second-hand British bangers and four brand-new machines – an MSS Velocette 500cc single; one of the last, 500cc overhead camshaft all-alloy Norton Internationals (which nobody wanted, believe it or not!); a Triumph Thunderbird and a 200cc Villiers engine two-stroke James Commander commuter. There were also several Ex-Police 1955 Triumph Thunderbird outfits, with sprung-hub rear suspension – the frightful sprung hub still specified for sidecar use – which were recently purchased at auction after the owners had finished with them, and there were a couple of forlorn mopeds sharing space with a few scooters.

As the men weaved their way through the assembled machinery they glanced about with ill-concealed contempt, but one of them (who seemed to be their leader) nodded approvingly as he patted the Inter Norton's fuel tank, quite obviously ignoring the pool of oil which sat in the drip-tray underneath the machine. They sidled up to the spares counter behind which I stood transfixed, uncertain whether to run away or to heartily welcome the strangers.

Suddenly, the Brochure Bearer made thrusting gestures at me with his out-thrust arms, obviously offering them to me for my inspection. I took them and he immediately snapped upright, then, following a hoarse cry from his immediate superior, all three of them bowed from the ankles, hissing like a bunch of pit vipers!

It was an impressive display, and – before I could stop myself – I in turn bowed and hissed back at them, muttering my thanks. Well, what did I know about their customs? This was my first sight of Genuine Japanese men, which I correctly thought them to be, and I had found the whole exercise a bit over the top; if not downright intimidating. But I still had not a blind idea who they were, or what the heck they were on about.

Apart from my thanks, which elicited Cheshire-cat grins all round, though I noted their eyes remained disturbingly hooded, nobody had said anything so I turned my attention to the colour brochures, which quite obviously featured motorcycles.

The name on the cover said HONDA, which I had never heard of before, but the illustration

1956-1960

and wording was, I clearly remember, *most* impressive.

The colour photograph which was featured on the cover showed a bright red, twin-cylinder motorcycle clearly ridden at high speed, the rider, oddly, lying down on the thing, his belly on the dual-seat and his short legs thrust straight out behind him!

The photo immediately put me in mind of an American oddball named Roland Free, who had ridden a Black Lightning Vincent on Bonneville Salt Flats in the early fifties to a speed in excess of 150mph, while wearing nothing but a tight-fitting bathing cap, swimming trunks and sandshoes!! He compounded this absurdity by placing his stomach on the rear mudguard and thrusting his legs out behind him, claiming that the lack of flapping leathers allied to the prone riding position removed drag and allowed for a much higher speed than might otherwise be expected.

Clearly, this had provided the inspiration for the cover shot on the HONDA brochure, but no-one explained how these riders managed – at, one assumes , a very high speed in top gear – to achieve such a riding position, how they got back down again, and how the Family Jewels survived such a pasting.

The cover illustration carried a Classic caption to describe the exciting range of motorcycles detailed inside. They were, according to the caption, and I quote verbatim:- "A superior chunk of high efficiency engine, for high speed thrill cuts through the wind motorcycling."

Quaint? If you thought that was quaint, you should have read some of the workshop and spare parts manuals which were to follow as Honda gained strength before their English improved!

If the cover shot was impressive, then the motorcycles displayed inside were out of this world when compared with the current crop of English and (extremely rare) German and even rarer Italian machines we were desperately trying to flog at the time. Many of the original designs of those brand-new British machines we had on display were, in fact, 30 and more years old.

Honda Dream, the brochure shrieked, featured *twin-cylinder*, 250cc and 305cc four-stroke engines with overhead camshafts(!), totally enclosed rear chains(!), twin rear-view mirrors(!), blinkers(?) and –wait for it – electric self starters(!!).

In this, the 21st century, you may shout 'what's new about all that?', but we *are* talking 1958 you may recall, just after the middle of last century.

Clearly, Honda was well and truly ahead of the game with those new machines, for I had never seen equipment levels like this before, and must have stood slack-jawed at the visions which unfolded before me at every turn of the page.

As I've said , there were 250 and 305cc OHC twins, but there was also a couple of brochures for the Honda Benly *125cc OHC twin* which arrived several weeks later, and was even more mind-blowing because the only 125cc commuter machines which were on hand in those days were single-cylinder two-strokes or the occasional 200cc, ohv Triumph Tiger Cub. BSA Bantam had its own engine – pinched from the German DKW as part of war reparation – while the others (and there were several of them) were fitted with 125 or 200ccVilliers engines. We are, of course, excepting motor scooters at this time.

However, though the new Hondas employed unheard-of equipment levels, their appearance was nonetheless very familiar. The engines bore more than a passing resemblance to the German 250cc NSU twins which had won several World Championships in motorcycle racing a few years previously, while the chunky, pressed-metal frames and leading-link front forks were almost identical to the 250cc, single- cylinder overhead camshaft NSU *roadsters*.

The general finish of the machines looked fantastic in print, with Post-box Red and Reckitts Blue dominant, the bikes fitted with matching dual-seats and their unusual, rectangular 'knife-edge' styling. I can't remember all of the technical specifications which may have been included, but the 250 employed the classic 54x54mm bore/stroke specifications, while the 305cc (which, because it was in the higher registration bracket, became the orphan of the storm) was over-bored to 57mm.

Contrary to popular belief, the 50cc C100 step-thru which really secured Honda's fortunes didn't arrive in Australia until early in August,1958, a scant few weeks after the first model left the production lines the first week of August, the bike later displayed on the Bennett and Wood stand at the 1958 Motor Show towards the end of August. That odd little machine shared its spot with the few other machines in Honda's – at the time – small range of motorcycles. That little step-thru was to prove to be the machine which saved the entire motorcycle industry world-wide, for I have always maintained that Honda was unarguably the motorcycle company which placed the whole world back on two wheels again. With more than 50 years gone

Ryde Motorcycles

and some 60 Million-plus machines later, the machine is still being made (in various guises, it must be said), often with an overhead camshaft engine and up to 110cc capacity, with varieties of the original machine being used by Postmen, Farmers, Commuters and a large variety of people from almost every field of endeavour you could think of.

Incredibly, Honda was to presage this scenario in the design of that first Cub's brochure, because that original brochure, which arrived with the first batch of machines, carried several photo illustrations of people riding it about who were clearly not your average motorcyclist but who were nonetheless actually mounted upon a 'sort of' motorcycle; however small and odd-looking that machine may have been.

That initial full-colour brochure from August 1958, with its most unusual illustrations, quite probably lead to that great American Classic promotion which was to appear a few years later, and which extolled the virtues of the little machine as never before, while suggesting to a stunned world that **"You Meet the Nicest People On a Honda!"**. The later American promotion, possibly following on from the original Honda brochure, would surely have been amongst the greatest publicity campaigns ever promoted.

So, Honda had arrived – the first machines had appeared in Sydney in April, 1958 – and the *Renaissance* of motorcycling had begun. It began in Australia, be well aware of that, for Honda arrived here a scant year before the machines were introduced into its next markets, which of course included America. The bikes – including the all-new 50cc C100 step-thru -were on display on Bennett and Woods' motorcycle stand at the Sydney Motor Show in late August of 1958, a few months before they were seen in the Netherlands, and almost a full year before they appeared in 1959 at the Earls Court Motorcycle Show in England.

Clearly, they had arrived first in Australia because of our very close proximity to Japan, but just how good were they, how well did they perform, what problems, if any, did Honda have in those very early days? We shall shortly see as we unfurl the Good, the Bad and indeed, the Ugly of HONDA and its arrival in Australia, the first nation – in fact the first city – in the world to import this brand new machine!

Honda arrived in Australia very quietly in very, very small numbers, to be followed almost at once by that bunch of quiet but determined Japanese who – I was later to learn – *visited every suburban motorcycle shop in Sydney* to deliver their pile of colour brochures and thus create interest before we were finally advised of the marque's quiet arrival in Sydney. I have been advised that there had been a delivery of similar brochures in the State of Queensland, however it was Bennett and Wood, the *New South Wales* BSA/Sunbeam distributors, who were the first people **in the world** to import Honda motorcycles.

It was an odd marketing ploy by the Japanese but was certainly effective, because the trio of short Orientals who announced Honda's very recent arrival uttered not a whimper when they arrived unannounced and handed me a bunch of colour brochures, and they said even less when they quickly departed. That non-existent whimper, we were not to know, took a little time to become a rumble, before it developed into a full-blown bang.

It has been said that the first stage of interest is confusion, and the second stage of interest is curiosity; both of which, and in particular the former, the Honda advance men had well and truly generated.

What were these bikes all about anyway; who were distributing them; what did they look like in the flesh; were we ever going to see the things; was it all a figment of one's overly fertile imagination; were the Honda reps likely to be heard from again – in fact did the machines which looked so exciting really exist??? These were questions we all asked ourselves and each other, but we had no idea where to turn for the answers.

For a start nothing had yet been heard from any of the major motorcycle importers about these new machines, which was no surprise because the whole industry was in a world-wide slump and the sudden appearance of a brand new name would seem to be a case of too little/too late. Almost everything on two wheels was made in England at the time, and in small quantities at that, while Moto Guzzi was seen in single-digit numbers and the two German entrants, Zundapp and BMW, were both on the brink of bankruptcy.

It's hard to believe today, but the arrival of the Japanese aroused some curiosity, but not much else, for they were initially referred to (and, I have to say, with some accuracy at the time) as 'Jap Crap.' If the British motorcycle industry was in its death-throes, how could the late entry of a brand-new *marque* from Japan be of any help at all? Exciting though these new models

Vintage Morris

appeared on paper, they could hardly make an impact on a failing industry, could they?

How wrong would that assumption be, for Honda was to save the industry almost as it was on the lip of the gurgler, with many great and famous marques either gone forever or feeling the cold draft of approaching doom at the back of their collective necks.

As we have noted, most people assume the little step-thru was the first Honda machine to appear, but it was in fact the *C70 250* twin, virtually identical to the machines in the brochure – but minus the electric starter – which first appeared in Australia.

The C71 models had starter motors fitted and they were accompanied by the C77 orphans, the 305cc over-bored machines which, unhappily, were in the no-mans-land of a higher registration bracket. The bikes were accompanied in their crates by small packets of colour brochures, because, strange though it sounds, there was some sort of import ban on colour brochures at the time.

According to my brother, who worked for Bennett and Wood at the time, in late 1957 a bright blue Honda stood on the showroom floor opposite his spare parts counter, and it bore a tag with the legend "To the Biggest Motorbike Shop in Sydney" attached to its handlebars. It had, so he said, done the rounds of just about every store in Sydney and had been returned with thanks but little else. It appeared that Bennett and Wood, perhaps out of desperation, had decided to become the new marque's distributor and they ordered a few of the machines *'on spec'* to see how they fared.

The company ordered twelve of the new Hondas and another twelve were ordered shortly thereafter. Bennett and Wood then became more serious and placed more substantial orders for the new Japanese machines, even as demand for the British BSA motorcycles they had imported for years was waning.

Our local Ryde Lions Club decided to hold a Motor Show in 1958 as a fund raiser on a large, vacant block near the Ryde shopping centre and had erected several large marquees to house the various vehicles they had hoped to entice. They were rewarded by the full support of all the local car dealers and the **one** motorcycle dealer in the area....which was, of course, Ryde Motorcycles!

I recall riding a small 175cc four-stroke Moto Guzzi '*Lodola*' to our display at the show, along with a couple of scooters, including a 200cc two-stroke Zundapp '*Bella*', a fairly large scooter with 12-inch wheels, telescopic forks and a quite punchy performance; a new Tiger 110 Triumph; The International Norton we still had in the showroom; a single-cylinder 600cc ohv Norton; a 200cc James commuter, one or two more I cannot remember... *and just one brand-new, bright red, 1958 C71 Honda Dream.*

The new Japanese motorcycle was delivered to the shop in one of Bennett and Wood's Harley-Davidson bun-trucks and it looked fantastic, with its full equipment levels, gleaming paint and chrome finish and smooth engine mouldings: but I have to confess we still surveyed it with some suspicion. So did the outfit's rider, who told me that this was the *first one* of that small batch of 'these new Jap things' to ever leave Bennett and Wood, which didn't mean much at the time, but which was to become quite propitious.

To make the most of the new, unproven machine, the C71 Honda was allocated pride of place on a raised plinth at the Lions Motor Show and I enjoyed immensely the startled looks of the passing peasantry as I plied the electric starter motor to fire the little engine up and then, as an unwarranted encore, to turn the blinkers on and off *ad nauseam*. The bike created a great deal of interest and, to our surprise and delight, ***I sold several of them, almost on the spot, as a result!*** I had no idea of the price of the new machine, and in fact didn't even know if it was for sale but there were people eager to place a Ten Pound holding deposit on them, so we were happy to accept the money – and the order – and to clean the mess up afterwards. Happily, there was no mess to clean up!

I cannot make that claim, for I imagine the facts cannot be proven, but it could well be that the C71 Honda machines for which I took the six (6) Ten Pound holding deposits may have been the first of their type to be sold – and personally registered, for I rode the new bike to the Motor Registry myself – anywhere outside of Japan.

In order to more closely examine the design of the unusual, pressed-metal, box-section spine frame on that little 250 twin we had on display, we removed the Honda fuel tank when the Motor Show was over, only to be horrified at the roughly-hewn, hand-beaten *underside* of the tank where it cleared the top frame section. We were then aghast at the legend, "C.C.Wakefield CASTROL" which could just be seen gleaming under the thin coat of paint which covered the underneath of the component. (N.B: Over the years many people have tried to assure me that this is a well-known *urban myth*. Let me attempt to assure the doubters that I removed the tank on that very first Honda C71 *myself* and saw its underside with my own eyes.)

Was this, I thought at the time, an early, pre-production prototype which had slipped away un-noticed in that first shipment from the factory, or could this rare and brand new marque, we wondered aloud, be using crate-loads of old Castrol oil tins in the manufacture of the base of its well-sculpted fuel tanks. If so, what horrors were we to find inside the unit construction engine/gearbox? We were to find out shortly thereafter! Those six, Ten Pound deposits were by then looking a bit like they may be sadly refunded, and in very short order!

Great though these new machines looked, the welding on many frame pressings and pipe-tube ends, the latter simply flattened out, instead of being scarped – or 'fish-mouthed' – to provide a neat fit against other tubing, left a great deal to be desired. True, the ends of the round-section, flattened tubing were well disguised by thick coats of black, baked-enamel, but I have often heard these rough finishes described as 'toothpaste' welding, or, more indelicately, 'bird shit', either of which were an accurate description of some very grim work indeed.

It has to be said that those early Honda engines would idle like well-oiled Swiss watches, but there were some cynics who suggested you could hear them wearing out, for the overhead cam drive chain and valve gear was noisy.

In head-on view, the 250cc C71 Honda 'Dream' was pyramid-shaped, the ultra-wide crankcases having the fat mufflers sweeping outboard of them with footrest hangers, rear brake pedal and centre-stand arm outboard of that. Allied to this were tiny, 16-inch wheels, which allowed minimal cornering clearance.

Just as well, I have to say, because the highly-polished and rock-hard Japanese tyres fitted to the first batches of machines had about the same grip on dry road surfaces as an ice-block, and were downright lethal in the wet. Furthermore, there were tramlines everywhere in Sydney in the late fifties, and they added their considerable danger to the equation.

You couldn't corner quickly on those early Honda machines even if you wanted to, but you could pull into a gutter and use its left muffler as if it were a prop-stand – in fact, if the bike was cranked over a few degrees from the vertical when you were riding it the mufflers would dig into the road surface with great enthusiasm and ease the wheels off the ground, with entirely predictable consequences!!

To make matters worse, the suspension system, though comfortable enough, imbued the bikes with a feeling akin to riding a horse at high speed as the machines would rock back and forth with abandon, the springs contained within leading-link forks on the front and oblong-shaped shocks on the rear seemingly bereft of any form of effective damping.

If you applied the front brake hard enough, the front-end would dive onto full bump and then patter about almost uncontrollably. It took several years before the Japanese learned how to make a halfway decent tyre, a shock absorber which employed any form of efficient damping, or a rear drive chain which lasted more than a couple of months!

True, the new Honda looked great and went acceptably well, but could have been a disaster to own for more than a few months, for it was an odd machine to ride.

The Dream – or *Nightmare,* as almost everybody called it – had a couple of extra tricks up its sleeve to trap the unwary. First of all, it had a gear change lever on the *left side*, where all British motorcycles had more 'normal' right foot change; it had an engine-speed clutch on the end of the crankshaft – spinning at four times the speed it would be if it was fitted on the gearbox main-shaft – and (horror of horrors!) the gearbox employed the dreaded 'rotary' gear-change.

That so-called rotary gear-change was tricky at the time, because you would push the pedal down from neutral to select first gear, then down again for second, down again for third, and down yet again to select top gear. If, or more often when, you pushed the pedal down again, you would be back where you started.... in neutral.

Then, *and this is the trickiest part of all*, if, in your confusion at apparently missing a gear, you pushed the pedal down again, it would select first gear once more, lock the back wheel, spin sideways, snap at least one of the rear chain adjusters, and then happily pelt you straight over the handlebars!!

This happened to many riders and it happened many times, so much so that if the rider of a brand-new Honda entered your spare parts department on tip-toe, his eyes agleam with tears and his bottom lip sucked it, you would reach under the counter and present him with two new rear chain adjusters and a steering damper knob. You could, if brave enough, suggest he make a visit to his Doctor for urgent

Vintage Morris

repairs or any other spare parts he might need for himself.

The ratio, as I remember it, was two sets of rear chain adjusters to one crankshaft, which, on the second occasion as you sailed over the handlebars would snap like a carrot and thus require a complete replacement. The crankshaft – Part number 13000-250-003 from memory, and supplied at once, with no questions asked – came in a neat little box and was completely assembled, with four main bearings, four crank cheeks, con-rods, big-ends, camshaft drive sprocket and oil seals. The replacement crankshafts, of which there were many, also featured substantially thicker crankpins (the original were a tiny 25mm, or one-inch, in diameter) and crank cheeks which were *slightly* better machined.

The crank assembly was fully pressed-up, as we've observed, but the machining of the small flywheels which formed the main-shafts and crank cheeks were originally rough-hewn from the solid and were covered with gouges and chatter marks from fast-feeding paring tools. This could be an indictment on the skill of the engineers and/or the haste with which the components were being machined. Perhaps demand was beginning to out-strip supply, or was Honda anxious to quickly introduce the new marque to a previously-shrinking marketplace?

The C71's little brother,125cc Honda Benly twin, was a sweet little unit and pretty well trouble-free, but the screaming little Sports variant of the 125 Benly– which produced its peak power of an amazing 15BHP at an unheard of 9500rpm! – was a beautifully sculpted machine from its alloy tank to its 18" wheels and huge drum brakes. Its performance was unheard of, for it would blow away any 250 (and most 350cc machines) which tried to give it a hard time, but its skinny, non-grip tyres could be even more of a handful than the shocking rim-protectors on the roadster 250 and 305cc models.

Honda improved, of course, and very quickly at that, with one of its finest machines, the Hawk, in both 250 and 305cc variants, appearing a few years later with a more acceptable semi-tubular and pressed-metal frame, telescopic forks, rear shocks that were so much better than the original oblong disasters, and other exciting dynamics.

Those new models employed twin-leading shoe drum brakes front – and *rear* – and much improved handling. The clutch had by then been moved to its rightful place on the gearbox main-shaft and the shocking rotary gear-change had also thankfully disappeared. The Honda Hawk was, in fact, a first rate motorcycle, which proved beyond question that Honda could learn very quickly indeed, for the machine was fast, well braked, a nice handler and, as a bonus, was also very reliable.

As we remarked at the start of this epic, the jewel in the crown was the quirky little 50cc step-thru, which achieved almost universal acceptance as cheap and ultra-reliable transport. It was a great favourite with Uni. students and nurses – especially those at Ryde Hospital – earning it a nickname as the Nurses' Bike. We sold a large number of the little bikes to many of the nursing staff (and not a few impecunious student doctors) who were seen riding the things about all over the place.

According to the literature which was in the pile of the original C100 brochures, the bike was good for some 45mph and around 180 miles per gallon of fuel – that's in the old money, of course – but I never had any reason to doubt the figures, then or now. It was also, according to the cute Japanese screed, "Quick like a squirrel".

I remember hearing of two *very large* employees of Bennett and Wood, who decided to put the first step-thru to the ultimate test by riding the device from a standing start at the bottom of the steep Wentworth Avenue hill to Bennett and Wood's assembly area and showroom at the top of the hill.

The rider was a certain Ken Pickering, the pillion passenger an uncertain Russ Burling, the latter quite sure he would have to abandon the little Honda while the machine was still in first gear. Burling had suggested he would have to jump off the little step-thru as soon as second gear was selected.

So the large, daunting duo took off, giggling like a pair of pre-pubescent schoolgirls, only for them to be amazed to discover the bike actually pulled away fairly smartly from rest and even accepted the change into second gear. The road flattened out a little halfway up the climb at Hunt Street, whereupon Pickering optimistically selected top (third) gear and the bike picked up a little more pace. Just a little, be it understood, but remember it was pulling two very, *very* large people (and itself!) up a steep hill, from a standing start, and with only a tiny 50cc overhead valve engine to power it!

The duo then turned into the layback and attacked the even steeper ramp to the second-floor assembly area of Bennett and Woods' building, which it successfully climbed, the tyres

Ryde Motorcycles

almost as flat as pancakes, the wheel rims almost scraping the road. The Honda Cub needed second gear at the start, and then into first at the very top of the steep ramp to the assembly area, but its performance – I have been assured by brother Don, who was there to witness it – was greeted with stunned looks and slack jaws at every turn.

Clearly, with just one person aboard, and hopefully a trim nurse at that, the bike's performance would be quite acceptable, and so the step-thru was thrust into a market-place it was later to dominate.

Honda, from such humble beginnings, has been here to stay since April, 1958, when the first machines trickled into Australia, the country which unquestionably saw the re-birth of motorcycling world-wide. It might support my argument that Honda placed the whole world back onto two wheels, just as almost every other motorcycle manufacturer on earth was on the slippery-slide to oblivion. The company's saviour, that trail-blazing step-thru, which arrived later in 1958, has changed little over the years, and is now manufactured in some 20 countries outside Japan. Australian Postmen have been using a variant of the little runabout – a close relation to the motorcycle-like 110cc overhead *camshaft* Trail Cub, but with more weather protection – since the early 70's and there seems to be no likely replacement.

Creeping up above that astonishing 60,000,000 machines made and sold in the intervening years the funny little step-thru has made, and secured, a niche for itself as a most amazing little machine, which has proved to be at once ultra-reliable and almost bullet-proof. It is far and away the most popular motorcycle ever made, whether we purists like it or not, and is in fact the most popular motor **vehicle** ever made!

There are some of the "Nicest People" along with some very odd characters riding these little things on the back roads and market places of Vietnam and many other Asian countries, just as you are likely to find similar characters in this country.

Is there yet another variant of that remarkable little bike in the breeze, do you think; a twenty-first century step-thru, perhaps? The enormous number of new Honda machines of all capacities, shapes and sizes shows no sign of abating, and Honda has embraced the 'new' scooter craze with some enthusiasm, so something far beyond the norm may again be seen in the marketplace.

Could there be, let's say, an enclosed, car-type two-wheeler on the drawing boards with gyroscopic stabilizer and hub-centre steering? Could there be a levitating **no**-wheeler???

Honda has done it all before, with the first eye-popping C71 motorcycle in 1958, and then the ground-breaking little commuter which arrived just a few months later, to then become so monumentally successful. Honda may well do it all over again, perhaps to place the whole world upon *no wheels* at all?

Velo 350

One of the sweetest motorcycles it was ever my good fortune to ride was a 'simple' single-cylinder 350cc MAC Velocette of 1953 vintage, which was just on four years old at the time. It was simple only inasmuch as it was a pushrod-operated, overhead valve design with just two valves in the newly-designed cylinder head.

The basic design had been around since the thirties, but the bike was catapulted into the early fifties by the adoption of an all-alloy head and barrel in 1951 and then all but perfected in 1953 with the addition of a neat swing-arm rear suspension, much improved front forks and the much-needed clean-up of the gearbox and timing-case castings which had occurred when the 'new' engine was cosmetically enhanced two years earlier. The bike also featured an odd two-level dual-seat, which allowed a pillion passenger to be accommodated half a head higher than the rider, for a reason which escaped me then, as it does now, for no-one else offered this design feature back then.

If the seat was comfortable in the extreme, it became even more so as the base of the rider's portion of the seat cracked and allowed the seat to droop onto one of the frame rails, assuming a better shape for a poised posterior than the designers originally intended. Unhappily, the 6-Volt voltage regulator was placed just under the seat, which meant that it had to be moved to a position slightly further along the frame rail – which then allowed the seat to droop even more and in fact become even more comfortable!

If the two-level seat looked odd to start with, then it became even odder in shape, and, though we were not to know this at the time, of course, it very much resembled the shape of the seats fitted to today's new batch of Harley-Davidson motorcycles. Come to think of it, the gap between the (normally) flat base of the dual-seat and the top of the rear guard was nicely enshrouded by the 'new' shape of that seat.

1956-1960

Of course we tried to correct the anomaly by removing the seat and trying to straighten it out and then weld some strengthening gussets underneath the thing, but didn't bother trying to remove the rubber padding or the vinyl cover before so doing. We were rewarded for our absurdity by the retch-making pong of heated rubber and the almost fatal stench of burning PVC material – if that is, in fact, what the material was.

We pretended we hadn't touched the seat as we gently bolted it back in place, and found, at once to our chagrin and to our delight, that it was almost exactly the same shape as if we hadn't touched the bloody thing at all.

Sweet though that little gem was it had a couple of quite odd traits, neither of which we could ever really come to grips with. First of all was the odd Velocette clutch, which many a former owner of this brand will say was not an odd trait at all, but in fact a clever feature of the machine's design. That's all right for them to say, but I could never – ever – come close to adjusting the clutch correctly when the time came for such a routine task.

You see, the countershaft (final drive) sprocket was mounted on the *outside* of the gearbox shaft, instead of being hidden in behind the clutch as on other machines. There were a couple of holes drilled in the face of the sprocket through which a small rod could be inserted, the bike simply wheeled back or forth to allow for the essential free-play at the clutch lever and to relieve pressure on the thrust bearing which resided just inside.

Over the three years I had access to the bike – it wasn't actually mine, but spent more time in my garage than it did in its owners! – I must have wheeled that little MAC Velo several kilometers back-and-forth, hither-and-yon, to-and-fro, left-to-right, right-to-left, A-to-Z, one-to-ten, and then back again, and again, and never got the bloody thing right! Once, I even cheated a bit by altering the little adjuster which was fitted halfway along the outer casing of the clutch cable, and even *that* didn't work! I was, in fact, chastised for being so presumptuous in doing so. The adjuster was there, the mechanic in question assured me, just for decoration

Down it would go to the local motorcycle shop and it would then be adjusted correctly in about thirty seconds while I watched the procedure and learned absolutely nothing from it. I was never charged for the service, the shop's owner obviously sympathetic of fools. It was all right for him, he used to race a small stable of the things and obviously knew the Velocette (from the little 250 MOV to the 500cc MSS) models inside out.

For some reason, he didn't want to know about that odd little LE Velocette, the 150cc – later 200cc – *side-valve,* water-cooled, flat-twin whose plodding performance was so beloved of the English Police. It could be used for creeping up upon the wrong-doer, who couldn't hear it arriving until it ran over him. This would have been a cunning ploy, for if the miscreant in question was not run over, there is every chance he could out-perform the LE (for Little Engine) in a quick sprint around the block.

That little MAC had a couple of other odd traits which were more than a little annoying. For some reason, and we never really found out what the problem was, the oil return in the crankcase-mounted oil pump could never fully scavenge the large volume of lubricant which would collect in the bottom of the crankcases. If the bike was sitting for any time on its prop stand, the excess oil would run trickle down from the inside of the engine to collect in the crankcase, dribble through the drive-side main bearing and run into the primary chain-case. From there it would simply piddle out onto the ground and leave a large puddle of oil for everyone to point to and tut-tut over.

On the other hand, if the bike was to be placed on its alloy centre stand the crankcase would simply contain too much oil, which announced its presence for all the world to see when you fired the thing up again. I can clearly recall the camping area on top of Mount Panorama being well blanketed with a heavy cloud of oil smoke one cool Easter morning on one occasion, to the consternation and shouted abuse of the many campers who, doubtless, would have preferred to be somewhere else at the time.

We were aware that the pump needed to be a very close fit in the crankcase to obviate any air leaks around the pump's body, and that its gasket needed to be similarly air-tight. We were also well aware that the feed line from the oil tank employed a small spring-loaded ball to contain the oil above it, assumedly to counteract a problem similar to that which we were experiencing. The old trick of removing the oil line from beneath the ball and slipping the lid of a Vegemite jar under the pipe overnight to check for possible leakage proved there was no problem at that point. We even tried a brand new oil pump, but with the same results.

What to do? We pulled the engine apart and checked the crankcase breather, assured

Vintage Morris

ourselves there was no blow-by of gas past the piston rings and drilled little holes into, and through, any – and all – of the strengthening ribs and gussets in the crank-case and timing case castings. Our hope was, of course, that oil which would collect there would thus drain into the cases more quickly and then be scavenged more effectively.

We then bolted it all back together again after fitting new piston rings, valve springs and exhaust valve, but we were astounded at the time to see that the two valve-spring collars were cracked almost entirely across!! One of them was so close to breaking in half that I could actually flex it and see the crack expanding. They were of course replaced at once.

Hey, guess what? When I fired the engine up and took the bike for a long squirt and came home again to leave it standing for a while, it hadn't made a blind bit of difference!

I might say the first time the oiling problem manifested itself I was not aware of it. I had ridden the bike down to the local grocer's shop (no Supermarkets in those days, folks!) to pick up a half-pound of butter and a small bag of sugar, and had, as usual, spent more than a little time chatting to the proprietor before strolling out to fire the engine up.

No matter how hard I kicked the thing over the engine refused to start, so, to demonstrate my undoubted riding skill I slipped the bike into gear, rocked the engine back onto the compression stroke, whipped the clutch lever in and trotted alongside it to run-and-bump the device into life. I had shoved the butter and sugar up my jumper and tucked the garment into the front of my waistband before doing so of course!

I was unaware that I had just trodden in a small pool of warm oil and, just as I nudged the dual-seat with my right thigh, my left foot slipped away and the engine simultaneously fired up. I managed to jog along for a pace or two before both the sugar and butter decided to remove themselves from their confinement and drop to the ground. The sugar bag split open, as you would expect, and I trod firmly into the centre of the butter with one stride and then onto the spilled sugar with the other.

The last view the amazed shop owner had of that little bike was of its rider still side-saddle, pursued by a huge cloud of white smoke and frantically shaking the remains of the once-pristine foodstuffs off the sole of a well-oiled left boot. It was a disaster, and in no way helped by my returning on foot to the shop, and it grinning proprietor, an hour or so later to buy – what was it, again? Ah, yes – a half-pound of butter and a bag of sugar for a cake my long-suffering mum was trying the make.

It has to be said, though, once fired up and running well that MAC Velo was a great little thing on the road; smooth and fairly punchy for its size, it handled extremely well and had a well-muted but punchy exhaust note. The new, more heavily-finned alloy head and barrel looked very purposeful, but the engine seemed to be little noisier than earlier Velocette engines with cast-iron heads and barrels. There is nothing unusual about that because normal engine resonances have often been amplified by the later adoption of alloy engine castings. The engine was easy to work on, which was perhaps just as well, but there remained no obvious reason for the strange oil problem, and thus no easy cure.

We could, and did, come to grips with it, however, by having the machine parked overnight on its prop-stand, the while employing a large drip-tray underneath the primary drive chain-case. When parking the bike for much shorter periods of time, it was always a good idea to have it on its centre-stand, firing the engine up again shortly thereafter, with the engine still warm. And no, neither we, nor anyone else, ever found the cause of that odd problem.

Speedway bike

It is a question I have asked many motorcyclists who have laid claims to have ridden just about everything on two wheels, and I have asked the question of these people, whether they are new to the scene or have been involved in this wondrous pursuit for many years. The question, quite simply, is 'have you ever ridden a Speedway bike?'

I have asked this question of numerous people, regardless of any of the numerous sexes to which they may pledge allegiance, or to any number of religious persuasions, and I have proffered the same advice to every one of them who answered in the negative. I have suggested to each and every one them that, were they given the opportunity to ride one of those slender over-powering, fiendish devices, that no matter how enticing the offer might be, please take my friendly advice for what it might be worth: Don't do it!

Those bikes are a bugger of a thing. Or at least they were, because unlike the latter batch of more highly specialised machines with their lightly-sprung front ends and lay-down engines, the earlier JAP-engine Speedway bikes of which I speak were fiendishly difficult things to ride, and the more one may have been used to riding the more 'ordinary' motorcycles on the road, the harder these machines were to ride. I know this only too well, for I once rode one for myself – briefly to be sure, but long enough to forever state that I would never ride one again. Never!

For a start, once the things were underway you couldn't sit on them because the little seat with which they were equipped was not only rigidly mounted and rock hard, but was much too small to fit anything onto it which was any bigger than a baked bean sandwich. This mattered greatly because there was absolutely no rear suspension of any sort (and precious little, if any, at the front wheel, either) which meant that any track irregularities one was forced to traverse were transmitted equally and undiminished from both wheels to a body already wracked by shimmering engine vibrations, and it found its way from there up one's torso, and along one's arms, to the wide, sweptback handlebars.

The phenomena which followed was usually referred to as the 'growing handlebars syndrome' which was very descriptive because the feeling was one of the handlebars grips growing in diameter until they felt like the size of a pair of grapefruit, and were thus seemingly un-grippable. One's hands would by that time be a blur as the vibrations made their way back along one's arms and up one's neck until one's head felt like it was becoming **two's** head. Besides which, it became impossible to focus one's eyesight on anything, for the twin orbs which one uses in this pursuit were freely gyrating about within their enclosing sockets as though they weren't attached to anything!

There were no brakes on those machines either, which meant that if one was confronted with some poor bugger who had fallen on the narrow, dirt track ahead, the only thing to do was to throw the bike to the ground and let Fate manage the situation from then on. This extreme measure was really quite an art, and most riders who had to do this would usually scramble back to their feet and trot onto the infield uninjured. The odd limp they displayed at this time was generated by the steel 'slipper' which was slid over a rider's left boot and was used to prop up a machine which might otherwise fall over if that 'outrigger' left leg was withdrawn for some reason.

There was also no gearbox to speak of, the quite substantial power generated from that simple 500cc push-rod, single-cylinder JAP engine delivered *via* a primary drive to the rear wheel through a simple clutch. There was only one footrest, which was on the right side and extremely low-slung at that because as I was once advised before an ill-advised ride on one of those odd mounts 'all you do is open the throttle to the stop, drop the clutch like a hot potato and keep turning left!' Yes, you could rest your *left* foot if you must, but only for a brief couple of seconds down whatever straight there may be, and then only by resting it on top of the crankcase or on the flimsy bracket which covered the frantically spinning primary drive chain.

To make matters even worse, the frames of those speedway bikes were very slim and thus very light, the wheelbase excessively short and there was little trail angle at the front forks to speak of. This was to make certain that the high-powered, ultra-light motorcycle was a very quick handler, able to turn into a corner sideway and very suddenly: quite unlike, say, a Ducati Darmah with its long wheelbase and subsequent 'slow' turning speeds.

That's slow ***turning*** speeds, not to be confused with high ***cornering*** speeds.

But it gets even worse because the front wheel rim was always a narrow, large diameter hoop, the skinny tyre very heavily knobbed and not much wider than one you might find on a 1940's telegram boy's PMG pushbike, or a latter-day 'Mountain Bike'. The rear tyre by comparison was much bigger and more heavily knobbed, the more to provide a modicum of traction, if not enough to stop the wheel from spinning madly and trying to drive itself around the outside of the bike. Naturally, this meant that a speedway bike ridden with any degree of enthusiasm would spend almost an entire race– even down any short straights which might be found on most shorter speedway tracks – almost sideways, most of the bike at ninety degrees to the front wheel, its rear wheel pelting a plume of dolomite loam and fine clay over the fence or into the face of any rider who happened to be unfortunate enough to be anywhere but in first position.

The rider at full pelt on one of these unwieldy machines always appeared to be hanging on grimly for his very life on a machine which would appear to be only just under control, at any time likely to pelt him on to a rough dirt surface which was flying by underneath him at an enormous speed.

Ryde Motorcycles

Consider this: Jim Airey was one of Australia's greatest ever speedway riders, and the absolute master of Sydney's Royale speedway on the 'old' Sydney Showground. The track was one of the finest in the world and it was just on 1/3 mile in length. A 'normal' race was three laps in duration which was of course was just on a mile long. Jim held the three-lap record on that Speedway track at a click under 59 seconds. Had the record been a neat 60 seconds then the **average** speed would of course have been 60 miles (100 Kilometres) per hour, but Jim's record stood at an *average* somewhat closer to **70mph!**

That's a mile from a **standing start** in under a minute, which means that to maintain this average the speed down the two 'straights' on the Sydney Showground must have been approaching 80 miles per hour in the old money, or 140 Km/hour!! And mounted on one of those frightful things which was leaping and cavorting about as though it had a mind of its own, and without benefit of a decent suspension system **or brakes**! Heroic stuff, indeed!

It should be noted that Jim is one of the very few speedway riders who never had a serious accident on any speedway track in the world, even though he won four Australian Championships (three on the Royale) and rode for some years in the highly competitive Speedway League in England. I asked him about this in 2010 when I was the on-course commentator at the 50th Anniversary short circuit meeting held on the Nepean Raceway outside Penrith, and he told me he had always 'ridden within myself, and taken no chances in winning races at the slowest possible speed.'

Did he say 'the slowest possible speed?' Yes, he did, so who knows what that three-lap record at the Royale would have been had Jim been really trying!!

I thanked Jim for the chat during the lunch break on Day Two – I tried to interview him over the course PA system but he politely declined – and fell to brooding later in the day about my own (early) experience on riding such a potent weapon as a JAP-engine speedway motorcycle, similar to the type Jim was to ride with such brilliance some 20 years later; a machine which I was talked into attempting to ride back in the late-fifties.

In those days Arcadia, which is in the Hornsby area, was out in the sticks and no-one knew it existed. No-one, that is, except for a few stalwarts who had carved out a rough, and entirely illicit, 'speedway track' in the bush where riders would often go to practice their craft.

This fellow had just bought a speedway iron from, I think, a well-known shortish rider called 'Porky' Levy, and he was anxious to take it to Arcadia to put it (and himself) through its paces.

We loaded up the Speedway JAP onto a three-bike trailer along with his short-circuit Velocette and drove into the scrub at Arcadia along a rough bush track. There were already some other riders there, the air rent with the sounds of several machines being ridden at a variety of speeds, while a light dust cloud hung in the air above. I helped him push-start the bike – which surprised me by firing up very easily in a couple of paces. He warmed the engine up for a minute or so by leaning the bike onto its low-slung right footrest, the rear wheel clear of the ground and spinning freely. The engine's external Pilgrim oil pump operated on the 'total loss' system, which meant that it would pump oil into the engine with some enthusiasm, but what was returned to the crankcases was then clearly to be seen piddling out of a hole in the engine and onto the track surface.

The tiny fuel tank was filled by about two cups-full of alcohol fuel – the speedway engines always ran a compression ratio of around 12 – 15 to 1, and could only be run on alcohol, or in later years, occasionally on nitro-methane, and usually ran for three, or occasionally, four laps. Once warmed to the task my mate dribbled slowly to the middle of the short 'straight' and then suddenly opened the twist grip to the stop, dumped the clutch and took off like a rocket, the bike side-on in next to no time.

Even though he didn't have a motorcycle licence (oddly enough, not many speedway riders did!) he could really ride a motorcycle, and he demonstrated his prowess in no uncertain terms by tearing up that track like nobody on that same surface seemed able to do. We filled that fuel tank several times as he returned to the track again after a breather, and then he invited me to have a ride. "After all," he said, "you've had your bike licence for about four years, and you reckon you can ride OK. Be a bit different, but shouldn't be too hard."

Famous last words? Famous last words indeed!

I had cunningly forgotten to bring my leathers with me, but he was un-phased as peeled his off and kindly loaned them to me. It was the usual two-piece outfit, the lightly-padded leather breeches augmented by a safari-length jacket. The waist was a good fit, but it was no surprise to find the pants too long, for the crutch was down to about mid-thigh, giving the distinct

1956-1960

> *"With the engine screaming underneath me he suddenly dropped the hanky and I did the same thing to the clutch lever."*

impression that I had suddenly filled my nappy, which was not far off the mark. The jacket was similarly too large, but the cankerous looking helmet was as tight as a jam jar lid. It hurt from the moment I put it on until we managed to drag the thing off again with a loud popping sound several minutes later.

With me astride the machine we rocked the bike back against the compression and he pushed me off. As instructed so to do, I bumped down on that tiny seat and dropped the clutch. It felt like slamming my backside onto a paving stone, but again the high-compression engine surprised me by firing up easily in a couple of steps. Everything about me seemed to be shimmering as the bike started to shake from one end to the other, just as I was doing.

As we have already noted, his friendly advice to me was to 'flatten the engine and then just drop the clutch,' but he had also advised me that I should lean well forward to get as much of my weight over the front wheel as possible to avoid the bike rearing up and looping the loop underneath me. I had seen this happen often enough at the speedway to know exactly what he meant, so I crouched there with my elbows almost behind my back, my head strained forward as far as it would go while he waved his hanky at me to signal the 'start' of my first-ever ride on one of those awful machines.

With the engine screaming underneath me he suddenly dropped the hanky and I did the same thing to the clutch lever. Amazingly, the engine continued to howl like a mad thing... but the bike didn't move off the spot! I thought the clutch must have been slipping badly, but then I could feel the rear wheel sinking beneath me and looked back to see it spinning madly, a rooster-tail of dirt being flung several meters skywards. Naturally I moved my body back onto the lunchbox seat and closed the twist-grip off about a notch or two. It was the worst thing I could possibly have done!

Suddenly the rear tyre bit, the bike reared into the air and turned sideways at the same time, and we were away in flash, the feeling by now more like riding an out of control pogo-stick than any form of motorcycle. Of course I quickly backed off and the bike slowed very suddenly, clearly through heavy engine braking from its very high compression. The bike was a little more manageable by now, so I cracked the throttle open again, and this time the bike was instantly side-on again as it leapt a small grass verge and flew onto the infield. Of course I tried to crank it to the right to get back onto the uneven track surface but the low-slung footrest instantly dug in and flung the bike sideways in the other direction.

How I stayed on the thing I am not sure, because for much of that hundred or more meters the only part of me in contact with the bike at any one time was a pair of white-knuckled hands, desperately hanging onto a pair of wide, swept back handlebars. I was half on and half off the bike for much of that time, and I ached like a boil almost from head to foot for days afterwards.

I finally managed to tame the bloody thing to the point where I could once more join the track and then began a much more leisurely tour. By now not entirely (or quite, but nearly) under control I managed to enter the final corner after about four laps at a fairly reasonable pace, but negotiated it like one side of a giant octagon by executing a series of four lurid, badly controlled slides, instead of describing the lovely parabolic arc my friend seemed to find so easy to do.

I climbed stiffly off that bloody awful device in the pits as he picked himself up from the ground but he was still in hysterics as I politely suggested he should henceforth garage his speedway bike though a small orifice and into an area in which the sun never shines.

One day I hope to be able to sit down with the immortal Jim Airey and ask him just how it was that he managed to survive for so long, and to be so very successful, when riding one of those highly-specialised Speedway solo motorcycles. They were too fast for anyone's good; they were most uncomfortable, ill-handling, too-powerful machines, which had none of the 'normal' luxuries like brakes, any form of rudimentary suspension and no other creature comforts. Not only was Airey perfectly capable of doing that, but this was achieved on an enclosed, dirt-surfaced, narrow, bumpy track, which became bumpier and deeply rutted as the night's events wore on. Better him than me, I have to say!

Ryde Motorcycles

Chain drive

At the turn of the 20th century, the very few, simple 'motorcycles' which were in existence were little more than an ordinary 'Safety Cycle' which had had a small industrial engine fitted, the pushbike's frame sometimes strengthened, but more often than not left entirely alone. These early examples of powered cycles which were to be seen in miniscule numbers clattering about the countryside were often cobbled together in a blacksmith's shop, an engineer's workshop, someone's garage or, very occasionally, in what passed for an embryonic 'motorcycle factory'.

The odd thing is that, even though those flimsy 'motorcycles' had initially employed a chain to take man-power from pedal to rear wheel, they almost invariably employed a large leather belt, or one made of a riveted canvas and rubber strips, cobbled together to form a crude belt, thus allowing the machine's tiny engine to provide the drive from a small pulley to a large pulley attached to the rear wheel.

Occasionally, there might be a small chain drive from the engine to a supplementary reduction-box, or a primitive 'clutch', with the final drive by belt. With the simple chain drive fitted to all bicycles at that time, it seemed a strange way to go about transmitting power from an engine to the driven wheel, but we are talking about the very early days of motorcycling, which was more than century ago.

But motorcycle drive chains have actually been around for more than 100 years, with the Phelon and Moore 'Panther' adopting this method of power delivery to the rear wheel way back in 1900. The early Scott motorcycles of only a few years later were similarly chain-driven. The company called it 'all chain drive' because they employed a primary chain drive to a simple two-speed gear-cluster as well, with final drive again by chain.

Shaft drive made an appearance at about the same time, with such highly advanced machines as the Belgian FN utilising shaft drive on their 1904 *four-cylinder* motorcycle, while also adopting a type of telescopic front fork and magneto ignition.

It is interesting to note that belt drive, albeit in a much more effective form, has made an odd re-appearance on a number of modern motorcycles, while shaft final drive seems to be in use on many more motorcycles than ever before. Apparently, the newer, notched belt-drive system is trouble-free and is said to perform very efficiently whether hot or cold, wet or dry, on sealed roads and also on dirt surfaces, with little or no maintenance required.

It would certainly be a whole lot better than being forced to piddle onto a troublesome final drive belt to cool it down – as the old-timers sometimes were forced to do whenever the large leather belt became too hot and started to slip in its pulley. It's true, for this happened often enough to be part of early motor-cycling's history.

During this extreme exercise, the errant rider would no doubt disappear – coughing and cursing loudly – in a cloud of fetid steam, the exercise achieving several results almost simultaneously. In the first instance, one's modesty would be assured at one's sudden disappearance into the cloud; then, I would assume, the sinuses would be almost instantaneously cleared; the belt would magically assume its erstwhile effectiveness, and the loud hissing (hissing!) sound and accompanying steam cloud would so startle the horses that there was no possibility of the gent being run over by a passing carriage. An added bonus would be that the rider, thus relieved in more ways than one, could then continue the journey so recently interrupted.

Interestingly, an erstwhile friend tells the story of a Police officer who came upon a Scottish motorcyclist sitting forlornly alongside a belt-drive Triumph motorcycle early last century, the bike clearly unable to proceed because the belt had obviously overheated. "You just piss on the belt!" the rider was told. "Works every time." Apparently the rider seemed a little embarrassed by this advice and was clearly reluctant to raise the kilt to administer the advised procedure.

"Stand aside," beamed the helpful minion, "I'll show you how it's done" Whereupon the Police officer, with hands on hips and nodding politely at the hapless rider, proceeded to cool the drive belt with the enthusiasm – and volume – of a large draught horse. "There you are," he smiled as the steam slowly dissipated, "all done, and be on your way now."

The friendly Police officer received a polite letter from the local Doctor a day or so later, thanking the officer for what ever he had done in assisting the Doctor's **daughter** to continue her ride home on the Triumph, and suggesting, as he would be out of town for a day or so, that the Policeman kindly repeat the procedure – whatever it was and at his daughter's request – in the lounge-room of the Doctor's home while he

Vintage Morris

was away. Into the fireplace, or perhaps a vase of exotic plants, might we assume??

It is interesting to note that BMW, of all marques, now employs belt final drive on the odd model, with chain drive on others (!) after having been committed to shaft drive across the range from the company's first machine back in 1923.

However, chain drive – though the term 'chain' sounds almost archaic, not to say agricultural – will almost certainly remain the final drive and/or primary drive mechanism for a great number of motorcycles for many years to come. It is an extremely efficient system of transmitting power, easy to manufacture, less costly to replace, and very nearly trouble free. If correctly maintained, that is!

Loose, mal-adjusted, badly-worn or poorly maintained chain drive systems have been the cause of more disasters, high drama or accidental humour over the last hundred years than probably all the other woes that have beset motorcyclist since the devices first appeared.

Take, for example, the rider of a WLA Harley-Davidson in Melbourne some years ago who, upon leaping and sliding about on that city's tramlines, suddenly had his badly-worn rear chain fly off and lie, as though carefully placed there, in the groove which is in the centre of the tramline to locate the flange of the tram's wheels. He quickly rode to the footpath and ran back to rescue the chain, but was horrified to see one of the captive vehicles run directly over it.

"Chunk!...Chunk-a-chunk,...Chunk-a-chunk... Chunk!!" it went, wedging the chain into the groove with some enthusiasm. The rider, no doubt sobbing aghast at the sight of his beloved chain being mangled and even then totting up the price of a new one, staggered back to the Harley and swiftly removed a pair of pliers from an open saddle bag.

"Chunk!... Chunk-a-chunk, Chunk-a-chunk... Chunk!" said the second tram as it, too, ran over the chain just prior to its owner arriving with the pliers. Try as he might, the rider couldn't grasp the chain firmly enough to drag it out of further harm's way and had to give way to yet another tram as it bore down on him, its clanging bell sounding more like a death knell than a warning device.

"Chunk... (Bastards!) Chunk-a-chunk, (Give us a Break!), Chunk-a-chunk...(Bloody Hell!)... Chunk!" went the third vehicle, its pounding wheels augmented by the cries of the owner of the thoroughly-dead chain as he flew back to the bike and swiftly withdrew a large screwdriver from his saddle bag. He at last managed to prise the chain from its bonds and carried the lifeless component to the footpath where he stood shaking his head at the grim sight. Though clearly dead the chain was by no means limp, for it was as stiff as a poker and, though its owner tried manfully to resurrect it, the chain, not surprisingly, could not be persuaded to assume its original function. Or its original shape, for that matter.

We were at the Sydney Speedway one night when one of the riders lost a primary chain in the second lap of one of the feature events. It lay dangerously close to the centre of the track, waiting for a rider to run over it next time round and pelt it over the fence at someone. A white-coated Official rushed over and grabbed the chain only to discover it was extremely hot – which it had every right to be – and he pelted the thing over the fence and into the crowd himself, blowing on his hand as he did so, and then thrusting the hand under his other armpit. He thereupon began to flap that elbow about like a one-winged bird trying desperately to lift himself off the ground. It was all very amusing stuff for us kids, who often employed this same technique to elicit loud flatulent sounds, as we then began to demonstrate to an amused assemblage.

The BSA was howling flat-out along the back straight on the old Mt Druitt racing circuit, tucked in behind Freddy Boyd on his Norton, when there was a sudden puff of smoke ahead as the primary chain flew off his bike and swished loudly past my helmet, missing it by no more than a coat of paint! Knowing how hot that chain would have been, and how quickly it hurled itself past us, it takes little imagination to know what would have happened had it just cleared the handlebars and wrapped itself around my neck. "Off with his head!" shouted the Queen of Hearts. Phew!

I took Freddy to task after he had pushed the Norton into the pits, and he cheerfully informed me that the chain was long since worn out, which was the reason he was using the thing on the race bike instead of his roadster! He said he couldn't afford a new one, and in fact had a box-full of various-sized, well-worn chains soaking in old sump oil in his garage. I pointed out that a chain soaking in oil couldn't actually repair itself, but he just grinned and shrugged his shoulders as he strolled casually away.

A bloke rushed into my motorcycle shop in Ryde some years ago. "Me bike's stopped running," he breathlessly announced, "It suddenly revved up

Ryde Motorcycles

and stopped driving." I trotted out to have look at his bike, a C50 Honda step-through, and found the engine still running. I snicked the gearlever into what should have been first gear, only to discover it was already in gear but, as he had already stated, the bike refused to pull away.

It was decidedly odd, and could point to expensive gearbox or clutch problems, so we wheeled the bike into the workshop where it was fallen upon by a couple of eager mechanics. The engine ran as sweetly as a well-oiled Swiss watch, but try though we might we could not get the machine to drive, even though it slipped quite smoothly through the gears as it sat on its stand.

My brother Andy removed the little rubber bung from the rear chain enclosure and looked up in amazement. "Where's your drive chain?" he exclaimed loudly. "Me what?" replied the bike's owner. "The chain that drives the thing," said Andy "it's s'posed to be inside this chain-case."

"I don't know anything about those things," said the bike's owner, "that's why I have it serviced by the local bike shop."

"Well the bloody thing's not there now, but it *was* there not long ago. You can't go anywhere without a drive chain, mate."

I grabbed a pair of pliers and trotted onto the street outside and, sure enough, there lay the errant chain in the gutter several meters up the road. I picked it up and it proved to be one of the most badly worn chains I have ever seen. Every pin was loose in the chain's side plates, it was bone dry and covered with a film of reddish iron oxide and it played a recognisable tune as I carried it back inside to present it to its startled owner. I think the tune, from memory, was 'Jingle Bells.'

It was a surprise to have had the chain disappear and leave no evidence of its departure, but upon removing the lower chain-case the mystery was solved, for there was a large gap torn into the front of the metal covering where it had shed itself from the final drive sprocket and speared onto the road. We checked the drive sprockets, which were of course worn but not too badly, fitted a new chain and sent the rider away with a little more expertise on the mysteries of self-propelled vehicles. We also suggested he seek another service centre for his little bike.

It is not only in the primary and/or rear drive that chains are used extensively on motorcycles, for there is many an overhead camshaft which is driven by chain from outside the confines of a cylinder, where it can be easily replaced by simply removing a side panel, or – like Honda and several others – driven from the centre of the engine's crankshaft where it is not quite so easy to replace. These chains are usually well lubricated and automatically tensioned to allow for wear and backlash and are mostly long lasting and trouble-free, whereas a rear drive chain is usually subject to the elements and the too-casual owner, like the owner of the C50 Honda, who might carry out no maintenance on the essential device at all because it is hidden from view within its fully-enclosing chain cover and the owner may be unaware of its existence.

Speed traps

Radar speed traps are becoming even more cunningly-placed than ever they were. It has been stated that every Police car and motorcycle we see has been outfitted with these fiendish devices, while it has also been said that they are often hidden in wheelie bins and roadside letterboxes, even concealed in innocent-looking, parked, privately owned (?) vehicles of various descriptions. The first, (c)rude radar cameras arrived in Oz more than fifty years ago, believe it or not, and must have ploughed billions of dollars into this country's Consolidate Revue since their introduction. They will probably be with us forever, or so it appears, for these devices, which are too often of questionable worth, continue to support local and National Governments alike, as they more than pay their way by generating an enormous income from unwary motorists for Statutory bodies everywhere.

I can clearly remember an early example of this scourge sitting on the side of the road on what is now the six-lane Prospect Highway, but which was no more than a highly-polished, high-crown blacktop of just one lane either way, with wide dirt shoulders on either side. Interestingly, the excuse for the wide dirt shoulders on major roads and suburban streets alike 50 and more years ago was (so they said) to allow horses a more comfortable surface on which to plod as they dragged their respective delivery vehicles about. The fact that there were not very many of those vehicles about back then would seem to be incidental.

How clever of Councils and other authorities to think of such a half-baked excuse to save money, and how very devious!

I was zipping along that narrow Prospect Highway on my way to the Blue Mountains on the old BSA one day for a brisk squirt over the top and down the other side, when I breasted

1956–1960

a small rise and beheld a queue of cars, and a couple of motorcycles, pulled up on the opposite side and sitting forlornly on the dirt shoulder. They were partly concealed in a small dip in the road which could not be seen when approaching from the West.

This small group of fellow road-users were attended by several Police officers gleefully licking their pencils and doling out speeding tickets as quickly as their eager hands could scribble them out. One of them, an extremely large Sergeant, seemed to be dancing an energetic jig as if he had supposedly surpassed his quota, or, I thought at the time, may have recently discovered he was standing on a large ant hill whose inhabitants had just announced their annoyance at his presence.

This was indeed curious, and so was I (some may say I still am!) so I whipped over the next rise and executed a neat U-turn to pull onto the shoulder just over the apogee and parked the bike on the dirt. It was clearly an early Radar Speed Trap in operation, but I was concerned that so many of my fellow travellers had been ensnared therein and I wanted to find out why.

The answer was not long in becoming evident, for the small sign (which was then required by Law, and may still be for all I know) bearing the legend "WARNING! RADAR SPEED TRAP AHEAD!" was very conspicuous by its absence. Perhaps, I remember thinking, the wind had blown the thing over or into the nearby weeds, but a quick *sortie* indicated it was simply not there at all!

Could it be that in their frantic dash from the Office to do their bit in assuring the Police Force should make a profit (?) from their efforts that the little sign was left in a broom closet somewhere; was it, I wondered, still languishing in the boot of one of the Holden Police cars which were so evident when the unwary swept into the net just over the rise? Whatever the reason was, it was at least very sneaky of the officers in question and quite probably illegal, not to say unsporting, as it so often is to this day.

Have we not all seen that little sign placed at the very wheel of the offending radar- equipped Police car, instead of a hundred meters or more up the road where, one assumes, it is supposed to be? Would it make any difference if it was placed a *kilometre* away? Probably not, for it would be a poor radar device which could not have picked up an enemy plane a great distance away, much less a smaller target almost within sight!

Be that as it may, I reckoned I should do my bit in assuring the safe passage of other road users and moved down the road to flag down the speedsters who were on their way to unintentionally donating even more funds into Government coffers. Some of the approaching motorists raised a thumb in acknowledgement and slowed down, others made an entirely different, and most unwarranted, gesture and sped on.

Served them right, I thought, I had done my civic duty in trying to prevent people committing an offence (the motorists, that is, not the Police!) and those who failed to respond deserved all they got. Or all they lost.

On reflection, some of those drivers could have been forgiven for wondering what the hell this short-arsed fool was doing on the side of the narrow goat-track waving them down when there was apparently nothing up ahead to concern them. But one does not ignore the flashing headlights of an approaching car these days, which is quite probably warning us of an Official Presence just out of sight ahead, does one? One certainly does not! Serve them right, I repeat, if they chose to ignore my almost frantic efforts at that time.

I had been on duty for some little time when suddenly my left arm was grasped in a vice-like grip and I was lifted onto tip-toe and spun around. My assailant was an extremely large Police sergeant! He was probably the biggest human I have ever seen (though most of them look big to me!) and he loomed so large I was struggling to see daylight past him. He glared down at me balefully, his little squinting eyes gleaming beneath a lone, long black eyebrow which looked like a giant caterpillar resting along his brow.

His face looked for all the world like one of the abstract Picasso paintings; the paintings often in a light purple tint, with odd-shaped ears and a large nose. In the Police officer's case, though glaring at me in full-face, his grotesque nose was so well broken it appeared to be distinctly in profile. His huge beer-belly would have easily won a Gold Medal in any International competition, but I noted his belt was several sizes too small, which may have helped account for the colour of his face. His hat was also several sizes too small. I was not about to advise him of these observations.

His slightly foam-flecked lips were the colour of goat's liver, and they surrounded a set of too-large false teeth a couple of shades on the yellow side. I couldn't help but notice that, although

Vintage Morris

Ryde Motorcycles

he wore the regulation long blue trousers, his breath was coming in short pants. He had thus, I assumed, spotted my efforts from afar and had shuffled up as quickly as he could to deter me.

He had certainly done that!

"What," he trumpeted, about a meter and a half over my head, "the Hell do you think you're doing?" I noticed that his lips moved, but the large teeth didn't. They were, unbelievably, so large they needed a conscious effort to stop them being spat several meters up the road. I wondered what would happen to them whenever he sneezed; perhaps he whipped them out first?

"I'm stopping these cars from exceeding the speed limit." I announced, hoping to receive some acknowledgement for my services. He looked at me with the same amazed expression you would expect if I had suddenly divested myself of my garments and stood starkers in front of him, or had decided to have a leak onto his boots. I thought for a second he was going to faint and that I might end up underneath him – a daunting prospect indeed.

"You're doin' what?" he bellowed, making my eyes water with the draught, "that's what **we're** supposed to be doin'! 'Snot up to you to do that"

He then offered to arrest me for some offence or other, but I hastened to point out to him that surely one could not be taken to task for trying to prevent people from committing an offence, and thus it could then hardly be an offence in its own right. He half closed one eye and gazed skywards as I could see him struggling with what I considered to be the logic of my statement. A few seconds later he nodded as though some Providence had provided him with the answer to his dilemma.

"Come on, you," he said, as he lead me down to where the BSA was parked. "Let's have a look at your bike!"

As any ageing Ulysses member will tell you, this was a common ploy of Police officers in the 'Olden Days', hoping (you would assume at the time) that they would find the machine out of registration, shod with bald tyres, or – as was too often the case – with an exhaust system which was on the far side of noisy. How they could define 'noisy' would of course depend on the sensitivity of the ears of the Officer in question, but in most cases Police ears could be very sensitive indeed.

Particularly if the BSA in question happened to be in an extremely high state of tune and fitted with a 'straight-through' absorption-type muffler with carefully measured exhaust pipe length, and a satisfying, if quite fruity, sound! Oh, dear.

"OK, fire it up!" he ordered, as we arrived at the bike and he lowered my feet to the ground again, and stood hands on hips.

So help me, in my urgency to comply with the demand I could not get the bloody thing to do more than kick back when I tried to boot it over, probably because in my panic I couldn't get the piston into precisely the correct position after its compression stroke

I kicked the blasted thing over time and time again and it wouldn't fire up until finally the smell of unburnt petrol filled the air.

Then, as I watched in total amazement, the copper fell to his knees and opened the small toolbox on the side of the machine to extract the tool-roll every self-respecting rider always carried with him. It was, he was soon to find, as complete a kit as you would ever need for any British motorcycle.

There were well-oiled spare cables for every control, a set of points, two spare spark plugs, a couple of globes, two connecting links for each chain and a chain punch, several valve cores and caps, a few spanners (including a plug spanner) and a screwdriver, a puncture repair kit and a pair of short tyre levers. The lot were wrapped in a greasy cloth to stop them rattling about.

Surprisingly, he nodded approvingly. "Nice kit," he said as he grabbed the plug spanner, "Let's have that plug out!" In short order he had removed the spark plug, blew on it very heartily and replaced it, rolled the tools up again and replaced them in their heart-shaped box.

Then, he shoved the bike off its stand, slotted the bike into first gear and trotted a few steps down the dirt shoulder and nudged the saddle with a horse-sized thigh. The engine fired up instantly and the Sergeant rode several meters down the road's shoulder side-saddle before swinging onto the seat and turning back. He gave that bike a fist-full of throttle and shot back to where I stood open-mouthed, the bike's rear wheel fish-tailing about on the dirt with unbounded enthusiasm.

I couldn't believe it!

He pulled up alongside me and climbed off, snicking into neutral as he did so. He then handed the bike to me, and I quietly slid into the saddle.

"Your bike goes real well," he announced, almost smiling, " I raced one of them before the war. Empire Star Beezer. I won a few races in the dirt on it. That's not a bad unit.

"Now listen you," he said somewhat more sternly, "Get on your bike and piss off! I don't like smart-arses playing silly- buggers with me. Did you get that?"

I assured him I did, and slipped into first gear. "Hey, thanks for that." I was forced to say.

He nodded in the direction of the Blue Mountains. "Get outta here, and don't let me see you again."

I have to say I got outta there as suddenly as I could and, happily, didn't see him again. But I must say, as one who has had more than his fair share of tussles with Police officers who are a bit strange about people who exceed some speed restrictions, however minor some of those transgression may be, he seemed to have been a reasonable enough bloke. However, I maintain that I was doing my civic duty in stopping a number of motorists, and a couple of motorcyclists, from committing the offence of going a little too rapidly on a narrow-guttered goat track which could be safely traversed at many a click higher than the 30 miles per hour posted limit.

Yes, even though his questionable tactics in not placing his warning notice where it could be easily seen, and then concealing his minions just over the brow of a small hillock to entrap anyone who breasted the rise a little too quickly, he was a whole lot better than some of members of the Constabulary I have had the misfortune to have come across. Besides that, he was a very smart, because he recognised the fact that my ordinary-looking BSA single was somewhat removed from the norm: it *almost* made my altercation with him worthwhile!

Out of the blue

There is a steep downhill lefthander at Mount Tomah, on the Bells Line of Road, which is very deceptive. It looks fairly tight on the entry, but surprises its attacker halfway through by straightening out on the exit.

When you know it well enough you come into that corner very late, so you can see farther into the bend in case some (other) idiot is scraping round from the opposite direction, and it also allows you to line up the fast exit earlier.

If the coast is clear you crank the bike over as far as tyre grip and clearance allow, lifting the bike up mid-corner and dropping it onto the opposite footrest for the fast righthander that follows as the suspension grunts onto full bump in the hollow before the steep climb ahead.

The handlebars twitch as the suspension re-adjusts itself and a fistful of throttle sees you spear up the apparently nigh-vertical climb ahead. Then, the machine is on tip-toe and you are almost weightless in the saddle as the bike breasts the rise and the road suddenly drops away again to dip into a very fast lefthander.

It's a great stretch of road and the joy of punting a potent, well-handling machine along it is cranking the bike hard over through a long series of vastly differing corners, from slowish to medium-paced and some as quick as talent, machinery and common sense allow.

Motorcycling is a handy and efficient means of transport. It's also great fun and with an element of danger, but one of its joys lies in cornering the device by laying it over into a corner at a greater or lesser angle, depending on how fast you are riding or how tight the corner is.

Or, very often a combination of both.

You bank a bike over to corner, you turn the steering wheel in a car to achieve the same aim.

You do not – cannot – crank a car over to negotiate a corner any more than you can turn the handlebars on a motorcycle to ride through a corner. Unless you are riding a motorcycle with sidecar attached, that is. It is really fundamental stuff, isn't it?

Not really, because I have observed, at very close quarters, two distinct instances in which riders of solo motorcycles have achieved the impossible. In both cases, and in vastly differing circumstances, these riders have cornered their upright machines by turning the handlebars like the tiller of a small power boat and thus zipping through a corner as though it was the most natural thing in the world to do.

We know this isn't possible, although occasionally we see expert Trials riders with handlebars turned to full lock with their machines climbing a steep rock face or into a very tight 'section' with the machine either upright or cranked over just a few degrees from the vertical.

But I'm sure no one told either of the 'novice' riders to whom I shall shortly refer that you couldn't hope to turn a corner on a solo by simply turning the handlebars, which is precisely why they were able to get away with the impossible. Perhaps you can achieve anything you like ... if you don't know it can't – or shouldn't – be done??

The first person I saw achieve the amazing feat of turning the bars on a solo to negotiate a corner came into our motorcycle shop at Ryde one day to have his sidecar wheel-bearing

Ryde Motorcycles

replaced. The third wheel fell off because he had removed the wheel to grease the bearings and had forgotten to tighten the axle nut when he replaced the wheel.

It happened just as he swung into the tight left-hander from Devlin Street, just outside our showroom window. He rode the machine to the gutter outside, graunching the axle against the kerb-stone as he did so. He then placed the wheel in the sidecar and rode the bike round the corner into the narrow laneway into the workshop, the sidecar by now very cleverly almost a meter in the air.

We didn't have the bearings in stock so we removed the sidecar and sent him on his way on what was now a solo motorcycle. None of us knew this at the time, but the man – highly experienced sidecar driver though he was – had never ridden a solo motorcycle in his life before!

He acquainted us with this fact as he was about to leave us and it was thus no surprise to see him gingerly move away dragging his steel-toe-capped boots along the concrete floor of the workshop. He made his way to a set of narrow bifold doors that lead into the narrow laneway outside the shop, then suddenly opened the throttle as he thrust his legs out in front of him like a pair of soft battering rams.

The bike shop straight through the narrow opening and leapt at the brick façade of a two-storey building only a few metres opposite. I ran after him shouting some gibberish I have (thankfully) long since forgotten and remain amazed to this very day by the miracle I was so soon to witness.

With a serious collision a split second away and the bike still upright, the rider reefed the handlebars full-lock to the left (as, of course, he would – had the sidecar still been attached) and took off up the lane at 90 degrees to his original direction, fending the wall off with his right leg.

This can't be done, we all know that, because the bike should have fallen over in the opposite direction, but the rider was clearly unaware of what he had achieved and was thus able to speed on regardless. And in ignorance, I have to say, of at least one of Newton's usually irrefutable Laws of Motion!

He snapped into second gear as the 600cc sidevalve BSA engine howled as it never had in its life before and shot away stirring up a small plume of gravel chips and lumps of dirt he dug out of the several large potholes he noisily traversed.

As he took off up that back lane a little old lady was making her painful way down, a well-filled shopping basket in her left hand and a walking stick in the other.

Our new solo rider, of course steered straight towards her!

She saw him coming and deftly moved to one side, but he immediately swung the handlebars and changed course again, once more heading straight for her.

She stepped to one side again, he moved the 'bars and headed for her as before, she stepped away again he moved the 'bars ...

Finally, with the bike almost on top of her, the LOL stood with her back pressed to a paling fence on the left side of the lane, her basket on the ground, her eyes tightly closed, her lips moving in what appeared to be a silent prayer, but which could just as easily have been a string of well-merited curses.

How that rider missed her I will never know, but he well and truly demolished her shopping basket and its contents, leaving her unscathed as he departed, pursued by a stream of abuse from lips which had suddenly found their voice again!

As an encore to this impressive performance, the rider then left a metre-high black crescent of powdered rubber along a once-pristine, cement-rendered wall he tried to climb as he passed between the old lady and a wooden telegraph pole he shaved with his right elbow!

From our position at the bottom of the lane, frozen as in a stage *tableau*, we could see there was clearly no room for this incredible manoeuvre and we stood, jaws agape and eyes bulging in silent horror and a high degree of admiration as the 10-second drama unfolded before us.

The BSA and its out-of-control rider departed the scene with never a backward glance and we rushed to the aid of a by-now semi-recumbent woman, tut-tutting and marvelling at her narrow escape. We apologised for the vanished rider and then tried to guess at what the contents of her wrecked basket used to be.

We stood her more or less upright and dusted her down and she blubbered her thanks as we led he inside the workshop to soothe her rapid, shallow breathing and racing pulse rate with a bracing cup of strong tea.

The tiller-steering rider appeared again a few weeks later on crutches, and a friend called in with a van while he was there. We loaded the sidecar into the van while the rider described how he had run wide on a left-hand corner and collected an oncoming car. He was, so he said, still trying to negotiate the corner while turning the handlebars.

"Bloody dangerous, these solos," he said, as a parting sally.

The second Tiller-Steering Solo Rider was attending my Learner Training School in 1972 and had come along hoping to learn to ride a motorcycle as "I've been for my car licence four times and never got my licence yet," she told me. "I had an accident twice while on test," she added, to my horror.

The Suzuki distributors, Hazell and Moore, through the good graces of the star International road racer, Jack Ahearn, had given my school five lightweight machines – two stepthru's, two A70 and one A100cc motorcycles – and these were available to students who hadn't yet purchased machines of their own.

The course was some 30 hours in length, over several nights and two weekends, and included lectures, whiteboard illustrations and then riding tuition on the quarter-mile, tar-sealed, go-kart racing circuit at Granville, where the Parramatta Speedway now stands.

We would then move out onto the track and let the riders loose for a few laps after they had familiarised themselves with the controls, how a machine felt when being wheeled about and many other basic instruction.

I was explaining to a young female rider how to use the front brake effectively and pointing out that you won't fly over the handlebars if you pull that right hand lever on with the bike upright, as I glanced up as one of the other students rode past.

It was the girl who hadn't passed her several licence tests and she was moving along quite well, as I was surprised to note.

I was even more surprised to watch her enter the righthand corner where we stood, take an unintentional late entry and turn the handlebars to full lock without cranking the bike over at all!

I was instantly reminded of that sidecar rider of a few months before as the stepthru she was riding swept round the corner as if on rails and took off towards the top hairpin at the end of the circuit's back straight.

She negotiated that corner at a fair speed while still entirely upright and I trotted onto the main straight to flag her down and explain (again) how to corner a motorcycle by leaning it over gently and allowing the handlebars to do their own thing. Which is, of course to turn themselves slightly, and automatically, into the corner as well.

"Hop on the back," I instructed her. "I'll show you what I mean."

"I don't think I like that very much," she confessed after a couple of laps, when she hopped off again and once more assumed control of the stepthru.

"Practise it, and gently, please," I suggested. "That's what you're here for. You'll soon get the hang of it."

"I'll keep an eye on you." I promised her – and myself.

She took off again, but much more sedately, and still insisted on cornering by turning the handlebars again, but I did note she was beginning to bank the bike over just a little as she came to grips with the 'new' method. Inside a couple of laps I was heartened to see she was at last banking the little bike into corners and making a good fist of it.

My attention was diverted while explaining to a student how to properly adjust a rear chain – simple maintenance was part of the course – and a half-hour went by with riders and their instructors zipping about and shouting good-naturedly to one another.

There were probably 10 riders on the track at the time and I noticed one moving very quickly (too quickly, I remember thinking at the time) as the stepthru overtook a couple of slower riders down the main straight.

I thought it was an instructor at first as the little bike was cranked over into the right-hand sweeper until the footboards scraped, and I marvelled at the grip of those skinny, highly polished Japanese tyres which, over 40 years ago, were almost lethal.

It took my breath away for a second and almost stopped it entirely when I saw it was the former tiller-steering student who couldn't pass her driving test(s)!!

I couldn't believe it! I still can't!

She braked for the tighter right-hander that followed, shot round the next corner, an opening left-hander, with sparks flying off the grounded centre-stand and took off for the tight hairpin at the top of the finishing straight.

I galloped across the infield to head her off, waving my arms frantically and shouting my fool head off, but she tore into that tight corner and came out of it again at about twice the speed of a racing go-kart, flying onto the straight at near-suicidal speed.

Halfway down the straight I managed to flag her down and she greeted me with a huge grin and eyes sparkling like luminous saucers.

Ryde Motorcycles

I discerned small flecks of foam in the corners of her mouth.

"Don't stop me now." she shouted, as she peeled her helmet off, displaying shoulder-width hair which stuck out sideways like a chimney-sweep's brush. "This is fantastic!"

She plopped the lid back on again, cinched the chin-strap up and found first gear somehow as she deftly swerved around me. She took off down the remainder of the straight and swept into the three open corners that followed, as I rushed to the hairpin again to stop her and was almost on the apex when she entered the corner even quicker than before.

Not surprisingly, the front end broke away, followed by the rear wheel, and the little bike slid to the grass, nudged the safety fence almost side-on and pelted her straight over the top and out of sight!!

So help me, I cleared that high fence without touching it and was horrified to see her lying face down in the tall paspalum, her body shaking. We were well insured, of course, but I hadn't expected anything like this to ever happen.

I confess I was in fear and trembling at what was going to happen next, but to, my surprise, delight and monumental relief she rolled over and sat up, laughing uproariously as she did so.

"Thank you, thank you," she gushed as she paused for breath.

"That's the best fun I've ever had. I can't wait to tell the girls." She hugged me and then kissed me fervently for a couple of seconds (it hurt because her helmet was still firmly in place) as she climbed to her feet and amazed up all by being entirely uninjured.

Best fun she had ever had, she said? Had she spent her life under a stone or in a cave somewhere? Was she a pale-skinned Arab who had grown up in the Sahara desert? Had she languished, unseen, in the back row of a harem somewhere?

If her idea of good fun was sliding sideways into a racing circuit safety fence and then being unceremoniously pelted over the thing, it certainly wasn't mine, let me tell you that.

Perhaps it was the unalloyed joy of cranking a bike over through a series of corners – now, that would be more like it – but I suggested that henceforth she should only ever be conveyed from point to point firmly strapped into somebody else's car. In the passenger seat.

Never, I suggester gently, as I gave her a C Minus Certificate of Proficiency, should she ever fling her leg over a two-wheel motor vehicle again, except, perhaps (and only perhaps) on the back.

Come to think of it, she could make a very exciting companion on the pillion for a hard blast down Mount Tomah and a couple of laps of Panorama one long weekend.

BSA fast cornering

There are few things on this earth quite so exciting or pulse-raising (for exciting or pulse-raising, read terrifying) as hurtling headlong into an open, fast corner on a road you don't know well enough, only to discover that the 'fast' corner you are attacking with such enthusiasm is not nearly as fast as it looks.

You've done all the right things on your approach, of course, including the so-called 'Classic, Open Racing Line' during your late entry on, or just after, the apex, which allows you to see further round the corner and sweep in on the exit, but you have just discovered to your horror that the 'fast' corner you have just flung the bike into tightens noticeably on the exit and that you are travelling about 30 clicks quicker than you should be.

Let's say you are cranked over onto the footrest, so urgent braking is out of the question – particularly front wheel braking of course – and the corner happens to be right-hander. It doesn't make much difference whether the corner goes one way or the other, because you can run out of road very quickly on a right-hander, while your exit from a corner going in the opposite direction might see you drifting across the centre line and onto the wrong side of the road. That's not too bad if there is no traffic about, because that extra piece of road can be very handy, but there is *always* that inevitable motor vehicle going in the opposite direction to you, and it is almost certain to be smack bang in the middle of your wide exit line.

In days of yore, when rabid enthusiasm and rampant testosterone reigned well above common sense, I confess it happened to me on more than one noteworthy occasion, both alone and in company, and it happened more often than not on the trust-worthy old stove-hot 500cc BSA single I campaigned vigorously for many a long year. It remains a daily surprise to me that I am still in the here and now to remember those occasions, and to be able to relate them anew.

I clearly recall one of the worst incidents of over-enthusiastic cornering, which happened on a run out to The Oaks, which is down Mittagong way, where I had expected to meet a mate of mine who was competing in an open-road 'Lance Watson Reliability Trial'. This was the type of Club-sanctioned motorcycle sports event which was held on a regular basis half a century and more ago through the auspices of the Auto Cycle Union (ACU) of NSW, an event which, as usual, attracted a reasonably large field of earnest enthusiasts. These 'timed' sporting events were usually held over a challenging variety of surfaces which might consist of rough bush tracks, *slightly* smoother fire-trails (which were not called fire-trails in those days) and the occasional short run between 'sections' which were connected by short squirts along tar-sealed roads. They call these events 'Enduros' these days.

On that occasion I had flung the BSA much too quickly into that decreasing-radius right-hander with what I was later to recognise as a perfect demonstration of a high degree of reckless abandon, added to an even higher degree of stupidity, which was allied to no knowledge whatsoever of the area in which I was riding. This is a recipe fraught with danger, as I'm sure most of us are all too well aware. To make matters worse I was alone at the time.

I had long since taken the precaution of raising the 'Iron Goldie' BSA's footrests on their splined shafts, re-aligned the gear and footbrake levers, and tucked the long 'silencer' much closer against the frame to allow for even more cornering clearance, but on this occasion – and once or twice when I raced the bike on the old Mount Druitt tar-sealed circuit – there was still nowhere near sufficient cornering clearance, as I was shortly to discover.

Fortunately, I had managed to quickly slot back into a lower gear, which ought to have helped a bit (but which didn't) and this meant that the sole of my boot was then trapped underneath the gear lever. The BSA was a British motorcycle, of course, with the gear lever on the right side.

So there we were, the bike cranked over until the muffler was shrieking as it was being ground away on the rough road surface, with the sole of my right boot gradually getting hotter and hotter. The God-awful, skinny Olympic 'Black Spot' – my nickname for them – 'Patrol' tyres with their square-section profile were scrabbling for grip and not finding much, while that blasted right-hander was still disappearing somewhere over my right shoulder! An intimidating rock face, with its small scattering of attendant shrubs, and a meter or so of dirt surface on its approach, was rapidly closing on us and we were in all sorts of strife because there was simply nowhere to go but earthwards. Or, should the worst have come to the worst, *Heavenwards*?

In those split seconds when disaster looms and there seems to be nothing to do but hang on to the bike and hope for the best, there are (too) many things which flash into one's mind besides your 'Past Life'. Should I stamp on the left-mounted rear brake pedal, you may swiftly muse, which would cause the back-end to step out, thus tightening the line, and automatically easing the tightness of the corner; should I just step off the bike and take my chances with the road surface; should I crank it over further and have the muffler jack the wheels clear of the road surface and have the bike slide into the rock-face first, instead of me; should I hang onto the thing for dear life, and indeed hope for the best?

These sudden crises are often over in a very few seconds, before one has the time to think of anything except what might happen next, and it happened in this case as well. With little input from me except a bunch of swear words shouted to the passing winds and the occasional high-speed prayer, that rock face quietly slipped past my left shoulder to be replaced by several small trees and some welcoming bushland, while the rest of the right-hander suddenly appeared once again over my other shoulder as the road straightened up, the bike by then almost teetering on the broken edge of the bumpy, lightly sealed surface.

But even then, with what felt like the contents of a 44-gallon drum of adrenalin still on the boil inside me, allied to more than a large dollop of idiocy and even more anger at throwing myself into this dangerous manoeuvre, I lifted the bike upright, slotted back a gear and tweaked the throttle against the stop to leap away again with renewed vigour!

The road was somewhat more open ahead as we picked up even more speed while the pulse-rate slowly dropped back to abnormal, and the anger at my stupidity subsided at a similar rate. Then, and only then, I rolled the throttle back and settled down to a more leisurely gait, quickly realising that I could have knocked myself about pretty badly only a few moments earlier while riding too quickly – *while alone* – along a quiet, switch-back road which I had never ridden upon before. It suddenly became a very sobering thought indeed, and I gave myself a hard time during the next several minutes as I bristled under my own stern lecture. What a jackass, but it was a lesson well learned: or was it?

Ryde Motorcycles

If there are tricky corners like that tightening right hander at The Oaks, which are traps for the unwary, then there are other corners which are a joy to traverse at quite respectable speeds, if you know where they are, and how to travers them at those quite respectable speeds!

One of the latter, a long-time favourite of mine, is the intimidating left-hander at the lower end of the steep drop down Mount Tomah when heading west on the great Bells Line of Road in Sydney's Blue Mountains. It is a very deceptive corner, which is actually very much faster than it looks because the adjacent rock face at the escarpment impinges upon the road from the left side, exactly on the apex, making it a near-'blind' corner. But immediately thereafter the road opens up on the exit, which allows that corner to be attacked much more quickly than would seem to be possible. That is assuming you dive into the corner late and come out early, of course – and certainly *not* the other way around!

I have zipped round that great bend on several different brands of machine over very many years, including many times on the trusty BSA, twice on my ex-Army 1944 10/12 Indian outfit, once with a lovely little 1953 Velocette 350 – which handled like a dream – just once while riding a modern-day Maxi scooter, and once aboard a heavily modified 750cc Suzuki 'Water Bottle' which I borrowed from the Distributors for a squirt to Bathurst at Easter in 1977. The Suzy was fitted with clip-on bars and rear-set footrests, triple discs, alloy wheels, a three-into-one exhaust, and multi-rate Koni rear shocks: none of which after-market attachments made much difference to the big machine's high-speed handling woes.

But the most memorable ride of them all was in around 1959 when I tried to beat my best time from Fairfield to Bathurst along what was, at that time, the twisting, tortuous, bumpy (old) road which has been 'improved' in later years by some gun-barrel straights, but at the expense of some nice corners.

As I came tearing down the Tomah area I espied a group of about five other riders pushing on ahead at a reasonable clip, but they were clearly not aware of the tricky left-hander because they all slowed – if only slightly – as they prepared to line it up. I swept majestically round the lot of them, and shot into the corner to snatch a higher gear after the apex and speared out of the now-opening bend, the plunger rear suspension bottoming out at the base of the road which then rose steeply ahead. One of their number blew his bike's horn at me as I zoomed past; he probably thought I was crazy, and he might have been right!

We shot up the hill which was rapidly approaching, and breasted the rise very shortly thereafter, the suspension by now on full extension, the bike almost on tip-toe, while I felt to be nigh-weightless in the saddle. The corner which follows in a nice open sweeper which allowed me a quick glance in the mirror to see if there were any challengers in close attendance: there were none.

Or there were none that I could see, that is, because I had earlier turned the mirror head sideways to reduce drag and help with streamlining. When pressing on swiftly on the open road, I always did that and gripped the tank firmly with both knees, tucked my elbows into my rib cage, wore gauntlet gloves to stop the wind whistling up my sleeves, wore very close fitting protective clothing with a tight neck strap, the slim-fitting, carefully-altered thick trousers tucked tightly into high topped boots... and kept my mouth tightly closed. Every one of these simple precautions, I always felt, helped add that little bit of extra performance to the slim BSA single, or whatever machine I happened to be riding at the time.

When riding a 'naked' bike like this, with the machine leaping about underneath me like a live thing, occasionally nodding its head and twitching its tail while trying to assert control, the wind tugging firmly at me the while, I often felt almost as though I was throwing *myself* into the corners and flashing along on my own down the long straights. The machine seemed then to form only a part of one entity, albeit a very large part, its presence allowing me to do this as though I was managing to achieve this nigh-blissful state all on my own.

On these occasions, I reckon I felt very much like a type of human/mechanical Centaur; not like one of those mythical half horse/ half man hybrids we see in Classic Fables or in ancient illustrations, but more like a serious rider feeling as one with the bike he – or she, of course – is riding.

There are few pursuits on this earth which come within a Bull's Roar of that feeling when the open road beckons, the weather is kind, the bike is well prepared and the mood is right. Well, now that I think of it, perhaps there *are* one or two, or even more, which *might* compare, but a hard squirt into the countryside on your motorcycle along with some mates still remains pretty much out there all on its own!

BSA piston

It was certainly no surprise that the piston went off as it did, because I should have known better, but when it decided to disintegrate it did so in a Very Big Way, even though it occurred when I was riding the BSA outfit sedately home in heavy traffic.

I had already checked the engine's recently-fitted, modified Gold Star BSA race cams by using a dial gauge to check the valve lift – which was considerable – and a timing disc on the engine's mainshaft to check valve overlap – which was also considerable – and had then decided to have the cast-iron cylinder barrel sleeved back from .030 oversize to standard.

As was ever thus, the process of converting a strong, but otherwise fairly ordinary, 500cc overhead valve ride-to-work engine into something very sporty indeed, if not almost race-worthy, was a seemingly endless process, and could only be done in bits and pieces as finances allowed.

The inlet and exhaust ports had recently been enlarged and highly polished, an over-large 50mm, VK+ inlet valve had been specially made, the valve rocker-arms lightened and fitted with rocker return springs, while special 'Terry' shot-peened Gold Star BSA valve springs, with the latest Gold Star BSA lightweight alloy collars, had also been installed.

The cylinder head still looked very ordinary from the outside, but inside the thing it looked – as best a lumpy-looking cast iron cylinder head could ever look – to be a Thing of Beauty: at least it did to me, for beauty, be it clearly understood, will forever be within the eye of the beholder.

At some 8.5:1 compression ratio, that locally-made piston was about as high a ratio as one would run on the very ordinary fuels which were around in the late fifties, and in the end would only run without pinking when I used the more efficient BP petrol/benzol blended fuels which were on hand from all BP service stations. But I didn't like the look of the very coarse grain which was clear upon the inner surface of that new piston. The piston was, of course, sand cast, which was the way it was done in those days, and very successfully at that. Naturally, sand casting is still in almost universal use to this day.

Even the Aussie 'backyard' engine tuners – who were many; mostly self-taught; entirely brilliant and often world-famous, often used the very fine Thames loam in the casting process, the clay-like loam/fine sand mixture being almost as fine as *Johnno's* talcum powder, which imbued an alloy piston – or any small aluminium alloy casting, for that matter – with a very fine surface texture. However, by the look of the inside of my new piston, the thing had been cast using small pebbles and some very coarse sand which someone had pinched with their bucket-and spade from Bondi Beach! Naturally, the exterior of the piston had been ground slightly oval on the Churchill grinder and looked to be fine enough, but again the inside surface was grim indeed.

I knew I was going to give the new cylinder sleeve a very hard time after it had settled itself down, so to be sure it stayed where it was I drilled two diametrically-opposite holes through the side of the barrel and just a few *thou.* into the new sleeve, and nipped a pair of short, self-tapping screws in place.

That new cylinder sleeve was going nowhere... or so I thought. But the piston had other ideas!

Against my better judgement I attached the new piston and re-assembled the engine, to find that, even on its first running after the detailed modifications, and still to be run-in carefully, the bike was clearly very much quicker than usual, because it jumped away like a well-tuned Bonneville Triumph; that high-performance British sportster providing the yard-stick by which everything else on two wheels was judged in the late fifties.

Honda had very recently arrived, but the machines were still unknown, viewed with some suspicion and were only lightweights, with lightweight performances, so they simply didn't count. But boy, how things changed for Honda, and for the entire world of motorcycling, within ten short years!!

I had ridden the outfit to work for only a couple of weeks, carefully allowing the new piston to reach its ideal 'heat set', and had yet to un-hitch the sidecar and give the bike a serious work-out on the open road when the piston suddenly, and noisily, exploded – for explode it did!

I was drifting along in heavy traffic at the time and had just moved into third gear, the clutch still dis-engaged (fortunately!) when the piston went off. I immediately knew what it was, of course, and cursed myself for not sending the inferior piston back to the local manufacturers at once, demanding a replacement.

We coasted into the gutter, found a local phone box – no Mobiles in those days, of course – and had Jack Pendlebury, our local picker-up and regular deliverer of damaged motorcycles to Ryde Motorcycles, tow me to work.

Ryde Motorcycles

We pulled the head off to discover there was no damage at all, which was a giant relief, but when the barrel was pulled off the mess which greeted us was absolutely jaw-dropping!

The blown-grenade, granulated remains of the awful piston lay like the aluminium equivalent of a broken windscreen, with many small fragments piled upon the top of the flywheels. The con-rod was bent into an Ess-shape, the gudgeon pin thus gouging a deep groove into the newly-fitted sleeve, which had then been pulled down the cylinder wall (against the pull of those small screws, I might add) to emerge into the crankcase on top of the spinning flywheels. From there the con-rod finished the demolition job by snapping part of the base of the sleeve away as it struck it during the normal arc of its travel.

Sobbing tearfully – well, not quite tearfully, but certainly fearfully – I pulled the crankcases apart, to discover that they were quite undamaged, but I pelted the entire crank assembly away, just in case the obvious nick on the flywheel's rim might somehow interfere with its balance factor, or, at worst, begin the irrevocable path to a major blow-up if the steel flywheels were to be even more damaged than they looked.

Mine must have been an early 1953 model B33 BSA because it was said that later in that year the original 7.375" connecting rod had been shortened by half-an-inch to 6.875", which was the same rod as fitted to the all-alloy Gold Star sports models. In the later modification, the gudgeon eye was lowered in the piston to allow more meat at the top of the piston, and this was done to help overcome the often-noisy piston slap which was always a feature of the earlier five-hundreds.

It happened that the renowned Barry Ryan had just pulled apart a 1955 BSA single which had been all but written off in a serious prang and was offering the parts for sale from his second-hand spares outlet in Sydney's Parramatta. I bought the bottom half and the more heavily-finned cast-iron barrel from him and gleefully pulled it all part, firstly to check that it had the shorter con-rod fitted – which it had – and that its piston (which was, amazingly, a beautifully-finished, 8.25:1 Hepolite unit, usually fitted only to Gold Star singles) was in first class condition, along with the crankshaft's main bearings.

I checked that the big-end was in perfect condition and noted that the cylinder bore was absolutely pristine, so I removed the main bearings from the newer crankcase and fitted them into my older cases. This was done to save the hassle of changing the engine number on the rego. papers, more than for any other reason; besides which, the inspectors at the local Registry office were known to be very suspicious of these changes, for stolen motorcycles were just as much of a hassle in those days as they have ever been.

After the engine was re-assembled I decided to fit a new 18-tooth engine sprocket from the 350cc **B31** single, which was two teeth down on the standard B33 five-hundred and was recommended for sidecar use. This was done so that the highly-tuned engine would be able to pull a sidecar more easily, while an incidental improvement was to result in a far, far more worthwhile road-burner as a solo machine. I might say the engine looked a bit odd with its fat cylinder barrel allied to the much thinner finning on the older cylinder head, but there was no way I was going to sacrifice that newly-modified cylinder head for anything more basic, strange though it may have looked when the engine was assembled.

Barry wanted to sell me the cylinder head as well – he wanted to sell the complete engine, of course – but I waltzed in one day with the heavily-modified cylinder head to show him what had been done, and he declared himself sufficiently impressed to withdraw his offer. So was I, for money was very tight indeed in those days, and I had already spent more than enough on the detailed modifications. Thankfully my wife at the time didn't know enough about engines to know that half of what was done was by no means necessary – at least not from *her* point of view!

Naughty of me? Yeah, I suppose it was, but hopefully in some way forgivable; beside which, while the necessary repairs were being undertaken I could then ride home on any one of the showroom's second-hand machines, which at the time included a late-model 500cc MSS Velocette, a 1000cc Square Four Ariel and a 'Series C', 1000cc Vee-twin Vincent Black Shadow, the latter a frightfully-expensive second-hand machine we simply could not sell to anyone at that time! It's very hard to believe, I know, in view of the Vincent's current legendary – if not Heroic? – status, but that was then and this is now: things do change with time, as we all know only too well. I must add, however, that the big Vincent, though a joy to ride home and to occasionally thrash about on during weekends, didn't really suit me – or, much more likely, I didn't suit the Vincent!

I well knew the trick to starting the engine – with the correct piston perfectly placed in the

Vintage Morris

correct cylinder – but it was never easy to fire up, even when employing the world's longest kick-starter; the bike was unwieldy (for me) to wheel about; the twin front brakes required a too-hefty squeeze on the handlebar lever to be really effective, and it was not an easy machine to ride at low speeds in heavy traffic because of its strange clutch. It really needed a man of somewhat larger stature that I if a Black Shadow Vincent was ever to give of its best.

However, it must be said that the big, hand-made Vincent was never *everyone's* motorcycle anyway, nor was it intended to be. I know it's a downright ridiculous statement to make in this day and age, with Vincent by now the most eagerly sought-after Classic motorcycle of all time, but again there it is!

Freud

If ever there was a person upon this earth who could be expected to understand the odd machinations of persons of the female persuasion, it was that great – if often misunderstood – shrink, Sigmund Freud. He should have been well aware of the manner in which their minds worked, even though he once claimed that 'women are not only a different gender to men, but they are in fact a different species of human being as well.'

Among other things, we all know that the female pelvis is different to the male's and that the femur is of a different shape at both ends, also that the female brain is smaller than a man's (not that it makes a blind bit of difference one way or the other) and that girls look a whole lot better than we poor blokes do, but it doesn't end there. Freud's final words makes it clear to us that he knew little more about how these fellow human beings function than we lesser mortal do.

As Freud lay upon his death bed, fitfully scratching himself while his unfocussed eyes stared dimly at the ceiling and his mouth replicated a large and inviting fly trap, one of the attending physicians, who badly wanted to know just how the female mind worked or – he is said to have stated – if it worked at all, was heard to ask the great man if Freud really understood women.

"Tell me, master," he asked breathlessly, as the other cohorts leaned forward, their eager hands cupped to their ears in the hope of gleaning some earth-shattering information from the master interrogator's reminiscences "as you have psycho analysed many thousands of women in your lifetime, surely you, of all people, should be able to understand them. Before you go, please tell us. How do they tick?"

The old man was said to have frowned at this hopeless question, shaking his head sadly and sighing deeply as he gathered every ounce of strength he had left in an effort – they thought – to drop a pearl of wisdom into the buffoon's lap. As the small assemblage leaned forward until they nearly fell as a group upon his horse hair mattress he answered the question with a four word answer.

"Vot do tzey **vont**?" he is said to have replied with a hoarse whisper and an upward inflection on the last word.

His attendants, who had every right to expect an answer of great pith and moment, were totally pithed off by this ridiculous piece of absurdity, and flew off in different directions, muttering to themselves, as they struggled into their frock coats and top hats, while leaving the poor old sod alone to giggle himself into his Next Experience. Whether he was right or wrong – or just having a jibe at his interrogators – we will never know, but we have all had our experiences with this large group of otherwise wondrous creatures, who continue to confound us poor put-upon blokes with their unusual behaviour, not to mention their often strange logic.

This odd pre-amble reminds me of the woman who was employed at one time in the establishment known as Ryde Motorcycles, the suburban store in which I worked for several years. At that time, business was fairly brisk, so much so that the store's owner/manager found it difficult to keep up with the essential paper warfare and had employed this quite attractive woman to handle much of the office work. She was a very attractive girl and was probably in her mid-30's, while I was somewhat younger. And almost as dumb about women then as I am now.

It could be argued that a rough and tumble suburban motorcycle store was no place for a woman to be found, unless her husband owned the place and she was forced upon us, because these were very blokey establishments, populated by blokes, and almost exclusively patronised by them as well. The very few women who were employed in small suburban motorcycle stores were always carefully placed on display, either in a corner of the showroom floor or contained inside a small glassed partition where she could clearly be seen. This usually resulted in a reasonable degree of decorum, which would otherwise almost certainly not have been the norm.

Ryde Motorcycles

The woman had only been in the job for a couple of weeks when I remember strolling into the office one day prior to lunch to espy her touching-up her lipstick and powdering her nose, the while pursing her lips and grimacing at herself in a small hand-held mirror. She then stroked her carefully quaffed hair with the palm of her hand, shook her shoulders and then stood up. It was fascinating stuff to behold.

She then smoothed her tight skirt over a pair of first-rate hips, glanced at the back of a leg to see if the stocking seam was straight, made a small adjustment to a bra strap, tweaked her tight blouse and then stared straight at me. "Look at me," she pouted, "you would never think that I was once a skinny kid, would you."

"No, you would not," I agreed, wiping a small trickle of saliva which had begun to seep from the corner of a mouth which, unbidden, had slowly creaked open. I really thought I had finally said something right to a female – which would have made a very pleasant change for me.

"Are you insinuating that I'm fat?" she demanded, suddenly glaring at me as my left trouser leg began to slowly shorten itself. Almost instantly the trouser leg resumed its normal length as well, and I blushed furiously, for all I had done was to heartily agree with her. Perhaps I should have known better, but all that had happened, I thought, was that I was entirely right in agreeing with her self-assessment. I was, of course, *right* and *wrong* at the same time. As far as women are concerned – if indeed they are concerned – this was not the first time I was in error, nor, sadly, was it to be the last time either.

Norma had been employed in the middle of 1958 and it was in that year we had the very first of the range of Japanese Honda motorcycles on display in the showroom. The rep from A.P. North, the Matchless and Francis-Barnett importers (who also very occasionally imported the three-wheeled Messerschmitt bubble-car – nick-named by me as the 'Mess o Schitt' –, and the wondrous but rare Maico Mobil scooter), came into the store one day shortly after Norma started work with us and he saw the Honda sitting proudly on it slanted plinth.

"Hey," he shouted loudly, "Look, it's one of those new Nipponese motorbikes. I had a Japanese girl friend once; one day she whipped out her boobs and said, 'here, Nipponese' Ha! Ha! Ha! Nipponese, she said"

While he thought this to be highly amusing, I did not, and it was too late to mention the fact that a girl had recently been employed and was well and truly within hearing distance of the showroom. He then leapt into the office to see how his awful joke had been received by the store's owner, just as she shouted "I heard that!" and he leapt out again very quickly.

"Gawd, there's a girl working in the office." he informed me. "I know that." I told him. "But, but, she wasn't here last time I called," he croaked. "Why didn't you tell me she was here?"

"You didn't ask me"' I gloated.

The office was a step up from the showroom and entered through a small door, while the girl's chair and desk sat in a corner to the right, where she was entirely hidden from view until one entered the office and looked in her direction. In other words, no-one entering the store could have known she was there.

Perhaps I could have pasted a sign above the door with the legend "BE WARNED!! – NEW FEMALE STAFF MEMBER ENSCONCED WITHIN" or with something a little less dramatic writ large upon it, if only to warn loyal clients and reps that there had been a major change to the store's personnel. It would thus have provided a warning that perhaps they should conduct themselves with a little more poise and decorum than they had ever shown before. However, I didn't think to do that.

I am not sure that Norma would have approved of the notice anyway, because she seemed in some perverse way to enjoy the fact that she was hidden away because when she left for lunch after the 'Nipponese' incident she flounced into the showroom with the corners of her lips trying desperately not to curl upwards, and a stifled tear forming in the corner of an eye with which she glared balefully at us. Through the showroom window I then spotted her with a hand held over her mouth trying to smother a fit of the giggles as she minced up the street to the local café.

On another occasion, the rep from Eric Moore, who imported Ariel motorcycles as well as a few Husqvarna motorcycles and the occasional Durkopp Diana, Iso and other rare scooters, was delivering a brand new Iso scooter to us, which was tied securely into his Harley side-box (or bun-truck, as they were called for some odd reason.) He had a hand to his crotch and had already begun to unbutton the fly on his overalls as he entered the showroom, and I felt for a moment that he was going to cock a leg over one of the bikes we had on display.

"Quick! Quick! I'm boilin' for a leak!" he shouted desperately as he leapt into the doorway which led to the office while waving everything

1956-1960

> *"I watched her dabbing at her eyes with a spotted handkerchief as she tottered up to the local café, her body almost doubled up with uncontrollable paroxysms of surprisingly raucous laughter."*

about. He leapt out again just as quickly and turned to stare at me, his mouth agape, his eyes almost hanging out of his head like a pair of multi-coloured ping pong balls. "Hey, there's a sheila in your office," he announced breathlessly, his face the colour of the topmost traffic light. "What's she doin' there?"

"I think she's taking care of the paper warfare," I innocently replied, "why do you ask?"

"A sheila's never been there before" he said in total amazement, as though he had never seen one of them before, "How long has she been there?"

He seemed absolutely thunderstruck, while I patiently explained that she had only recently been employed and that we hadn't thought to make the announcement over the radio, or to take an ad in the *Herald's* personal columns. Besides which, I added, even though he had always made a dramatic entrance into our store (and, I assumed, many others as well) and announced his presence with an array of words of which any nineteenth century sailor would be proud, we did expect that, from now on, he would enter the premises with a little more dignity?

Again Norma swept into view a short time later as she affected an exit from the office, but this time her face was bright red and she was obviously trying desperately not to guffaw into our faces, but she could hold back no longer and fairly shrieked into a thunderous peal of unbridled laughter as she staggered down the three marble steps from the showroom onto the footpath outside.

I watched her dabbing at her eyes with a spotted handkerchief as she tottered up to the local café, her body almost doubled up with uncontrollable paroxysms of surprisingly raucous laughter. I remember thinking at the time that this would surely stuff up her carefully applied make-up, and it would serve her right if it did!

There was a great day's Classic motorcycle racing at Oran Park several years ago and I was watching the day's proceedings from the balcony outside the Press Room. For a change, I was not involved in the race commentary at that time, because I usually handled that job at Amaroo Park and Bathurst, and only once or twice at Oran Park, so it was a more relaxing time for me. I was standing alongside Eric McPherson, one of our greatest local and International riders, who had won many races on dirt and road racing tracks pre-war and who had – among other things – officially represented Australia at the Isle of Man and other circuits in Europe in the late forties and early fifties.

Eric had long retired from the sport, but was still a keen observer at these types of meetings, where the exciting sights and sounds of those four-stroke engines would rend the air as few two-strokes ever seemed able to do. As I recall it was a very close race and I looked about to see that the lovely Lyn, my latest wife, was not out there as well, but was in fact in earnest conversation with Eric's wife, Ruby.

I trotted inside to politely suggest that she was really missing something and was dismayed to note that she was less than interested in the event, so I turned to Ruby, who was knitting what looked like a singlet and asked outright why she was not at Eric's side and enjoying the spectacle herself. She looked up at me with a somewhat angry expression and shouted "I hate the bloody things!" and then harrumphed back to her knitting as though that all too short conversation was well and truly over. This really caught me by surprise, for here was a woman who had married Eric when they were kids and had supported her man for a great many years in this dangerous sport, and who had sometimes accompanied him through his International campaigns.

She had no doubt lain quietly in bed some nights while he worked on a machine in the garage until the early hours, we could be well assured of that, and had *apparently* supported Eric in all his endeavours over a great many years, not only as a great racing motorcyclist, but during his many years of working in the trade.

But in all that time she had 'hated the bloody things?' Had she then suffered in silence – although knowing the feisty Ruby that is not very likely! – and simply followed him about, putting up with whatever slings and arrows may have been hurled in their direction every time he fronted the start line in any one of his many hundreds of races? Had she feared for his life every time he threw a leg over a high-performance racing machine, or ridden his MSS Velocette home daily after he had retired

Ryde Motorcycles

from racing and was then working for P and R Williams, the Velocette and AJS importers?

The first time I managed to convince my current wife to climb on the back of a motorcycle – it was a 1952 Sunbeam S7 I was riding for a Classic road test report – she complained bitterly about how uncomfortable the thing was and swore never again to be seen in such an awful position. She could hardly be blamed, I suppose, because the bike had a simple low-travel plunger rear suspension system and her seat was a near-bullet-proof sponge rubber pad bolted directly atop the rear mudguard.

But the next machine she straddled was a 4-cylinder 550cc Honda I was riding at the time, and she declared it to be 'a little better, though not by much, but at least I had clean underwear on and the insurance was up to date.' Lyn is still with me after some 30-plus years, which I find amazing, but then Ruby stuck with Eric for decades no matter where he went, and was never *heard* to complain – other than to me, and thankfully only once. As far as I am aware, that is!

It could never be said that women and motorcycles should not co-exist, because there are probably more women riders about these days than ever before, and girls have always ridden motorcycles, as many a photograph from almost a century ago will attest, but you can't help but wonder what goes on in that grey matter lurking behind those great looking faces as they seem to gleefully leap onto the back of you bike, or sit with you on a baking hot day at the motorcycle races, when they may well much prefer to be at a (dreary) flower exhibition or a (dull) fashion parade.

Not too long ago, I fired a small sample of whatever wisdom I have learned over too many years when I was forced to advise a young stud, who had broken off with yet another girl he had known all too briefly, of the error of his ways. He was complaining to me that this one was (yet again) much too fussy, so I leaned forward and addressed an area of around his shirt pocket.

"Lemme tell you something my boy." I pontificated, "You are going to have to learn to put up with them, and with their strange ways. That's all there is to it"

"And why," he arrogantly retorted, "should *I* have to put up with *them?*"

"Because, my boy, **they**... have to put up... with... **you!**"

Some blokes say sometimes you can't live with them, but you sure as hell can't ever live without them.

Bike displays

Unlike a suburban car distributorship where stock is always on display outdoors, it has been the tradition for decades to announce a suburban motorcycle distributor's presence by wheeling a selection of machines from the showroom onto the footpath outside in the morning, and then wheeling the lot back inside again in the late afternoon. This was always done in the fond hope that one or two, if not several, of the bikes would not need to be wheeled back inside later on because their new owners had smilingly leapt upon their latest purchases and ridden off into the sunset.

Some of these dealerships, like Sydney's Ryde Motorcycles, displayed no more than about fifteen examples daily of what were later to become "Classic Motorcycles." Others, like one well know store in the Sydney suburb of Blacktown, currently wheel out about a hundred of them in the morning, and, often as not, not quite so many back inside during the afternoon.

For some of those establishments this procedure is a fairly simple process; you just roll a bike off its stand, wheel it outside and trot back inside to do the same thing... over an over, and then over again. But at Ryde it wasn't quite so simple, because the exit from the lower of the two small showrooms was down three steps onto a fairly steep footpath which was lightly coated with badly broken asphalt. This material embraced two smallish patches of a sadly unkempt, grass-like foliage, the two small areas, each of which measured about two meters by four, slightly sunken beneath the surface of the ragged footpath. Between the two garden plots (?) was a concrete layback, which was very handy indeed when it came time to wheel the bikes back in again.

Did I just say **wheel** them back in again? Yes, I believe I did, because that's what we did. It was much easier to do this than to kick the engines over, wait forever for them to warm up a bit, and then to ride the bikes back inside. The engines needed to be well warmed up, because no-one would want to have an engine not at its best and perhaps conking out half way up that narrow ramp we used, just because the engine was cold and unhappy about the task. That never happened, so I don't know what that would have been like, but I'm sure it would be no fun at all, because there is no way even the longest-legged rider amongst us could get his foot within about a meter of the ground at any time he rode along

Vintage Morris

the narrow, and often slippery, ramp we used for the job.

The two showrooms were a bit on the small side, the upper one displaying about eight or ten brand new bikes, the lower one up to about twenty-five or so second hand mounts. It was only the second hand machines which were wheeled out on a daily basis, and they were never wheeled out during wet weather.

But because the lower showroom was fairly small, and somewhat narrow, with the bikes shoved very closely together, it was easier to face the first few machines to be ridden outside, grab the handlebars, reef them off their centre stands (or rear stand if it happened to be an earlier Triumph or Panther) then stroll backwards for a step or two. After assuming a measure of control when the machine was then clear of its fellows, it was then a fairly simple matter of just riding the bike down the ramp and heaving the thing back onto it stand.

It was always as well to be aware that a bike could topple over if the soil in the garden plots was a bit on the soft side, so if this was on the cards the occasional 4" x 2" timber support, specially made for the job, and painted a matching green, would then be employed.

It was only the AMC machines – the AJS and Matchless singles and twins – which came equipped as standard with prop stands which sprang up when un-laden, and they always needed those trim little wooden devices to stop them slowly subsiding into the ground whether it was hot, cold, wet or dry.

But it was not quite as easy a job as it would appear to be, because British motorcycles of that period were somewhat notorious for leaking more than their fair share of oil, and the ramp could often have more than few drops of oil on it, so it was prudent not to try to brake at any time during that short, sharp and surprisingly swift descent for fear of either sliding sideways off the thing, or carrying the plank with us onto the footpath below. I cannot recall what the terminal velocity was by the time we reached the garden bed, but the rate of acceleration down that plank/board/ramp was fairly swift. So, too, was the sudden stop at the bottom, which did no favours at all for the soil in the beds.

Late in the day, when it came time to wheel the bikes back inside again, was where the real drama unfolded. Yet again, the quickest, but by no means the easiest way to slot the various machines back into their positions in the showroom was to secure the ramp in place, wheel the bike in question down the layback and onto to the road way, then gather whatever strength you may possess to wheel the thing swiftly up the ramp ***backwards*** while facing it from the front and steering the thing with the handlebars!

As you can imagine this is easier in the telling than in the execution, for it meant you only had one shot at getting it right. Often there was a helping hand, with someone dragging the bike in from the rear, while nimbly climbing the steps backwards, and in so doing exhibiting a level of expertise which might almost be equalled only by an internationally renowned circus performer.

The helper would **never** run backwards up the ramp, for fear of slipping on the surface and then being run over in the most painful possible way, and if this had ever happened, the victim – probably with just one hand – would then have to assist the original pusher up from under a machine which had suddenly toppled over on top of him.

That is assuming the 'helper' hadn't suddenly quit the scene as he minced off on tip-toe, knees locked tightly together, his eyeballs hanging out like organ stops, with his lips tightly pursed as though he had just had an enthusiastic suck on an under-developed lemon.

But that helping hand was not always available, and that made the exercise all the more entertaining. While I no longer wake in the early hours of the morning screaming about it, I often simply don't believe I was ever able to do this.

I well recall one occasion in which it had begun to sprinkle with rain just before I was about to wheel the very last motorcycle up that ramp unaided. I had already wheeled about ten of them back inside, assisted by a grumbling store owner on several occasions, but everyone had by now disappeared. The swine were probably enjoying a furtive cup of tea, or a bracing ale or two, and may well have been in ignorance of the sudden change in the weather. Then again they might have all retired for the day and could have been grinning at me from the comfort and warmth of their various inner sancta.

The bike was wheeled out to the roadway, I accelerated as best I could in the short space available, and the bike began to run up the ramp cleanly enough, but when I arrived on the ramp myself shortly thereafter, it was to find that several drops of oil had arrived not long before I did, and the wet plank was as slippery as if it had suddenly been coated with ice! There was virtually no traction at all on that slippery surface, and I must have run the equivalent of at least 500 meters on that blasted ramp, my legs disappearing like humming bird wings, while that confounded bike slowly, ever slowly, inched its way into the showroom.

> *“ By now my lungs were screaming for air, my legs aching like twin boils, my heart thumping like a jackhammer. ”*

I couldn't find the air to shout for help, and I reckon it took the strength of utter desperation to be able to finally get the bike's rear wheel onto the level showroom floor, and then, after what seemed like an eternity, finally into the showroom itself, followed very shortly afterwards by my panting self.

By now my lungs were screaming for air, my legs aching like twin boils, my heart thumping like a jack hammer. During that drama, which probably took all of about 30 seconds but seemed like about five minutes, I had jettisoned one wool-lined boot, the other was hanging half off, and my left sock, which was also half off, was probably the most heavily lubricate item of footwear on the planet. Oh, and I was laughing like a loon as well – hysterical and decidedly nervous laughter though it was.

What was so funny, you may sigh deeply and ask? I once saw an early Charlie Chaplin silent movie, in which the little tramp was roller skating and trying desperately to assist a large man to learn the craft as Charlie was pushing him about. But he was trying to push the bloke **sideways**, and making very little headway, Charlie's legs thrashing about beneath him. And at the most inopportune moment, while halfway up that ramp, the long-forgotten scene flashed into my head. It was very funny when I first saw the movie: it was not quite so funny when I experienced a similar situati on myself!

Fortunately the bike was a 350cc single-cylinder AJS, otherwise I would never have been able to get the thing up the ramp and into the showroom alone, nor for that matter might I have attempted to do so. Prior to this episode, I had wheeled a Triumph twin up there on my own with no problems, been assisted with a 1000cc Square Four Ariel, and pushed a Vespa scooter up; the Vespa done the right way round.

Why was the scooter shoved in head first, you might very well ask?

The Vespa in those days had its engine hanging well off the right side of the rear wheel, and was thus very badly out-of-balance. It drove through its three-speed gearbox directly to the centre of the wheel through a cruciform mechanism. This was a clever design, but that engine hanging so far off the centre line meant the scooter would fly round right hand corners with ease, but it simply didn't like left handers at all, and had to be held down with some determination because it always wanted to pop back up again.

Just to complicate matters the gears were selected by a left-hand twist-grip, in concert with the clutch lever, of course, so if you did manage to fight the thing backwards up a slippery ramp, there was no guarantee you would not unintentionally slip the bike into gear on that short journey, with the most obvious consequences.

There was no way anybody would ever attempt to wheel such an unwieldy device as this backwards up a steep ramp, even at a pace slightly above walking speed. In fact, it was probably the only machine on the showroom floor (there was often at least one Vespa on display) which nobody would attempt to pull off its centre stand by pulling on the handlebars while facing the machine head-on.

No matter how hard you tried, or how ready you were for it, the moment the rear wheel hit the floor again, you knew the little monster would flop over onto its right side, swiftly crossing your arms as it did so, and doing no favours at all to either wrist!

Perhaps I should have thanked my lucky stars the Japanese invasion had not yet begun in earnest, for the first of them was the 250cc C71 Honda of 1958 vintage, which always sat upon its plinth as a new machine, followed shortly thereafter by the little step-thru. Had the four-cylinder CB750 Honda been around in those days, it could have stayed inside, or outside forever as far as I am concerned, because there is no way I would have been seen shoving one of those things backwards up a plank unless at least *four* helpers were on hand! And if four eager helpers had been there, they would have done it all on their own while I stood by and supervised the operation.

Maimed and limbless

There was once a charitable organisation grimly referred to as the "Civilian Maimed and Limbless Association", which has hopefully changed its name to something a little more acceptable, for that original title has long since been abandoned, while associations of that type, no doubt set up to assist those of us in one or another of those grim situations, are of course still with us.

The company had several powered vehicles which were either on loan, or owned by, people who were suffering one or more of those afflictions so well described in the organisation's original title. These odd contrivances all seemed to be driven by that 197cc Villiers engine which 'powered' almost every small commuter motorcycle which existed at that time. Quite apart from those 'invalid carriages', the Villiers engine was used with great success in this country by James, Francis-Barnett, Norman, DOT, Tandon, Ambassador, Cotton, Excelsior, Sun, the later Swallow Gadabout scooters, and several other one-offs which appeared from time to time and which *disappeared* just as quickly. That little Villiers engine could drive any one of those lightweight bikes at around 90 Kays or more flat-out, which meant they were more than capable of keeping up with traffic in those days.

There were many more *marques* in England which used these engines, but few of them made their way to Australia, and it is sad to note that those other brand names just referred to have also disappeared, even though they were plentiful enough back in the fifties. Probably none of them are known to the new breed of motorcyclist, and may well be just a hazy memory to Ulysses members and other grizzled veterans.

The shop at Ryde in which I worked used to service these odd little vehicles, which, far from just being footpath-bound machines which we see today, were actually registered as road-going vehicles, albeit with special dispensation given to their odd controls and their sometimes even odder designs. They were of course custom built, and sometimes this would appear to have been done in someone's garage, for there seemed to be as many unusual design features as there were people with those disabilities. Again, they could tootle along at around 85-90 Kays if pressed hard enough, although handling may have been a bit of a problem. And as for stopping them in a hurry? Well, that may be why you don't see them on the roads anymore.

One fellow we saw on an irregular basis had no arms, so he would lie on his belly on his little machine, a long handle under his chin, which he would push to either side to steer the device, push up to accelerate and lean on to apply the brakes. He could kick the little engine over easily enough, and then swing aboard the device to lie down, using his right foot to change gear, his left foot to augment the braking power from that long, oddly shaped 'handle-bar', while his 'hand' signals were actually 'foot' signals, displayed by the simple ploy of hanging one foot or the other out in the breeze. I cannot recall how he operated the clutch

I never could work out how he managed to stay on the thing without rolling off it, for the 'bed' on which he was so precariously perched seemed to me to be quite flat. He was a bit reckless – or perhaps often out of control? – because he seemed to ride/drive the device pretty well flat-out everywhere he went, and he could be seen weaving in and out of the traffic stream any time he went past the store. The store's mechanic, Ernie dal Santo – who, unhappily, has recently passed away – suggested there had been "some work done" on the machine's engine, much of which he did himself.

There was a fellow from the organisation who often called into the store; he had only one arm and a strong limp, and he described himself – with great seriousness, and an entirely straight face – as a 'ball point pen and cigarette lighter mechanic', a trade of which I can find no reference anywhere.

It may have been listed on the back page of the first year apprentice's handout,

"The Journeyman's Gazette", assuming there was such a publication, but I never saw a reference to the job anywhere, nor did I ever see an advertisement for a position of that type. Perhaps I never looked in the right places?

He also flogged what he happily referred to as 'girlie calendars', and would pop in to see us around September to show us the layout for next year's epic, hoping we would decide to buy a bundle of them with our name emblazoned upon the various pages. They were all pretty harmless paintings of the so-called Gibson Girls, all of whom were very scantily clad, but showing no more than some impressive cleavage and several acres of thigh.

On one occasion Norma, our new girl, was in the office, and he flashed his wares at her. "What do you think of that little lot?" he asked lecherously, "Trim, aren't they?"

Ryde Motorcycles

"Don't show those things to me," she retorted, "Are you going to tell me that those girls pose for that man while wearing next to nothing?"

"Oh, no," he replied, "I have been advised that he is nearly always fully clothed."

"Not him, you fool," she snorted "The girls. Are you telling me that those floosies pose for that man Gibson with most of their clothing gone?"

"Not at all," he replied, with a wink, "I hear he paints them entirely from memory."

She was not remotely amused, and told him so, while we lot sat there giggling into our hands like so many village idiots.

We serviced a number of three-wheeled devices, some with one front wheel, while others (which, I suggest, were a far better design) with both wheels in front while the single rear wheel was driven through a three-speed gearbox by that ubiquitous Villiers engine. That little two-stroke engine delivered a reasonable amount of power in those days, while usually allowed those invalid carriages – for so they were called – to at least keep out of the way of other road-users, and they could manage to keep up with much of the traffic if the going was heavy enough.

As I recall, it was only on a couple of occasions that one of the organiser's members came in to buy spare parts for his machine, but his conveyance was quite different from the others, because it was a genuine, full sized 500cc single-cylinder Matchless motorcycle which had a sidecar attached. This fellow told me he had suffered some brain damage as a result of an industrial accident and had difficulty walking, but he had a set of shoulders shaped like an Arnott's Milk Arrowroot biscuit and was thus as strong as a bull.

The first time I spotted him was one day when he climbed off the outfit and shuffled painfully up the front steps, assisted by a pair of stout walking sticks, and moved, stiff-legged, to the spares counter.

After I had attended to him, he shuffled outside again and threw his purchases, and his sticks, into the sidecar and then proceeded – as everyone else did who ever owned a British single would proceed– to retard the ignition timing by using the little lever on the left side of the handlebar – then he leaned down and 'tickled ' the Amal carburettor several times to raise the fuel level, eased the piston to just over the compression stroke with the aid of the exhaust valve-lifter and swung onto the kick-starter.

Ho-hum, there's nothing new about this, you might say? Perhaps not, except for the fact that he actually kicked the engine into life in just on hit, but he pushed that kick-starter pedal down **by hand!** If I hadn't seen this myself, I never would have thought it possible, because I had by then kick-started many a lumpy British single and I knew full well that it took a fair bit of effort, a degree of skill and/or practice, allied to all the weight one could summon if you could manage to fire up an engine of that size in just one kick.

Or, as in his case, just one *push!*

And then, as if it was the most natural thing in the world to do, he hand-lifted first his left leg, then the other, into position, made the usual very personal adjustment as he settled into the single saddle, snicked into first gear and roared away. But instead of moving up to the corner where there was a break in the median strip, which everybody else did, he executed a swift U-turn, savagely bounced the outfit over the wide concrete strip outside the store and accelerated briskly down the steep Victoria Road hill! That exhibition was almost as hard to believe as his single-handed demo on the kick-starter had been. I wondered aloud if he did that sort of thing everywhere he went.

One of the invalid carriages which Ernie serviced was owned by a man who had tiny arms like little flippers which sprang almost directly from his shoulders. No, he was not a 'Thalidomide' victim, for this was several years before that disaster occurred; his was just one of those grim abnormalities which occur from time to time.

His carriage was different from most, because it had a near-normal seating position, but a platform was mounted at about 45 degrees when measured from the front axle, which allowed him to lean back fairly comfortably as the steering handles were then placed at what would be almost at neck height to most people. The device had been brought into the workshop because it was mysteriously conking-out, but it would then start up again and move away with no problems at all once it had stood idle for a few minutes.

It was later discovered that a little piece of fluff had blocked the air-bleed hole in the petrol tank, which resulted in an air-lock which would dramatically slow down the rate at which fuel would flow into the carburettor, but of course no-one knew this at the time and it was not an easy problem to detect.

Ernie carried out the normal tests, cleaning the spark plug, points and carburettor, then checked that there was a good, fat spark from the flywheel magneto (Villiers had far and away the best of all flywheel magneto/generator systems) and all seemed well.

He ran the engine for a time in the workshop and revved it up one or twice, and again everything seemed to work well, so it was time to take the odd device for a road test. It was obviously difficult to climb into the thing and even more difficult – not to mention uncomfortable – for Ernie to control the machine at that odd angle, but he lurched down the side lane and out into the traffic stream, steering the thing, as best he could, with his fists just under his chin.

A bus driver stopped and motioned him to move across in front of him (should I mention here that it was more relaxed and *much* more courteous time back in those days of the mid-fifties?) and Ernie opened the throttle to the stop to check that everything was OK, only to discover that the thing conked out again, the engine spluttering and backfiring like a series of loud pistol shots, while two-stroke smoke and chunks of heavily-oiled black material was flung out of the muffler, to add to the smoke.

Immediately the bus driver leapt from his vehicle and ran to the rescue of the apparent invalid, aided in this pursuit by a nearby pedestrian, and they shoved that carriage down the incline as hard as they could, Ernie shouting encouragement as the little engine tried manfully to keep running. And then there seemed to be just enough fuel in the carburettor to the engine to kick over smoothly, but then it mis-fired again.

Suddenly, without a word of explanation to anyone, Ernie threw off the tartan blanket which covered his legs, flung up that long steering handle and leapt athletically out of the carriage to run alongside it to assist the perspiring duo to shove the confounded thing down the hill.

The helpful pedestrian fell flat on his face as the device suddenly picked up speed, the bus driver shouted "You bastard" as he waved his arms about and stamped his feet, and glared at the big black spots on the front of his once-pristine white shirt, while the carriage, with Ernie back inside the thing and by now coasting in neutral, sped down the steep hill and disappeared from view!

It was some little time before the carriage re-appeared, being driven quite strongly but at a much reduced pace. Apparently, if the carriage was being driven at very low revs, the carburettor could still keep enough fuel in it for the engine to run cleanly and smoothly, but under higher *engine* speeds the fuel would soon cease to flow effectively and the engine would of course simply cut out or run erratically.

After that it took no time at all before Ernie could diagnose the problem, and he was able to pluck out of that air-bleed hole a surprisingly long piece of string-like fluff, the engine from then on (and without the benefit of any kind of road-test!) running as close to the smoothness of a well-oiled Swiss watch as any Villiers engine could ever be expected to run. Which, when I come to think of it, is not very close!

Kick starters

Owners of modern-day motorcycles and scooters, are probably unaware of what a priceless boon the ubiquitous electric starter has become. Virtually every machine of a reasonable size is equipped with this device, so much so that there are probably thousands of motorcyclists riding today who have never had the opportunity to fire up the engine of their iron steed by using any other method than simply pressing a button and waiting for a second or so before the machine bursts into song.

There is nothing new about electric starters on motorcycles, of course, for the Indian company in America was many years ahead of its time, by having an electric starter (in effect a dynamo which could be earthed out to 'motor' and spin the engine till it fired up) on its big vee-twins as far back as 1914, and the German DKW 500 two-stroke twin employed a similar dynamo/starter electrical component back in 1939. Incidentally, Indian also invented the throttle twist-grip we so fondly employ – too often with unbounded enthusiasm – to this day.

When Honda first showed its 250 and 370cc OHC twins to Australia back in late 1957, the first machine – the C70 – arrived unannounced with a simple kick-starter, but within a few months all the later C71 models, followed by the new 125cc twins which arrived several months later on, arrived with starter motors as standard equipment. There was even a starter motor fitted to some of the 50cc step-thru machines (arriving even later, in early August) which is certainly one of the main reasons for Honda's unparalleled acceptance world-wide.

But the humble, if almost entirely universal, kick-starter was adopted as the preferred method of firing up your machine by everything out of Britain (there were very, very many of them!), and by the few German and even fewer Italian motorcycles which were so prevalent in Australia – and probably elsewhere – from the

Ryde Motorcycles

immediate post WW2 years. This was the *status quo* until the Japanese crept up on everybody, including every one of the numerous factories, the various distributors, and their customers, in the late fifties and knocked them all for a loop.

Ah, yes, the humble kick-starter of fond memory. What a bugger of a thing that was! But it was all we had in those days, so we simply learned how to use the thing, and how its inconsistencies – from machine to machine – could be so easily tamed once we learned a few simple tricks.

Even the most difficult of Big Singles would fire up so easily in one long kick if you knew exactly where the piston was supposed to be, retarded the ignition timing lever (?) and knew that the engine would spring into life if you shoved the pedal down hard enough. If one was timid in this approach, or the piston was on its way *towards* the compression stroke instead of just past it, or the ignition timing was not sufficiently retarded, the engine would assuredly kick back viciously, often firing your leg off the kick-starter pedal and probably tearing the crutch out of your trousers for good measure, just as an example to others.

The 1000cc Vincent twin was always a challenge, because of its odd cylinder angles, and its so-called 'long' and 'slow' firing intervals, and a 'first kick' start was – at least for me, with these short legs – not always achievable. This is probably the reason Vincent had what is the longest kick-starter this planet has ever seen fitted to a motorcycle; it was the best part of 18" (45cm) long, and it could quite possibly have been used to kick start the Queen Mary cruise liner had the worst come to the worst!

On the other end of the scale was the world's shortest kick-starter, which also featured a folding pedal at its top. A Velocette was no harder to start with this too-short, folding pedal but you really had to be dead certain of the piston's location just after the compression stroke or you could kick the thing over all day and it would never fire up. It also had a deadly trick up its sleeve for the unwary. It caught me out once – just once! – which could have been a disaster.

Two things occurred almost at once not long after I fired up the little 350cc MAC Velo one morning and my (first) wife climbed, complaining as usual, onto the pillion. The bike was resting on its stout prop stand and she, again as usual, stood on the nearside pillion footrest before swinging her leg over and settling down, which of course meant heaving the bike up with its added burden as I slipped into gear and took off briskly, as usual.

Two right-handers later and nicely on the boil I lined up a favourite left-hander and cranked the bike into it, to suddenly discover that the prop-stand was still down!! Of course it dug in and spun the bike almost completely side-on, whereupon – almost out of control -it flopped over to the right. I tried to dab my right foot to the ground but discovered, to my horror, that the errant kick-starter crank had slipped up the inside of my trouser leg and I simply couldn't move my foot off the right footrest!

OK, there I am, trying to flick a badly bent prop-stand up out of harm's way on the bike's left side, at the same time trying to lift my foot off the footrest on the other side to remove that accursed kick-start lever from inside my trouser leg, while fighting a minor tank-slapper as we are spearing, only just under control, towards oncoming traffic. I am also being heartily abused by an irate pillion passenger who is belting me about the head with one of those little wicker baskets which were all the rage with newly-pubescent females at the time!

It was all over in a matter of a few seconds, as we unintentionally shot up a service station driveway to escape and it suddenly occurred to me to back off the throttle and pull in the clutch lever. Mercifully, we pulled up – side-on, I might add – and I bent to drag that bloody lever from my strides as the attendant came flapping over the see how we felt about the incident. My wife leapt off the bike and began savagely abusing the man for some reason, as if it was in some way his fault, which I confess was a profound relief. Until she turned her attention back to me, that is!

Of all the tongue lashings that was probably the worst; on second thoughts, I'm not so sure about that, sometimes they all seem to merge into a blur and are not necessarily dimmed by the passage of time. Thankfully, she flounced off and leapt on a bus which happened to be standing at a local bus stop, and was still shouting at me as the door mercifully closed to diminish the sound of the tirade. It didn't stop it, for that was not possible – it just diminished it.

But the oddest, and the most difficult, of all the kick-start pedals belongs, surely, to the pre-electric start BMW models. This pedal was operated by kicking the thing *sideways* and was mounted, for good measure, on the bike's *left* side. There may have been some large individuals who could start one of those motorcycles while normally seated, but I never met anyone who could. For my part, the only way I could ever fire one up was to have the bike on its centre-stand in the gutter while I stood on the footpath facing the bike. I once tried to start a 500 twin with the bike off its stand while it was facing uphill, but this was entirely impossible. For anyone, I suggest, regardless of shape or size.

Those machines were fitted with a very efficient twin-leading shoe front brake which was designed to perform as its best while the bike was moving forward. It simply didn't work **at all** if you tried to hold the brake on while facing uphill and trying to use a pedal on the bike's left side which operated sideways!

I called into the Yamaha distributors to pick up the brand-new CR500 single for a road-test report to find three exhausted stalwarts gathered about the bike. The big Japanese single was not fitted with an electric starter.

"You can't take the bike," one of the men announced gloomily, "we can't get the bloody thing to start."

"You have to be sure the piston is in the right phase before you kick the engine over" I advised them, "or it will never start."

"Yeah, we know that," said the largest, and sweatiest, of the trio, "there's a clear Perspex window on the side of the cylinder head, and when a little silver dot appears in it, that's when you kick it over. I'll show you." He straddled the bike, hauled in the valve lifter lever and slowly eased the kick-starter pedal down, while the other two crouched alongside the bike peering at the little window. It was almost comical.

"Slowly, slowly," advised one of the observers, "Hang on, there it is!" he shouted triumphantly, as he straightened up. "Kick it over"

I've never seen such a half-hearted effort at kicking over a Big Single so the engine, instead of gleefully bursting into life, just went "Choof! Choof! Choof! Choof! Fart! Fart! Burp!"

There was a distinct smell of unburnt petrol in the air as I offered to try for myself. The bike, with many a giggle and sideways glance, was handed over.

This was not the first 500 single I had ever started, rest well assured, so I moved the piston to the top of the compression stroke, eased it over with the assistance of the large valve lifter and heaved myself onto the kick starter pedal with all the grunt I could muster.

"Hey, what about the little silver dot?" one of the men shouted, as, at the very end of the pedal's travel, the engine burst into life. "To hell with your little silver dot," I gleefully shouted, "That's how you start a 500 single."

The three faces showed absolute amazement, and three mouths creaked noisily open as I swear one of the three actually bowed while another crossed himself and looked towards the heavens.

"How the hell did you do that?" one of them asked. "We've been trying to do that all morning." I climbed off the bike and handed it to the smallest of the trio, who was still about twice my size (which is not hard to be). "Forget all about your little silver dot," I pointed out, "this is how you do it." I talked him through the whole procedure, and I was nowhere near as surprised as he was when the engine started first kick.

So they of course all tried and mostly managed to fire the engine up in two or three kicks, to the cheers and enthusiastic applause of the others. I rode that bike out of McCulloch's warehouse in Seven Hills like some sort of conquering hero, but there was nothing brilliant about my performance. The bike had much smaller flywheels than the old British singles, which required a very enthusiastic swing on the starter, but it was only my long experience of riding an army of old British bangers which allowed this apparent miracle to occur.

Modern riders should all fall to their knees and thank their various Deities for the fact that the electric starter motor is here to stay – as it should be – for they have missed nothing.

Lost classics

We have all been there, and could be excused for sitting with our collective heads in our collective hands, be-moaning the now-priceless, if 'useless' things which slipped silently – and with some relief, as often as not – through our collective fingers. Many of these things, like old treadle sewing machines, garish jukeboxes, slot-machines, wooden-box radios, padded chairs and lounges, old china and crockery dinner sets, various corny *objets d'art* and cast-off gramophone records of jazz classic or great Opera singers, are often eagerly sought-after by collectors nowadays, when once they were consigned to rubbish bins or pelted out in Council clean-ups.

If one goes back half a century, or in some cases even less than that, each and every one of us could easily recall how, as they used to say 'one man's trash is another man's treasure', but this old saw never seemed to apply to the trailer-loads of useless stuff we gleefully flung out, or left behind for someone else to attend to.

This irrefutable rule certainly applied to rattle-trap old cars and trucks, old pushbikes, small industrial and lawn mower engines, plus a great many more seemingly useless items: including, it must be said, 'clapped-out' old motorcycles. Ask any member of the Ulysses Club, or anyone else who has spent a great part of their life involved with motorcycles, about the older 'Classic' machines which slipped through their fingers and you are sure to elicit one, or more, of several strong reactions.

At the very least you could expect to see a forlorn expression, a sad shake of the greying head, a shrug of the shoulders and a deep sigh; you would probably see an errant tear rolling down someone else's grizzled cheek; you may well see a clenching of teeth – false or otherwise – and a sharp intake of breath from yet another veteran, followed by a short list of machines which unfortunately Got Away.

At the worst you could expect to see an extreme reaction!

You may, for example, be surprised to see your victim storm away stamping his feet and waving his arms about in an alarming fashion; another could grab you by the shirt-front and tell you to mind your own bloody business; someone else may offer to kick your arse around the block for asking such a rude question; or he may – in extreme cases – fall to his knees and bay at the moon like some lonesome, lovesick wolf.

He may grab your elbow and escort you swiftly through his front door, insisting you never darken his doorstep again, and as for his daughter's hand in marriage? You can bloody well forget about that, mate!!

Lost Classics? Motorcycles we wish we still had hidden away somewhere, or are in the process of secretly restoring? Sadly, no.

It has, in fact, happened to us all. It has happened to me (several times over), it has happened to almost everybody who pounded those older machines over this nation's roads. Even the highly-steamed Editor of this august series of articles has had several motorcycles slip away from him which I am sure he would gladly have had in his garage today. But perhaps this was not the case many years ago, when motorcycling was just climbing back to its metaphorical feet after falling to its lowest ebb in the late fifties and into the early sixties.

As far as those of us in the trade in those days were concerned it was, quite frankly, All Over. The motorcycle industry was almost dead and buried. Some of the greatest names in all of motorcycling had gone to God, or were feeling the cool breath of a rapidly approaching doom, while the Japanese had just begun to make their presence felt and were, at that time, very much an unknown quantity.

In Britain, Velocette had gone, so too had Ariel, BSA, the AMC machines – Matchless and AJS – you could say Norton as well, though it was struggling on at the time, and a small army of lightweight, commuter machines including James, Excelsior, Francis-Barnett(another of the AMC marques) among many others had also gone to the wall. Vincent had gone some years earlier, along with Sunbeam, but, happily, Triumph struggled on and today has reaped the rewards of its determination and will to survive.

Some people may argue it is a new Triumph in name only, for it is cast in a similar mould to many others machines in the market-place, but let's not go there; let's just insist that Triumph has evolved along with the market's dictates and it deserves every bit of success it now enjoys.

In Germany, the two-stroke twin Adler (copied and improved later by Yamaha and Suzuki) had gone, Zundapp had floundered, Horex , Hoffman, Victoria were also gone or on the way out, while BMW – hard to believe though this is today – was hanging on by its corporate fingernails in 1960 and was only saved by a giant injection of funds from some of the country's leading banks.

What of the Italians? Other than in Grand Prix road-racing (where they were all but unbeatable), the Italian roadsters were very rare indeed, with very few finding their way to this country. Moto Guzzi was a rarity in those days, while Ducati was entirely unknown.

I wouldn't say I wake up screaming in the early hours of the morning after having nightmares about the motorcycles I wish I still had hidden away somewhere, but I can very clearly remember – if the mood takes me, and I want to upset myself about it all – the machines which today are revered Classics and which I might have had. If Only.....

Back in 1959 a chap came into our suburban shop in Ryde, wanting to trade in his Vincent 'Black Shadow' on a brand new BMW R60. I took the big Vee-twin for a squirt and was less than impressed with it. The steering was a bit heavy, it was hard to start, there was a bad misfire in its front cylinder, the brakes weren't working terribly well (they were always tricky to adjust correctly) and the typical oil-leaks from the valve lifter and clutch cables as they entered the huge alloy castings had allowed the lubricant to piddle out and bake itself, and its coating of road grime, into black streaks.

1956-1960

No, we really weren't interested in trading in the Vincent (??) I told him and he better go away and try someone else. He came back a couple of days later and we grudgingly took the bike off his hands and sent him off on his new BMW. We traced the misfiring to a faulty slip-ring in the machine's magneto and fixed the oil leaks as best we could, but no-one wanted to buy the thing (!!) for it sat on the showroom floor for months and even more months. I rode it home on regular basis, just to 'keep it in tune'.

Some poor fool finally bought the thing. If he still owns it, I'll bet he is beside himself with ill-concealed glee, while I could mourn its loss if I felt so inclined. What price a Vincent "Black Shadow' in pristine condition today? Try about $60,000 or more!

About the same time a fellow called into the shop with a late-model all-alloy Square-Four Ariel 1000. It was burning some oil, manifest by a light puff of blue smoke issuing from the left muffler. I pointed out that the left front big-end bearing was the last one to be effectively lubricated, because the oil pump was located on the far *right* side of the engine inside the timing case. The big-end, I suggested, could be on its way out.

When the engine was stripped, this proved to be the case and we suggested it would need a crankshaft re-grind or be built up with hard chrome and re-ground, and it also needed a re-bore with four new pistons. How much to do the job? No less than *Seventy Pounds*, if I remember aright.

The bike's owner was horrified at the thought of paying more for repairs than he considered the bike to be worth and told us we could keep the thing. I replied that we had a workshop full of old machines we could not get rid of and that he should return ASAP and take his totally dismantled – and thereby useless – machine with him.

He returned a couple of days later with a trailer and I clearly recall helping him lift the bike into it, fling the petrol tank on top of it and then proceed to gleefully pelt the cylinder barrel, the massive crankcases and the engine's entrails in as well, watching as several alloy cylinder fins were snapped off in the process. Who cared? The bike was worthless and was then on its way to the rubbish tip at Top Ryde, the tip now resting underneath verdant and pristine parklands.

The Ariel Square Four is now a revered Classic, though not yet in the Vincent's class, and good examples of the model fetch equally good money.

I wonder if I could zip up to Ryde with a metal detector some moonless night and try to locate the thing? I'd say not, for the rubbish tip/parkland is adjacent to the local Psychiatric Hospital. A short bloke with a metal detector, torch and shovel, in the dark, with a black beanie on his head and with boot polish smeared on his face, would probably arouse some suspicion. Beside, the best I could hope for in that hopeless exercise would probably be an old metal bucket and then I'd probably end up being helpfully escorted inside the joint. How on earth could I have explained what I was doing there in that strange guise as I was carted off, strapped into a wheelbarrow, and gibbering with fear?

I don't go near the place anyway, even in the light of day, just in case. Just in case!

The AMAL carburettor spares book contained a large, mesh-filled device that looked like an air filter, but which it coyly described as a 'flame trap'. You could screw the device onto the carburettor instead of its bell-mouth to help contain any small flame which may erupt in the event of the 'long, swinging kick' not firing the engine up.

It's true, I promise. The pre-war Rudge and the much later ES2 Norton 500 single were both prone to spitting back through the carburettor if you didn't kick them over with some enthusiasm, and this was often followed by a small tongue of flame licking out of the bell-mouth. The more learned of us knew how to locate the piston in precisely the correct position to ensure a successful result any time you kicked a bit single into life, but many owners never really got the knack of it at all.

If we occasionally missed, an errant small flame would then be sucked inside the engine on the next kick.

A fellow pulled into the gutter outside our store one day riding a 1949 ES2 Norton to buy a packet of the once-ubiquitous gas goggles. After his purchase, he strode back to the bike and heaved it off its footrest then proceeded to (try to) start the engine again. He must have kicked the thing over a dozen times, but all it did was go 'Choof! Choof! Choof!' and point-blank refuse to start.

I strolled out to show (off to) him how easy it would be to start when the piston was in the correct position, but before I got him he tried again with the same result, except for the wisp of flame which suddenly appeared under the tank.

Vintage Morris

Ryde Motorcycles

He dropped the bike onto the kerbstone again, where it rested on its footrest. "Fire! Fire!" he shouted, "The thing's on fire!"

"No, it's not!" I tried to assure him. "Kick it over! Kick it over!!"

That's exactly what he did. Before I could stop him, he raised his foot, shoved it against the bike's petrol tank and kicked the thing onto its side! I rushed into the street, heaved the bike upright, slipped it into first gear, rocked the thing back onto the compression stroke, spun it around (trying the ignore the small stream of flame which was by then running down the road) whipped the clutch lever in and trotted downhill to run-and-bump start the engine.

It started in about three steps and I rode the bike back, side-saddle, and offered it to him, the engine ticking over sweetly.

"Thanks, mate," he said through tightly clenched teeth, "I'll take it from here." So saying, he reached into a small bag he was carrying and removed a small screwdriver. I thought he was going to carry out an adjustment of some sort, but he set about removing the number plated and rego holder, which he stuffed into the bag and then walked stiff-legged away.

"It's all yours," he shouted over his shoulder' "I'm sick and tired of the bloody thing!"

I assured him we didn't want it but he didn't want to know about that. We left that Norton outside the shop for days, hoping somebody would pinch the thing, but nobody ever did, so we were forced to bring it inside the workshop where it languished in the dark with perhaps twenty or more other orphans.

There is now a ready market for a nice, plunger-sprung Norton of that vintage, but that example now languishes under a large concrete slab along with several other machines of its era!

I could go on and on (many of you will say I have already done so, including the Editor!) but I could mention the rare four-cylinder MV 750S California which Bob Jane offered me for $4400 in 1976, but which I couldn't afford at the time, or the Black Shadow Vincent in the Norton frame which I rode for a time at Ron Angel's in Melbourne, or the all-black Munch Mammut which sat for some months under that same roof in Richmond. Oh, yes: what about the 500cc1938 Triumph Tiger 90 single, or the four-valve Royal Enfield of the same engine size and vintage which a friend of mine found in a shed and which we virtually gave away?

Back in 1974 the well-known Melbourne agent, Ron Angel, had on display upon a raised plinth a 750cc 'Desmo' Ducati Imola vee-twin, the machine which the Italian Bruno Spaggiari rode into second place in the Imola 200 in Italy. It was one of two factory-prepared machines which filled the first two places in the event. I was working with Ron Angel in that store in the mid-70's and was thus able to admire that genuine big fire-breather of a machine on a daily basis. The bike was on display for some weeks before it was sold for a pittance to a young hopeful from Melbourne, who traded-in a TZ250 Yamaha racer, but the young rider never raced the bike with any real success.

It is entirely possible that the Angel Ducati may be the only one still in existence, for it is still very much alive, but how it got to be where it is now is anyone's guess! That factory 'Imola' Ducati currently languishes in a major European museum, where it was insured some years ago for no less than 200,000 Pounds, which is the best part of half-a million Oz dollars.

I trust you will excuse me, folks, for I have just started to feel more than a little sick; I think I might go outside and lie down on the roadway outside the local bus stop. That Imola Ducati could easily have been mine if I had had the brains – and the money – to have bought the thing when it was put up for sale. Of course that mean hanging onto it for some years, which might not have gone over too well with the Little Woman.

Mount Druitt

Hey, I once won a motorcycle race on the old 500cc single-cylinder BSA. Well, perhaps the motorcycle wasn't quite so old at the time, because the race I won was held on the old Mount Druitt circuit back in late 1956, so if I am correct, my calculations indicate the 1953 model was by then just on three years old. OK, it was *only* a Merrylands Motorcycle Club day, which might be said to take the shine off the win as bit, but there were *twelve* other starters and I was very much last away, so again a win is a win is a win. Readers who may have accidentally stumbled upon some of my previous pieces and actually been caught furtively reading them may well remember that my simple-looking 500 single appeared to be just your everyday ride-to-work hack, but this was certainly not the case.

The 'normal' B33 employed a cast-iron cylinder head and barrel, with a low compression ratio piston, 'soft' cam timing, smallish bore carburettor

1956–1960

> "*Mount Druitt was one of the very few genuine road-race circuits in existence in New South Wales*"

and was very much the 'roadster' model in the range of BSA singles and twins. On the other hand, the 500cc **B34** Gold star BSA (which shared the same bore x stroke measurements) was very much your punchy sports/racer, with all-alloy cylinder head and barrel and it naturally used much more potent cam profiles, a larger bore carburettor, higher compression ratio pistons and lighter valve gear, with special valve springs which had the inner set of springs wound in the opposite direction to the outer springs, into which they were a light 'interference' fit, and were shot-peened to reduce surface tension This was done to help overcome valve bounce at high engine speeds, and to allow for better control of the overhead valve gear. Oh, and a somewhat larger inlet valve was also fitted. Close-ratio, or better still, medium-close gears could be specified to make the best use of the greatly enhanced engine performance now available.

The special high-performance engine components could easily be fitted to the 'cooking' engine of the every-day **B33,** and were used to great effect in serious road racing, these machines winning many Clubman (and the occasional, more serious 'Senior') events in open road racing meetings. These highly-tuned B33 machines were often referred to – quite accurately – as 'Iron Goldies.' My BSA was one of those, but with a few extra mods (like rocker-arm return springs and lightened valve gear, to allow the overhead valve gear to more accurately follow the modified Gold Star cam profiles) to make the engine even more efficient. It looked like an 'ordinary' Beeza single, but this was very definitely not the case – as many an owner of a hard-ridden twin-cylinder machine of somewhat larger capacity often found out to their chagrin and dismay.

My then-wife usually showed little or no interest in the motorcycle Club's activities, but for some odd reason had decided to come along to the Mount Druitt circuit on the day, and had brought our two-year-old son with her, so my sidecar remained firmly attached to the BSA until we arrived at the circuit, whereupon she drifted off somewhere. The sidecar was then swiftly detached, a tuned-length megaphone fitted, the necessary adjustments made to the large-bore carburettor (three size bigger main jet, throttle slide with a shallower cutaway, the throttle needle clipped into a lower position) and the lights removed.

A quick squirt along the rough grass area inside the circuit, which posed as the pits – and which in fact, *was* the pits, for the '*pits*' existed in name only! – indicated that the megaphone, as expected, assuredly cut in with a bang at higher engine revs. 'Straight-through' exhaust pipes were great for better acceleration, while a correctly tuned megaphone exhaust was much better for more power at higher engine speeds.

And so we were ready to put the bike through its paces on a race circuit for the first time.

Mount Druitt was one of the very few genuine road-race circuits in existence in New South Wales, for there was only the 'occasional' Gnoo Blas meeting held on the 'open road' circuit at Orange, the rarely-used and now long-forgotten L-shaped Lackersteen airstrips, the most unsuitable Parramatta Park (used only once for motorcycle racing, and that was a disaster) and of course, the finest one of them all, Mount Panorama at Bathurst. The enclosed race track at Catalina Park was only opened somewhat later, in 1960. There were wartime emergency airstrips scattered about outside Sydney's outer western and southern suburbs at Marsden Park, Wallgrove, Schofields, Hoxton Park, Picton, The Oaks, Pitt Town, Castlereagh and Mount Druitt, and many of them were used for what they called 'sprint' racing. There were, of course, many others which disappeared as the urban sprawl of Sydney crept ever outwards.

The two best known, and most often used, of these airstrips were 2.9 Kilometre asphalt strips at Castlereagh and Mount Druitt; the racing simply conducted by flashing up one side of the strip, diving round a set of old oil drums which formed a left-handed hairpin bend at one end, then howling along the other side of the strip to a similar set of oil drums at the other end. Sprint racing indeed, for winning those events was usually the exclusive province of the swiftest machines raced there on the day.

The airstrip at Mount Druitt, which was also used for sprint racing until 1948, ended up being a very different track indeed. The strip was originally the 'traditional' 2.9 Kilometres in length and was a very acceptable 50 meters wide when used during the war, but a fellow called Belf Jones hired the strip out from 1948

Ryde Motorcycles

and extended into a very fast, 2.25 mile (3.60 Km) open circuit by utilising just over two thirds of the long airstrip. It was used as a serious road-race circuit for just 7 years thereafter, the Speedway Control Bill of 1957, allied to encroaching suburbia, putting paid to this very popular venue in 1958.

The circuit was shaped a bit like somebody's right leg, albeit with a very skinny thigh, a fast, 400 meter long finishing straight at the top of a shallow rise leading onto a downhill, slightly adverse-cambered left hander, then a series of right/left, right/ left corners, each corner somewhat faster than the one before it, before a sweeping, full-bore right hander which lead onto about the centre part of the airstrip itself. It then ran down to a tight hairpin round the old oil drums before spearing back along the other side of the strip (the skinny thigh) into a very fast left-hander (the knee joint) which led the riders off the strip and onto the approach to the top of the circuit again. A short, slightly uphill, straight led to the medium-paced right-hander called Dam Corner, which then took riders along a very short straight – the corners were not *quite* an ess-band – to the tricky, opening-then-tightening left-hander (in fact almost **two** corners in one, forming the foot) which led the riders back onto the finishing straight.

It was a very entertaining track to ride upon (and even more as a spectator, when some of this nation's finest riders were in action upon it!) and was considered by most riders to be almost as good as the Mountain circuit at Bathurst. Almost, but not quite! It was very fast, the lap record for motorcycles standing at a very respectable 1 min.42.3sec – that's an average of just under 80mph (130Km/h) – which is fast indeed for a fairly bumpy circuit of 3.6 Kilometers, which had grass growing here and there through cracks on the track surface, and the record was just a whisker faster than the 1 min.43 sec lap record for racing cars. The outright lap record was shared by Geoff Duke from England, the visiting 500cc World Champion Gilera 4 rider, who rode at the Mount in 1955, and Jack Ehret, on the viciously swift 1000cc Black Lightning Vincent.

Naturally, this lot were the furthest things from my mind as I fronted the start line with the punchy BSA single. The flag dropped and the field was away; all but me, that is because the races in those days were all run-and-bump push starts. I almost ran out of my ill-fitting firemen's boots at the start because that blasted BSA clutch would not fully disengage, and was left panting at the line until the official 'pushers' arrived to help me shove the bike away. I was furious at this, because the rest of the field was by now well into the series of fast corners which led onto the airstrip.

It had pelted with rain earlier in the day, but the top of the circuit was by now bone dry, so I was looking forward to belting the bike around the track to see what it could actually do when confronted with a genuine road race. I knew too well how it went on the open road, but this was of course to be something entirely different. We flew into that first left hander and I wasn't at all happy at being left like an idiot at the start, so I screwed the throttle to the stop and I wound the engine out almost to valve bounce in each gear as we shot down those descending corners to arrive at that fast right-hander flat out in top gear, the engine well and truly on the megaphone.

Perhaps I should have known better, because I often stood as a spectator on that corner, and knew how badly the track was drained at that area, but that thought certainly didn't cross my mind at the time because I was closing up a little on some of the more cautious riders. Suddenly I was into that corner and going like the clappers only to see that water was flowing across the apex with some enthusiasm, and it was carrying with it some twigs, shreds of dead grass and a *posse* of small stones!

Under those circumstances the narrow 325x19" front tyre had every right to aquaplane, and it did just that, the handlebars crashing to a full-lock, vicious tank-slapper five times before I was able to drag my left hand off the 'bars and screw down the friction damper knob. It was perhaps a dangerous thing to do, but there was no alternative, because the front end of the bike by now had a mind of its own and there was no other way to assume some form of control over the thing. We slid out sideways and almost clipped the 'safety' fence which separated the two sides of the strip, before we once more found ourselves on a dry surface. The last I saw of the Club's flag marshal on that corner, a bloke called Ron Beaver, was his legs in the air like the letter V as he fell, headfirst, over the other side of the fence!

He came up and abused me in the pits later in the day, and then confessed that the first time he raced there he had done almost the same thing as I did, though the track was dry at the time, but he had actually *crossed the strip* just past the fence and had then been confronted by

1956–1960

> *"The gulf between racing a motorcycle and riding swiftly on open roads is an enormous one, and it was never more proven to me that when I dived into the right-handed Dam Corner on the second lap of that race."*

some of the faster riders coming straight at him in the opposite direction!

I had to slacken off the steering damper for the slow hairpin corner at the end of the strip and tighten it up again for the blast up the straight and in to the fast left-hander, only to loosen it off again for the slower corners which followed. During that race, I reckon I must have played a tune on that confounded (life-saving) steering damper knob almost as often as I pulled in the clutch lever to change gears.

The gulf between racing a motorcycle and riding swiftly on open roads is an enormous one, and it was never more proven to me that when I dived into the right-handed Dam Corner on the second lap of that race. I had just overtaken another rider before the entrance to that corner and had gone into it much more quickly than I had on the first lap while I was still recovering from the near-disaster on the fast sweeper. I had changed back to second gear and my foot was still under the gear-lever (those levers were on the right hand side on British bikes) as I cranked the bike hard over into the corner. The footrest was well and truly on the deck, the sole of my boot scraping the roadway as well and getting hotter by the second as I couldn't get it out from under the lever. The BSA footrests were mounted onto a splined shaft which allowed me to lift them to their maximum height, which allowed for greater cornering clearances, but on the open road, no matter how hard I rode the bike, there was always daylight clearly visible underneath them. But on the racing circuit that footrest rubber was being ground away to a sharp point in no time flat, with those awful, skinny tyres scrabbling for grip on the rough surface!

That late entrance put me offline for the following double-apex left-hander with the result that we speared off the track on the exit and dropped into a water-filled hole, which enveloped us with a cloud of brown steam and little pebbles, but we emerged from that without a hiccup and pressed on to slip around the outside of another rider on the following left-hander, the inside footrest this time grinding its way into the road surface.

A couple of laps later it was all over and I had won the race! The very first, and only, motorcycle race I ever won, although I did manage a third place in a later race that day. My wife returned later, and I asked her what she thought of my wonderful effort in winning my first race, but she gleefully replied that she missed it because she was picking some (suspect) mushrooms with our young son at the time!

At the end of the day I bolted the sidecar on again, and simply drove us back home. Perhaps motorcycle racing has improved markedly over the intervening years, but I venture to say that these days you couldn't drive an outfit to a race track, detach the thing, enjoy a full day's racing on the solo, then bolt the device back on again and ride it home afterwards – even if it was a simple Club Day!

Brother Andy

My brother Andy joined the regular Army at 15 years of age in the Army Apprentice School at Balcombe in Victoria to study fitting and turning, oxy and electric welding, metallurgy, refrigeration engineering, armaments and a host of other manual skills. He excelled in them all, and added new skills as he went along.

At the date of his retirement he was still working – as a civilian – for the Army at Moorebank, Sydney and, after some 47 years, still riding a motorcycle daily. His mount at that time was the super-fast, thinly-disguised 'racer' 250 Suzuki two-stroke, a genuine rocket-ship of a bike which was all the rage in those days. He had made a name for himself for (among many other things) re-designing temporary pontoon bridges and their means of location to the barges upon which they rested and the tracks which were laid upon them. The wall on his living room is adorned with numerous commendations for the work he has done over many years, and he has been invited to make his services available to the Army as a consultant, but as he himself says, he is "less than on the far side of remotely interested." That, for my brother, says it all.

To try to engage Andy in casual conversation could often be a fruitless exercise, for – unlike

Vintage Morris

Ryde Motorcycles

me – he is a man of very, very few words. He is much taller than I am, as is everybody else on the planet, except for seven of the cast members of my Theatrical production I tour as often as I can, but I often joked to him that my arms are longer than his because my hands are closer to the ground. He has never found that even faintly amusing, as I'm sure you don't.

I recall we were once lifting a heavy welding set off the back of a flat-bed truck but I couldn't take my share of the weight at the appropriate moment, and the heavy box slid slowly down the front of his shin, barking off a long strip of skin in the process. Andy pelted the case to the ground, rolled the ruffled skin back more or less into its original position and, as blood began to trickle down his leg, he fixed me with a baleful glare and growled just one word between gritted teeth. The word he uttered? "GROW!!"

> "*Those were the good old days, before expressions like 'Dickhead' were accepted into polite society, but then he turned at the door and described me as a 'Gold plated imbecile', which was certainly bad enough.*"

For some obscure reason, I found this highly amusing, but he did not. He does possess a fine sense of humour and can be very entertaining in his own, dry way, but I could understand why he didn't find that particular incident I any way amusing.

Those were the good old days, before expressions like 'Dickhead' were accepted into polite society, but then he turned at the door and described me as a 'Gold plated imbecile', which was certainly bad enough.

On another occasion, back in 1960 when we were racing go-karts, I was thrashing one of our very swift karts sideways around Sydney's Londonderry tar-sealed track in practice and came back into the pits where Andy was waiting to take his kart for a squirt. A fellow standing near the pit gate proffered his advice as I rolled to a stop. "Runnin' too rich, mate!" he suggested smugly. Andy looked at me and muttered "Paramount" to which I nodded in agreement. Long forgotten now, but back in those days Paramount News was perhaps the biggest newsreel company in the world and its slogan was "The Eyes and Ears of the World." A man of few words, indeed, my brother Andy.

Skilled engineer though he became, it was of course not ever thus. He bought his 1953 AJS 500cc single not long after he sold his motor-scooter, the 200cc German Durkopp Diana he purchased just after his 18th birthday. The Diana was one of the finest of the mid-fifties scooters. It was also one of the very first 'five-port' two stroke designs; the system still in use with sports two-stroke motorcycles for many years thereafter. He bought the AJS when we were living in Fairfield, an outer Sydney suburb, and he rode that AJS everywhere, including his daily trips to Moorebank, as wse have noted, he was working as an engineer.

One damp morning he couldn't get that AJS engine to start, no matter how hard he tried. He kicked the engine over a dozen or more times, and then we pushed the thing up and down the street until we were bright blue in the face and it still wouldn't start. I suggested he ride my BSA *outfit* to work because he was running late, and I pointed out that, as he had never ridden an outfit before he needed only to turn the handlebars, tiller-like, to turn into corners, but I advised him to be very, very careful of left-handers. Very careful....very careful!

I lectured him several times over about 'tiller steering', the perils of riding one of those lop-sided things and warned him over and over again to be very careful of left-hand corners, very, very careful of left-hand corners, very careful...

"Once, mate, just once." he said mournfully, as he booted the BSA engine into life. "I got the message the first time, OK? Watch out for left-hand corners, was that it? Tiller steering, did you say; tiller steering it is. Oh, and watch out for left hand corners. Over and out." Clearly, he thought he had absorbed the message: I, on the other hand was not quite so sure.

He gingerly eased his behind onto the bike's dual seat and made it slowly down the driveway, but I had forgotten to tell him that I had had the brake-drums carefully machined and had the special MZ41 racing linings fitted with extremely close tolerances. The end result was that the first application of brakes first thing in the morning would always lock both wheels; it was very odd, but from then on they worked perfectly. As he rode the outfit onto the roadway both brakes of course locked up and almost unseated him, but he then accelerated fairly briskly away, bravely waving a hand as he left.

I watched as the outfit slowly breasted the high crown of the narrow street and then moved onto the right-hand side of the road as Andy tried manfully to crank the bike to the left, which it of course steadfastly refused to do. It continued on until, at just above walking pace, it nudged the gutter at someone's driveway and pelted him over the handlebars. He thought he had absorbed my stern, hasty lecture on tiller steering but obviously had not. By the time I had trotted up to where he was dusting himself off, Andy was back in the saddle again and roaring angrily away. His first left-hander was at the end of our street and he turned into it a bit too closely, and a bit too quickly for a novice, with the result that the sidecar wheel hit the kerb and then reached for the stars as Andy again cranked himself into the corner – and almost into the sidecar itself – while running wide on the exit as an approaching car zoomed past in a cloud of dust and dead leaves, its horn blaring loudly.

He was gone, but by no means forgotten, and at home I passed a strip of emery cloth through the magneto points of the AJS a couple of times to clean them up, the engine fired on the first kick and I rode the bike to work at the motorcycle store in Ryde. When I got home again that night Andy was waiting for me at the dirt-floored shed which passed for our garage, and he was not a happy man. I parked the AJS with some uneasiness and asked him how he went – as if I didn't know, for it was writ large upon his face!

"Ben Dover." He said, with no pre-amble at all, which was not unusual for him. "Ben who?" I queried, in all innocence. "Don't joke," he said, "I'm gonna shove that outfit of yours where the sun doesn't shine." I thanked him for the offer, which I of course declined, but the bike looked OK from where I stood, so I had to assume he hadn't run into anything he shouldn't have, or allowed the reverse to happen to him.

I managed to evade him until he had settled down after dinner, but then he unfolded a tale of woe which would have reduced a Grand Inquisitor's Senior Torturer to tears. He said he had run wide on nearly every left hand corner he encountered, sometimes in heavy traffic, and on one occasion had to flag down a Council truck and elicit the help of no less than four labourers lurking therein to help heave the outfit out of the bottom of a steep ditch.

"Those brakes," he said, "have them fixed will-ya? I dragged them on hard once to miss some idiot backin' out of his drive and locked 'em up. Did a three-sixty. To the right, thank Christ! I ended up bloody near in the sidecar. Hey, did you know the left handlebar rubber slips off the bars?"

"Yeah, I know." I assured him. "I'm not sure why it does that; I've tried everything, but it's always been the same. It makes left hand corners a bit of a challenge sometimes, particularly in the rain with a bare handlebar and a spare rubber between your fingers. I thought of gluing the rubber to the bars, but thought I might get the grip half on before it would be stuck in place where I couldn't get it on any further. Or off again. I must say I'm used to it by now."

"Look at me scone-grabber," he said, again with no reference to anything, as he displayed the blackened palm of his left hand. "Wrapped some insulation tape round the bars. Did make a bit of a difference, because then I could hang onto the bars more easily. Bloody hard work uncurling me fingers to pull the clutch lever in, though. Lucky it wasn't on the front brake side." He strolled away, shaking his head sadly.

"Hey," he said, as a thought crossed his mind. "I dunno who decided to build the first sidecar," he mused. "But whoever the clown was, he should be bent over and have his arse kicked till his nose bleeds, then be led away to design something else just as ridiculous and then lie down forever. Preferably in the middle of a major Highway!"

It must be recorded that Andy could find no love for any form of three-wheeled transport, although he always enjoyed the spectacle of sidecar racing. He often remarked that he could have used one of those 'acrobats' who hang out of 'those bloody lop-sided things' on that day long ago when for the first time, and very assuredly the last time, he tried his hand at driving a sidecar to work.

Andy's AJS

In the late fifties my brother Andy owned a 1953 AJS, an OHV 500cc single with jam-pot rear shocks, tiny (if highly effective) drum front brake, Burman gearbox which had a cast-iron clutch centre with thin splines which were known to shear off if they were not carefully (and frequently) inspected... and a slightly bent frame. While the former were standard features on the AMC singles, the bent frame was a legacy from a previous owner. Before it was correctly

Ryde Motorcycles

aligned again it endowed the bike with an odd propensity to flop into right-hand corners with the rear wheel stepping out, while it didn't like left-handers at all and had to be held down with some determination or it would try to pop upright again. We've all ridden bikes like that in years gone by – or most of us have.

Another feature of the 500 singles was their tendency to premature wear on the valve-spring collars where they came into contact with the engine's hairpin valve springs in the alloy cylinder head. The tappet clearances could sometimes disappear, for they were said to be adjusted at *nil* when cold, but with no pressure on the pushrods, thus allowing them to spin freely. This meant that, if tappets weren't correctly adjusted, the valves might be 'riding' and thus not fully closed when resting on their seats.

In other respects the bike was a good example of the typical, honest 500cc single-cylinder British motorcycle, any and all of which, along with their owners, would benefit greatly from simple and regular week-end maintenance.

Despite Andy's protestations, I decided the time was ripe to pull the rocker cover off one weekend and inspect the valve gear. We duly did so, and sure enough the valve collars were so badly worn they were beginning to bend over on the ends where they made contact with the hairpin valve springs, and the springs themselves were worn almost halfway through at the same point of contact!

He was contrite, of course, so we proceeded to pull the head off to replace the springs and collars. I had taken the precaution of bringing home the replacement parts I was sure we'd need, along with the copper head gasket, the thick, wire-reinforced Klinkerite gasket for the large alloy rocker cover, the rubber tappet inspection cover seal and the pushrod tunnel rubbers. Oh, yes, and Rolls-Royce (?) engine jointing compound. Not gasket cement you'll notice... this was RR after all, so it was called engine jointing compound.

By no means in the same league as the modern gasket sealing compounds, the Rolls-Royce 'compound' was as good as it got in the fifties, and this goes a long way to explaining why British machines were notorious for leaking oil. I suggest now, as I did then and have done for years, that whatever oil leaks existed in some British machines, they were more often the fault of the gasket sealing compounds, or the gasket materials, rather than the machines themselves.

To digress further, this was evidenced by the fact that Triumph motorcycles of that period never employed a gasket on the engine's large timing case cover and it never leaked oil. It was only when a local manufacturer began to supply a gasket for the joint face that owners complained of oil leaks from the timing case!

Where were we? Oh, yes, we pulled the head off, ground the valves in (who does that, these days?) carefully reassembled the new springs and collars, cleaned the various faces and carefully re-assembled the top-half. We had already polished the chromed pushrod tubes and replaced their tubular sealing rubbers in the head along with the thick O-rings at their base. Oh, and I had also decided to pull the barrel off and replace the piston rings, if only because we didn't know if they had ever been replaced, and this time was as good a time as any to do so. I was pleased to note the original piston was fitted, a snugly-fitting, wire-wound component, its expansion when hot controlled by a 'split-skirt' design, which allowed expansion to be controlled by closing the slot in the skirt of the piston. The very close tolerances made possible by adopting the wire-wound piston neatly overcame the problem of piston slap, which was evidenced in many other British designs.

The engine was by now sparkling in the noon-day sun as we replaced the head and barrel and the large alloy rocker box, nipped everything up and marvelled at our expertise.

I suggested we run the engine for a while to allow everything to settle in before we adjusted the tappets so my brother gleefully sprang to the kick starter. He jumped on the device several times but nothing happened, so we whipped the new spark plug out and checked the strength of the spark by prodding the kick starter while holding the plug lead against the alloy head.

There proved to be a fat, purple spark at the plug lead and there was plenty of fuel in the carburettor – evidenced by it dripping out and running over the top of the gearbox. How we managed not to be consumed by flames is a mystery to me now, though it escaped me then!

So we screwed the plug back into the head and kicked... and kicked... and kicked again... but nothing happened, not so much as a wheeze or a groan, much less a bang and engine running sounds!

About this time a neighbour rode by on his pre-war Francis-Barnett Cruiser, the fetching 250cc two—stroke single with pressed-steel engine covers, large alloy muffler, wide leg shields and heavily valanced mudguards, the lot finished in

Vintage Morris

gleaming black with heavy gold pin-striping; it was very much his pride and joy, a fact of which he kept us very well informed.

I never saw this man without a large, Sherlock Holmes-type pipe in his mouth, the pipe's stem curled over the bottom lip, a huge, bell-sized bowl filled with a pungent, grey material emitting the foul stench which announced his imminent arrival almost before he came into view.

I cannot say for certain but, as I never saw him remove the pipe from his mouth, he may well have filled the bowl with his liquid lunch and sucked it through the stem.

He rode his bike up the drive trailed by a stream of smoke from the large, black muffler which emerged from the fat alloy component directly under the exhaust port and another stream from that rotten pipe, to do a neat feet-up turn in the drive and heave the bike onto its rear stand.

"Whotcha doin'?" he asked. "P'raps I can help." I noticed that explosive consonants, like 'p', 'b' and 'd' and 'f' were accompanied by small mushroom clouds of smoke and gurgling sounds from the bowl of his pipe, while the embers would be disturbed for a second and then settled again quickly.

One of the worst pongs on this earth is a rotten potato, but that bloke's foul pipe would be surely listed among the top ten which followed, and it would be closer to the top than the bottom.

We three pushed that confounded AJS up and down the drive several times, that man's blasted pipe belching away too close for my comfort, but the engine still refused to fire; in fact, it was a bit easier to push with the exhaust valve lifter open and there was something odd about the way it behaved when we were pushing it.

We went into the garage for a breather – thankfully The Pipe stayed outside – and we were discussing the problem when I glanced at the benchtop. There hidden from the casual observer by a small piece of water pipe and a scrap of paper, were the engine pushrods!

How the hell we had assembled the engine without the bloody pushrods in it I will never know, but there they were shyly grinning at us, as if enjoying a game of hide-and-seek!

"Look here," I shouted, waving the offenders around for all to see. "The pushrods! No wonder it won't start. The valves won't work without these," I added quite unnecessarily.

"What a priceless pair of clowns youse are," The Pipe puffed furiously, as he gestured to the Francis-Barnett. "You should get yourselves a two-stroke like one of these. No valves in these things... no pushrods, neither."

> *"The rear wheel hit the wall, spun violently for a split second, then gripped and shot away underneath, to neatly flip the bike on its back, the owner spreadeagled beneath it."*

"They never give you no trouble," he added double-negatively as he rolled the bike off the stand.

"Look at this," he said, as he gently prodded the kick starter. "First kick every time!"

The engine coughed back through the carburettor and almost stalled as The Pipe blipped the throttle desperately, while clouds of smoke leapt from the exhaust. Then, with another couple of bangs and a rasping sound it settled down again.

"There, first kick!" said an obviously relieved Pipe, whose demo had almost come unstuck, "I'll see youse two tomorrow."

With that he lifted the hand-gear-change lever into first, opened the throttle to the stop, and dropped the clutch.

The bike took off like a rocket *backwards* into the shed!!

The rear wheel hit the wall, spun violently for a split second, then gripped and shot away underneath, to neatly flip the bike on its back, the owner spreadeagled beneath it.

We rushed up to stop the engine and lift the bike off its incumbent, who staggered to his feet wearing a look of utter amazement. In fact, as I was later to remark to my stunned brother as we re-assembled the AJS engine, I will guarantee he would never again see a well-grizzled visage with such an utterly astonished look imprinted upon it. The poor bloke was at once slack-jawed and goggle-eyed, a small dribble of dirt-encrusted spittle at the corner of his mouth, his yellowed teeth bared in a Gargoyle's grimace which he clearly hoped would pass for a smile. It certainly would *not*.

It was plain for all to see that he must have felt the whole world had suddenly stopped and gone into reverse!

We tried, without much success, to hide the laughter which was bursting out of us as we dragged the man to his feet and dusted him off – our garage/shed had a dirt floor – and lifted the bike onto its wheels again.

It was then I noticed that his pipe had disappeared!

Ryde Motorcycles

Perhaps he swallowed it, or it might have shot up his nose, or down the front of his shirt, or up the leg of his trousers, or it may have taken the Heaven-sent opportunity to blow up in his face (which was very dirty, as the pipe itself had always been) but the pipe had absolutely disappeared and he didn't seem to have noticed!

Well, we helped him to stand more-or-less upright, we placed the handlebars in his hands, then led him pipe-less down the drive to show him where his house was, and we even waved him goodbye as he tottered off, wheeling the bike home again. He glanced at it fitfully from time to time, then looked back at us, doubtless wondering what the device was going to do next.

That man didn't ride his bike again for weeks, and search though we might, we never found a trace of that man's pipe!

"What the hell happened?" my brother wanted to know after the man had staggered off. "I've never seen anything like that before."

I explained it to him simply, because that's what it was... quite simple.

Because the piston alone controls the incoming and outgoing gases in the two-stroke design, rather than cams and valve gear as in a four-stroke, it doesn't matter whether the crankshaft is running forwards or 'backwards'. With many of the earlier, slower-revving two-strokes, the 'soft' ignition timing was such that a piston rising very slowly could easily be thrust back down the cylinder again in the opposite direction to its normal rotation if the charge fires and there isn't sufficient impetus for the piston to go over the top of its stroke and down the other side as it should. Therefore the engine will run quite happily 'backwards', if not with quite as much impetus as if it was revolving in the correct direction.

I had heard of the phenomenon but had not witnessed it until our friend tried to show off by easing the piston up the cylinder without enough grunt to be sure the engine was running as it should.

I suppose it served him right, but I did feel sorry for Pipe-less who, I may say, remained pipe-less for quite some months. I saw him with the occasional (small) pipe clenched in his teeth, but he never, ever, rode his bike with a pipe in his mouth again.

He rode his bike often enough after that, to be sure, but I did notice that every time he fired the engine up he booted it over very heartily and then, as he moved off, he always eased the clutch in very gingerly indeed to be sure he moved off in a forward direction.. That's not so surprising, when you stop to think about it.

Easter 1960

These days you can purchase any type of dead chicken you wish, whether it be uncooked, from Kentucky Fried Chicken (KFC) with all its secret spices, or perhaps from Country Fried Chicken (CFC) in the bush, from a Red Rooster outlet, your local snack bar or greasy spoon, Charcoal Chicken, Coles, Woolies, or in any number of eateries and you can sink your choppers into the stuff on the side of the road somewhere at any time of the day or night, seven days a week.

This was not always the case, because half a century and more ago, before Colonel Sanders arrived in Oz with KFC in late 1968, the only chooks you usually saw were moving about and clucking at one another in fowl-houses in peoples' backyards. The only time you actually *consumed* one was at Christmas time when your dad chopped the head off one, plucked it, gutted it, and gently placed its remains in the oven to be shortly consumed with all the extras during a fattening lunch.

If you were fortunate enough you never got to see most of this, but you might have felt a little guilty as you chomped on your portion of this delicious creature, or perhaps couldn't eat it at all if you happened to know which one of your 'pets' it was which had so recently got the chop.

This is why, at Easter time in 1960, accompanied by with my old riding mate Big Fred, I was to be seen riding briskly upon my BSA motorcycle while conveying a pair of protesting (live) chickens to Palm Beach for a BBQ: in a string bag which lay, mostly concealed, within the confines of my leather jacket.

I was not going to be involved in any way during their preparation before those birds were to be eagerly consumed, nor was I to consume any part of them but if chicken was to be part of the menu at that BBQ there was no other way to manage this than to bring along your own fare. Someone was to do this, and as it was no secret our family had a large population of these birds in our quarter-acre backyard then it was suggested that I provide the company with a couple of free samples.

Prior to the trip to Palm Beach Fred and I were off to the races at Bathurst. Again, it may be hard to believe, but the motorcycle scene was in a very sad and sorry state in 1960, with many of the better-know British and European factories gone, or hanging on desperately as sales fell away to almost single-digit figures,

1956-1960

the Japanese only just beginning to make their presence felt.

It may be a surprise to learn this as well, but there was only one local motorcycle magazine being published at the time, called "Motorcycling in Australia", while the thin, green Victorian AMCN was the only newspaper: they were both a bit 'hit-and-miss', the magazine appearing on a now and again basis, the newspaper usually about every two or three weeks – and sometimes longer than that between editions.

But there was drama aplenty in the couple of days prior to the BBQ, both on the way to Bathurst and then while riding to the BBQ itself, so it was more by good luck than good management that Fred and I made it to Palm Beach at all. Most of our trips were memorable enough to be remarked upon at some length, but certainly one of the most memorable was also one of the shortest, that 50 Km blast Fairfield to Palm Beach, a ride set up by that disastrous trip to Bathurst a couple of days before.

My riding mate, Big Fred and I, covered several hard fought rides back in those days when traffic was probably a bit light on, and there were fewer motorcycles to be seen anywhere, the big fellow on his Black Shadow Vincent and little me on the potent "iron Goldie" BSA 500cc single. Let me say, and in not just in passing, that the Vincent had more than an edge in performance over the BSA, even though my bike was always tuned to nigh-perfection and had enjoyed the 'luxury' of the addition of many Gold Star components, a much enlarged inlet valve and highly polished ports. A high compression piston and tuned-length exhaust pipe, allied to a perfectly matched set of medium-close ratio gears added their considerable input to the bike's very spirited road performance.

I must have made up for the difference in the bikes' performances by riding with some desperation, for at worst Fred, who waited for no-one, was always in sight, but more often than not I would be tucked into the considerable slipstream which sat, vacuum like, behind the huge bulk of Fred and the big Vincent. If I missed the 'stream he was off and away, and I had to ride like crazy to haul him back in again.

It I was occasionally faster through the corners he would sail imperiously past on long straight stretches, holding his nose and shsking his head sadly from side to side. The old, serpentine road to Bathurst presented a challenge which isn't there anymore, because the gun-barrel straights and wider expressways have made the trip at once easier if somewhat boring.

So we set out in the early dawn on Good Friday for the blast to Bathurst, expecting to arrive in the town and have breakfast before the local incumbents had thawed out sufficiently to take up all the tables in local cafes. The trip was pretty well incident free and we were making very good progress -as we dropped onto the plains on the other side of the Mountains. I was in front, but only just, having hosed Fred off through the Pine Forest, the big Vincent crackling in earnest pursuit.

Naturally, the B33 BSA had no rev-counter fitted, but it could run swiftly to an indicated 75mph in third gear well before valve bounce when changing 'by ear' and had been clocked, in full road trim, at 93mph through the electronic timer on Schofields airstrip on the previous weekend. The performance is somewhat modest by modern standards, it must be said, but it was in every respect a true road-going 'Iron Goldie', and a very swift one in its day.

I had wound the BSA out well in third gear, but was by no means flat out, and had grabbed top gear just before we breasted the rise in the middle of a jittery right-hander, the bike on tip-toe and me all but weightless in the saddle, to suddenly espy a pall of dust across my right shoulder about 100 meters ahead. I couldn't see what it was, but it was coming along fairly quickly so I sat up, slotted back a gear and slammed the brakes on.

Suddenly, just as the dirt road which was the Portland turn-off came into view on the right, a utility truck shot on to the road ahead and skidded to a halt to be enveloped in a cloud of dust, the truck by then broadside-on in the centre of the Highway. There was no more than a meter of tar surface ahead of the ute, so with only seconds left and nothing but sharp reflexes upon which to rely, I slotted back to second gear and released the brakes as I headed desperately towards the front of the stalled truck. I almost made it, but the front wheel slipped off the side of the road and into some deep gravel, as I executed a textbook tank-slapper and was unceremoniously pelted over the handlebars.

As I flew through the air at about 20 Km/h while entirely upside down and marvelling anew at the miracle of wingless flight, I caught a brief glimpse of Fred flashing along in the grass on the opposite side of the road behind the truck before the Vincent inexplicably leapt clear of the shrubbery and appeared to go into a shallow orbit. In that very swift second or so, Fred

Ryde Motorcycles

appeared to me to be travelling very swiftly at near tree-top height.

I landed almost head first into the tall grass, to the accompaniment of a wonderful Light Show and some sweet music which seemed to be the First Movement of Mozart's great 'Eine Kleine Nachtmusik' Suite. It was great stuff, but was over almost as quickly as it started, because I sat up shortly thereafter and looked dazedly about to see Fred riding back to the scene of the accident, standing on the Vincent's footrests with his pursed lips forming the letter 'O' and one hand massaging his crotch.

My bike was upside down in the middle of the road directly behind the truck, resting on its handlebars and the raised rear mudguard bracket, its dual-seat a few paces away, while the vehicle's erstwhile incumbents were running about in the tall grass searching for me. I saw Fred jump off the Vincent to then heave the BSA bike upright and put it onto it stand, just as the two men spotted me. They rushed over and dragged me to my feet, with no thought at all as to whether or not I might be injured, and then sternly rebuked me for **'not giving right of way to traffic on my right!'**

Fred stormed onto the scene, grabbed one of the men and swiftly silenced him then turned to the other, somewhat larger man who had made the mistake of shaping up to him. He gave this fellow a stern, wordless lecture as well, then moved straight to me as they picked themselves up from where they lay and shuffled painfully back to their truck as they supported one another. They then drove morosely away in their rusted old rattle-trap, no doubt well chastened by their experience and (hopefully) the wiser for their very swift lesson in road craft.

Safety helmets were not worn much in those days, but I was wearing one simply because it was warm and waterproof and would stay where it was bolted without being blown away by the wind. It was a frightful Romer pudding basin, which featured a cork-lined metal dome, the shell made from spun aluminium, the rider's head held remote from the shell by a webbing harness.

Suddenly I felt a headache coming on, and there seemed to be an enormous pressure bearing on my head, the chinstrap almost strangling me. I undid the clip and took the lid off, to my enormous relief, but was horrified to see the top of the shell was flattened and there were two or three deep depressions of about 50mm each on top as well, those dents causing the helmet's cork lining to come into contact with the webbing and then to impact on my head.

The Romer helmet confirmed to the accepted standards in those days – so there is no question that, shocker though it seemed to be, that French helmet certainly did the job it was designed to do. Perhaps I should have kept it to add credence to this tale, but I flung the helmet away and clamped the flat cap on my head which I always carried with me when riding.

We walked over to see what it was that launched the Vincent into that gigantic leap, to discover it was a meter-square concrete casting for the inspection of a drain of some sort. The casting stood proud of the dirt surface by some 200mm or so and was shrouded by tall grass, but luckily it had had its cover removed for some reason, the lid leaning against the casting and pointing towards Fred's approach as he flashed through the tall grass. It thus made an ideal launching ramp for Fred's performance, but we were sobered by the thought of how it might otherwise have been if the concrete lid had *still been in place*, or stacked in the *opposite* direction!

WE stood the BSA up to note that nothing was bent or broken so we re-attached the seat and mopped up some fuel which had piddled out of the tank cap's breather hole along with a small trickle of acid which had run out of the inverted battery, then proceeded – at undiminished pace, I might add – into Bathurst.

That comparatively simple accident could have been a great deal worse, but it did little more than set the scene for the incident which was to occur only days later during that 50Km squirt to Palm Beach. People were delegated to bring a whole raft of foodstuffs, sweeties, wine and the like to the BBQ, and it fell to Fred to bring along the grog, while I said I would bring along a couple of plump chickens. I grabbed a couple of chooks from the fowl-house and I shoved them feet-first in to a large string-bag, which I then hung on a doorknob until they settled themselves down a bit.

Nobody knew the chickens I was to provide were going to arrive alive, because there was no way I was going to be involved in preparing the birds for the hotplate, either at home or at the venue: besides, I thought I quite a gag to turn up at the festivities with a couple of live chickens in tow. I must say that, after the joke had been accepted and everyone had recovered I quite expected to bring them back home again. So I stuffed the string bag down the front of my over-large leather jacket and zipped it up, leaving

1956-1960

> "*But there has never been a cartoon canary born that went "Pook, Pook, Pook, Pook, Awwwkk" in its entire life.*"

the chickens' heads out of the same hole from which my head projected so they could enjoy the scenery on the way. They squirmed about as bit initially, but soon settled themselves down for the trip.

I called into Fred's place on the way to find him ready and waiting, sitting on a large wooden beer keg. He fired the Vincent up and set the keg on top of the fuel tank, with a towel folded up underneath it. The keg was thus secured between his huge thighs and bulging arms, and was further located by Fred resting his square chin upon it.

The trip was free of incidents until we dropped down onto that old, once-lethal De Burge Bridge on the road to Gordon. Rain had started to fall and the highly polished timbers of this death trap were gleaming through the balding road surface. Standing on the footrests as I rode over the rough surface I watched in awe as Fred fought a lock-to-lock series of slides one-handed in the centre of the bridge while his left hand held the keg in place. We should have been riding a little slower over the bridge's ice-like surface, but that would never have occurred to him.

We got through that one OK, but disaster struck during the long, fast descent into Mona Vale. I was only about 20 meters behind Fred when it happened. With little warning, I saw the Vincent suddenly swing onto as full-lock broadside to the right, and in an instant Fred simply flung to keg to its fate as he straightened the bike up again and I immediately buttoned off. The keg kept up with us for several seconds as it flashed up the bank and slammed into an over-hanging slab of sandstone, whereupon it slipped down the bank to the road again and nudged itself playfully against the Vincent' primary drive case. Fred kicked the keg clear and it rose up the roadside cliff-face again to slam once more into a large sandstone boulder and come crashing back onto the road, this time directly underneath the Vincent's crankcase.

The Vincent's rear wheel was wrenched clear of the road, and Fred was jerked out of the saddle with only his hands still on the bike, while the wooden keg, by now foaming from several cracks, was spat from under the rear wheel as a cherry stone might be when ejected from between finger and thumb. It flew straight back at me and slammed into the bike's front wheel and exploded upon impact. Solidly built though wooden kegs assuredly were, they were never designed to withstand the abuse which was meted out to that particular one, so it had every excuse to go off like a large hand grenade.

Naturally I came off, the bike and I sliding swiftly down the road, our progress unimpeded by the beer froth upon which we were aquaplaning. I don't know what the co-efficient of friction of beer suds on asphalt might be, but I reckon it would be quite high, because it seemed as though I was never going to stop sliding, as I chased a recumbent Fred down the steep hill for longer than I would have thought necessary. And all the while I couldn't come to grips with fact that I/we had just managed to endure **two frightful prangs in three days**! That is many more than I have ever had in such a short space of time.

I slid to a painful stop and spun around once or twice not far from Fred was lying, the two bikes almost coming together as one, on the side of the road and only a few meters ahead. There seemed to be some dickey-birds chirping somewhere, which you usually see only as cartoon characters when someone is knocked rotten, but instead of chirping they were emitting a series of decidedly different sounds.

But there has never been a cartoon canary born that went "*Pook, Pook,Pook, Pook, Awwwkk*" in its entire life. I sat up and it went off again "*Pook, Pook, Pook, Pookawwwkkkkk*", by now seemingly to be very close by. Fred was sitting up and peering about him in a dumbfounded manner, as though unsure of where he was, and besides, his lips weren't moving, so it certainly wasn't him – and thank Gawd for that!

"*Pook, Pook. Pook,Pook, Awwwkkkkk, for Chrissake,*" it went again, this time with much more urgency. Suddenly, I caught sight of a movement under my chin and looked fearfully down to see what it was. Fred suddenly snapped upright, a hand the size of a Christmas ham cupped to his ear. "The chickens, it's the bloody chickens!" he exclaimed.

He had obviously heard them as well, and sure enough there they were, apparently uninjured, the two of them with their enquiring heads poking out of the top of my jacket, their beaks agape and their beady little eyes almost hanging out of their tiny heads.

"*Pook, Pook,. Pook, Pook, Pook, Awwkkk, Pookawwkkk, they're awake Mabel,*" said one of them.

"*Pook, Pook, Pook, Pookawwwwkkkk, thank Christ for that, Agnes!*" shouted the other one. They could easily have whispered to one another because their heads were close enough together, but so far there is no record anywhere in history of chickens whispering to one another, so why would they start now, particularly after the drama they had just been through.

Fred staggered down to pick the bikes up and prop them against a dirt bank as a pungent odour quietly began to become manifest. "Phew!" Fred exclaimed, holding his nose, "someone has dumped a load of fertiliser here."

"Yeah" I said, as my eyes began to water, "and it's getting stronger." "*Cluck, Cluck, Cluck, Cluck, not a word*" said one of the chickens, this time quietly enough to be almost a whisper, as they both fell silent and looked guiltily about them.

That pungent odour was by now beginning to rapidly overcome me as it swiftly festered itself into a grim putrescence as Fred trudged back up the road, pointing at the front of my trousers. "Pooh, what's that stuff?" he enquired, his eyes bulging. "Chicken shit," he volunteered, "that's what it; chicken shit." I cranked my head over the now-silent chickens, to perceive a trickle of green slime sliding down the front of my pants.

Of course he was right, but there was much more to it than that. When I unzipped my jacket the sudden input of fresh air upon the inside of the jacket resulted in a stench of almost overpowering proportions. I was horrified to behold a grim and sickening sight. One chicken, obviously suffering from a grim gastric affliction, had cacked itself hugely, while the other looked as though it had laid at least two complete eggs and another, half-assembled one. To add to this felony, the chickens had apparently danced a jig upon the mess and had thus stirred it into a fetid, raw omelette, the likes of which I hope never to smell again.

With teeth firmly clenched and gasping for breath, I reached into the morass and extracted the now-silent and entirely embarrassed chickens and flung them to the side of the road, still within the confines of their string bag. In an instant they were up and gone, the last sight I saw of them was their tail feathers as they minced off on tip-toe into the bushes, clucking madly at themselves while slowly extricating themselves from the bag which still managed to be glued to them.

"*Pook, Pook, Pook, Pook, Awwkk, What a Relief, Agnes!*" one of them gleefully clucked

"*Pook, Pook, Pook, Pook, Awwwkkk, Yeah. Serves Him Right. The idiot!*" replied the other.

What a mess. One wrecked shirt, the jacket lining not much better, the keg gone, no chickens, the Beeza forks and steering head bent, the trail angle all over the joint (which was to result in a shortened wheelbase and some distinctly odd handling traits) and the prospect of having to make the rest of the journey on the back of a madman's Vincent.

To make matters worse, my (new) shirt was a sports number with no buttons, and it had to be taken off over my head. Along with a singlet!

As if that wasn't enough, the lime in the fowl/foul omelette was beginning to frizzle the hairs on my chest and set the skin a-tingling as it cooled off and started to coagulate. Fortunately, there was a trickle of water running down a small drain so I was able to remove the worst of the crap from my chest, but the shirt had to go so I flung it savagely after the departed chickens, and gingerly tore the stained lining out of the jacket.

The BSA headlight was busted, the handlebars slightly bent, while a few more scars and dings were in evidence, and the front wheel couldn't be turned from lock to lock because the guard touched on the frame down-tube, but it was at least rideable, and had to be a logical alternative to a swift journey on the back of the Vincent.

The relief with which our late arrival was met soon turned to scorn when it was discovered that the keg was not with us, and the chickens had disappeared as well. Nobody wanted to hear the story, but they all wanted to know what I was doing wandering into the joint stinking like a combination of glue factory, chook-shed and brewery with my chest bared to the breeze and my leather jacket carried at arm's length on the end of a stick.

I managed a swift shower and was able to borrow a robe, but had to make the journey home without a front guard and with that cloying, cold leather jacket glued to my borrowed singlet. Easter weekend in 1960 remains a memory, but not a particularly happy one. Two serious prangs in just three days is way beyond anyone's average, and we were both lucky to have escaped with little more than a few bumps and bruises.

Omodeis

1961-1968

History

One of the most popular suppliers of specialised clothing, accessories, spare parts, tyres and almost everything and anything a motorcyclist might ever need could be obtained from one of the smallest specialist stores in the country, W.F.Omodeis, which was situated on 473-475 Pitt Street in Sydney. Amazingly, that small outlet operated from that one location for the best part of a long, seventy – that's 70! – years.

It was a small, double-fronted store with two narrow entrances and two large display windows, and it never employed more than about three or four people at any one time, but the enormous amount of specialised motorcycle equipment it turned over in a year was absolutely astounding. In the area between the two doors stood its trademark motorcycle wheel, mounted upon one half of a car's rear axle housing, and it bore the famous slogan, boldly emblazoned on its never-used, brand-new tyre: "OMODEIS. At Your Wheel To Serve." Almost every second person who ever strode into that small store gave that wheel a good spin or two, which must have resulted in that pristine tyre covering many thousands of miles while never touching the ground or ever leaving its original location!

W.F. (Bill) Omodei operated what was said to be the first petrol station in the country to have a (hand-operated) petrol pump, the fuel raised from its storage in large drums by a long pumping lever into a carefully graduated glass container atop the pump before being fed by gravity into a car's fuel tank. His early fuel outlet was opened in Tamworth not long after World War One, before he moved to Sydney shortly thereafter to open his highly-specialised motorcycle store in the late twenties. Although the store was always better known as an 'accessory house' and usually advertised itself that way, it was more a 'universal provider', for it could provide not only a great variety of clothing and other accessories, but a huge range of motorcycle spare parts, and – surprising though this might be to many enthusiasts – *complete motorcycles* as well!

As early as 1932, Omodeis advertised in the Sydney Morning Herald to advise its country and Interstate clients that they could write in to enquire about the 16-20 page 'fully illustrated catalogue', which would then be immediately posted away to them 'free, and entirely without obligation'. The interior of the store couldn't be used as a showroom, but Omodeis indicated that they could import Norton, Dunelt, and occasionally Scott, motorcycles should anyone wish to purchase one. But a purchaser would need to take delivery of the machine while it was still in its crate, take it home to assemble it and be responsible for its servicing from then on.

The most surprising piece of the history of these motorcycle importations was that Omodeis took delivery of not one, but **two,** of the *extremely rare*, water-cooled, three-cylinder Scott motorcycles in the thirties. The machines were really pre-production prototypes, for they were made in England in very small numbers indeed, and were never popular because they were very expensive and, it was said, a bit on the lumpy side to wheel about, and not much better to ride.

The first three-cylinder Scott motorcycle the company imported was the 750cc version, which arrived in 1934, the second one, the 1000cc rarity, arriving a couple of years later. Omodeis may have used these two machines as part of a publicity campaign, because they were both exhibited, fully assembled for a change, on the floor of that tiny establishment: they must have taken up an enormous amount of space, and would certainly have been in everybody's way, but once these unusual, rare machines were picked up by their enthusiastic owners, they were taken away and were never seen again! How those two large machines made their long journey to Australia, much less to Omodies, remains a mystery!

This information was imparted to me while I was working for Omodeis, from 196i-ish to 1968, by the then-manager Reg Hardie, who had worked for the company for more than fifty-five years from the thirties until it closed in the early 1990s.

I never met Bill Omodei, but his son Aub, who managed the store after his father's death, was very active in its administration, and not only from the store, but 'on the road' as well. It appears it was part of his early duties when old Bill ran the place, because Aub (whom everybody, including me, called Bill, incidentally) often visited suburban motorcycle stores as a rep for the company. I first met him in the mid-fifties when I was working for Les Rudd at Ryde Motorcycles,

Vintage Morris

Omodeis

when he strolled into the establishment one day and introduced himself as a 'traveller from Omodeis.' I checked the sample prices of some of his stock items, and ordered much of our spare parts, accessories and other stock from him from then on.

When I left Ryde in late 1961, after the infamous 'credit squeeze' had closed many suburban dealerships, he had apparently visited the store on his rounds, found I was no longer working there, took a note of my phone number and rang me to offer me a job, which I of course gleefully accepted.

As a client entered the Omodeis store, he would find himself facing the left side of the short counter if he was looking for clothing or accessories, or the right side if he was looking for spare parts. But whatever his fancy may be, he could be well assured of being attended to almost as soon as he made his appearance through either front door, and to leave the premises not long afterwards pretty well satisfied with his purchases.

The store always carried an enormous range of spare parts, as well as just about every item of specialised clothing or accessories any rider would ever need, including made-to-measure one-piece road race leathers. And it wasn't only the visiting rider who was well looked after by the company, because an almost never-ending stream of letters arrived daily from clients or motorcycle agencies throughout the country and Interstate, with enquiries for either an enormous range of spare parts, or to ordering specialised 'Aero' leather jackets, gloves of various types, boots, leather jeans or breeches, goggles and a host of other motorcycle accessories too numerous to remember, much less to enumerate.

When we were not flat-out attending to clients at the counter, we were equally as flat out packing parcels to send by post or rail half-way around the country, or by van to suburban dealerships. If a suburban motorcycle agency rang through an order before 10 o'clock in the morning, they could be certain that the order would be picked and packed almost at once, collected by a contracted delivery company and deposited upon the dealer's countertop the same afternoon. It used to be called 'service', but I don't know what it is called today, or even if it quite exists as once it did.

However, the company was never looked upon with favour by the major motorcycle importers, who were all members of the now-defunct Motorcycle Importers Federation, because Omodeis was seen by them as some sort of parasitic organisation which had somehow attached itself to these large companies, and was thus impinging upon those peoples' inalienable right to supply their own goods to the public at whatever prices the market would bear. This of course flew in the face of the fact that Omodeis was in existence many years before most of them had arrived on the scene, and that the offended companies were beginning to supply the same goods and spare parts to the nation's motorcyclists which Omodeis had been supplying to them for decades.

An example is the Clark Cable Company which, along with Bowden, supplied carburettor, magneto, clutch and brake control cables to most major motorcycle manufacturers. As just one example, a **Clark** cable purchased from the company for, say, a 6T Triumph clutch, was precisely the same as one which could be purchased from the distributors in a 'genuine Triumph' spare parts box, and it sold for less than one-third the price of the 'Triumph genuine article', for Clark supplied the same cables to the factories, to be labelled as 'genuine' as they exported to Omodeis. The same applied to handlebars for most of the British motorcycles, along with control levers, footrest and other rubbers, which were supplied by original manufacturers to the various factories as genuine spares. They were exported to Omodeis for sale as simple, 'over-the-counter' spare parts, with never a claim to them being in any way the genuine article. Little wonder the major distributors were off-side with that small company with its giant turn-over.

Almost every second day a large truck would pull up outside and deposit at least two, and often more, very large, and entirely immovable, crates upon the footpath. There was never enough room inside to unpack them, so it was all hands to the pump as we quickly opened the crates up and dragged the material inside, to be carefully – very carefully – checked against the pile of invoices which seemed always to be located nearby. There was never an easy – that is, quick – way to check the enormous amount of AMAL parts which might arrive in one large crate, but they would need to be swiftly removed and stacked in a convenient corner until time could be delegated to checking the items thoroughly. Once emptied, the crates were always nailed closed again and left on the footpath overnight. By some mysterious alchemy, the empty crates were always gone by the next morning! Upon my enquiring about this whimsy, Reg Hardy told me they had been doing that for as long as he had been employed by the company, and the crates *always* disappeared overnight!

If it was always busy during week days, then

Vintage Morris

Saturday mornings were something else again, because a never-ending stream of motorcyclists seemed to arrive from about 9.15 until well after 11 o'clock, with customers often standing at least five deep around the counters. It was not unusual to be serving at least two or three people at once, with some of them (unintentionally) stuffing the system by being directed to the spare parts side for some odd bits and pieces they may need for their bike, and then asking to try on a safety helmet or a pair of gloves, which was often quicker to attend to on the spot (or perhaps half-way between!) than directing them to the other side of the store a few paces away.

The store's manager was a lay preacher, and he often rang various food suppliers to ask for donations for Church Fetes and the like. He once asked me to ring someone about donating some fruit juice for one of his Church's activities, and I was amazed to hear the CEO extol the virtues of the company which had supplied him with most of the gear he needed when he was young Uni student well before WW2! I mentioned this to Reg Hardy, the manager, and he told me that this often happened to him as well.

In the later years, we outfitted a central alcove as a 'Silent Salesman' in which we placed a seemingly never-ending range of motorcycle magazines, alerting the distributors, Gordon and Gotch, to sending us whatever new motorcycle magazine were published. We air-freighted two English magazines and a specialist newspaper from England as well, which we added to the pile of about fifteen or twenty titles, each and every one of which were sold through the store by the truck-load.

Sadly, the Gas Company, which owned the building from which Omodeis operated for all of seventy years, gave the company just *four weeks* to vacate the premises because of the new extensions planned for their building, which left the small company with the big heart with nowhere to go, and it was thereupon forced to close its doors forever. It was a monumental tragedy to a company which had served the motorcycle community for all those years, and it was a sad loss to each and every one of us as well. I had left the company some years previously, but I felt the loss of that great little store at least as much as everybody else did who ever visited that little gem of a store.

As a footnote to this story, no matter where I go, and not only in the motorcycle movement, there will almost invariably someone, somewhere, who will come up to me and ask: "You used to work at Omodeis, didn't you?", then mention that they had bought all their specialist gear from that shop for years. I always find it quite amazing, as well as an uplifting, warming experience.

Choppers

One of the highlights of the four Daytona Speed Week tours with which I was so closely involved in the late seventies/early eighties was the marvellous Rat Hole Chopper Show, which was held on the beachfront, well away from the Daytona track.

It was always a stunning display of a large number of fantastic-looking motorcycles, any one of which had had many thousands of hours – and dollars! – spent upon their construction, but not one of which was worth a red cent in terms of its practicality. They were truly magnificent Show Machines, let there be no doubt about that, but would have been useless for any form of transport because it's a fair bet that not one them could have been fired up and ridden home in their current state.

Among the many fantastic motorcycles on display was a very special, multi-coloured Triumph machine which springs to mind. Among many other modification, which were far too numerous to be listed here, it had had its primary drive's alloy chain-case cover removed, the chain patiently pulled apart, pin by pin, to have the links platinum plated before it was carefully re-assembled. The outer plates had previously been **gold** plated before being carefully pressed back onto the link pins.

I had 'cut' many kilometres of motorcycle drive chain into a variety of lengths over very many years, so I knew very well how that process worked, and also knew how long it took to break several links with the highly-specialised Reynolds 'chain breaker' tool. How long it took to remove hundreds of those links one-by-one is anyone's guess, but it must have taken weeks to do so. It is also anyone's guess as to why someone would go to that trouble in the first place!

If that gleaming ½ x ⁵/₁₆" primary drive chain was an impressive sight, I was even more staggered when I saw that the much longer ⅝" x ⅜" rear chain had been similarly pulled apart and *completely* gold-plated! The bike was able to be wheeled about without any problems, but it's a safe bet that neither chain could hope to transmit any power. If it was possible to start that Triumph engine, much less attempting to ride the bike away, it would assuredly have been a suicide mission, for the chain (s) would almost certainly have exploded into a thousand shrapnel pieces once any power was transmitted through either of them.

Omodeis

I couldn't guess at the cost of that gold plating, or the time taken to gently re-assemble the drive chains, but I felt that there should have been a small bagful of gold dust left once the two chains had been pressed back together. The link pins would naturally have been slightly thicker than normal so some of the gold plating would likely have been peeled off when the pins were tapped gently back through the rollers. Perhaps there might be a refund applied to that small bag of gold, I suggested? The machine's owner had no idea of costs – or of any residual gold dust, for that matter – and he didn't show the slightest concern for any of it.

Perhaps he went to the extra trouble of wrapping each of the link pins with tape so they wouldn't be electro-plated, with any residual gold which may have been stuck on the tape able to be saved? This would have taken an enormous amount of extra time, but have probably been much less costly once surplus gold had been patiently remove, and would certainly have made the re-assembly much easier.

He, and his fellow exhibitors – of which there were many – told me bluntly that they had no intention of watching any of the races, which I found to be very odd indeed, but then they had arrived to display their fantastic motorcycles, and that was that, while we had travelled halfway round the world to see the Daytona Speed Week for ourselves, the Chopper Display simply (for us at least) a bonus.

I was amazed to see that many of those eye-watering, sparkling machines had their various alloy castings heavily engraved with some of the most fanciful, tattoo-like designs I have ever seen anywhere, many of the casting then either gold or silver plated. Some of those detailed engravings had then been patiently detailed by being over-painted with matching or contrasting enamel, often in a multitude of dazzling colours, which made their fantastic engravings stand out in even more detail. Again, these very artistic designs had possibly been finished off by clever tattoo artists, as their owners had been.

Each and every one of those marvellous motorcycles were heavily festooned with fanciful, non-standard adornments and they all glistened blindingly in a multitude of colours and hues, most of which Nature herself could never have envisaged.

I was assured – I trust correctly, but to my ultimate dismay – that very few of them, if any, still had their engine internals in place. I suppose it might have made sense, but then again I'm not so sure. I just feel that even a special display motorcycle ought to be ridden now and again, but that's just me.

But I couldn't help compare those marvellous machines at Daytona with the efforts of a local lad, who built his own Chopper in Oz many years previously, and he did so with his very own hands – which was very obvious as he patiently imparted that information to me the first time I saw the thing. And this Chopper, I might add, was no Show Pony, for it was ridden almost daily, and looked like it, but why and *how* he had managed to ride the shocker – and survived unscathed – still escapes me!

The poor thing had begun its life as a rigid-frame M33/BSA motorcycle of about 1953 Vintage, the machine a single cylinder overhead valve model designated by the factory as the marque's sidecar model. It differed little from the 'solo' B33, but mostly in its lack of rear suspension and the colour of its fuel tank. Typical of BSA, as well as other British manufacturers, the M-model could be specified with plunger rear suspension while the B-series could be ordered with no rear suspension. Odd, isn't it?

Clearly the basic BSA frames were very similar, but the M-series followed the WW2 BSA Don-R M20 side-vale machines in having a full-cradle frame, whether sprung or not, while the fully-sprung B33 had the sidecar mounting lugs brazed onto its frame in the same manner as the rigid frame M-series. It thus remains a mystery as to why BSA bothered with the rigid frame at all! Perhaps it was simply the cost – or was it that most 'sidecar' models in most factory catalogues used the dull, and plodding, outmoded, *side-valve* engine – as BSA themselves did? The *overhead valve* engine was far more efficient, which would certainly have resulted in a better on-road performance.

And yes, I know it's confusing, but that's where all the Brits were coming from in those days, for even a four cylinder 1000cc Square Ariel (among others, like the 1950s Norton Dominator twins) could be specified with a rigid frame.

Incidentally, for those of us who were forced by others to fit a sidecar to a sprung B33 BSA in the interests of family transport, the spare parts manual listed a special set of heavier springs for the plunger-type rear suspension. These could be allied to heavier front fork springs and longer fork bushes, again to accommodate the extra load of a sidecar, as well as the side-thrusts generated when cornering. My own B33 was of course fitted with the heavier suspension components, but not only to haul a sidecar around. The stiffer suspension worked very well in keeping the wheels glued more firmly to the road surface – at the expense of a small degree of discomfort – and made an obvious difference to high-speed handling when the bike was ridden with some enthusiasm as a solo.

Back to the Chopper, you fool, I hear you groan; and not for the first time!

The Chopper's engine featured that slight leak from the oil seal behind the timing case where the magneto drive spindle entered, the oil smear as usual coated with a film of dirt evident as the bike pulled into the gutter outside Omodeis store in Pitt Street, Sydney. I hadn't seen the bike before but I had recently sold its rider a very popular 'megaphone' silencer, in which the bright red, tapered 'pepper-pot' silencing component could be readily detached. Of course the pepper-pot in his bike's 'silencer' had been 'readily detached', the strident exhaust note rattling everyone's eardrums who stood within 100 meters or so of the bike.

And what a delight it was as the engine sobbed with relief – as did we all, including the policemen who was rapidly approaching, his index fingers thrust firmly into his ears – when he finally turned it off. I clearly heard the copper suggest none too politely that perhaps the rider ought to invest in a new silencer.

They debated this energetically for a time until the chopper owner was forced to produce the pepper-pot from a shoulder-bag he was wearing and grudgingly replaced the 'silencing' device in the end of the open megaphone.

The bike had a slightly dented tank and was painted a strange violet hue, but it looked very odd for its engine sat much closer to the ground than usual, because the front forks had been raped (yes, raped, not raked!) to a ridiculous angle. I subsequently heard from him that he had achieved this by the neat ploy of heating the steering head with a welding torch until it was almost red-hot before reefing the thing forward to a much greater angle by inserting a large crowbar into it and heaving upon it!!

A pre-war 21" front rim was fitted with a thin 3.00 block-pattern tyre, which looked not unlike the front tyres fitted to modern-day Mountain Bikes, but the rear wheel was something else again. The heavily-chrome plated steel rim was about 6" across and it was fitted with a fat, square-section *car tyre!* The rim must have originally belonged to a wire-spoked sports car, for it was laced to – of all things! – one of those God-awful sprung hubs for which Triumph was infamous, and for which its famous designer, the odd Edward Turner, should have been struck off the sane list forever.

Rather than adopting a plunger-sprung frame, which most British factories did, or the far, far better swing-arm design, which was initially fitted to Royal Enfield machines from late 1947, Turner stuck with that strange design (which had the short-travel suspension components located within the rear hub itself!) from 1947 to 1955.

Triumph's first swing-arm frame was introduced in 1954 with the arrival of the all-new, very swift Tiger 110, but Triumph Thunderbirds which were supplied to NSW Police for sidecar use were still fitted with that peculiar sprung hub rear suspension as late as 1955. The Mk.1 version of the sprung hub, with its large, pushbike-like cup-and-cone bearings, was a genuine shocker, the later Mk 2 only fractionally better.

As a kid, I remember an English road test journalist who wrote in 1949 of a sprung-hub as 'a fitment which enlivened the ride' of a Triumph thus equipped, although he did suggest that the act of simply sliding one wheel out and replacing it with another which had a suspension medium built into it, did result in a 'very slight improvement' in rider comfort.

Besides this, having ridden more than a few Triumphs fitted with sprung hubs, I knew only too well that the 'very slight improvement' in comfort was attended by in-built, very poor handling. The added 'comfort' was also very easily negated if one abandoned Triumph's excellent sprung single saddle and ordered their thin, rock-hard, dual-seat which was listed as an 'optional extra'. That narrow and unyielding seat, listed from late 1949 to 1953, was a real bone-shaker whether it was attached to a rigid frame or a sprung hub.

Be that as it may, the poor bugger had stuffed the BSA's carefully-calibrated trail angle mercilessly and compromised the front suspension at the same time. He then had another brain snap in patiently modifying the car's wheel rim to accept that Mark One (yes, it was a Mk 1) sprung hub; just two of the several facts I mentioned to him as he stood grinning by my left elbow.

"Choppers are all the rage," he shouted as he fired the bike up to ride off. "You see if they aren't."

With that he cranked the bike over and rode it briskly over the tramlines which were still in place at the time. It was no surprise to see the bike jumping all over the place, the fat rear tyre chirping as it scraped against the alloy rear guard which was too narrow and attached much too closely to it. The bike straightened itself up with little help from its rider but still appeared to be almost out of control as it weaved drunkenly about while he dragged his feet along the ground for as far as I could see him.

A few weeks later he rode up on another motorcycle. "Where's your Chopper?" I asked, not unkindly. "Me downtube dropped right out of

Omodeis

the steering head," he whined. "Then the crankcase hit the ground and I got pelted off of it. Twisted me frame as well." Was it his own frame which was twisted, I wondered silently, or was it the bike's?

I of course sympathised with the youth, but didn't bother to mention that his action in heating the frame's steering head and then bending it grossly out of shape had almost certainly compromised the brazed joint which located the frame tubes. The extra pressure which would then be generated at that point of maximum stress would have all-but guaranteed the serious problem he had experienced.

Expensive display Choppers are one thing, and no doubt have their place in motorcycling, but dangerous, home-brewed modifications such as the one that young man attempted are very much another.

Honda P50

It was during one of my thankfully rare train trips to an Interstate location some little time ago that I chanced to overhear a fellow traveller breathlessly remark to another sufferer at his right elbow that he had recently discovered a pristine example of one of the rarest machines Honda had ever made. This piece of intelligence would be enough to arouse interest in even the most jaded of us, so it instantly aroused my attention. Even though I was fitfully involved in reading the current issue of the entirely worthwhile '*Australian Motorcyclist Magazine*', I craned forward with some subtly in the eager anticipation of hearing something of great importance to me, and even, should Fate so decree, to fellow readers of that publication, for whom I write a faintly humorous monthly column.

Imagine my shock, indeed disgust, when this rare Honda turned out to be nothing more nor less than that frightful P50 motorised bicycle, a thing which bore a more than passing resemblance to a lumpy and distinctly over-weight pushbike, but with a small engine hanging out of the left-side of the rear wheel. That shocker had a set of large pedals where they would normally be mounted on a run-of-the-mill pushbike, and it employed an open frame much like those odd ones of yore on pedal cycles which were intended to be ridden by elderly, plump females wearing voluminous skirts.

The frame tubes were of course somewhat more robust, and the front-end sported a leading link fork like the earlier step-thru machines, but it was still simply a large pedal cycle with a tiny motor fitted inside the rear wheel. It drove the rear wheel through an entirely mysterious system which I have never had the slightest interest in finding out anything about.

It was of little more than passing interest to me, but it was of *some* interest, if only because I was about the re-live the nightmare of being seen on (only) one occasion to be actually riding one! It was many years previously, I might add, but that fiendish little bike could be added to the vast number of good, bad, great, distinctly odd, woeful, extremely fast, too big, unwieldy, marvellous but often entirely unforgettable machines I have ridden about this Nation's roads for more than half a century. Happily, I point-blank refuse to add that little monstrosity to my list; oxymoron though that 'little monstrosity' phrase might be.

I know it sounds a bit like the local Baron disowning a wayward black-sheep of a son who appears at the Manor door in the early hours of a wet and blustery Sunday morning. The errant lad might have had a screaming bundle wrapped within a small laundry basket, while accompanied by a toothless, one-eyed, snivelling lady of ill repute who featured a screwed-up face, a withered hand and an obvious hump… but there it is.

I mention this simply awful little moped because it may deserve space within this august piece if only to show some of the odd thinking which can permeate the most brilliant mind, even the minds of the designers of some of the finest motorcycles this planet has ever seen.

One bright and sunny summer morning in 1967, a new employee of Omodei's rode up and dismounted outside the store and strolled inside, peeled off his gloves one finger at a time and casually asked me to "come outside and what I've got!" He usually rode his very swift 250cc two-stroke Bultaco 'Metralla' to work and he seemed to be quite excited about his new acquisition, so I hurried out to see what new contraption he had obtained. In a word, I was very curious to see what had taken his fancy for, apart from owning that potent little Spanish motorcycle, he seemed to have quite an eye for some of the new and exciting machinery which was just beginning to arrive from Japan.

Try as I might, all I could see outside the store was a large pushbike which seemed to have an engine in the rear wheel, and which almost entirely filled that available space, the large alloy casting which contained the donk held in place by spokes about 60mm in length and almost as thick as pencils. For a split second I thought it was a BSA Winged Wheel, which was simply a rear wheel (or a front wheel, or **both** should you be brave, or crazy, enough) made by the British company in 1953 and which you fitted to your pushbike by the simple ploy of removing a rear wheel and slotting the device into the sub-frame in its place.

In fact BSA actually made a complete machine with suitably strengthened frame tubes, the front end with a kind of crude trailing-link suspension, the little 40cc two-stroke motor fitted permanently in position, a small fuel tank sitting directly above it on its very own personal carrier. Believe it or not, the BSA Winged Wheel was introduced at the same time as the company's first post-war all-alloy 350 and 500cc Gold Star singles, the Sports touring and racing machines which were far and away the most successful push-rod-engine motorcycles ever produced in England.

Rest well assured, the BSA Winged Wheel – as a complete machine – is **never** mentioned in any BSA Owners' Club meetings anywhere on the planet!

During the fifties there was also a Cyclemaster powered wheel, and an even rarer Powerwheel, both of them, as their name indicated, simply a strengthened pushbike wheel with a small two-stroke engine, and sometimes its fuel tank as well, fitted inside the wheel and in fact taking up most of the space therein. There were also numerous clip-on engines which either sat above the front or rear wheel of your cycle and usually drove directly to the tyre by a small grindstone attached to the end of the crankshaft, bearing on (and often prematurely wearing *out)* the tyre's outer tread.

But no, on closer inspection it was none of those, and my jaw suddenly became as limp as a month old celery stick and dropped onto my chest with a dull thud, while my head swam as I beheld the name **HONDA** proudly emblazoned upon the unusual device!

"It's a Honda," I cried hoarsely, as my hand flew to my throat (perhaps it should have flown to his?) "Where the hell did you get this thing from?" I added, ending the sentence with a preposition. "I bought it from a bloke up the street" he smugly announced, with a hint of entirely misplaced pride in his voice. "It's the only one I've seen anywhere. (*I was not surprised: my italics.*) That's one reason I bought it. It goes about 200 miles to the gallon, and I'm gonna save a motza by riding it to work every day."

Perhaps it could have covered that prodigious distance on such a small amount of fuel for all I knew, but I fondly imagined you would be pedalling the thing for about half that distance to help achieve that figure, while providing a large amount of pedal assistance – your backside out of the saddle – while climbing hills. Blast that for a joke! Oh, and the device was absolutely flat-out at around 40 Km/h!

Clearly, and as usual with all things Japanese in those days, Honda had had a very long look at several similar designs – in particular the Winged Wheel – which had appeared almost 20 years prior to their introduction of that odd P50, but there were nonetheless several improvements in that much later design.

The bike, or at least its wheel-mounted engine, was remarkable, because while it was a single-cylinder 50cc unit it featured an ohc (yes, folks, that's an overhead *camshaft!*) engine, where all the previous types were simple two-strokes, the engine not unlike the little donks fitted to the much more acceptable step-thru designs which were to be seen almost everywhere. Front suspension was of course a much better, and more effective, design, while the engine unit, the head and barrel of which hung well out of the centre-line on the bike's left side, was very neat and looked very purposeful.

It must be noted that 1967 was a fairly grim time in motorcycling history, because almost all the major factories in England and Germany had disappeared, while the number of great scooters (from Germany, Austria and Italy) which had been on the road seemed to be dwindling away, being replaced by many of the smaller commuter machines from Japan, or by the dozens of step-thru machines from Honda and Suzuki.

"Hey" he said, nudging me in the ribs to break my reverie, "Would ya like to ride it?"

Ride it? No, I would not, thank you very much for the kind offer, but no thanks I would *not* like to ride it, I sniffed, as I strode purposefully inside, my mind still trying desperately to deny the machine's existence.

But for some ridiculous reason, for which I still cannot provide any excuse, I was to change my mind later in the day when I had to commute to the other and of town on a personal matter and time was pressing, because I had to do this entirely within the strictly specified period which was referred to as my lunch hour. The rules of that otherwise happy store were quite strict, and any business of a personal nature had to be accomplished entirely within your *own* time, while personal phone calls were strictly forbidden. True!

"How do you fire this thing up?" I queried, as I sat on the newly-lowered saddle later in the day, the proud owner smiling at me the while. "Oh, you just pedal it for a bit and it does the rest. Then away you go," he cheerfully advised me. So I sprang to the pedals and tried to get underway, but it was nowhere near as easy as thought it

Omodeis

might be. So help me, it was just like trying to heave a pushbike off the mark while both brakes were still on.

I huffed and puffed as I strained on those pedals for what seemed like a hundred meters, but which was probably no more than about five or ten, and then it seemed to me that the pedalling became a little easier as I discovered that the engine was actually assisting me to get underway. I opened the throttle to the stop, but not much seemed to be happening as I wobbled uncertainly into everyone's way, still pedalling furiously to get to the other end of town and back in under an hour without being run over by somebody in an invalid carriage which was badly in need of a service.

The climb up Castlereagh Street was achieved by standing on the pedals to assist that little engine, and I would like to have said that an obese and palsied dwarf, shuffling painfully along with the aid of a pair of stout canes, rapidly overtook me during that exercise, but that didn't actually happen. Of course it could have: no, it didn't happen, but I would not have been surprised if it had.

Later on, I found that trying to start that device while pointed uphill was more than I could manage, though I strove with every ounce of power I could manage in attempting to do so, so I had to wait for a change of lights to run the P50 downhill, execute a tight U-turn and then scurry off as quickly as engine and pedals could carry me. I was never happier to hand a motorcycle back to its owner than I was when I finally leapt off that thing: and just for the record, the bloke was back on his fire-breathing Metralla in about four days.

I was not in the least surprised to note this, though I never asked him want happened to the P50. For a start, I didn't want to embarrass him, but secondly, I simply didn't want to know. That first Honda P50 came and went in no time flat, but Honda than went on to build the P50A, and several versions thereof, which were **genuine** mopeds, the engines where they should have been in the fist place – between a rider's ankles.

The design of the average moped, including some very sporty, more highly tuned versions (the term moped derives from the fore-shortening of the expression '**Mo**tor assisted **Pe**dal cycles', for what that's worth) consists of a pair of stout pushbike pedals to allow for easy starting, and this applied to the little P50A as well. Those same pedals would almost certainly have to be used by the rider of the little device to provide additional power when climbing hills, or attempting to get out of everybody's way at other times.

There can't be much doubt that the P50A filled a crying need somewhere on the planet, perhaps in the backblocks of many an Asian market-place, and it was probably quite successful in its niche, but I thank the Good Lord that none of them seemed to have made their way into this country!

Priestley

The modern motorcycle is a highly-sophisticated design, bristling with advanced technology, as it has nearly always done. Even the most ordinary of motorcycle has shown the way in engine design, suspension and transmission efficiency to the more plebeian motor car, leaning much more towards aircraft technology that the more humble four-wheeler.

It's true that rampant technology was not part of the two-wheeler's simple design when the first of those 'motorcycles' – motorised push-bikes – spluttered about at the end of the nineteenth century, but the recent advances in many fields has thoroughly overtaken the design of the modern machine just as it has with many modern devices..

To this day, since John Stanley invented the so-called safety cycle before the end of the nineteenth century, replacing that unwieldy penny-farthing with a diamond-frame and headstock design, the motorcycle frame as we know it remains virtually identical to that very first 'safety cycle.' Singer, of sewing machine fame, then patented the curved front fork we still see on pushbikes, which allowed for the essential 'trail angle' which thus resulted in far better control of his solid-rubber tyred machine.

Everything else on two wheels followed this advance, and that includes modern motorcycles, whose trail angle – with telescopic forks – is determined by tracing a line from the steering-head angle to the roadway, and a vertical line from the front axle. The difference between the two points of contact is the trail angle, and what a monumental difference this angle makes to the handling and – depending on the length of a motorcycle's wheelbase – to cornering speeds.

Of course there have been several departures from the norm in frame design over the years, including the once-fashionable cantilever rear suspension – which is more than 80 years old, though purportedly new – but essentially the bicycle frame of the early 1880's remains fundamentally unaltered whether the machine is a pushbike or a high-performance motorcycle.

Remember that British Playwright and author J.B. Priestley, who visited Australia some 50 or more years ago? His complexion was very much of the 'Peaches and Cream' variety so much a feature of the Poms, whether male or female. I recall a TV interviewer asking him about Priestly shaving with an old cut-throat razor when they first met in the latter's Hotel room.

"Have you ever thought of using a more modern electric shaver?" Priestley was asked. "And throwing that old razor away?"

"I once purchased a face mower," the man replied, forever denigrating the electric shaver. "For I felt that with progress *comes a better design and a better, more efficient product*. I was at once amazed and horrified to note it took me at least three times as long to have an agreeable shave, dear boy.

"And when I then came to adding an after-shave lotion to my face with the agency of a small wad of cotton wool, I suddenly assumed the jolly face of dear old Santa Clause. Only half the whiskers had been removed; the rest I quickly whisked away with the OLD cut-throat. That light stubble left behind by the mower picked up the fine strands of cotton wool and aged me by many years in an instant. Would you call *that* progress?"

We aren't about to dive into a story of the late J.B. Priestly, but his point about progress *per se* is a moot one. He used a razor which did the job with great efficiency, and had tried a newer instrument which didn't really do the job. But times have changed, and by now (were he still alive) his cut-throat razor might well have disappeared to be finally replaced by a 'mower' with which he would be entirely happy.

If our motorcycles have been incorporating the safety cycle frame design for more than a century, is that because (as Priestly might have thought) there is simply nothing better out there, or have we in fact not bothered to look hard enough at another, albeit revolutionary, advance on that basic and currently archaic invention.

In fact there is something which could be infinitely better 'out there' and it has been put to good use, on a somewhat limited scale, for more than 80 years.

It is the hub-centre steering system.

This design was utilised way back in 1920 by the Ner-a-Car motorcycle and the four-cylinder, shaft drive, American Militaire from 1914. The Militaire was somewhat unwieldy through its prodigious weight and very long wheelbase, but the Ner-a-Car was a machine which proved to be incredibly stable at less then walking speed, and just as stable, even over some very poor road surfaces, at its maximum speed; which was not particularly high. There were several other examples of hub-centre steering in those early days of motorcycling, but the safety cycle was much simpler – cheaper? – to manufacture and was thus adopted by most manufacturers.

I rode a 1922 Ner-a-Car many years ago, and I remember sitting on the enclosing saddle, which was more like an office chair, while taking instructions from the machine's owner. "You can ride the thing anywhere you like with your arms folded," he told me with a wink, "and you will be very surprised at how the thing feels at any speed."

The sprung saddle was placed directly above the petrol tank, and its upright handlebars which sprung up from a position directly behind the huge front mudguard, ended up about knee-height, seemingly clamped to a thin steel broom handle. I didn't much like the look of the agricultural steering linkages, or the feel of the bike, but once it moved no more than a small pace or two I was totally in awe of its amazing stability. It employed an under-powered, 300cc two-stroke motor, but it moved along well over some very broken road surfaces, one or two of which were dirt.

I was not about to ride the thing with my arms folded for very long, but I was happy enough to try this for some distance with hands resting on my knees, within very easy reach of the wide handlebars. I could even corner the bike on smooth roads without touching the bars, simply by leaning gently into the corners as though my hands were firmly wrapped round a solid set of handlebar rubbers.

I doubt if I have ever ridden a motorcycle, large or small, which could approach the Ner-a-Car for its inherent stability at any speed, from a slow canter to about 50 Km/h. It jumped about a bit, of course, because the suspension was awful, but this made the bike's stability all the more remarkable.

Readers who viewed a Batman movie several years ago might have been intrigued to note that the 'Bat-Bike', which was ridden with such enthusiasm by the Caped Crusader, or his stand-in, featured hub-centre steering. It should also be noted that the 5-meter long Johnny Allen Triumph 'motorcycle' which in 1956 held the world land speed record was far, far too long for the rider to control it with a set of ordinary handlebars. So it, too, featured a form of hub-centre steering, which allowed for precise handling at the enormously high speed of 345Km/h the machine reached, but also at the near-walking pace at which it was ridden through the pit area.

A fellow called Doug Waye campaigned a very long and strange looking drag bike he called the 'DragWaye', which was originally fitted with a 1000cc Square Four Ariel engine, but which was later fitted with a Volkswagen engine. The bike was a 'slingshot', for it was several meters long,

Omodeis

with the rider perched at the very back, behind the rear wheel. His seating positon was a bit like that of a modern-day Cruiser.

Someone nick-named the device the Flying Bedstead, possibly because of its unusual, box-girder, low-slung, space-frame construction. The handlebars sat just ahead of the rider, in a fairly normal position, the steering controlled to the distant front wheel by a simple hub-centre steering system. It was reported by Waye that the odd-looking device was (again) amazingly stable at very high speeds, but could still be steered with great precision at walking speed.

One has only to watch those high-performance motorcycles ridden in Moto GP races to note that the diamond-and-headstock frame has gone about as far as it can go, for these viciously swift machines are often seen only just under control with their handlebars shuddering violently as the riders accelerate out of fast corners. This is particularly obvious on the fast entry from the left hand sweeper onto the finishing straight at Phillip Island.

Steering problems experienced with early motorcars which employed 'tiller' steering, in which a bar sat, often horizontally, in front of the driver and was used to steer the device were at once arm-wrenching and dangerous. At any reasonable speed over poor road surfaces, the tiller would shimmy violently in the driver's hand and the vehicle would have to be brought almost to a standstill before it could move off again. This type of steering mechanism was used by Oldsmobile, Rambler, and even Henry Ford's first vehicle, his 1896 Quadricar.

Tiller steering was replaced in motor cars by a steering wheel and hub-centre steering just before, or slightly after, the turn of the twentieth s century. What a giant leap into the future that move became! This type of steering is still used with outboard motors.

But what about the Elf, and Bimota, both of which machines used hub-centre steering in Europe some years ago – but with limited success? That is quite true, but the design has been used to great effect on some racing *outfits* as well, including the Skinner Laverda which swept all before it in sidecar racing in Australia back in the early seventies, the machine campaigned with what was claimed to be a bog-standard, 1000cc Laverda Triple engine.

The hub-centre steering design has been used by Jack Difazio in England on many solo machines, as well as sidecar mounts for years, and there was once a BMW flitting about the streets of Sydney with a Difazio front-end grafted in place. It looked distinctly odd (as all hub-centre steered machines do) with its long front swing-arm and upright shocks, while a long rod seemed to be shoved through the middle of the front hub, with cranked steering links everywhere. It also looked as though something very important was missing from the front-end as well: these were, of course, the telescopic forks.

There are a few viable two-wheelers doing the rounds today which feature hub-centre steering, one of them a small Italjet scooter! – but we will probably never see my favourite Hobby Horse adopted until Honda abandons the 130-year-old design with its headstock, diamond frame and telescopic forks and dives headlong into the old-fashioned principle of hub-centre steering.

After all, this is the company which firmly placed the whole world back on two wheels, and I predict they will – in fact they *must* – inevitably embrace the hub-centre steering concept. They will then, equally as inevitably, be followed by everybody else who ever wants to win another motorcycle race.

Then, like everything else which has ever been proven in the cut-and-thrust of motor racing, no matter how many wheels are employed in this pursuit, it will then appear, heralded as if by the Trumpeting of Angels, as if it were Honda's Brand New Invention, and it will then appear upon every two-wheeler, from your savage road-burner to your bread-and-butter motorcycle as well. You think not? Bet on it; it must soon arrive – oh, and remember the name Vyrus from Italy: already here, and winning races!

Monday at Omodeis

If Saturday mornings were absolutely flat-out at Omodeis from about 9.15 on the dot until well after 11am, then Monday mornings were something else again, because it was a little more on the quiet side if no less interesting. 'A little more on the quiet side' didn't mean for a moment that there wasn't plenty to do, because there was always a lot of new stock to be brought forward, and there was always a steady stream of customers coming into the place at the beginning of each week.

There might have been a motorcycle race meeting somewhere in the Sydney area the previous weekend, or a bunch of riders may have blasted off for a squirt into the country and returned needing some parts to service or repair one or more of their bikes, while sometimes a party of country or Interstate riders would roll up just to check us out. The latter were often clients from far afield who may have come to town to watch the races or, as often as not just to see, so they would say, what we actually looked like!

The company was justifiable popular with

motorcyclists everywhere, but it was never in the good books of the once- burgeoning *Federation of Motorcycle Importers*, simply because Omodeis didn't import motorcycles after the War, and were thus firmly shut out of this organisation's criteria. But the company *did* import a great many motorcycle spare parts to augment its large range of clothing and accessories, and it sold them at much lower prices than those charged by Federation members. Therein lay the source of irritation.

Many of the items the company imported were brought in directly from the companies in England which manufactured 'genuine'- the so-called original – components which they supplied under contract to the various British motorcycle factories. These components included handlebars, control cables, gasket sets, engine and gearbox parts like valves and their springs, AMAL carburettors and a host of spare parts for them, control levers and electrical items like light bulbs, and ignition contact points and condensers, among many other essential spare parts which would have been sold quite legitimately by importers as genuine items.

One particular Monday morning followed the previous weekend's motorcycle race meeting conducted on the tight and unforgiving road race circuit in the bush-like outer Sydney suburb of Amaroo Park. As usual I had been the on-course commentator at the meeting, not only calling all the races but trying to keep the crowd entertained between events by reciting a large number of faintly comical anecdotes, along with the occasional technical dissertation.

Whether or not I was successful in the latter pursuits I cannot say with any certainty, but I held that very busy, and almost entirely ad-lib gig, at Amaroo Park – and at Bathurst over the Easter holidays as well – for many years so I suppose it worked well enough. There was a small group of customers around the counter and I was holding court that morn as we discussed the meeting at some length, the store's Manager as usual not particularly keen on this quite normal occurrence. But as he said, he had to put up with it because he felt it helped bring some people into the establishment who might otherwise not visit the place. And after they had discovered who, and what, Omodeis actually was – and who I was, for that matter? – who knows what products they may buy while under our roof?

One of the fellows had proudly parked his sparkling new 650cc BSA Spitfire Mk.111 out front, the sports mount resplendent with its chrome plated mudguards and the large-capacity fire-engine red petrol tank with huge, matching side panels. He had only owned the bike for a couple of weeks, because I remembered him riding a 500cc AJS twin up until that time. We were all ogling the bike as it pulled up, and were lavish in our praise of his choice of machines when he strolled nonchalantly up to greet us.

The bike looked most imposing, but perhaps not quite so impressive to the Potts Point Dowager who had parked her jet black Mk.V Austin Vanden-Plas Princess (the poor man's Rolls Royce) in front of the store while she strode imperiously into the AGL offices next door to pay her gas bill.

She came out again to find the BSA parked with its rear to the kerb and in a position which wouldn't allow her to get her car out of its tight parking spot, so she thrust her head into the store from the footpath outside, her bulldog-like jowls wobbling with indignation.

"I say" she snorted, "will the chap who owns that blood red bicycle please remove it so I can get my car out. Is the man in there?"

"Is that your red bicycle?" I jokingly asked the fellow who owned the Spitfire. "The lady would like it moved so she can get out and go home to her high tea and cucumber sandwiches."

"I don't own a bloody red bicycle," he said grimly, doing his best to ignore the woman. He turned back to the counter, muttering to himself.

"No, she didn't say a bloody red bicycle, she said a **blood** red one." I goaded, "and I think it must be yours."

While we all found this more than a little amusing, he clearly did not, and neither did the Duchess. "I have been hemmed in by that person," she said, "and I wish to depart. Will he have the good graces to remove his bicycle and let me leave, please?"

"Go on, better move your bicycle mate, don't upset her any more than you have to. She might stride back into the Gas Company and complain about us." I advised him.

He turned without a word and stamped out to move his bike. "It is a *motorcycle*, not a bicycle," he hissed at her through gritted teeth. "Some bicycle."

"It has two wheels, therefore it is a bicycle," she sniffed at him, as she informed him of this quite undeniable fact. "If it had had three wheels it would be *tricycle*."

Almost as he went out to move his BSA another bloke walked in flourishing an engine valve. He walked up to Mal who was the other assistant in the store. "Have you got an inlet valve for me ES2 Norton?" he enquired, handing the valve across.

Omodeis

Mal disappeared into the depths and came back shortly thereafter to hand the man his valve back again. Unlike me, Mal was always a man of very few words.

"Stiff!" is all he said as he handed the valve back to a clearly disappointed customer. Mal then turned his attention to the bloke who had just moved his bike (onto the footpath, I might add!) and was coming back inside again.

This wasn't nearly good enough, because you can't be that off-handed to anyone, particularly a good client like that fellow was. I asked the Norton owner if he had a lathe at home, or if he knew someone who could machine a blank valve for him. "Yeah, I've got a brother who is a fitter and turner," he said, by now looking a bit more hopeful.

I pointed out that we had a couple of boxes full of Dufor blank valves (made by Duly and Hansford) which were in either Valve Chrome Plus for inlet valves or the more specialised KE965 for the exhaust, and I knew we only had the VK+ in stock at the moment. The valves were all around 55mm – over 2" – in head diameter, with a long stem which could easily be machined to the right length, and the stem was also somewhat thicker than normal. But with a sample valve such as he had it would be a simple matter to have his brother machine a valve for him, no matter what type of engine it was meant for.

"How are you for valve springs, and a gasket set; what about some new valve guides?" I asked him, not forgetting the essential gasket cement as well. Oh, and while he as was about it, how were all his control cables? He left the shop delighted with his bag of spares parts, but he didn't need any of the cables I recommend he might like to replace.

As it happened, the bloke had wheeled his BSA onto the footpath because it was about to rain, and rain very heavily at that. It was, after all, a near new machine and it looked great – but it had not yet begun to show the problems it was soon to demonstrate with seized pistons, a problem which plagued the first of those models, but which was swiftly overcome by a recall for the fitting of replacement parts. "Can't leave it out there in the wet," he suggested, "and what if it's gonna be a hailstorm?"

"Well, you can't leave it out there all night, and you can't wheel the thing in here." I told him, "you'll have to ride it in the rain at sometime and this is as good a time as any."

"I haven't got any waterproof gear," he wailed, "that's what I came in here for."

In short order he slipped into a pair of waterproof pants, which he thought were much too long until I pointed out to him that he should try them on a conveniently placed chair to see that they would ride up to the correct length when on his bike. He peeled them off and tried on the matching jacket, but again found the sleeves to be a bit on the long side. I suggested he sit on the chair again and thrust him arms out at near full stretch, which he did to then discover the sleeves were of course a perfect fit.

He already had a helmet, even though they were not yet required by law, a good set of gauntlet gloves (for which he bought a pair of 'waterproof' over-mitts) and his boots were solid and as waterproof as boots were in those days – which was not very waterproof at all. He piled his purchases on the chair again as he paid for them and we then continued our conversation. The thunder was pretty loud and the rain really lashing down, so he hung around for a while as we served a few more people, had a swift cup of tea, packed a few parcels and chatted between times.

He had an illicit read of a couple of magazines, bought one of them which he shoved up his jumper and then slipped his helmet back on. It was still raining as he strolled outside and wheeled his bike onto the roadway, which I thought was fairly brave of him for it was, after all, obviously his pride and joy. Then he kicked the engine into life, executed a neat U-turn and zoomed off into heavy rain towards Central Station.

He came back again about ten minutes later.

"I forgot these bloody things," he shouted, pointing to the waterproof gear he had recently purchased, but which was still on the chair where he dumped them earlier. I thought he'd be back sooner rather than later because it was only a few seconds after he had swiftly departed that I noticed he had left the lot behind.

"I forgot the new gear, because I'm not used to dragging the waterproof stuff on, that's what it is," he muttered as he pulled the gear on over his sodden clothing, "But I won't be doing that again."

He took an age to struggle into his protective gear, which by now was perhaps not quite so protective, because it was as wet on the inside as it would been on the *outside* had he been wearing it when he left. He then strode outside, waved forlornly at us and rode off. He was so wet and uncomfortable underneath that I don't know why he bothered wearing his new gear at all!

Nicknames

There was a kid in Wooloomooloo, where I grew up during the war, who bore the unfortunate nickname of 'knackers' – even his mother called him that! – while there was another kid who was a bit on the plump aide who was forever called 'Bubbles', which was arguably a whole lot worse. There was a kid at school who had a funny lump of sandy, white hair which stuck up at the back of his well-freckled head, where his hair parting ended, an errant thatch of hair which he could never tame. He was endowed with the nickname 'Cocky' of course, and I cannot recall him ever being called anything else, for I never heard his first name called out, even by our teachers at roll-call.

There have been great nicknames endowed upon people who have been featured in some of the finest literature ever written, including the immortal Sir Toby Belch, one of Shakespeare's most enduring characters. Nicknames, whether laced with scorn, ridicule or simply due someone's great sense of humour, have probably been around since the times when men lurked, half-terrified, within the confines of their numerous caves. "What's in a name?" Shakespeare's Romeo asked his Juliet, "that which we call a rose by any *other* name would smell as sweet." Had Juliet a nickname, Romeo may well have asked her what's in her 'nickname', for it's safe bet that, as Sir Toby had been given one, so might she also. I wonder what it was. 'Brittle' comes to mind.

With the ever-increasing line-up of new models and often confusing nomenclature from only a very few motorcycle manufacturers, the nicknames which were very often applied to most of the earlier motorcycles seems to have disappeared these days.

These nicknames were usually very corny to say the least, while some of them were somewhat descriptive, if a little cruel – and however accurate – at times.

For those of us old enough to remember the scores of motorcycle manufacturers which used to proliferate in the dim past, most of us can clearly remember that the Matchless models glorified in the nickname 'Much Less', while its almost identical clone (except for the juxtaposition of magneto and generator on single-cylinder models) the AJS, was referred to almost universally as a 'Jazzer'. This had nothing to do with the way the AJS models rode over rough road surfaces, be assured, for the AJS/Matchless machines employed the same frame and suspension. Both were very comfortable and handled acceptably well, in particular the mid-fifties machines with their soft dualseats and dual-diameter, 'jam pot' rear shocks.

But the two marques were a great example of badge engineering, and came in the form of 350 and 500cc singles, or 500cc – and later 600cc – vertical twins, the twins enjoying one of the most beautifully designed engines to come from England. It is a fact that most Matchless owners claimed that any AJS model was a reject Matchless, found wanting somewhere on the (same) production line. Not true, of course!

BSA was either a Bloody Sore Arse or a Bloody Sure Accident, but why anyone would suggest an arse was more likely to be sore from riding a BSA about or that you get into trouble from riding one escapes me, but the expression was more likely an odd term of endearment than a slur on the marque. The once-ubiquitous BSA Bantam rejoiced in the nick-name 'Phantom Bantam', while some of the Bantam's competition amongst the small commuter machines carried their own nicknames as well; Francis-Barnett was a 'Frantic Bastard', the Excelsior was an Eggshells for Sure, while the little James (of fond memory) was simply a Little Jimmy.

Harley-Davidson was usually either a Highly-Dangerous or a Hardly-Rideable, with its other American compatriot, the long-suffering Indian, glorified as an Inter Ya. In those days of yore, there were few Harleys about which were not WLA surplus, which it must be said were not amongst the easiest to ride (I have ridden more than a few), while Indian was even rarer – though again mostly ex-Army – and originally had its twist-grip throttle control on the **left** side!! The Indian was even more difficult, not to say dangerous, to ride. Fortunately this odd quirk was easily rectified by swapping the piano-wire cables across from the carburettor to the distributor spark advance and *vice-versa*.

I can't remember Velocette or Sunbeam enjoying the dubious honour of any form of nickname, though a friend of mine once referred to his Velocette as his 'Old Fella'. Make of that what you like. Oh, and the 350cc flat-twin Douglas was simply a Dougie.

Norton's range of machines glorified as Nought Ons, with no reason given for that title except for a possible attack of the whimsies. Royal Enfield was, quite unfairly, commonly called the Royal Tinfield. That *soubrique* could have been applied to the Model J at a pinch, that very ordinary 500 single with high-mounted front mudguard, alloy con-rod with simple white-metal big-end bearing and very pedestrian performance. But Tinfield could never be used to describe the fine 500cc Bullet singles with their brisk performance and advanced swing-arm rear suspension (probably the first on a British touring machine in 1948!), the much later sporty 250cc Crusader or the even finer range of vertical twins from the 500cc models to the 700cc Constellation Superbike with its 120mph top speed, potent (double 7" drum) front brakes and great handling.

The 600cc single-cylinder Panthers – and the later 650cc variants – were, because of their

Omodeis

prodigious pulling power as a sidecar mount, always referred to as a Grunter. Panther's rare siblings, the 250 and 350cc singles, hardly rated a mention, much less a nick-name.

The Ariel was referred to as an Airy Ole, the punchy 1000cc Square Four variant – the only four-cylinder British machine made at the time, which very sadly departed in 1959 – either a Squaffer or a Squariel, while the ever-popular Triumph began as Trumpies and then became, for most admirers, the Trumpet.

The very rare 600cc Scott two-stroke twin and (almost) forgotten 350cc EMC 'split-single' two-stroke were all but invisible in those far-off days, while the Czech Jawa, though popular enough as a commuter, escaped notice as well. The fierce, fully-sprung, 350cc two-stroke twin DKW of the mid-fifties, rare though it was in this country, but a very, very exciting ride whenever you had the opportunity, became, simply, a Deek

Among the other, few Europeans, which sold in single-digit numbers, BMW (almost as rare a machine in those days as the DKW, believe it or not!) was always a Boomer – it's a Beemer these days – while the even-rarer Moto-Guzzi was of course a Gutsy. The German NSU was a Snoo, while the Austrian Puch was, perhaps inevitably, a Pooch. Zundapp escaped without a nick-name, while the very early Ducati was – and remains with some people and for some unhappy reason – a Spew Catty.

The King of the Castle, the 1000cc Vincent HRD, was always a Heard, while the later, road-burning Vincent Black Shadow was simply, and reverently, a *Shadow*! (Ooohh! Whisper it, he bought himself a "Shadow", shhh!) With the notable exception of my riding mate, Big Fred, who had one of these potent roadsters, I gave those big black things – few as they were – a wide berth on the road.

Nor did the Japanese escape the often unfortunate tags which were applied to the very many motorcycles which had gone on before them.

The first of the few – which became, as the flood gates slowly opened, the first of the many – **Honda**, bore the nick-name On Ya, (as in Honda Dream, On Ya Nightmare) an apt description of those first unwieldy machines, while the next arrival, Suzuki, became a Sez Youki and the next from Japan became a laughing stock as the Yamaha-Ha. Who's laughing now, I hear you ask.

One of the finest Japanese machines to reach these shores, the late and well-lamented Bridgestone, became the Kidney Stone, while perhaps the saddest nick-name of all belonged to those early Kawasakis. They were referred to then – and occasionally now – as Cack–ya-Dackies, or, even worse, as Crack-a-Slackie. That first nickname could well be descriptive of the monstrous, ill-handling and under-braked 500cc three-cylinder Mach 3 Kawasaki of 50-odd years ago – the bike also referred to as the Widow Maker – but Crack-a-Slackie?? The mind boggles!

That very first Honda Gold Wing motorcycle I road-tested for Revs magazine way back in 1974 was branded by almost everybody as the **Lead Wing** – that's lead as in base metal, *not* Lead as in 'ahead of the pack'. It was perhaps an unfortunate name to bestow upon that first example of a very advanced design, which just might have been close to the mark at the time. It's hardly a Lead Wing today, however!

The portly, 750cc water-cooled Suzuki triple, one of which I rode for several months back in the seventies, though it was a bit too big for me, was – and remains – the Susie Water Bottle. The rotary RE5, which nearly sent the company broke in the early seventies because it failed to sell, was called the Lunchbox, no doubt in view of the round, if distinctly odd, tin-canister shaped instrument binnacle on the handlebars of the first model. It was clearly a very clever, metal pun on the rotary theme, even if no-one knew that at the time.

There may well be very many nick-names which people now apply to the ever-increasing range of motorcycles from an ever-increasing list of countries – including China, and India, the latter still manufacturing an enormous number of the well-revered 350 and 500cc (Royal) Enfield machines – and it might be of interest to find out what some of them may be.

There are probable many people out there who apply pet names to their various machines – I know a girl who rides her 'Vera the Vespa' scooter everywhere – which is quite different from bestowing a nick-name upon them, because a pet name is usually a form of endearment, while a nick-name may well be anything but that!

Wet Monday

There were two or three customers standing about in Omodeis that rainy afternoon, all being served (at once, of course) when another bloke wandered in, scooped up a handful of motorcycle magazines and sidled up to me at the counter. "Let's have twenty hex-headed 2BA set screws, will you, mate? About a half-inch long" he asked, his trusting expression clearly hoping that we could easily accommodate him; which of course we could, because those little screws were fitted to a large range of British motorcycles.

I went over to the serried rows of boxes which

contained a large variety of screws, nut and bolts and dug out several from the box which held a large quantity of the set screws he wanted and brought a handful back to the counter. I counted out about ten or so, then palmed one of them, holding it between finger and thumb on my left hand as I counted the others out with my right. Suddenly I snapped my left fingers and one of the little screws quickly leapt out of concealment and began to spin violently upon the counter top, as though it might be driven by some mysterious force. It jumped about, scattering a few of the other screws in so doing, as it gyrated around, spinning at high speed.

"Christ!" the customer shouted, his eyes sticking out like dogs' balls on a canary. "What the bloody Hell's going on. Look at that, willya?" Holding my hands up as in mock surrender, and assuming a suitably horrified face, I jumped back and shouted "Stand back! Whatever you do, don't touch it. It's another one of those blasted 2BA screws which has become magnetised. We have a few of them arrive like that sometimes. But that's the fourth one this week. Phew, it usually only happens now and again. Don't go near it, wait until it stops, and I'll neutralise it. The thing will be all right then."

"I don't want that bloody thing on *my* BSA," the bloke gasped, his face a perfect study for any actor who needed a lesson in how to swiftly don an amazed gaze, as the screw continued to jump about and spin madly, while clearly beginning to slow down. One of the other clients, who had obviously seen what I had done, excused himself and trotted to the front door, one hand over his mouth as he tried in vain to smother the raucous laugh which was soon to erupt from him as he staggered onto the footpath outside. "See that?" I asked the bloke, as I pointed to the fellow doubled up outside the shop. "Those things have an aura which affects people in many different ways. That bloke is in hysterics. Some people actually burst into tears. How do you feel?"

"I've never seen nothing like that in me life before," the man gasped double-negatively, as the little screw began at last to slow down, and then to stop. While he stared goggle-eyed at the little screw as it whirled about for the last time and stopped, I couldn't believe he had reacted as strongly as he did, so I added a *Finale Ultimo* to the gag by rubbing my hand vigorously over my nylon/wool blend jumper and then pointed a finger at the little screw. "Don't move, mate," I said, "I'll neutralise the thing and you can use it then." Having unloaded that lot of nonsense on the unsuspecting customer, I slowly slid a finger in the screw's direction when suddenly, when about forty thou from it, a sudden flash of static electricity erupted from my finger tip to the head of the screw with a soft cracking noise."Ow!" I shouted, for the spark stung a bit, and then I gingerly picked the screw up and handed it to the bloke. "It's OK, it's quite harmless now" I assured him.

"I don't want the bloody thing," he retreated, his eyes fixed on the harmless little 2BA screw, "It might do that again."

"Yeah, I s'pose it might" I said, as I threw it into the waste bin – from where I could retrieve it later. "Better get rid of it." I finished counting out the rest of them, the customer watching very intently in case another 'magnetised' screw suddenly decided to start leaping about. I was not about to encore that tired old gag (which sometimes worked, as it did this time, but more often than not didn't) in case he discovered what I had done, and I was congratulating myself on the success of that particular exercise when the store's manager – not well known for his sense of humour – called me in to his office.

"What's going on out there?" he demanded, as the customer left, nodding at the two grinning customers who had so enjoyed that innocent pantomime. "What's all that laughter about; you've done that screw spinning thing again haven't you? Look, you have work to do. You can't stand about telling jokes all day. It's not all about entertaining the customers, you know."

"Why not?" I retorted, "a few gags now and again never hurt anyone. These people come back again and again, so it's not harming anyone. Besides which, I'm still serving those other two blokes ("Clients" he butted in) – er, clients – so I better get back to them."

On that occasion he probably had some reason to be a bit shirty, because he often left his daily glasses near the counter when he donned his reading glasses to cost a bunch of overseas invoices, and earlier that day when he did this I had sticky-taped white paper inside the lenses, upon which I had drawn a pair of bloodshot, crossed eyes. I knew he would be busy with his pile of invoices for some hours, and I was going to fly another awful gag by donning his glasses when the next client came into the shop, hoping to elicit a strong reaction from him when I looked at him and he saw those glaring eyes. It backfired, because I was in the toilet when the next customer came in, and was just coming back to the counter when the manager emerged from his office, rubbing his eyes as he reached down and put on his 'ordinary' glasses.

"It's OK, I'll look after him." I cried, but it was by then too late because he had slipped his glasses

Omodeis

on, and then *he* became the recipient of the hoot of laughter which I had expected to get. He took them off again, and peeled the paper eyes out of the frames as he strode purposefully back into his office, leaving the grinning customer to me. His dignity was fearfully ruffled and I got some innocent fun out of his near-frantic efforts to remove a lump of the sticky tape from his finger, which still had one of the fearsome eyes stuck to it. He was not amused and told me so several times thereafter, so that gag disappeared without trace from then on.

Hey, it was more than half a century ago, and thankfully I don't do anything quite as a silly as that anymore, but I always felt there was nothing all that wrong with a bit of harmless fun to while away the hours; not that Omodeis was in any way a boring place in which to work, for I still cherish (almost) every minute I spent in the place.

That same afternoon a rider limped into the store, the while spitting on his palm and rubbing it over a pink patch of bare skin on his elbow. "Just slipped off me bike up the road," he said by way of explanation. "I'm alright, but looks as though I'll need a new headlamp rim and footrest rubber. Gimme a handlebar rubber as well, will ya? Bloody wet roads; came off in the tramlines in Railway Square, turning into Pitt Street."

"Sorry to hear that," I remarked, quite sincerely. "I did the same thing myself some years ago, in that same spot, when they still had loose, three-inch square wooden road blocks as a road surface. They were laid right through Railway Square in those days; in the middle of the tramlines as well. It was like riding on ice when they were wet. How's your sealed beam light unit?" I added. "Better switch on your headlamp and see if it's working. It could be busted as well." He trotted outside and switched the light on, which glowed for a few seconds and then want out again after a sudden flash.

He came back in again, shaking his head sadly. "How did you know about me headlight?" he asked. "It's gone all right." "Well, the sealed beam unit is all glass," I told him, "and all it needs is a crack in it to allow air in which stuffs the vacuum and the filaments will burn out almost at once. Better to find out now than when it's night time. Be a bit late then to be looking for a new headlamp unit."

"Thanks for the info on the light unit, mate, better gimme a new one with the rim, and the rubbers as well," he said. "I can fit 'em outside the shop." It should go without saying that there was many a simple repair job carried out in the gutter, or on the footpath outside Omodies, often with assistance from one of us. I turned to one of the two boxes of 'wet weather spares' we always wheeled out of a darkened corner when the roads were wet, one box for British machines, the other for bikes made in Japan, because we knew that the occasional rider – either new to the game, or inattentive after months of dry weather – could spend a few seconds bike-less and sliding on his backside down the road when inclement weather struck. It gave us absolutely no joy to do this, but facts were facts, so we were well prepared.

Typically, A British machine like his AJS might need a headlamp rim, perhaps sealed beam unit, almost certainly handlebar and footrest rubbers (the foot-peg would almost always shove itself through the end of the rubber) and possibly a new set of handlebars as well. If crash (for crash, read 'safety') bars were fitted, a simple repair to a bent bar could usually be carried out in the street with an owner pulling on one side while I heaved mightily upon the other, or better still to lean the bike against the nearest telegraph pole and simply shove the bike against it, using the bike's weight to effect a simple job of straightening the bar out. This could only be done once, of course.

We had two different types of safety bars for BMW motorcycles, one of which wrapped itself very neatly over the horizontal cylinder barrels and heads – but I cannot remember ever selling one of them. Clearly, the BMW's pots hanging out in the breeze were vulnerable to accident damage, but I never heard of a cylinder barrel being snapped off in an accident: other than twice at very high speed during races,that is, once at Amaroo Park and once at Bathurst. I have seen more than one flat-twin BMW with scrape marks on its rocker box covers, so the cylinders are clearly stronger than they appear to be.

It was quite a different situation with Japanese machines, in particular with Honda. The great 305cc Honda Hawk (1961-68) which followed the 1958 Honda Dream, was the first Honda to have telescopic forks fitted, but it continued to use the engine as a stressed member, which meant there were no frame rails or front down-tubes to which safety bars could be attached. If one of them was dropped in the wet, you could bet it would need at the very least a new blinker lens, or complete blinker assembly, and certainly a new clutch or front brake control lever blade – if not a complete unit with switch box and integral wiring. The fat mufflers should have helped cushion the impact of a bike falling onto its side, but this was negated to some degree by the folding footrests these machines featured. The later CB Honda models could have safety bars fitted, as could the range of Yamaha and Suzuki machines, because of their more 'normal' pipe-tube frames, but in each case the fragile design of the handlebar control levers would almost inevitably result in them snapping off.

This was a great deal worse than it sounds, because these alloy lever blades were contained within diecast-alloy circular switchboxes which were clamped to the handlebars. It all looked very neat, with the wiring hidden as it was located within the handlebars, but unhappily the fulcrum point where the levers pivoted was very much the weakest point because the casting in that area of maximum stress was far too thin. All too often the piece snapped clean through, leaving the front brake – or worse still the clutch – lever inoperable, and the switches no longer working, which meant you couldn't ride your bike at all! If you were smart enough to nip the levers up so they were just tight enough to remain in place, the lever could then rotate under stress and neatly sever the wires where they were threaded through the razor-sharp grooves machined into the handlebars.

But it gets worse again, because the lever blades all *looked* to be the same shape and size, but were supplied to the Japanese factories by a variety of small manufacturers, which inevitable meant that the holes for the pivot point and the nipple hole for the brake or clutch cable would almost certainly be slightly different. For example, a control lever assembly supplied by Igotta Ichiwan's factory might have the holes for the pivot point and control cable nipple up to 3-4mm further apart than a near-identical unit supplied by the small factory owned by Iusuli Krakaslaki. Clearly, this meant that you had to buy either an Ichiwan or Krakaslaki control lever blade, for they were not interchangeable! What a King sized pain that was. But these factories compounded that felony by often providing control lever assemblies which looked identical to components which had been supplied *by them* only weeks previously, but in which the two holes *were sited differently again!!*

The owner of a Japanese machine might need to supply engine and frame numbers, and just as often a 'sample of type' to be sure of getting the correct lever blade to fit his bike.

It couldn't go on like that, because we always needed to see a 'sample of type' and even then might not be able to supply the correct replacement part, which was real nightmare, but this dilemma was solved to quite some degree when a huge crate full of hundreds of universal lever assemblies for many Japanese machines arrived at Omodeis one day – along with bags and bags of spare levers. I helped to unpack them all and carefully labelled them before placing them into stock. I never knew where they came from, but they were clearly stronger than the original items and of a far better quality. The new stock was replaced on a regular basis because the news had apparently spread into outlying areas with resultant orders from all over the country. It simply meant that the components we had imported (and imported several times again thereafter!) from that unknown source were so similar in construction that a broken lever blade could be instantly replaced because they were all the same dimensions. What the reaction of Igotta Ichiwan and Iusuli Krakaslaki to the importation of these components has thus-far not been recorded – at least not to my knowledge – but I doubt that they would have been very happy about it. Serves them right, I say, the unfeeling swine!

Audition

The so-called–'credit squeeze' imposed by the Menzies Australian Government in 1960 virtually wiped out many of the smaller suburban motorcycle distributors across the Nation. Some of them closed their doors forever, while most of them managed to survive only when they were forced to dismiss some of their most valued staff members. The latter occurred simply because the sales of new and/or second hand motorcycles dropped off alarmingly because prospective purchasers couldn't have ready access to the credit they had until then taken for granted.

As a natural sequence, the sales of accessories and specialised clothing had also dropped off, although the sales of spare parts picked up because owners were then spending money on re-furbishing, maintaining or repairing their older machines; bikes which might normally have been traded in on a later machine, or even a brand new one.

Unhappily, the squeeze coincided with the downturn in sales in general following the intro-duction of the dreaded Mini-Minor, the Japanese factories – spearheaded by Honda's arrival in Australia just two years previously – not yet making the dramatic in-roads into new motorcycle sales in this country; or anywhere else, for that matter.

Whether or not I was a 'valued member' of Ryde Motorcycles I cannot say, but the fact is that I was tearfully dismissed and had to scratch around to find whatever job I could, even if it was outside of the motorcycle trade.

Omodeis

I managed to secure employment outside the trade for the best part of a year, staggering about in a job I disliked intensely, although it must be said that there was a reward of some sort because of the nature of the job itself. I was aching to get away from it all, and it was at my lowest ebb when Fate flung me a lifeline, in the form of an unknown phone call from an equally unknown personage.

How they managed to get my phone number was something of a mystery to me at the time, but one day after I had delivered my charges to their respective houses and parked the bus outside, I arrived home to be told by my widowed mum that somebody from some motorcycle shop or other had rung me and wanted to offer me a job. At the time I was living in Fairfield and driving a bus for the Spastic Centre (which was a world away in Mosman), and it was my job to pick up nine little kids of about ten years of age, and two adults, deliver them safely to the Centre by 9 am every Monday to Friday, then pick them up at 4pm to drive them home again.

During the day we drivers were required to shuffle about and do whatever we were asked to do, from moving the kids about between therapeutic centres, to sorting through bundles of festering clothes, busted toys and crockery, and other bric-a-brac which had been donated to the Centre rather than being placed outside next to the bin with the other household garbage. It was a bugger of a job and it was very poorly paid, as you might expect to be the case with any charitable organisation.

One of my more onerous tasks was to occasionally hop into a large Hessian bale and leap up and down upon a huge, overly ripe heap of aluminium caps from glass milk bottles in an effort to squash them down; this would then allow more room within the large bag – after I had leapt out of it for a few seconds -for another truckload of the things to be added, so that I could then leap up and down on top of those as well, before the bag was finally brim-full of the grimly festering things. I would by then be totally exhausted and have to be assisted out of the bale by a couple of stalwarts with pegs on their noses, my clothes stinking like a Vintage rubbish tip.

During this pursuit, I often wondered why nobody ever bothered to rinse those sparkling aluminium caps out before they enthusiastically placed them in the Centre's specially provided containers for re-cycling. Had these people known that some poor idiot was soon to be seen dancing a *fandango* upon them while in the heat of the sun, I trust most of these people would have bothered to give these caps a quick squirt under the kitchen tap. Perhaps these well-meaning citizens thought the yellow or brownish encrustation which finally adorned these things several days after their removal might of itself be recycled into a form of strong cheese, perhaps a lethal bait for itinerant rats, or possibly an insect deterrent of some sort?

During my lunch (half) hour the following day I trotted up the road to make a call to the mysterious motorcycle store, to discover, at once to my surprise and delight, that it was, of all people, Aub Omodei who answered the phone. Omodei had called into the Ryde store every couple of weeks to hawk his wares, and had sometimes stood quietly about while I attended to some customers. When that happened, I noticed he often wrote notes in a small book he carried with him, the book into which he entered my orders for products he was offering.

I was soon to learn he was actually making notes of my 'performance', but I had no idea I was actually *auditioning* for him on those occasions.

When I rang him he told me he had called into the store and was 'dismayed' to learn I had left, but he had, he said, been 'suitably impressed' by my 'ability behind the counter', and my 'cheerful demeanour', and promptly offered me a job, which I just as promptly accepted. I started work there just on ten days later.

Aub Omodei owned and managed the store, with only one other employee in the place at the time, and that first day I strolled into Omodeis at just after nine o'clock I noticed the bloke who was standing behind the counter have a less than furtive look at the large Railway clock which stood on the wall just inside the front door. He then had a much more obvious, long hard look at his wristwatch as well, and then glanced at me with arched eyebrows. I noticed this display, of course, and was somewhat alarmed by it, but chose to ignore the performance.

"Hi lad, how's it going?" I asked, as pleasantly as I could, as I shook hands with him. I had been in the trade for some years prior to that of course, knew a bit about it, and felt I didn't have too much to learn from this bloke (except, of course, how they carried out business in that particular establishment) so I needed to tell him at once that I wasn't going to be sniffed at like a newbie who had just arrived on the scene. Well, as it happened I had quite a bit to learn and I was soon to discover that it was to be on the most basic level.

"First thing we do in the morning is sweep the place out," he said, "and we use this bottle to do so." He produced a large glass bottle with a screw-on lid which had had several holes punched into it, and flourished the thing under my nose. I had seen the occasional bottle before, and was about to remark upon this as well, but said nothing. I almost flippantly asked him how you sweep the place out with a bottle, but a natural feeling for the fitness of things stopped that retort at my lips before I uttered it.

"This is how we do it," he pointed out as, bottle in hand, he lead me upstairs. He screwed the cap off the bottle and carefully filled the bottle to the brim, screwed the cap back on and then marched me downstairs again.

"Now you sprinkle the water onto the floor to settle the dust. You do it like this" he said, suiting 'the word to the action, the action to the word' as Shakespeare wrote in Hamlet's advice to the players, while I stood quietly by shaking my head in disbelief. "Now let me see *you* do it," he said, as he stood to one side, hands on hips.

It was a delight to be back in the motorcycle trade, and I really wanted – in fact needed – the job, but I had to put a few things into perspective before the day was over, and I wanted to do it without upsetting anyone and without suddenly losing the job I was looking forward to enjoying. "Let me get this straight," I said, as kindly as I could. "I know I am brand new to this particular establishment, but are you trying to teach me how to shake water out of a bottle? I think I've actually done this once or twice before, and managed to do it quite successfully." He didn't look too happy about this subtle, arrogant admonition, and began to tap the toe of his right foot to the floor as the corners of his mouth drooped down.

"Oh, Reg," Aub called from the office at that moment, "come and have a look at this new invoice from England. There is crate load of Amal parts and another of control cables on the wharf. I need you to handle this at once."

The bloke huffed and puffed a couple of times, as I sprinkled some water to the floor to placate him, nodding at him the while, then he turned on his heel and flounced into the office. I noticed Aub looking over the man's head as he bent to look at the sheaf of invoices, and I was relieved to see him wink at me and nod his head in what I assumed to be some form of tacit approval. Hugely relieved, I went about the task, displaying to the world my newly-acquired skill of water sprinkling and then swept the place out with some enthusiasm, even finding a rag to over-act outrageously as I dusted some shelves which I felt needed attention. They were actually spotless.

A customer came into the store and I immediately walked up to him. "What can I do for you, me boy?" I helpfully enquired. "Have you got a back chain for me 1959 Fundaberg – that's *Thunderbird to you and me* –Triumph?" he asked with a smile.

"I believe so," I answered, having previously noted several large boxes of Renolds Transmar ½" x ⁵⁄₁₆" primary drive chain alongside a similarly large pile of ⅝" x ⅜" rear chain boxes – each in 25-foot rolls – while, happily, there were several cut lengths of various chains in brown paper bags on a neighbouring shelf. I was well aware that the rear chain for that Triumph Thunderbird was five-foot-three-and-one-half-inches in length, and the last price I knew of a year earlier had been nineteen-shillings-and-eleven-pence-ha'penny per foot, so I was nonplussed as to work out this price without the aid of that indispensable little book known as the "Ready Reckoner." Happily, there were a couple of them lying about.

When I stooped to that little pile of cut chains it was a relief to see that one of them was clearly marked Triumph Thunderbird, ⅝" x ⅜" rear, with the price still clearly marked on the bag, though it was half smudged underneath a large grease stain.

I straightened up to find my fellow employee standing over me, again with hand on hip, as he pointedly held one out to take the little packet from me. "Go in and see Mr Omodie, will you?" he said, "you should have seen him when you first came in."

"I was too busy learning how to pour water out of a bottle." I said, and was rewarded for this fatuous remark by seeing a slight grin on Aub's face when I turned and walked into the office. I spent some little time in there being shown the ropes by this quite pleasant man, who pointed out that the other bloke had never had any other job in his life, was very good at it (which proved to be quite true) and that he could be very conservative and a bit impatient at times. Aub was so right about that, too.

There were several rules in that establishment which I fell into without much trouble, though some of them were impossible for me to put into practice. I had no problems with wearing a white shirt and crisp tie every day, and I suppose the strict, to the minute lunch hour was OK as well, but I could never call 'Mr Omodie' anything but Aub. I used to call him Bill, as in W.F.Omodei, but Bill was in fact Aub's father, as Aub reminded me when I went to work for him. "Don't worry about it," he once told me, "everyone calls me Bill. I don't bother mentioning it." He was that sort of bloke.

I found it too stiffly formal to always refer to clients as 'sir', although I sometimes used that formal title if it was a Police officer or someone who was new to us. Unhappily Aub passed away about two years after I started working there, and the place (which was actually owned by the Omodei family) was automatically managed by Reg, with whom I endured a reasonably professional relationship, if not any real friendship.

If my train was a little late at times and I arrived just after nine, he could never, ever, overcome his

Omodeis

habit of looking at the wall clock and frowning, and I would always follow this in counterpoint by looking at my wristwatch and shaking my head sadly. Apart from that, I enjoyed working there, and liked the great camaraderie which always existed between myself and our very many customers. Reg was always stiffly formal, and that was OK as well, but it simply wasn't my style.

The company had been in that same location for over 50 years, but it was suddenly given its marching orders in the early eighties by the Gas Company, which owned the building, and it had only one month's notice to quite the premises. When it folded up its tents and moved on, it was never to be heard of again. What a crying shame that was, for that tiny store served the motorcycling community , both locally and State-wide, the latter through the Postal and Rail networks, at least as well, and at least as effectively, as any of the very much larger establishments with which it competed on much more than equal terms.

Access

One of Australia's most remarkable motorcycle stores traded very successfully from the one outlet, and at the same address, for more than five decades. It was a small, pristine, double-fronted establishment which catered to the needs of countless thousands of motorcyclists over those many years, while turning over more much highly-specialised merchandise than many of its larger competitors could ever hope to achieve.

During the second world war its employees were precluded from any form of Military Service, the tiny store, along with many, very much larger engineering and heavy-industry companies, being officially listed as an 'essential service'. This was fair enough, for it was clearly necessary to have the population of such a large city as Sydney as mobile as possible, and for a variety of very good reasons. Even though the motorcycling population may have been small, the company could certainly be relied upon to keep as many of Sydney's (two)wheels moving about as possible.

For all of those fifty and more years, Omodeis stood next to Sydney's Gas Company in Pitt Street. Its enormous inventory included motorcycle acc-essories, specialised clothing (including, in its later years, one-piece leather racing suits made to measure) and a huge list of spare parts. Anything from saddlebags to handlebars and carburettor parts, control cables and their attendant control levers, gaskets, chains and re-banded sprockets, cylinder re-boring, batteries and a host of other essential too long to list here could be obtained from this one little store.

Towards the end of its long tenure there was also a magazine rack which bulged with every motorcycle magazine printed in English, with a standing order with the distributors to send every new publication to the store as soon as it would become available. Among numerous others, there was also a weekly motorcycle newspaper from England which was air-freighted in, hot off the presses.

The company was simply called Omodeis and, tiny though it was, and never employing more than three people at any one time, it served the needs of many thousands of motorcyclists throughout NSW, and of course elsewhere, as few other outlets of its type ever did. Suburban dealers who rang an order through before 10.30 on any morning could be certain of that order arriving at their premises the same afternoon at around 4.30pm. Orders from the country or Interstate would be despatched by post or rail immediately upon receiving a letter and/or order. It is doubtful if that type of service is readily available today.

In the early pre-war years the company imported motorcycles as well, including Norton, Dunelt and Scott. The Scott was usually a water cooled, twin-cylinder two stroke of 500 or 600cc capacity, but just one of the very rare **three-cylinder, water-coolled** 750cc Scott two-strokes was on display at Omodeis in 1936, with another of the even rarer 1000cc Triples on display several month later. Less than 20 of these unusual machines – including several prototypes – were ever built, and how the Australian company ever managed to obtain even one of them remains a mystery.

With no facilities for servicing or other forms of maintenance, it was made clear to prospective purchasers that a motorcycle would arrive and be sold while still in its wooden crate with the essential servicing left entirely up to the new owner, to whom the machine was delivered, or who would pick up his crated machine and happily drive away with it in the back of a ute or trailer.

The company was a magnet for motorcyclists of every conceivable shape, size and Nationality and for so very long. I was privileged to work there from 1961 to 1968, and it was very rewarding indeed. There was a steady flow of customers every day, and it was by no means unusual on a Saturday morning to find the customers standing four or five deep around the counters and to be serving several of them at once. Doesn't happen much these days, does it? That level of service, I mean.

There would be someone trying on a few different helmets, another checking the size of a pair of gloves, someone else slipping on a leather jacket, or waterproof trousers, while others would be gleefully departing with a rear chain for a Triumph Thunderbird, perhaps a set of engine gaskets for a single-cylinder AJS, or a clutch cable for a BSA twin. Maybe it was a blank VK+ (Valve Chrome Plus) 'Dufor' inlet valve from Duly and Hansfords which was soon to be carefully machined from a 'sample of type' and fitted to a pre-war Sunbeam, or an American Big X Excelsior. As I said, all shapes and sizes, and that meant **motorcycles** as well as riders!

So vast was its clientele that the store's manager, who doubled as a lay preacher on Sundays, would often ring a food supplier asking for donations for his local Church Fete, and find the person he was speaking to was a former customer, sometimes from as long back as 30 years previously! The donations were always forthcoming. I rang on his behalf on several occasions, and sometimes even senior management would express surprise that Omodeis still existed and from whom they – often as young students at Sydney University – had purchased most of their motorcycling needs many years before.

If it was a great place in which to 'work', it was naturally a great place for numerous comedic episodes, not all of them intentional. There were a few tragedies as well, a couple of which involved well-known clients as they competed on racing circuits, and a couple more well-known to us who suffered major injuries on the road – and not all of them on just two wheels. That is life in general, for all families large or small are under the control of some of Kismet's capricious moods.

A young Asian student from Sydney Uni rode up one day on his brand-new Vespa, and strolled in all smiles, his top row of teeth almost entirely covered with gold, his little eyes framed by large spectacles with thick, ink-bottle lenses. He bowed ever so slightly and lisped, with no preamble, just two words. "Pear Grubs," he said, his hypnotic teeth gleaming.

"Pear Grubs?" I remember thinking, what the hell did we have to do with pear grubs? I was just about to refer his complaint to a local green grocer when he raised a hand and made what I thought was an obscene five finger gesture. I had never been rewarded with such a gesture then, or since, but it transpired he simply wanted a *pair of gloves* and this was the quickest, and simplest, way of getting his message across. When he left a short time later, he placed his leather-clad palms together in a prayerful attitude then turned to me and bowed again. Another happy customer I would have thought, but I never saw him again.

A nubile blonde minced up to the counter one day and said " I need a jockstrap for my boyfriend. He told me to ask for one here." I was about to suggest she go to the sports store Mick Simmons, which was block or so away, but with a (knowing) smile asked her what size she wanted. With a (melting) smile she cooed "Eighteen inches," which I confess took me aback. "You know," she added "those elastic things you use to tie your luggage with."

I know her boyfriend was having a lend of her – for which no man on earth could blame him, the swine – because he had sent her to get an 'occie-strap,' luggage elastic, or to use its correct title, an Aerolastic, of the appropriate length. We had no shortage of those things and they lived in a couple of boxes just under one of the tall counters.

"They're downstairs" I said smugly, "I'll go down and get a couple." With that I took several steps to where one of the boxes lay, bending my knees as I did so and thus pretending to go downstairs into the non-existent basement. I rummaged around for a while and re-emerged, straightening up as I did so to make it appear I had just come back up again.

As she was paying for them, another employee, the late, lamented Robert Radnidge, of no little fame, strolled casually behind me with a large cardboard box over his shoulder. "Look out for the stairs!" she shouted as Rob approached what she thought was a flight of stairs. He apparently levitated across the gaping hole where the stairs were thought to be, and grinned over his shoulder at me as he vanished behind one of the fixtures. The girl looked at me as I raised my eyebrows in mock surprise, then she half-closed one eye as she stretched to tip-toes and leaned across the counter to where she could then clearly see the box containing the Aerolastics.

She said nothing, but unfortunately I have seen the look she gave me upon the faces of several other females I have known over too many years, and it was not a sight I was comfortable with or would ever wish to see again. Unhappily I still see that fearsome expression from time to time.

She flounced out of the place and fixed me with another of Agatha Christie's 'baleful glares' as

Omodeis

she crossed the road outside, slapping her thigh with her purchase as she went. I felt sorry for her boyfriend, but equally as sorry for myself in case I had unintentionally upset his apple cart and he came in to tell me all about it.

There are a thousand stories from the portals of Omodeis. This has been one of them.

YDS-1 Yamaha

A fellow I knew breathlessly remarked upon a very early, little-known – if in fact quite interesting – YDS1 Yamaha, which was brought into Adelaide in 1961, or thereabouts, as an off-road "Ranch" bike called *'Liberty'*, after the name of the company, Liberty Motors, which imported them. Or at the very least, modified the original machines.

It was a very swish-looking 250cc twin-cylinder two-stroke which was equipped with a large rear sprocket, some engine protective bolt-on panels under the frame, rear and tank-top carriers, high-mounted mudguards and upswept exhaust pipes which were in the style of the 'Scrambles' machines which they had built in quite small quantities for a few years prior to that time. It remains uncertain if the add-on, Ag-bike bits were fitted by Liberty as 'after-market' bolt-ons – which is very likely – or were fitted in the Yamaha factory, which is unlikely. The design was by then four years old, the first machine of this type built in 1957, having been copied from the 250cc German Adler which had so recently gone to God with almost everything, and everyone, else.

Along with Suzuki a year or so earlier, the very rare – and long forgotten – Tohatsu, and the first-rate Bridgestone sportsters some years later, the upswept, Scrambles-type exhaust design which was featured on the Liberty 250cc twin was something of a fashion trend in those days.

The gold-and-cream coloured machine was apparently intended to be used as a farm machine, and has been recognized as a very early example of this type of motorcycle; a bike strictly intended for use on the land, for it lacked some of the essentials to allow it to be ridden with safety on the open road. There is no doubt it would have filled either task admirably, and, one assumes, might have been a popular mount, but Yamaha themselves are said to have **no knowledge at all** of the 'Liberty' machine's existence!

If that 250cc off-road **YDS-1** Liberty/Yamaha was little-known at the time, even in Adelaide, much less the rest of Australia, then its sibling, the **YC-1**, was even rarer. The first example of the 'other' Liberty I ever saw rolled uncertainly into the gutter outside Omodeis one day not long after I had begun working there; which would have been around 1961, at about the same time as the YDS-1 appeared in Adelaide. This was many years before Yamaha's first, well-trumpeted **DT175** off-roader appeared. It remains the only one I have ever seen.

The bloke who clambered off the thing had clearly been brand new to motorcycling, because he seemed very uneasy as he pulled up and struggled to climb off the bike: large though he was, and small as the bike was, he looked to be very uncomfortable indeed.

Perhaps it was an off-spring of that off-road 250 twin, for the machine he rode carried the Liberty name writ large upon the fuel tank but the machine carried no other identification upon it which we could find. But it was actually a 175cc *single-cylinder* two-stroke, which I later learned was an enlarged version of Yamaha's first-ever motorcycle, the 125cc YA-1 from 1955, the Japanese design pinched from the near-identical pre-war/post war German DKW RT125.

The 175cc YC-1, clearly a logical progression from the little 125, was first built by Yamaha in 1956, but was totally unknown outside of Japan at that time. It was, I suggest, no better known when we saw that first Liberty motorcycle pull into the gutter outside the store several years later.

There was a small disc underneath the imposing Liberty name on the 175cc bike's fuel tank, but it carried no other identification. The small plate which covered the ignition points, and which, in later models, would have Yamaha imprinted upon it, had nothing on it but the same odd Yamaha logo.

Contained within the small red plastic disc was that strange logo which took me some little time to work out, but it suddenly clicked when I realized what it was: it was, of course, Yamaha's then-trade mark of the three tuning forks, which none of us had ever seen before, but which spoke of its involvement in the music industry. This meant nothing to me at the time, but, as a serious singer, I knew what a tuning fork was, but to see three of them crossed in that odd manner looked very strange indeed! It might have helped were we to look at the factory ID plate, which would normally have been wrapped round the frame's steering head, for it should have borne the Yamaha name somewhere upon it, but it simply never occurred to us to check that out.

Vintage Morris

1961–1968

The rider told me that the bikes had recently been imported by Dalgety, a company well-known at the time for supplying a large range of farm machinery, and he also mentioned that he had never ridden a motorcycle before. If the unknown bike's sudden appearance was a surprise, then the admission of his ineptitude as a motorcyclist was not.

At that time, it must be noted, there were other odd Japanese motorcycles appearing from time to time: the transverse Vee-twin, shaft-drive Lilac was one, the BMW-like, flat-twin Marusho (which built Lilac machines) was another, along with the occasional Meguro, which looked not unlike a cross between a 500cc single-cylinder Ariel Red Hunter and a G80 Matchless – so, too, did the 350cc Cabton, which faithfully copied the Ariel Red Hunter engine, but without any sign of Matchless. In effect, Meguro became Kawasaki when the companies merged, Meguro actually building the British BSA ohv 650 twin under license to the Brits, which finally emerged from the mists as Kawasaki's W1, the BSA-look-alike 650 twin. The oddball two-stroke Tohatsu (who still make a large range of excellent outboard motors, it should be remembered) was another, if a very rare, two-stroke machine.

The rarest one of all, which I heard of occasionally, but only saw very briefly when one of them pulled up at the lights outside Omodeis just once, was the late fifties *three-cylinder two-stroke Olympus-King*, which pre-dated Kawasaki's 500cc Mach 3 by some years. The three, heavily-finned cylinders were horizontally disposed, its spark plugs assumedly exposed to road grime and water which would have been flung up from the front wheel, while it sported telescopic front forks and up-to-date swing-arm rear suspension. When the three-cylinder Japanese bike stopped at the traffic lights I rushed outside to have a swift look at it, but it took off like a rocket seconds later, filling the air around it with a cloud of two-stroke smoke. I would like to have known much more about the Olympus-King, and whether or not the camera manufacturer Olympus had anything to do with its manufacture.

I had not heard of the Liberty brand at that time, of course, so I naturally assumed it to be just another Japanese motorcycle, but whether it was actually imported directly from Japan, which might have been a bit rude of Yamaha, or through the Liberty company in Adelaide, I have no means of knowing. But the bike was clearly an off-roader, with its high-mounted mudguards, bash-plate under the crankcase, rear carrier and large-diameter rear sprocket. It carried no blinkers or mirrors, and just a simple speedometer, with only a single-filament tail-lamp globe and no brake light switch because, one assumes, a brake light might not be all that necessary when flapping about the paddocks chasing livestock around.

But a warning stop-light would surely have been a necessity in heavy Sydney traffic, and that applies to its non-existent blinkers and mirrors as well.

For many years thereafter I have had some people attempt to assure me that the Liberty of which I speak did not exist, for only the little-known 250cc twin was said to carry the Liberty trade-mark, but the 175cc single certainly existed, at least in NSW, even if in very small numbers.

I also heard – at a later time, and from the bloke at Dalgety – that the bikes had been fitted with rubber main-shaft oil seals, which were of course ruined by the mineral based oils which were used in the lubricating system which was common place in those days. This would have resulted in a gas leak at the shafts which would allow air to enter the engine's crankcase resulting in a lean mixture. This would have thinned out the fuel mixture and wrecked the big-end assembly in no time flat. Before Yamaha designed the 'Autolube' system of a separate oil pump and its attendant oil tank, mineral-based oil was mixed with petrol to provide an entirely safe form of lubrication: it should have specified a vegetable-based oil anywhere rubber was being used. Had the oil seals been made of a material like Neoprene or other synthetics (which clearly happened with later machines) the problem of them being dissolved by the wrong type of oil may not have occurred.

This may well be the reason why the YC-1 disappeared without trace, long before anyone knew anything about it; except for a few cow-cockeys, that is, who were said to have buried more than one or two of them in their driest paddocks.

It is also fair to assume that farm bikes were the rarest of the rare in pre-war times, because the rigid-frame, poorly-sprung machines which were about in those days would probably have seen many a rider spend more time face-down in the dirt than he would riding the range. These machines were certainly not ideal for farm work.

If that 1961 YDS-1 Liberty/Yamaha was an early example of a farm-bike, then it was by means the first of its type.

In the late forties P and R Williams imported

Omodeis

the semi-advanced LE Velocette into NSW; the very cleverly designed, well-sprung little machine somewhat ahead of its time, while being equally *behind* the times. I say *'semi-advanced'* because this unique little motorcycle employed an advanced, swing-arm rear suspension, first-class front forks, comfortable sprung single saddle, foot-boards with integrated leg-shields, felt-lined box-section frame, rubber-mounted engine and shaft drive, all of which allowed for very smooth running and very precise handling. But it bucked convention by being badly under-powered by a very old-fashioned, water-cooled flat-twin, **side-valve** engine of only 150c... and it employed an even more old-fashioned *three-speed hand gear-change*!! In 1948? Come on!

This was clearly a backward step, because Velocette was the first factory on earth to employ the now-universal 'positive stop' foot gear-change mechanism, which they introduced on their KTT racing machines as far back as 1929. Besides which, after the war old-fashioned side-valve engines were still in the occasional catalogue, but were swiftly falling out of favour.

Starting the LE was by a long hand lever, which also doubled as the method by which the little bike could be hauled onto its centre-stand and off it again, but that side-valve engine, what the heck was that all about: oh, and what about the ancient hand gear-change lever?

Why then a hand gear-change, and no kick-starter, you may ask? The machine was intended, it was said, as a Gentlemen's Commuter, the absence of a kick-starter and the hand gear-change suggesting that a Gentleman who may – or may not – have decided to leave the Rolls at home and commute upon this neat little bike, might not sully his white spats, or his patent leather or suede shoes, with scuff-marks engendered by kicking an engine into life, much less operating a foot gear-change pedal.

Oh, and the exhaust of the trim little bike was so well-muted that you couldn't hear the thing running, and the engine was similarly silent; in fact, it sounded like a small sewing machine, and developed about the same amount of power. I had ridden two or three of them in the dim, dark ages – should I say 'of course?' – and was very impressed by their eerie silence, smoothness and great comfort, but I couldn't find any performance to speak of.

Fortunately, later models enjoyed an engine boost to 200cc, but not much more power while, by 1958, the LE employed a kick-starter and four-speed foot gear-change, but the bike was still a poor performer. I doubt if it could have dragged a very large gentleman up a shallow driveway, while a one-legged man, recently discharged from Hospital and struggling with his newly-acquired crutches, might kick his hat along up a steep hill in front of him at a far greater speed than that little machine could ever have managed.

OK, so what am I on about with that LE (the initials stood for 'Little Engine') I hear you shriek?

Let me tell you why. I was strolling past the P and R Williams shop-front one day in the early fifties when I beheld a large notice board prominently displayed in their front window. Upon it was a range of black and white photos depicting several LE Velocettes being ridden enthusiastically by felt-hatted men with elastic-sided boots as they rode quietly amongst a flock of sheep on an unknown station.

The sheep looked as though they couldn't have cared less, the comments written on the large display board suggesting the bike was so unobtrusive that it could be ridden into the midst of a flock of otherwise twitchy sheep without disturbing any of them. It also suggested that fuel economy was part of the machine's charm, its shaft drive and comfortable ride yet another. I must say the riders all looked relaxed enough, the machines clearly moving about.

But there was no word mentioned about how the bike – and in particular its rider – would fare in the midst of a herd of *cattle*; especially during breeding season. It's a safe bet that the bike could not have accelerated quickly enough to out-run a rampant bull, which could result in that randy beast having its way with a hapless rider without the bull breaking into more than a casual trot.

It may not have been the first farm bike to have seen duty on the land, and was never intended to be used in anything remotely like that rough-and-tumble pursuit, but the little LE Velocette was very surely the first one we know of which was at least *tried* on the land. How it managed to perform is anybody's guess, but I doubt if it was very successful. The machine's speed was, however, not an issue – except in a desperate attempt at escaping a rampaging old bull.

As a footnote, no fewer than fifty (50) British Police forces ordered many hundreds of the later Mk 3 series LE for patrol bike duties – along with a large range of spare parts – which assured its longevity until the mid-seventies. A very nice little machine, to be sure, but not one for the land, and certainly less than ideal if one was in a hurry to go anywhere.

www.ingramcontent.com/pod-product-compliance
Lightning Source LLC
Chambersburg PA
CBHW081420300426
44110CB00016BA/2329